Real-Time Operating Systems Concepts

Real-Time Operating Systems Concepts

Prof. Dineshwari Bisen

ARCLER PRESS

www.arclerpress.com

Real-Time Operating Systems Concepts

Prof. Dineshwari Bisen

Arcler Press
4164 Lakeshore Road
Burlington, ON L7L 1A4
Canada
www.arclerpress.com
Email: orders@arclereducation.com

ISBN: 978-1-77956-964-6 (Hardcover)

ABOUT THE AUTHOR

Dineshwari Bisen, is presently working as an Assistant Professor in IT Department, Western College of Commerce and Business Management, Sanpada,Navi Mumbai, with 14 years of teaching experience. She has completed MCA, PGDCA andADCA. She has worked as a Member of Vigilance Committee, University of Mumbai. She filed and published 1 patent and 8 research papers presented forpublication in various conferences. The books authored and published by her are'Fundamentals of Database Management System, FYBSc IT, Semester-I, University of Mumbai','Open Source Technologies, Semester-1' and text books on'Data Science for Beginers' and'Machine learning Concept,Methodogy, Tools and Applications'.Her interest areas are Programming, Database, operating System, and Technology.

TABLE OF CONTENTS

LIST OF FIGURES

PREFACE

Computing systems increasingly need not just to execute correctly but also within strict time limits. From automotive control systems and medical devices to aerospace navigation and industrial automation, numerous safety-critical applications need computations to be executed in real-time. In these settings, correctness is not only determined by logical results but the timing of task completion. Any delay or missed deadline can put safety, efficiency, and reliability at risk. Real-time systems therefore represent a specialist and demanding domain of computing, where both performance and predictability are no less important than correctness of function.

Central to these systems is the Real-Time Operating System (RTOS) that controls resources, schedules tasks, communicates, and synchronizes under hard timing constraints. In contrast to general-purpose operating systems that aim for fairness and throughput, an RTOS strives for determinism and low latency. The architecture and implementation of RTOS notions demand a good balance of hardware capabilities, software algorithms, and application-specific needs. An understanding of these principles is essential for engineers and developers that are creating mission-critical applications where the failure is unacceptable.

The *Real-Time Operating Systems Concepts* textbook attempts to deliver a structured and in-depth discussion of RTOS concepts, architectures, and applications. It gives an overview of real-time computing basics, the formulation of operating system principles for real-time needs, and the breakdown of the elements of RTOS design. By its treatment of scheduling, memory management, communication, and reliability, the book offers an entire primer for students, practitioners, and professionals interested in designing or building real-time systems. The chapters follow a consistent order with the fundamentals beginning in the first chapter and the more advanced ones on communications systems and security matters concluding last.

Chapter 1 explains real-time systems. It addresses the distinction between soft and hard real-time systems, the relevance of deadlines, and usages in fields such as embedded systems, robotics, and telecommunications. The chapter provides perspective on why there are real-time requirements and sets the stage for the need for special operating systems.

Chapter 2 deals with real-time operating system basics. It describes the fundamental concepts of process management, scheduling, and resource allocation as they are taught conventionally and how these concepts must be adapted for real-time usage. It identifies the difference between general-purpose OS functionality and RTOS design specifications.

Chapter 3 discusses RTOS architecture and components. The chapter identifies the kernel, scheduler, interrupt handler, timers, and communication subsystems as the pillars of an RTOS. It describes monolithic and microkernel architectures and how determinism and performance are affected by modularity and efficiency.

Chapter 4 talks about the scheduling of tasks in real-time systems. It talks about static and dynamic scheduling algorithms such as Rate-Monotonic Scheduling (RMS), Earliest Deadline First (EDF), and priority-based preemptive scheduling. It discusses the predictability, resource utilization, and computational overhead trade-offs.

Chapter 5 introduces inter-task communication and synchronization. It describes mechanisms such as semaphores, mutexes, message queues, and mailboxes. The chapter also outlines the limitations of avoiding deadlocks, race conditions, and priority inversion in real-time systems.

Chapter 6 addresses time management in RTOS. Real-time systems do indeed need proper timekeeping, and the chapter summarizes clock management, timers, event scheduling, and time-triggered mechanisms. It stresses the necessity for exact time services to handle synchronization and deadline enforcement.

Chapter 7 deals with memory management for real-time systems. It explains partitioned memory, stack management, and dynamic allocation methods. The chapter explains how fragmentation and nondeterministic memory delays must be avoided in order to obtain deterministic execution.

Chapter 8 discusses interrupt handling and I/O management. It mentions the key role of interrupts in the processing of external events as well as the design of interrupt service routines (ISRs) with minimal latency. The chapter also addresses device drivers and direct memory access (DMA) in efficient I/O processing.

Chapter 9 addresses real-time communication systems. It covers the protocols and mechanisms by which distributed real-time systems can be made to communicate reliably. Fieldbus systems, real-time Ethernet, and wireless protocols that try to minimize latency and jitter are addressed.

Chapter 10 concludes with RTOS reliability and security. It examines the growing necessity of making real-time systems secure against cyber-attacks, as well as ensuring fault tolerance and robustness. The chapter discusses redundancy, watchdog timers, and safety certifications required in sectors such as automotive and aerospace.

The intention of this book is to act as a resource for students, researchers, and experts involved in the concept and use of real-time operating systems. For electronics, computer science, and engineering students, it provides a sound foundation in RTOS concepts with immediate application. For software engineers and system architects, it offers technology guidance in real-time solution design and development. It may be useful for researchers to explore more topics such as communication systems and security in real-time systems.

CHAPTER 1

INTRODUCTION TO REAL-TIME SYSTEMS

Contents

INTRODUCTION

In computer science, real-time systems are computing systems that react to input events within a given time frame. This is a significant aspect in systems where time is crucial, including embedded systems, aerospace control systems, and real-time operating systems (RTOS). In short, a real-time system must ensure the execution of some tasks within hard deadlines, thus distinguishing it from ordinary computer systems where timeliness is not of concern. Meeting these deadlines late will have serious effects, such as system crashes or safety hazards. Thus, the most typical feature of real-time systems is not necessarily their functionality but rather that they can respond accurately and in time, which points to a mix of hardware and software with specific design for reliability in performing tasks that are time critical. Moving to a more detailed classification of real-time systems, they are divided into two broad categories: hard real-time systems and soft real-time systems. Hard real-time systems demand rigorous adherence to timing constraints, so that any procrastination would lead to catastrophic effects. For instance, in medical devices such as pacemakers, failure to execute within specified time constraints might result in life-threatening ailments. In contrast, soft real-time systems allow some latitude for timing constraints, so that delays would depute performance but not lead to catastrophic effects. An example is in certain multimedia applications, where timing is required but there is leeway in replaying audio or video streams. These classifications must be understood in order to properly design systems suited for their respective applications and the particular roles they play within greater operational environments within industries. In addition, issues inherent in real-time systems extend beyond the enforcement of deadlines in a strict sense. One such interesting aspect is the addition of non-functional attributes such as performance efficiency and reliability that have to be included along with timing constraints. With technology advancements, application variability and interaction complexity demand advanced mechanisms to represent and manage these non-functional specifications. For example, NoFun notation provides a basis for modeling non-functional properties of software components so that they are harmonized properly with the real-time requirements. Such frameworks are very useful in the design and construction of real-time systems to enhance performance and improve real-time computing trade-offs (Guti et al., 1998). Therefore, a proper definition of real-time systems should not just consider timing but also how they must effectively compete in a busy technological world in order to be efficient and reliable.

Explanation of Real-Time Systems

Real-time systems are a system that accepts input and gives output in some time duration. They are most important for applications where timing matters, like embedded systems, robots, and even financial trading systems. Hard and soft real-time systems are the points of differentiation here. Hard real-time systems guarantee that the critical tasks are completed within a bounded time frame; any deviation from these time constraints results in failures of catastrophic proportions. A few applications of such systems are aerospace control systems and medical instruments, where delay can risk human lives or damage property.

Soft real-time systems, while being interested in time bounds, have some tolerating capability for misses of deadlines. This subtlety is most applicable to systems such as multimedia applications, where quality degradation is acceptable, but responsiveness remains the issue to maximize user satisfaction. The intricacy of real-time systems typically arises from their requirements for both correctness of operation and system performance. Real-time systems not only have to respond suitably to input but also have to respond within specified temporal limits. Since real-time computing is coupled with high-end technologies such as Cyber-Physical Systems (CPS) in larger numbers, the importance of robust real-time mechanisms also increases. The problems involved in ensuring reliability and security in real-time systems are aggravated by this integration. For instance, varied risks can be evolved due to unforeseen interactions between parts or from external cybersecurity attacks. Mitigating these risks requires firmer frameworks that are able to monitor system activity at all times so that any deviation from expected function is detected and rectified immediately, thus serving to protect user safety and system integrity (Wagner et al., 2023) (Figure 1.1).

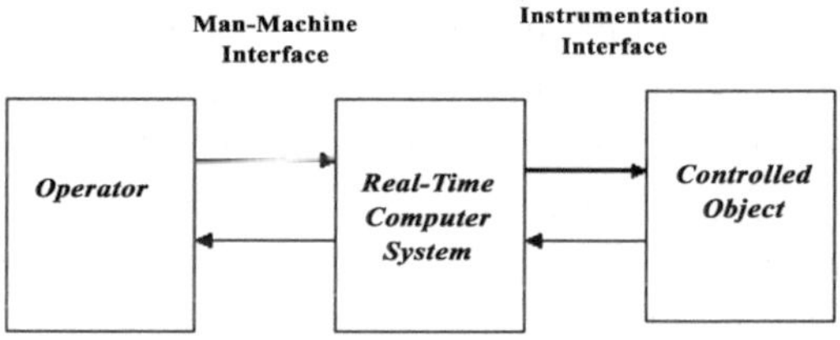

Figure 1.1. *Real-time system.*

Source: https://users.ece.cmu.edu/~koopman/des_s99/real_time/rts1_fig1.gif.

In this context, Protective Shells have been designed as an advanced means of defending real-time systems during their runtime phase. The protective layer proactively checks systems for anomalies and activates countermeasures appropriately, thereby ensuring enhanced safety and security. Protective shell is not an addition, but an integral part of contemporary real-time system design. By utilizing advances in explainable artificial intelligence (XAI), such shells can render their decision-making processes understandable, thus allowing human operators to interpret system behavior. Such transparency is useful in avoiding unwanted and unexpected outcomes, usually the reason for safety incidents (Schmidhuber et al., 2008). Lastly, the design and use of safeguarding shells are a significant advance in realizing the full potential of real-time systems in a secure and protective setting.

Characteristics of Real-Time Systems

The real-time systems are characterized by their ability to complete tasks within defined time constraints, a feature that sets them apart from ordinary computing systems. Not only is the accuracy of the results in real-time systems significant, but also so is their timing. This suggests that a system may be ineffective if it provides accurate results after a deadline period of importance. The aspect of time has the hard and soft requirements; hard real-time systems should obey strict timing constraints under all conditions, while soft real-time systems can tolerate small latencies. The distinction emphasizes the operating demands in varying applications, from industrial process control to consumer devices, emphasizing the need for precise timing devices in developing effective real-time programs. The second significant property of real-time systems is their predictable scheduling behavior, which becomes crucial to deal with activities that run in parallel. Scheduling activities in real-time systems can be classified into various algorithms, such as rate-monotonic or earliest deadline first, that schedule activities based on their priority.

For instance, in the context of safety-critical systems such as aerospace systems where failure to respond in time would lead to disastrous consequences, these real-time scheduling algorithms play a crucial role in order to provide system reliability. In addition, predictability provided with real-time scheduling enables system designers to achieve performance analysis and resource allocation in a more effective way. This ensures that computational facilities are best utilized, in line with the severe requirements of programs that demand correctness and prompt response time. Besides scheduling, resource management in real-time systems is another essential aspect that underscores complexity.

Resource management must cater to both the computation and communication aspects of the system. In systems where multiple tasks compete for limited resources, it is critical to ensure that the actual real-time demands of the more important tasks are not ignored. For example, in a vehicular network, as highlighted in the recent work, energy and bandwidth management become vital concerns for maintaining the required Quality of Service (QoS) levels of data and audio applications in real-time systems (Audu et al., 2016).

Moreover, the combination of power-saving considerations with the real-time realm, as indicated by the advent of wind-driven base stations, is a sign of persistent endeavors towards green technology while maintaining rigorous performance demands (Bajaj et al., 2016). This multi-faceted resource management approach ultimately encourages overall dependability and usability of real-time systems in various applications.

Importance of Real-Time Systems in Various Applications

The significance of real-time systems is achieved in varied application domains such as telecommunications, motor control systems, and medical devices. Real-time systems are designed to process inputs and deliver outputs under tight timing constraints, preserving system reliability and functionality. In automotive systems, for instance, real-time systems support life-critical functions such as anti-lock braking systems (ABS) and adaptive cruise control. These qualities are premised on timely data gathering and reaction to changed conditions, emphasizing the severity of consequences resulting from delays in processing. Additionally, telecommunications cannot overstate the significance of real-time systems, which maintain the quality of voice and data conveyance, which is paramount to free communication. Real-time systems ensure that time-critical data is processed smoothly, which enhances system performance and satisfaction. But another place where real-time systems play a most important role is in medical devices.

Devices such as infusion pumps and pacemakers need real-time capability to monitor physiological signals and execute life-sustaining interventions. For example, failure or a delay in such devices may be lethal to patient safety. The application of real-time systems in healthcare not only facilitates immediate medical response but also aids in the management of large volumes of data streams generated by sensors connected to patients. This enhances the provision of healthcare as a whole since fast analysis and decision-making may be indispensable in emergency situations. Real-time systems further facilitate remote monitoring, with healthcare professionals remotely controlling patient health, ultimately enhancing outcomes. Moreover, the growing importance of real-time systems across domains such as robotics and internet of things (IoT) helps highlight their universal applicability. In robotics, real-time systems enable autonomous machines to interact with changing worlds by reacting to sensor inputs and sending commands in a timely manner.

This holds great utility for applications as diverse as industrial automation through to service robots in healthcare environments. Similarly, the proliferation of IoT devices calls for efficient processing and communication of real-time data. With increasing IoT networks, there is a need for systems that can handle big amounts of data while delivering low latency. The systems should meet the high requirements of real-time performance in terms of providing reliability and efficiency on various platforms. The advances in real-time systems also provide opportunities for growth in smart cities and infrastructures of connections, further cementing their indispensable position in modern technology and society.

1.1. TYPES OF REAL-TIME SYSTEMS

Real-time systems are broadly categorized into two fundamental categories: hard real-time systems and soft real-time systems. Hard real-time systems are characterized by the stringent requirement that tasks must be completed within a predetermined deadline, and non-compliance with it could result in disastrous harm. Flight control systems of aircraft and biomedical equipment monitoring patient vital signs are a few examples of hard real-time applications. Their predictability and reliability are of utmost importance as they are employed to accomplish safety-critical missions for which a slight delay can have disastrous implications. On the other hand, soft real-time systems emphasize timeliness but can tolerate some slack in meeting deadlines, accepting some lapse without calamitous consequences. Examples such as video streaming and online games are typical examples where there is a better user experience using a constant stream of data without the same level of urgency as hard real-time systems. In addition to the underlying difference between hard and soft real-time systems, there are embedded real-time systems and networked real-time systems. Embedded real-time systems are subsystems of larger electronic or mechanical systems and function as an expert control module. An example of this is the anti-lock braking system (ABS) of an automobile, which keeps a continuous lookout for wheel speed and applies the brakes to prevent skidding. They tend to be designed with stringent resource requirements and power constraints. In contrast, networked real-time systems execute on interconnected nodes, where communication and timely data exchange are essential. These systems are likely to require sophisticated synchronization protocols to ensure prompt data transmission between distributed components, which might be especially critical in application areas such as industrial automation and smart grids. Utilization of embedded and networked components indicates a growing trend in real-time system design, which requires seamless integration and uniform performance across complex configurations. Finally, real-time system applications with critical implications can be observed in the field of healthcare, the most prominent being the utilization of real-time continuous glucose monitoring (RT-CGM) systems. These systems are worth their benefits for diabetes patients by providing real-time data to support effective control of the condition. A study highlighted the cost-effectiveness of RT-CGM for intensive insulin-treated patients, which shows the worth potential of improving health outcomes and reducing diabetes management-related complications (Alshannaq et al., 2024). In addition, the use of real-time monitoring within clinics is able to avoid dangerous hypoglycemic attacks by allowing timely data-driven decisions, exemplifying the significant influence of real-time systems on patient health. These advances not only attest to the technological competence of these systems but also to their critical role in enhancing the quality of life of patients, ultimately to enable the ongoing development of healthcare technologies in patient safety and results (Figure 1.2).

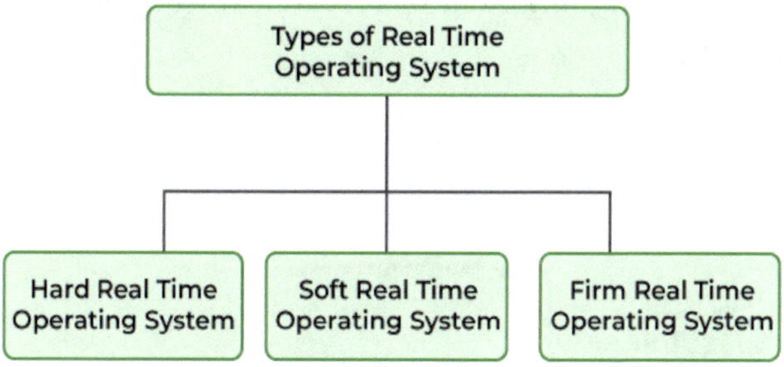

Figure 1.2. Types of real-time operating system.

Source: https://media.geeksforgeeks.org/wp-content/uploads/20231004143321/Operating-System-1.png.

1.1.1. Hard Real-Time Systems

Architecture in hard real-time systems is predominantly a key to missions where timely execution of tasks is crucial to functionality and safety. These systems are designed to offer assurances that all tasks must be finished within some time limits, which is important in applications such as aerospace, automobile, and industrial automation. For instance, the systems deployed in military hardware, such as the Army Fault Tolerant Architecture (AFTA), are tailored to satisfy severe requirements like high computational throughput and hard real-time responsiveness. AFTA not only puts pressure on the necessity of reliability and maintainability but also on the fact that the underlying technology can be economically manufactured and effortlessly integrated into existing operational frameworks (Alger et al., 2025). The consequences of having such rigid design constraints underscore the importance of precise task scheduling and resource allocation in hard real-time systems, which critically influence their overall performance and dependability in mission-critical environments. One key feature of hard real-time systems is that they have deterministic characteristics, with predictable task completion times. This determinism is addressed in multiple manners, including rate-monotonic and earliest deadline first scheduling, which are calculated by priority sequence of task execution. The scope extends beyond mere performance measurement to influence safety-critical operation where failure can have disastrous implications. In military contexts, the system design needs of low altitude helicopter control or tank systems present the challenges hard real-time systems can cause to operational efficiency and mission success (Alger et al., 2025). As such, the building of resilient algorithms and scheduling environments capable of satisfying the stringent requirements of hard real-time computing remains an ongoing area of research for researchers and engineers in the area (Figure 1.3).

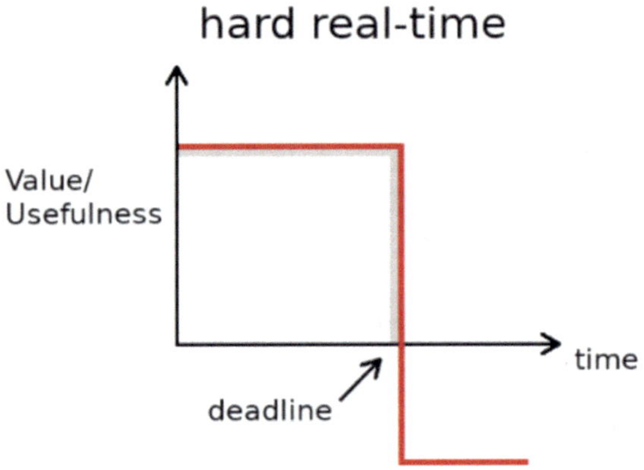

Figure 1.3. *Hard real-time systems.*

Source: https://www.allaboutcircuits.com/uploads/articles/Real_Time_Embedded_Systems_01.png.

Despite the advantages offered by hard real-time systems, there are problems, particularly in the area of integration with today's computing environments. Virtualization technology based on containers offers a probable path to realization of optimum system performance, with conditions attached. Although such technologies offer assistance for multiple isolated applications being co-deployed on shared assets—facilitating efficiency along with asset management—the technologies do not usually incorporate the inherent real-time support necessary for hard real-time systems. This limitation is of great concern in automated companies, where the ability to always meet deadlines is non-negotiable, especially in connecting applications from different vendors. Consequently, studies must address this limitation, coming up with solutions that optimize the real-time aspects of container-based worlds so that they remain applicable in companies where strict compliance with deadlines is required.

1.1.2. Soft Real-Time Systems

Soft real-time systems play a pivotal role in situations where timely responses are imperative but not always essential. Unlike hard real-time systems, whose absolute deadline guarantees play a vital role, soft real-time systems favor responsiveness and overall system performance. For soft real-time systems, late arrival or misses by deadlines are tolerable, provided they do not lead to significant loss of the quality of service. Soft real-time systems exhibit this elasticity in general, with continuous audio and video streaming being inevitable but imperceptible delays being acceptable. The inherent elasticity of soft real-time systems offers improved utilization of resources and the ability to deal with varying workloads, and so they are applicable to situations that need both performance and elasticity. Computer-assisted surgery (CAS) is one such use of soft real-time systems. In this context, soft real-time capabilities facilitate real-time assessment of tissue motion and morphology under procedure conditions, which is critical to make the procedure outcomes successful. Successful intra-operative monitoring of soft tissues has been observed by recent research to enhance the navigation capabilities of a surgeon substantially, hence resulting in improved accuracy of minimally invasive surgeries (MIS) (Figure 1.4).

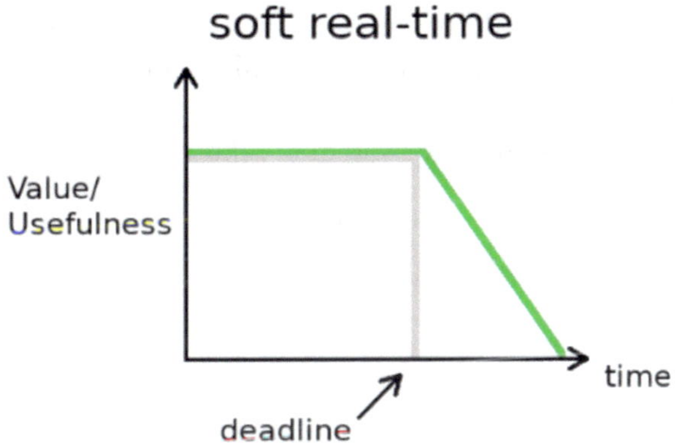

Figure 1.4. Soft real-time systems.

Source: https://www.allaboutcircuits.com/uploads/articles/Real_Time_Embedded_Systems_01.png.

With surgery trends progressing even more towards MIS, responsive and adaptive systems become increasingly vital. Optical techniques employed in 3D reconstruction of soft tissue surfaces demonstrate how intricate CAS procedures can be enabled by soft real-time systems, taking advantage of the capabilities of dynamic and adaptive technology in a high-risk environment (Bartoli et al., 2013). Moreover, the development of artificial immune systems (AIS) is a prime example of the growing emphasis on computational paradigms that are consonant with soft real-time structures. Through imitation of biologic immune processes, AIS models are well-suited to deal with complex computational problems through adaptive means. In recent years, there has been a growing research interest in creating immune-inspired algorithms that help in real-time data processing and analysis, highlighting their future feasibility for use in soft real-time applications. This coalescence of ideas is particularly valuable as demands on computer systems continue to escalate, encouraging innovation in ways that continue to perform despite decreased timing demands. The creation of AIS highlights the robust nature of soft real-time systems, providing avenues for research and implementation that address a wide variety of computational and engineering issues (Abbod et al., 2010).

1.1.3. Firm Real-Time Systems

Hard real-time systems are essential in environments where time is important for ensuring the integrity of operation but where the consequences of missed deadlines are less catastrophic than they are in hard real-time systems. They are characterized by their ability to tolerate random deadline misses without catastrophic failure. Instead, a missed deadline in a firm real-time system typically results in a reduction of service quality or loss of significant information, but not the complete system breakdown.

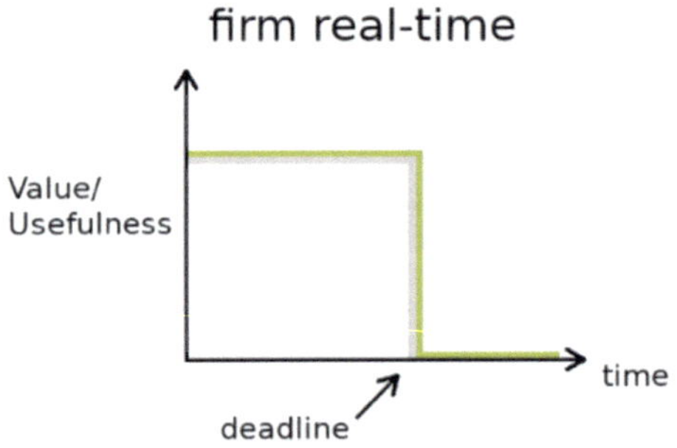

Figure 1.5. Firm real-time systems.

Source: https://www.allaboutcircuits.com/uploads/articles/Real_Time_Embedded_Systems_01.png.

As an example, in the application domains of streaming multimedia or telecommunications, timely delivery of data is important, but the system can typically recover from occasional delays with little long-term impact. Understanding this trade-off allows engineers to design systems that are both robust and efficient, targeting the needs of applications requiring some such compromise between strict timing requirements and resource usage. Engineering principles constituting the basis for firm real-time systems need to be taken into account for maximizing control over resources without fully losing some temporal constraints. Scheduling methods here are essential, as they decide how tasks are given priority and executed within the limits of the computational area. Approaches such as Rate Monotonic Scheduling (RMS) and Earliest Deadline First (EDF) are often employed to ensure that high-priority tasks are accomplished under their deadlines without degrading the overall system performance. Further, the developers of a system must also address the challenges of multithreading and concurrent processes, especially in mapping these features to the target hardware architecture. The requirements of dependable real-time scheduling and safe multithreading point to the complexity of implementing a reliable firm real-time system that is capable of fulfilling its aimed operation targets without compromising system integrity (Broenink et al., 2003) (Figure 1.5). In addition, the emergence of more distributed architectures in company real-time systems creates further design issues, not least of which are fault tolerance and real-time communication. Since such systems are often composed of numerous interacting modules that run in parallel, coordination among them must be maintained using advanced techniques to allocate resources and schedule networks. Incorporation of fault tolerance strategies is also important since it enforces the systems capability to withstand unexpected failures that may arise while in operation. Furthermore, as demand rises for embedded systems in various industries—ranging from the automotive to telecommunications—developers must navigate a complicated matrix of trade-offs between performance, reliability, and efficiency. This cross-disciplinary design environment reflects the requirement for continuous improvement of methodologies and practices devoted to solid real-time systems in order for them to keep up with the evolving demands of today's applications (Aldin et al., 2009).

1.2. COMPONENTS OF REAL-TIME SYSTEMS

The core of any real-time system is its main elements, which are interlocking to deliver timely and determinist responses. They are made up of hardware elements, including processors and I/O devices, and software structures responsible for dictating real-time behavior. The hardware must be capable of performing tasks within specified time durations, at times requiring special processors or task-switch-friendly architecture. The software of a real-time system is made up of real-time operating systems (RTOS) that offer task scheduling, resource management, and inter-process communication. Components of real-time systems also need to meet stringent reliability and fault tolerance needs because even minor delays lead to total failure. This interchange between hardware capabilities and software structures is significant in managing time-critical applications, which are the pillars of good real-time systems. Scheduling algorithms in the real-time systems decide the sequence of task execution and in what order of priority. Various algorithms have been designed for different types of real-time constraints, such as hard or soft deadlines (Figure 1.6).

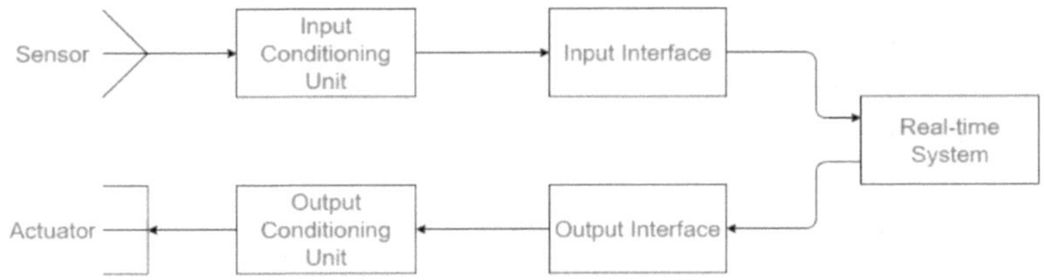

Figure 1.6. Basic model of a real-time system.

Source: https://www.geeksforgeeks.org/operating-systems/basic-model-of-a-real-time-system/.

Certain other popular scheduling algorithms include Rate Monotonic Scheduling (RMS) and Earliest Deadline First (EDF), which address the sequencing of tasks based on priority and deadline, respectively. The choice of algorithm directly affects the efficiency and determinism of the systems and is therefore a consideration that should be kept in mind by developers. System responsiveness is also generally quantified using Quality of Service (QoS) measures that quantify timeliness and reliability. By the use of effective scheduling methods tailored to specific application needs, real-time systems can offer the dependability and performance necessary for applications ranging from industrial automation to embedded systems, thus being an essential component of real-time systems (Anastasi et al., 2009). Real-time systems can also execute under advanced networking environments, such as in industrial automation and most IoT applications. The integration of standard off-the-shelf networking protocols with real-time capabilities facilitates higher communication and interoperability among system components. This paradigm allows flexible, self-contained, and dynamic behavior because devices can share information effortlessly with very stringent real-time requirements. As a case in point, the increasing visibility of embedded real-time systems has introduced new methods for facilitating self-configuration and diagnosis that result in plug-and-play capability. However, challenges to QoS must be addressed to guarantee that real-time applications are provided with the bandwidth and latency they need to run optimally. With the improvement in the technology, development of architectures that are capable of negotiating QoS and examining the temporal character of services is essential for enhancing the functionality of real-time systems in complex industrial environments (Szücs et al., 2011) (Figure 1.7).

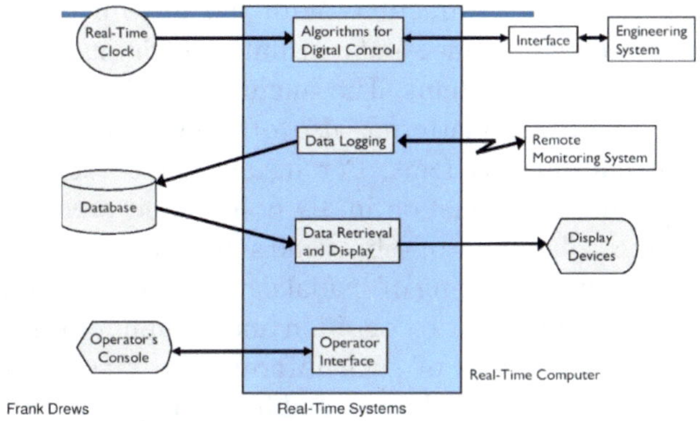

Figure 1.7. Typical components of an RTS.

Source: https://external-content.duckduckgo.com/iu/?u=https%3A%2F%2Fimage3.slideserve.com%2F6796645%2Ftypical-components-of-a-rts-l.jpg&f=1&nofb=1&ipt=7efa12cc37055b1e87944aad77a8a541296 40ee95443b0f75ca4dcdcc646a25f.

1.2.1. Hardware Components

Hardware components in real-time systems form the critical infrastructure that provides for performance, dependability, and functionality. Hardware choice influences not only the speed at which processes run but also the performance of the systems in satisfying real-time constraints. Critical components include microcontrollers, processors, memory, and communication interfaces that collaborate for addressing stringent time requirements that are inherent in real-time systems. Particularly, the resource-constrained environments have embedded systems whose processing power is limited. The designs of the systems must be given adequate attention and optimization to allow them to handle the processing load as a result of complex tasks, e.g., control algorithms and sensor data, prevalent in robotic and automated systems. Hardware reliability increases increasingly as electronic devices get more sophisticated. Minimization has been realized with very integrated circuits, but at the expense of higher fault vulnerability. Hardware faults can seriously make real-time system reliability very complex, particularly in applications where fail-safe operation is paramount. Emerging methods such as Software-Implemented Hardware Fault Tolerance aim at addressing these problems so that systems are able to enjoy dependable operations without extensive hardware modification. Such solutions can enhance fault tolerance but add new problems with regard to task scheduling, as timing constraints will become harder to satisfy with the use of such levels of abstraction. With the growth of technology, the interaction between fault tolerance and real-time scheduling will remain a vital issue in designing reliable systems. The integration of hardware components with sophisticated software platforms also offers the grounds for high-level functionalities in real-time systems. For instance, the use of deep learning methods like semantic segmentation in 3D point cloud processing has a long way in elevating the capabilities of robots and self-driving cars. The technology is based on the effective processing of spatial data obtained from sensors such as LiDARs, which facilitate object recognition and mapping of the environment. However, real-time processing of such information is considerably difficult owing to its sparsity, disorganized form, and high computational requirements. As described in contemporary studies, good performance on hardware with limited resources like the NVIDIA Jetson devices can be achieved by leveraging efficient algorithms and optimized training methods, facilitating good real-time use of advanced functions in practical applications without compromising efficiency or reliability (Haidar et al., 2024).

1.2.2. Software Components

In the context of the real-time system, software components play a crucial role in preserving the reliability and efficiency of operations. They are executable modular components that may be independently developed, tested, and maintained. Their design demands careful attention to timing constraints, wherein any lapse would lead to system failure with catastrophic consequences. Because most real-time applications require responses within tight time deadlines, the software entities have to exhibit not just functional correctness but also correct timing. This kind of performance-reliability tradeoff highlights the importance of using strong scheduling algorithms as well as fault tolerance techniques. Moreover, with increasingly more complex real-time systems, the software entities have to be conformant to higher-level requirements, through the integration of traditional static analyses with dynamic resource scheduling for optimally improving their performance in various operating environments. The software composition introduces special challenges, particularly when dealing with mixed-criticality systems. These are systems in which multiple software components of varying safety-criticality execute on a shared computing platform. The composition demands a framework that delivers timing assurances at multiple assurance levels to all of the components. Resource reservation in conventional real-time systems has been cautious and yielded low resource utilization but not at the cost of safety. However, recent explorations of mixed-criticality systems reveal new means of alleviating those issues, such as the synthesis of necessary feasibility tests for such systems.

Not only do such tests provide formal means for assessing the performance of critical components overall, but they contribute to a more dynamic utilization of computational resources as well. By emphasizing special characteristics of mixed-criticality systems, researchers have established developments in resource optimization with regard to critical timing constraints. Fault tolerance combined with scheduling is a vital topic area within software components in real-time systems. Although hardware miniaturization and growing complexity make hardware faults more likely. Software-Implemented Hardware Fault Tolerance methods have now been viable means to enhance system robustness against such failures. However, their integration complicates satisfaction of timing constraints further and thus makes scheduling more complicated. Software fault tolerance and timing properties' interaction calls for more research to achieve interaction in an all-encompassing manner. To address this, researchers are proposing coupled scheduling-failure analysis models that explain the formal interactions between these two inextricably linked aspects. These new paradigms aim to address emerging research in this area, with the goal of informing the development of future real-time systems that are efficient yet reliable, allowing for the safe operation of safety-critical applications within a wide range of domains, including automotive and industrial control systems (Chwa et al., 2021; Reghenzani et al., 2023).

1.2.3. Communication Protocols

In real-time systems, efficiency and effectiveness of communication protocols are accountable for accomplishing timely and reliable data transfer among system components. Communication protocols define conventions and rules of data transmission that enable devices to smoothly communicate within time-constrained environments. Minimizing latency and delivering data transfer within given time boundaries is one of the main objectives of communication protocols in real-time systems. This becomes particularly important in systems such as those found in car systems, aerospace, and industrial automation, where delayed communication can lead to catastrophic failures. Compliance with predetermined timing requirements and message priority allows communication protocols to facilitate the operational integrity and success of real-time systems and thereby underscores the importance of stringent design and implementation standards in this field. Moreover, the usability of communication protocols contributes significantly towards system performance as well as user experience. Security features complexity can lead to usability problems, which can be harmful in smooth communication and data sharing. Recent research has clarified that poor usability in security features will exclude the intended users from systems and provide means of access to violation of sensitive information.

Hence, there is a need to maintain a balance between robust security features and user-friendly interfaces while designing communication protocols. By being capable of handling issues of usability such as memorability, feedback, and context of use, protocols can be secured and made accessible. This not only guarantees that sensitive data is kept secure, but it also facilitates a more accessible arena where users can interact with technology in an effective manner, showcasing the intersectionality of security and usability in real-time systems. Besides, new paradigms that integrate various design methodologies, such as Kansei Design (KD) and User Centered Design (UCD), may play an essential part in more efficient communication protocol design. These methodologies focus on user preference and need centered design, which is important when designing protocols to facilitate effective communication while working towards environmental awareness. By coordinating user values and connecting them with design solutions, developers can enhance the Eco-design process in such a way that communication protocols become sustainable and user-centric. As proposed in previous research, extending an understanding of user interaction in the case of real-time systems can lead to innovative design solutions that are both efficient and environmentally responsive. This integrated approach highlights the need for incorporating users' viewpoints into designing communication protocols, with a long-term goal of enhancing real-time systems.

1.3. CHALLENGES IN REAL-TIME SYSTEMS

Real-time systems are characterized by their timing requirements in which correctness of system functioning and punctuality of the output are of prime concern. One of the biggest challenges in designing such systems is specifying that the systems are responding within specified deadlines. This is particularly complex in systems where there are multiple tasks to be executed in parallel. For instance, autonomous flight systems, which are increasingly being integrated into the National Airspace System, require real-time capability to conduct obstacle detection and avoidance for safety of operations. The need to minimize disruptions while optimizing technological capabilities presents significant challenges, as indicated in recent research commenting on the sophisticated problems that must be addressed for ubiquitous adoption of autonomous systems in aviation contexts (Lodding et al., 2011). Disastrous failure can occur if these timelines are not met, emphasizing the synergy between timing and functionality in real-time application development. Another significant problem in real-time systems is their multidisciplinary demands of problem-solving methods for efficient development. Researchers in fields such as systems biology have utilized collaborative models to achieve breakthroughs, but the same models need to be used when addressing problems in real-time systems.

Integrating effectively entails collaboration among experimentalists who design the hardware and software components and mathematicians who design the algorithms needed for real-time capabilities. Creation of web-based software which facilitates collaboration, like the Google Wave protocol, is an example of what technology can do to facilitate research groups which are creating real-time systems to collaborate over data and understanding in real-time. The collaborative platform can solve problems with regard to the distribution of experimental data and system standardization. Lacking these cooperative frameworks, the growth of robust real-time systems may be dramatically hindered, as various specialists must coordinate their activities towards common goals (Swainston, 2010). Finally, real-time system validation and verification present unique difficulties that call for stringent methodologies. With such systems typically operating in mission-critical systems, mistakes or delay in the systems response may have disastrous results. Making the systems correct and reliable is further made harder by their dynamic environment of operation, necessitating adjustments and adaptations at all times. Such processes as formal verification, in which mathematical proofs are employed to prove correctness, may be required but are inherently resource-consuming. Furthermore, even with the introduction of automatic testing tools, real-time systems typically find it difficult to cope with the hurdles of simulating huge environmental conditions comprehensively. It is critical that there be robust validation tools in such systems to guarantee performance and safety levels so that they function optimally under the unexpected conditions that are inherent in real applications.

1.3.1. Resource Management

Effective resource management is crucial to the successful deployment of real-time systems since it directly affects system reliability and performance. Resource management means strategic utilization, scheduling, and coordination of computational resources to assign adequate resources to satisfy system needs without contention or inefficiency. In real-time systems, since the timing of resource allocation is as critical as the quantity of resource allocated, resource management dynamics become more complex. Techniques such as priority scheduling allow systems to allocate resources based on urgency, thereby catering to time-critical operations. Not only does this reduce delay, but overall system responsiveness and stability are also improved. As new technologies emerge, the practice of resource management must continuously improve to cope with emerging challenges in real-time systems so that systems are efficient and resilient against potential failure. Moreover, advancements in technologies such as multi-agent systems present new challenges and possibilities for real-time management of system resources. Utilization of such systems for coordinating to aggregate for decentralized decision-making will enhance flexibility and responsiveness through coordination of various agents. Such a decentralized process, however, demands robust mechanisms to resolve conflicts as well as coordinate activities efficiently. A concentration on the development of Village Knowledge Management Systems (VKMS) can serve as an example for real-time systems that integrate resource management for multiple agents so that knowledge sharing and strategy are permitted for effective utilization of resources (Gupta et al., 2025). The need for change in resource management strategies identifies the importance of adaptive models that can respond to evolving market conditions and varying operating needs, thus increasing efficiency and productivity. In the energy industry, effective resource management becomes increasingly significant as it also influences economic viability and operational sustainability. Previous research has shown that the application of supply chain management practices can decrease profit margins and operating efficiency in energy production and storage operations significantly. For instance, with the use of utility-scale batteries combined with wind power, the generation capacity can be converted to a more stable source, making its involvement in real-time market situations more effective (Saran et al., 2009). Utilizing real-time information and sophisticated analytics, systems are able to adjust the charging and discharging cycle of energy storage in conformity with the prevailing market conditions to ensure that the resources are utilized optimally. This resource strategic management not only guarantees optimal returns on investments but also promotes sustainability in the energy sector, underscoring the underlying connection between the management of resources and contemporaneous system success.

1.3.2. Timing Constraints

Timing constraints are responsible for ensuring tasks are executed under given deadlines in real-time systems. As opposed to other computer systems, whose correctness relies largely on the correctness of the output, real-time systems require both functional correctness and temporal correctness. The two requirements make the system harder to design because the synchronization of task execution must satisfy rigorous timing requirements. Schedulability analysis thus becomes an essential tool for managing these constraints. Through intense investigation of task workloads, engineers can decide whether each task can finish its deadline under varied conditions. The Digraph Real-Time task model with resource sharing (DRTRS) offers an abstraction in this regard, focusing on timing properties of relevance rather than on functional details and hence making temporal correctness analysis of real-time software easier (Zhuo et al., 1963) (Figure 1.8).

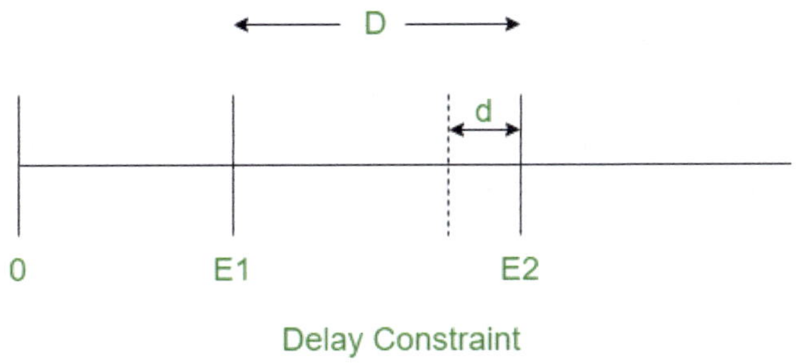

Figure 1.8. Delay constraint.

Source: https://www.geeksforgeeks.org/operating-systems/timing-constraints-in-real-time-system/.

The intrinsic unpredictability of modern-day streaming applications brings extra complexity to real-time systems' timing constraints. Adaptive behavior due to mode switching in such applications can cause critical degradation of predictability, particularly at mode switches. To counteract such issues, effective temporal analysis during mode switches is vital. The Mode Aware Data Flow (MADF) model is a significant innovation in modeling the intricate behaviors of adaptive systems. By establishing a new protocol, the Maximum-Overlap Offset (MOO), MADF enhances predictability through self-mode transition analysis. The method minimizes timing interference and enables improved understanding of temporal dynamics in mode switching. Hence, employing methods such as MADF is essential so that systems can have a capability to maintain strict timing constraints under different operating environments (Niknam et al., 2018). Ultimately, a comprehensive approach to timing constraint control will be required so that real-time systems can continue to be trustworthy. The intersection of schedulability analysis and adaptive application behavior creates a call for ongoing research in this field. With growing system complexity, supporting timing constraints in a timely manner necessitates creative approaches, such as the MOO protocol, which prevents processor overload and allows for independent examination of task switching. This development not only aims to maintain hard real-time constraints but also to create a climate where predictability and performance can coexist. With changing nature of real-time systems, a better understanding of timing constraints and their impact will continue to play a vital role in the design and implementation of effective and reliable systems in numerous applications, and hence the relevance of temporal analysis in itself (Niknam et al., 2018; Zhuo et al., 1963).

1.3.3. Fault Tolerance

Fault tolerance in real-time systems is a primary concern for ensuring operating reliability and continuity under adverse conditions. It is a quality most critical when system failure would be catastrophic, such as in autonomous systems or infrastructure.

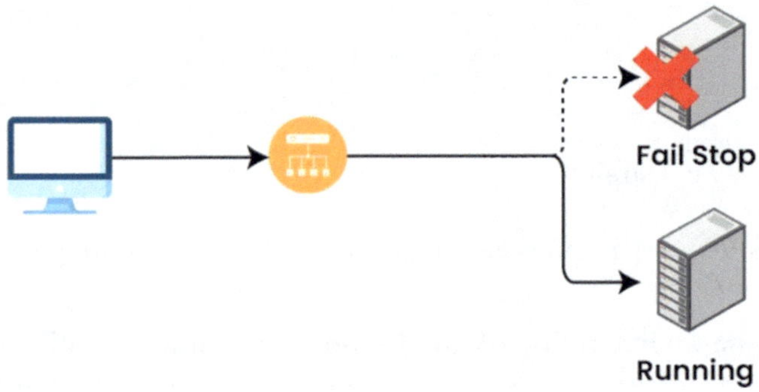

Figure 1.9. Fault tolerance.

Source: https://media.geeksforgeeks.org/wp-content/uploads/20240726124218/What-is-Fault-Tolerance.webp.

Most critical is that the system is able to detect, restrict, and recover from faults without degrading performance. Efficient fault tolerance mechanisms minimize downtime and maintain system functionality, thus meeting real-time requirements. As system complexity and interdependence grow, traditional fault tolerance methods prove insufficient and necessitate the creation of new frameworks and approaches to dynamically address failure in real-time applications. Implementing machine learning techniques into fault tolerance frameworks is of immense potential to facilitate the enhancement of system robustness. Predictive modeling helps real-time systems anticipate failures before they happen so that proactive measures can be initiated. For instance, machine learning classifiers such as a Random Forest can analyze system behavior patterns and forecast impending node failures to provide timely intervention. By using these techniques, systems can redistribute tasks and allocate resources effectively based on predictive data, thus reducing system disruption. As exemplified by existing research, developing fault tolerance strategies with the aid of machine learning does not only improve prediction accuracy but also facilitates a more adaptive response to failures when they occur, influencing the reliability of real-time systems (Niranjan, 2025) (Figure 1.9). Furthermore, real-time data pipeline optimization complements the fault-tolerance design guidelines by ensuring data availability and usability even with component faults. The integration of sensor data, models of computation, and decision algorithms illustrates the requirements for scalable, fault-tolerant data processing systems. Real-time settings are replete with challenges like data latency and transmission faults that can significantly impair the functionality of autonomous control systems. To address such issues, solutions like edge computing and stream processing can enhance both fault tolerance as well as efficiency. These technologies ensure that critical streams of data are maintained, and computation work gets distributed efficiently, which enables robust real-time decision-making resistant to potential system faults (Gaddam et al., 2025).

1.4. APPLICATIONS OF REAL-TIME SYSTEMS

The applications of real-time systems are critical across most fields, particularly where there is a great reliance on processing and acting in real-time. In industrial automation, for example, real-time systems guarantee the automated operation of machinery by guaranteeing that signals of control are dispatched and carried out within specific time constraints. This capability is imperative to providing safety and efficiency in production processes, where mistakes or delays can create costly downtime or even danger. Furthermore, advances in hardware and software programming methods, such as OpenMP, have made it possible for parallel processing to develop, allowing enhanced performance in real-time embedded systems. These developments offer improved response time and computation capability, particularly as systems become more integrated with advanced machinery and diverse data sources, emphasizing the revolutionary impact of real-time systems on industrial processes (Quiñones et al., 2017). For car systems, real-time systems are critical to ensure safety and reliability. Modern automobiles also rely heavily on embedded real-time systems to monitor performance, govern engine management, and aid the driver through options like adaptive cruise control and anti-lock braking systems. These applications have very rigid timing constraints to read sensor data and apply control actions in half a second. As there is greater complexity in automotive environments with features of autonomous driving, there is an even greater need for robust real-time systems. Through the implementation of methodologies that prioritize safety and time promises, developers can design systems that are either meeting or exceeding safety promises, hence establishing more confidence in autonomous technology. This revolution not only enhances vehicle performance but also has a promise of significant reduction in traffic accidents due to human and mechanical failure (Abdi et al., 2017). Healthcare applications are significantly enhanced using real-time systems, particularly in medical equipment and monitoring systems. Various life-critical processes, such as patient monitoring and robotic surgery, rely on fast and accurate data processing of data collected by hundreds of sensors. Real-time systems ensure crucial information is conveyed instantly to healthcare providers, enabling them to make decisions in emergency situations instantaneously. For instance, heart monitoring devices ought to provide real-time feedback throughout to warn medical staff of imminent changes in a patient's condition, potentially saving lives. Second, telemedicine helped by real-time systems facilitates consultation and diagnosis from any location, enabling patients to receive timely treatment anywhere. The continued advances in this area exhibit the key role that high-performance real-time systems play in relation to improving patient outcomes and enabling improved healthcare services (Quiñones et al., 2017).

1.4.1. Industrial Automation

Real-time system integration has played a crucial role in the industrial automation industry to enhance productivity and operational efficiency. Embedded real-time systems, which play a vital role in contemporary manufacturing environments through the timely and reliable control of processes under automation, are widely used in these environments. The trend is supported by advancement in networking technology technologies such as Ethernet and wireless communication technologies such as Wi-Fi and ZigBee, which facilitate immediate communication between various components of an automation system.

Figure 1.10. Industrial automation.

Source: https://etimg.etb2bimg.com/photo/116799139.cms.

Another important aspect of contemporary industrial automation platforms is their use of service-oriented architectures (SOAs) that are capable of dealing with elastic and autonomous components that provide self-configurability and diagnostics. The use of these technologies, however, creates problems where real-time support and ensuring the levels of quality-of-service (QoS) for applications based on stringent timing and reliability in execution become the concerns (Anastasi et al., 2009). To deal with the timing challenges of software-intensive systems, the estimation of software component execution times becomes an important task in industrial control applications. Accurate estimates of execution times are required to quantify non-functional properties of real-time systems since they affect the reliability and performance of the system directly. However, the generation of accurate execution time estimates is hindered by the unpredictability of software behavior in the actual system. To address this issue, new approaches have been proposed, including techniques based on algorithms that loop around the analysis of repeated code blocks for creating detailed timing models specific to processors (Gamer et al., 2014) (Figure 1.10). These answers enhance the reliability of timing predictions, ultimately enabling smooth incorporation of timing analysis into the software development environments of industrial automation projects. Use of effective real-time systems in industrial automation, apart from ensuring effective performance, provides a robust platform for future technological progress. The evolving world of industrial automation emphasizes the importance of adaptive and dynamic systems with the ability to cope with increased demands of production processes. Researchers and practitioners are thus always seeking means of boosting real-time capabilities through more effective architectures that facilitate QoS requirements negotiation between services. This ongoing development enables industrial systems to make efficient allocation of resources and eliminate interference among simultaneous operations, leading to better temporal behavior and overall dependability (Anastasi et al., 2009). Through it, then, the close integration between real-time system design and software performance analysis is set to revolutionize industrial automation, forging the way to more responsive, more intelligent manufacturing environments.

1.4.2. Automotive Systems

The integration of real-time systems in auto technology has revolutionized the operation of vehicles, making it safer and more efficient. Modern automotive systems rely heavily on real-time processing of data to support critical applications such as anti-lock brakes and advanced driver-assistance systems (ADAS) to function perfectly under varying conditions. The systems must respond to sensor input and environmental factors in real-time in a bid to prevent accidents and improve driver control. The design of such systems is particular in nature, i.e., it demands strict scheduling algorithms that guarantee the production of timely, reliable outputs. Additionally, there is the need for interaction between multiple systems present in a car that necessitates the in-depth examination of hard, soft, and firm real-time paradigms, as our mobility is slowly becoming automation and associated technologies as mentioned by Gomathy et al. (2025).

Within the automobile environment, sophisticated object detection technology has played a fundamental role in facilitating vehicle autonomy. An example is the application of real-time image processing-based systems, which allow vehicles to recognize and respond to various objects on their path. An example is the You Only Look Once (YOLO) algorithm, which has gained popularity for its efficacy and accuracy in object detection. With frames from in-car cameras, vehicles can see real-time changes in their environment that would ultimately result in safer driving conditions. Present trends indicate growing interest in the application of YOLO in the automotive sector, particularly for use cases like road traffic regulation and navigation of self-driving cars, as stated by Gheorghe et al. (2024) (Figure 1.11).

Figure 1.11. Automotive technology.

Source: https://www.fujitsu.com/global/imagesgig5/automotive-banner-800x450_tcm100-6604331_tcm100-6286607-32.jpg.

These advancements underscore the need for systems that are processed in real-time and need to balance speed with accuracy. Progress in real-time automotive systems continues to underline the importance of safety and reliability in engineering paradigms. With vehicles becoming increasingly more connected and autonomous, establishing robust testing and validation frameworks is essential to ensure such systems act predictably across various conditions. This encompasses not only formal simulation techniques but also on-road test environments that emulate different driving conditions. Furthermore, the integration of new technologies such as IoT and AI into vehicle systems is anticipated to raise their complexity, necessitating a cautious investigation of the attendant performance trade-offs. By concentrating on design good practices that address such parameters, designers can enable the continuous improvement of automotive systems without compromising stringent safety regulations and operation efficiency in terms of the principles described by Gomathy et al. (2025).

1.4.3. Telecommunications

As telecommunications advance, the need for real-time systems has become much more critical in this domain. This is due to the need for dealing with massive amounts of data in real-time becoming more vital in applications such as network management, security, and massive-scale sensor networks. Traditional DBMSs rather rely on a store-then-process mechanism, where data needs to be indexed and stored prior to being able to process it. On the other hand, data stream management systems (DSMSs) support real-time processing of streams of continuous data, and thus reliable and high-performance real-time systems are imperative in telecommunications. As firms aim to take advantage of this technology, operating dynamics and constraints of existing systems need to be grasped so that enhanced performance and reliability are achieved within telecommunications infrastructure (Muratore et al., 2014). Cutting-edge platform innovation is also necessary in creating telecommunications. These innovations encompass the Enhanced Storm, which takes advantage of the current strengths of Storm infrastructure to build upon inherent shortcomings. Enhanced Storm is compatible with native relational algebra and database operators, which enhance real-time data stream processing. Though maintaining fault tolerance and scalability that earns Storm a wide appeal, Enhanced Storm provides a high-performance solution especially tailored for dynamic scenarios. When such innovative systems are adopted by organizations, the potential to leverage real-time processing of information becomes a value-add that can facilitate greater responsiveness and agility in telecommunications applications (Muratore et al., 2014) (Figure 1.12).

Figure 1.12. Telecommunications.

Source: https://valenta.io/wp-content/uploads/2022/11/How-do-Telecommunications-Companies-Benefit-from-Process-Consulting-1.jpg.

Additionally, the open network APIs push has facilitated expansion and integration in the telecommunications sector. At the forefront of these is the

Parlay API, a leading technology that has attracted third-party innovators to create network-hosted apps. By opening up telecommunication networks to short-lived and niche applications, it fosters an ecosystem that thrives through innovation and rapid deployment. The successful phases of the API release and industry acknowledgment affirm its relevance and potential impact. Simulation and prototyping on real-world network execution platforms are essential in ensuring the technical feasibility of the Parlay APIs, hence revealing its advantages as well as its drawbacks in facilitating interoperable systems in telecommunications. These efforts emphasize embracing real-time systems that promote telecoms to be more adaptive and responsive to market demands.

1.5. FUTURE TRENDS IN REAL-TIME SYSTEMS

The development of real-time systems has grown exponentially with the growth in technology, especially by the integration of the Internet of Things (IoT). With more connected devices spreading all over, the characteristics of real-time systems are also expanding to support tremendous amounts of data generated by the devices. The effective deployment of the same information not only enables real-time control and monitoring but also enhances decision-making in different sectors of the economy like healthcare, transport, and industrial automation. According to Saurabh et al. (2023), deployment of IoT resources facilitates the collection and processing of data in real-time, which is critical in realizing utmost operational efficiency. This shift towards increased connectivity stresses the importance of developing robust real-time systems that can handle complex data exchanges, ultimately producing more responsive and intelligent environments. Another chief advancement of future trends in real-time systems is the evolution of edge computing with great benefits in latency and bandwidth usage. By calculating closer to the source rather than relying on cloud infrastructure in the middle, edge computing lessens latency and improves responsiveness of real-time systems. This is specifically important in those systems requiring real-time feedback, e.g., autonomous vehicles and smart factory. Furthermore, combining edge computing with existing systems holds potential as well as challenges, including security, interoperability, and concern for resource sharing. According to Saurabh et al. (2023), overcoming these challenges is imperative to maximizing the potential of real-time systems and ensuring the dependability of intelligent systems in increasingly complex environments. In the future, the merging of real-time systems with state-of-the-art technologies such as artificial intelligence and machine learning promises a revolutionary transformation across various domains. Smart real-time systems that incorporate high-end analytics have the ability not only to react to events but even predict and respond to future situations, thereby enhancing overall operational effectiveness and efficiency. The implementation of such intelligent real-time systems would necessitate robust systems of data management and decision-making that can cope with the dynamics of a changing environment. Methods that result from advancements in sensor technology, big data analytics, and human-machine interfaces will have a central role in this development. As relates, the fortification of geotechnology in planning procedures suggests the prospect of an era in which real-time systems are incorporated into comprehensive strategic decision-making in various areas, thus transforming our engagement with technology as well as the environment.

1.5.1. Integration with IoT

The integration of Internet of Things (IoT) into real-time systems has revolutionized industries across the board, with healthcare and supply chains leading the way. In the healthcare sector, the application of biosensors linked by multi-hop IoT networks has revolutionized real-time patient monitoring. Positioning biosensors at advantageous locations in medical facilities enables practitioners to continually take and feed health-related data to centralized servers.

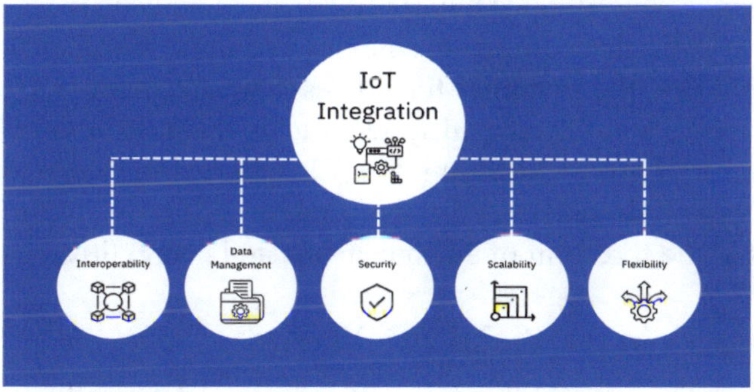

Figure 1.13. Integration of internet of things (IoT).

Source: https://external-content.duckduckgo.com/iu/?u=https%3A%2F %2Fthin-aer.io%2Fwp-content%2Fuploads%2F2023%2F05%2FIoT-Integration-1536x802.png&f=1&nofb=1&ipt=a0dfac03e4cd506d4655b215d16bd678e8ad2278d6fb8cf8599decd67da002cd.

Such alignment not only enhances the degree of surveillance by healthcare professionals but also transcends geographical positions since it enables them to receive critical information irrespective of where they are. This technological advancement, as described in relevant literature, is central in bridging traditional healthcare barriers, culminating in an ever-interconnected and efficient healthcare system (Uddin et al., 2024). The need for IoT integration is equally evident in the inventory management, particularly for Small and Medium-sized Enterprises (SMEs). AI-based inventory management systems via IoT technology have been extremely successful at controlling optimization of inventories and lowering operation expenses. With the help of IoT sensors and cloud applications, SMEs are able to achieve real-time inventory monitoring, which subsequently offers greater accuracy, reduced stockouts, and reduced carrying costs. Empirical data verifies that application of such systems leads to significant performance improvement in the form of a 25–35% increase in inventory accuracy and a 20–30% reduction in carrying cost. This paradigm shift not only enhances better demand forecasting but also mechanizes the process of reordering, thereby allowing companies to utilize resources more efficiently and effectively (Ugbebor et al., 2024) (Figure 1.13).

Further, the existence of IoT in real-time systems enables greater collaboration among stakeholders, leading to improved operational efficiencies in industries. In healthcare and inventory management, access to real-time information encourages anticipatory decision-making whereby businesses are capable of addressing problems as they arise. Seamless sharing of information via IoT networks enhances the supplier-buyer relationships and enhances supply chain responsiveness overall. As more businesses are implementing the utilization of IoT technologies, the potential for process improvement is 10 times more, resulting in a future with automated systems achieving maximum efficiency and reducing costs. This groundbreaking use of IoT in real-time systems ultimately signifies an essential transition in the strategies for operation, positioning organizations at the forefront of advancements and competitiveness.

1.5.2. Advances in Artificial Intelligence

The artificial intelligence (AI) landscape has changed drastically, especially with the emergence of deep learning and machine learning algorithms that allow for real-time processing of data across different fields. These technologies allow for the processing of complex data by machines and generating decisions at unmatched speeds, making them ideal for applications that need instantaneous responses. The application of AI in real-time systems not only adds functionality but also enhances efficiency, resulting in an even broader range of applications in robotics, medicine, and driverless vehicles. With these technologies on the horizon, there is a growing need for interdisciplinary collaboration to fully leverage the potential of AI, ensuring human capability complements machine capability. The quest for developing hybrid intelligence systems that leverage human intelligence, and artificial intelligence highlights the importance of systematic design knowledge in driving such solutions (Calma et al., 2019).

Also, high-dimensional sensing has come to play a crucial role in AI more and more. As the worlds transition into data-oriented paradigms, the ability to sense and process vast amounts of data in a limited time is of utmost importance. High-dimensional sensing (HDS) techniques have been more prominent in computer vision, robotics, and real-time computing because they can process intricate visual data and environmental interactions. With the rapid growth of AI technologies, it is now even obvious that algorithmic structures need to be developed that can facilitate real-time decision-making. For instance, application of advanced models to enhance machine vision for autonomous vehicle systems demonstrates a requirement for innovative solutions to processing and collecting data. This evolution creates avenues towards systems that not only fulfill the requirements of real-time performance but also maximize accuracy in data interpretation and decision-making processes (Arguello et al., 2022) (Figure 1.14).

Figure 1.14. The integration of AI into real-time systems not only enhances functionality but also increases efficiency.

Source: https://assets.everspringpartners.com/dims4/default/fb976e9/2147483647/strip/true/crop/686x360+171+0/resize/1200x630!/quality/90/?url=http%3A%2F%2Feverspring-brightspot.s3.us-east-1.amazonaws.com%2Fdf%2Fee%2F106592af4d508f76b29662e456db%2Fadvanced-ai.jpg.

Ultimately, the convergence of AI breakthroughs presents enormous potential for designing high-level real-time systems. The emergence of socio-technological aggregates that combine the effectiveness of human mind with the computability of machines constitutes a groundbreaking advance in the way that complex tasks can be solved. By establishing mutual collaboration between human operators and AI systems, organizations can achieve higher outputs that both could not produce on their own. While practitioners and researchers seek to determine the relevant dimensions of system design for such hybrid intelligence systems, the implications of these unifications become paramount to learn about. Guidelines for system developers will become the critical solution to bridging the gap between these advancements and practical implementations, turning real-time systems not only functional but also continually improving as they adapt and learn (Calma et al., 2019).

1.5.3. Development of New Scheduling Algorithms

Designing new scheduling algorithms is one of the key areas in real-time systems efficiency and reliability improvement. It is motivated by the increasing complexity of applications, such as manufacturing and computing environments, where timely execution is critical. Algorithms must compromise among various performance parameters, such as time to execute, using resources, and using energy. Specifically, adaptive scheduling techniques, which alter parameters in real-time based on varying system loads and environmental factors, have been efficient in managing such demands. As industries increase, scheduling algorithms are being specialized based on specific situations, such as job-shop and flow-shop scheduling issues, to enable maximum processing under diverse conditions (Werner et al., 2018). These advances pinpoint the necessity of continuing to enhance scheduling techniques in order to be able to keep up with advances in technology and user demands. The incorporation of real-time kinematic (RTK) positioning technology, yielding high precision in certain applications like agriculture and construction, points to the demand for robust scheduling algorithms. The necessity of simultaneous concurrent user inquiries in Network-based RTK (N-RTK) systems exposes additional computational challenges. The proposed layered framework utilizing Grid Computing is a manifestation of innovative scheduling mechanisms which can manage advanced algorithms without sacrificing responsiveness (Yin et al., 2009). Smart scheduling mechanisms on which such systems rely for optimal efficiency are capable of distributing resources dynamically based on requirement and capacity. This adaptability not only enhances the general performance of the RTK systems but also anticipates other developments in real-time scheduling techniques in other areas. In researching other algorithms, studies have demonstrated huge advancements in hybrid models that merge conventional scheduling techniques with modern computational models. Hybrid models can answer a broad spectrum of scheduling problems by leveraging heuristics and optimization techniques. For example, application of bi-objective optimization in scheduling can guarantee trade-off between opposing objectives such as minimum makespan and optimal resource utilization (Werner et al., 2018). With this multi-faceted aspect, algorithms are able to create innovative solutions based on increasing demands of real-time systems, particularly those with flexibility and responsiveness requirements. With innovation in scheduling algorithms, programmers are now able to make sure that real-time systems continue to be able to cope with diversified operation demands, thus paving the way for even more effective and more trustworthy programs in various sectors.

SUMMARY

In closing the topic of real-time systems, it is necessary to admire the intricate dance between trust and automation, especially in high-risk settings. The examination of the variables for instilling trust in real-world automation systems shows that while theoretical studies place a heavier emphasis on reliability and competence, operational trust in real-world circumstances significantly relies on the users' understanding of the automation deployed. The difference draws attention to the need to build systems, though technically good, that are also transparent and straightforward to operate and facilitate a trusting relationship capable of withstanding the stresses of practical use. The implications extend far beyond measurements of performance to operator psychology and point to a key area for future investigation as emerging technologies become more complex (Balfe et al., 2018). Furthermore, progress in real-time systems emphasizes that there is a need for continuous and accurate data processing capability. As an example, the ability to analyze real-time breath volatiles demonstrates the applicability of transportable mass spectrometry in health diagnosis. Such advancements have the potential to change patient treatment by enabling immediate reactions to clinical conditions, demonstrating that real-time data analysis is no utopian idea but a real requirement of the medical field. With scientists refining detection methods that are becoming ever more sensitive and transportable, it is clear that efficacy in operations and prompt response are front-of-mind priorities among real-time systems (Liam et al., 2016). Lastly, the implication of the integration of conclusions on real-time systems is that technology deployment must be multi-dimensional. A successful real-time system must possess robust technology, thorough knowledge of user trust fundamentals, and optimal methods of data aggregation so that it is effective in real-world applications. The future for real-time systems is bright with great possibilities, but it also challenges researchers and developers to supply solutions that are user-centric in sympathy yet strict in performance standards. It will be crucial in adopting a synergistic approach to tackle the complexity of automation so that technology and trust synergize well in the application range from transportation to healthcare (Balfe et al., 2018; Liam et al., 2016).

In real-time systems, the fundamental concept is focused on predictability and response of the tasks within very tight time constraints. The systems are characteristically known for processing inputs, executing operations, and producing output within a given time period, which is very critical in applications such as embedded systems and industrial automation. Real-time systems' concept of time goes beyond the execution; it includes deadlines and system responsiveness. Real-time behavior is affected by task deadlines, priority scheduling algorithms, and resource contention between the running processes. Understanding these factors is essential in an effort to create systems that are able to maintain their effectiveness under varying operational loads so as to support the main purpose of these systems during situations where reliability and timeliness are critical. The organization of real-time systems typically involves distinct categories: hard, soft, and firm real-time systems. Hard real-time systems execute under rigid schedules with missing deadlines having the potential to cause catastrophic failures, for instance, in medical devices or aerial systems. Soft real-time systems, however, leave avenues for deadline flexibility by attaching greater significance to overall system performance rather than hard-nosed punctuality, usually found in multimedia systems. With such classifications, designers are able to select appropriate methods to meet performance specifications with regard to constraints of the system. Also, inclusion of concepts such as scheduling tasks—statically or dynamically—assumes a core place in optimizing the flow of execution so that priorities run is always addressed economically in time. Coupled with scheduling complexities, real-time systems also face resource management and fault tolerance complexities. The allocation of computer resources, including CPU time and memory, must be well planned so that it does not lead to bottlenecks that cause deadline misses. Over-provisioning and resource reservation can be utilized to counter these threats, and the system can be made more resilient under varying operating conditions. Fault tolerance is also very important; systems not only have to recover from failure but should recover in such a way that operational integrity is not threatened. Redundancy and graceful degradation are approaches by which systems can continue to function at acceptable rates even in cases of partial failures. This pairing enhances the performance and resilience of real-time systems, which is a service of fulfilling expectations in its use in various industries.

REFERENCES

1. Abbod, M. F., Al-Enezi, J. R., & Alsharhan, S. (2010). Artificial immune systems: Models, algorithms and applications. https://core.ac.uk/download/8010.pdf (accessed on 29th September 2025).
2. Abdi, F., Caccamo, M., Mancuso, R., Tabish, R., et al. (2017). Restart-based fault-tolerance: System design and schedulable analysis. http://arxiv.org/abs/1705.02412 (accessed on 29th September 2025).
3. Abou Haidar, S., Chariot, A., Darouich, M., Joly, C., & Deschaud, J. E. (2024). Are we ready for real-time LiDAR semantic segmentation in autonomous driving? https://www.semanticscholar.org/paper/a31de1588768894323d531d32ca5d6ff8a754c2e (accessed on 29th September 2025).
4. Adams, A., & Blandford, A. (2003). Security and online learning: To protect or prohibit. https://core.ac.uk/download/1786.pdf (accessed on 29th September 2025).
5. Aldin, L., de Cesare, S., & Lycett, M. (2009). Semantic discovery and reuse of business process patterns. https://core.ac.uk/download/8018.pdf (accessed on 29th September 2025).
6. Alger, L. S., Babikyan, C. A., Butler, B. P., Friend, C., et al. (2025). Advanced information processing system: The Army fault tolerant architecture conceptual study. Volume 1: Army fault tolerant architecture overview. https://core.ac.uk/download/pdf/42811478.pdf (accessed on 29th September 2025).
7. Alshannaq, H., Ahmed, M., Norman, G., & Simmons, D. (2024). 1036-P: Cost-effectiveness of real-time CGM vs. self-monitoring of blood glucose in people with type 2 diabetes on intensive insulin therapy in Australia. *Diabetes*. https://www.semanticscholar.org/paper/a7ed9efdadc3091c197c4debe462a2618b9bb7d0 (accessed on 29th September 2025).
8. Anastasi, G. F., Checcozzo, R., Cucinotta, T., Lipari, G., et al. (2009). A real-time service-oriented architecture for industrial automation. https://core.ac.uk/download/pdf/54933057.pdf (accessed on 29th September 2025).
9. Aoussat, A., Bouchard, C., & Rasamoelina, F. (2013). Towards a kansei-based user modeling methodology for eco-design. https://core.ac.uk/download/29137353.pdf (accessed on 29th September 2025).
10. Arguello, H., Brady, D. J., Katsaggelos, A. K., Rodrigues, M., et al. (2022). Editorial: Introduction to the special issue on deep learning for

high-dimensional sensing. https://core.ac.uk/download/568121758.pdf (accessed on 29th September 2025).

11. Ashjaei, M., Behnam, M., & Papadopoulos, A. V. (2020). Real-time containers: A survey. https://core.ac.uk/download/296708949.pdf (accessed on 29th September 2025).
12. Audu, G. A., Bhattacharya, S., & Elmirghani, J. M. H. (2016). TDMA-based MAC (CVTMAC) in green vehicular networks. https://core.ac.uk/download/46665406.pdf (accessed on 29th September 2025).
13. Bajaj, K., Bentley, S., Nadir, N. A., Papanagnou, D., et al. (2016). Characteristics of real-time, non-critical incident debriefing practices in the emergency department. https://core.ac.uk/download/83049577.pdf (accessed on 29th September 2025).
14. Balfe, N., Sharples, S., & Wilson, J. R. (2018). Understanding is key: An analysis of factors pertaining to trust in a real-world automation system. *Human Factors, 60*, 477–495. https://www.semanticscholar.org/paper/8caf539a3691bec075e0c15fb79b9e717c438cca (accessed on 29th September 2025).
15. Bartoli, A., Groch, A., Kolb, A., Audette, B., Bachta, P., Bailey, C., et al. (2013). Optical techniques for 3D surface reconstruction in computer-assisted laparoscopic surgery. https://core.ac.uk/download/16670017.pdf (accessed on 29th September 2025).
16. Broenink, J. F., & Orlic, B. (2003). Real-time and fault tolerance in distributed control software. https://core.ac.uk/download/pdf/11458244.pdf (accessed on 29th September 2025).
17. Calma, A., Dellermann, D., Ebel, P., Lipusch, N., et al. (2019). The future of human-AI collaboration: A taxonomy of design knowledge for hybrid intelligence systems. https://core.ac.uk/download/211327088.pdf (accessed on 29th September 2025).
18. Chwa, H., Baek, H., & Lee, J. (2021). Necessary feasibility analysis for mixed-criticality real-time embedded systems. *IEEE Transactions on Parallel and Distributed Systems, PP*, 1–1. https://www.semanticscholar.org/paper/67a0236bbafbdeabc3574178496f2c7b61c8fcfc (accessed on 29th September 2025).
19. Consoli, S., & Darby-Dowman, K. (2006). Combinatorial optimization and metaheuristics. https://core.ac.uk/download/29139966.pdf (accessed on 29th September 2025).
20. Crouch, C., Geller, B. D., Turpen, C., et al. (2018). Sources of student engagement in introductory physics for life sciences. https://core.ac.uk/download/215477910.pdf (accessed on 29th September 2025).

21. Cui, J., Hasselman, F., Olthof, M., & Lichtwarck-Aschoff, A. (2025). Understanding types of transitions in clinical change: An introduction from the complex dynamic systems perspective. *Journal of Psychopathology and Clinical Science*. https://www.semanticscholar.org/paper/139b000ff58440b8e7eea0cfff0b76769bfd9a3a (accessed on 29th September 2025).
22. Eliazar, I., Metzler, R., & Reuveni, S. (2019). Poisson-process limit-laws yield Gumbel Max-Min and Min-Max. http://arxiv.org/abs/1808.08991 (accessed on 29th September 2025).
23. Franch Gutiérrez, J. (1998). Systematic formulation of non-functional characteristics of software. https://core.ac.uk/download/224976303.pdf (accessed on 29th September 2025).
24. Gaddam, H. N., Kommi, M., & Alla, C. V. K. (2025). Real-time data pipeline optimization for autonomous control systems. *2025 6th International Conference on Artificial Intelligence, Robotics and Control (AIRC)*. https://www.semanticscholar.org/paper/85948e4d256c6508576358cc465ab3d7768cb76a (accessed on 29th September 2025).
25. Gamer, T., Oriol, M., & Stattelmann, S. (2014). Execution time analysis for industrial control applications. http://arxiv.org/abs/1404.0847 (accessed on 29th September 2025).
26. Geertman, S., & Stillwell, J. (2000). Geoinformation, geotechnology, and geoplanning in the 1990s. https://core.ac.uk/download/51004.pdf (accessed on 29th September 2025).
27. Gheorghe, C., Duguleană, M., Boboc, R., & Postelnicu, C. (2024). Analyzing real-time object detection with YOLO algorithm in automotive applications: A review. *Computer Modeling in Engineering & Sciences*. https://www.semanticscholar.org/paper/8c63fd804551cc5a67de88fc8d4257595474ad0b (accessed on 29th September 2025).
28. Gomathy, C. K., & Puneeth, P. (2025). Real-time systems in software engineering: An in-depth perspective. *International Journal of Innovative Research in Science, Engineering and Technology*. https://www.semanticscholar.org/paper/3603dc936451fbf43b7cebbdb9b4489f4460d5f6 (accessed on 29th September 2025).
29. Gupta, A. K. (2025). Managing knowledge, creating networks and triggering innovations for sustainable agriculture. https://core.ac.uk/download/pdf/6443470.pdf (accessed on 29th September 2025).
30. Heaney, L. M., Ruszkiewicz, D., Arthur, K. L., Hadjithekli, A., Aldcroft, C., Lindley, M., Thomas, C., et al. (2016). Real-time monitoring of exhaled volatiles using atmospheric pressure chemical ionization on a compact mass spectrometer. *Bioanalysis, 8*(13), 1325–1336. https://www.semanticscholar.

org/paper/a11ef69b4b3cd9746e3b6d862878dbada104bfef (accessed on 29th September 2025).

31. Hellenthal, J. W., Planken, F. J. M., & Wegdam, M. (2001). Validation of the Parlay API through prototyping. https://core.ac.uk/download/pdf/11470417.pdf (accessed on 29th September 2025).

32. Jayamaha, N. P. (2003). Distributed generation on rural electricity networks: A lines company perspective (Master's thesis, Massey University). https://core.ac.uk/download/148645495.pdf (accessed on 29th September 2025).

33. Lodding, K. N. (2011). Mapping a path to autonomous flight in the national airspace. https://core.ac.uk/download/pdf/10562941.pdf (accessed on 29th September 2025).

34. Muratore, L. (2014). Large scale data streaming. https://core.ac.uk/download/19792153.pdf (accessed on 29th September 2025).

35. Niknam, S., Stefanov, T., & Zhai, J. T. (2018). Modeling, analysis, and hard real-time scheduling of adaptive streaming applications. https://core.ac.uk/download/388644081.pdf (accessed on 29th September 2025).

36. Niranjan, M. K. (2025). Adaptive fault tolerance using machine learning for dynamic distributed systems. *International Journal of Scientific Research in Engineering and Management*. https://www.semanticscholar.org/paper/3192d7e4d8ff29b99f3a2abb82d6cda9ec609641 (accessed on 29th September 2025).

37. Quiñones, E., & Serrano, M. A. (2017). Time-predictable parallel programming models. https://core.ac.uk/download/87661654.pdf (accessed on 29th September 2025).

38. Reghenzani, F., Guo, Z., & Fornaciari, W. (2023). Software fault tolerance in real-time systems: Identifying the future research questions. *ACM Computing Surveys, 55*, 1–30. https://www.semanticscholar.org/paper/c5cca4b8115f5450c46992a310d871a6b5ba226c (accessed on 29th September 2025).

39. Saran, P., & Siegert, C. W. (2009). Using supply chain management techniques to make wind plant and energy storage operation more profitable. https://core.ac.uk/download/4418175.pdf (accessed on 29th September 2025).

40. Saurabh, K., et al. (2023). IoT resources and their practical application: A comprehensive study. https://core.ac.uk/download/591405272.pdf (accessed on 29th September 2025).

41. Schmidhuber, J. (2008). Driven by compression progress: A simple principle explains essential aspects of subjective beauty, novelty, surprise,

interestingness, attention, curiosity, creativity, art, science, music, jokes. https://core.ac.uk/download/62914586.pdf (accessed on 29th September 2025).

42. Swainston, N. (2010). Wave omics: Bringing experimental data to online collaboration. https://core.ac.uk/download/pdf/289324.pdf (accessed on 29th September 2025).
43. Szücs, A., Prinz, A. A., & Sharp, A. A., et al. (2011). Dynamic clamp with StdpC software. https://core.ac.uk/download/2716549.pdf (accessed on 29th September 2025).
44. Uddin, R., & Koo, I. (2024). Real-time remote patient monitoring: A review of biosensors integrated with multi-hop IoT systems via cloud connectivity. *Applied Sciences*. https://www.semanticscholar.org/paper/e187cf6986df3d0d8064fb2e854301cb1a85f646 (accessed on 29th September 2025).
45. Ugbebor, F., Adeteye, M., & Ugbebor, J. O. (2024). Automated inventory management systems with IoT integration to optimize stock levels and reduce carrying costs for SMEs: A comprehensive review. *Journal of Artificial Intelligence General Science (JAIGS)*. https://www.semanticscholar.org/paper/6c8d556a19b475f65816f316b50bc710d318f1e8 (accessed on 29th September 2025).
46. Wagner, L. (2023). Mitigating emergent safety and security incidents of CPS by a protective shell. https://core.ac.uk/download/591055277.pdf (accessed on 29th September 2025).
47. Werner, F., Burtseva, L., & Sotskov, Y. (2018). *Algorithms for Scheduling Problems*. https://core.ac.uk/download/478121663.pdf (accessed on 29th September 2025).
48. Yin, D. (2009). A framework for network RTK data processing based on grid computing. https://core.ac.uk/download/10894600.pdf (accessed on 29th September 2025).
49. Zhuo, Y. (1963). Federal taxation: Formal stockholder vote held controlling in determining when a plan of liquidation is adopted under Section 337 of the Internal Revenue Code of 1954. https://core.ac.uk/download/62552356.pdf (accessed on 29th September 2025).

CHAPTER 2

FUNDAMENTALS OF OPERATING SYSTEMS FOR REAL-TIME APPLICATIONS

Contents

INTRODUCTION

The foundation of modern computing is operating systems (OS), which are the essential bridge between software and hardware. An OS manages hardware resources, provides support for user input, and provides an environment to run applications. In real-time systems, the reliability and responsiveness of the operating system are most vital since such systems typically must strictly adhere to timing constraints. Real-time operating systems (RTOS) are used with the motive of supporting time-critical activities efficiently, offering functionality such as task scheduling, interrupt servicing, and resource management. Task scheduling in terms of urgency and importance, an RTOS ensures that critical tasks are given appropriate priority to maintain performance and system stability, which is crucial in transportation and automation sectors. The development and implementation of real-time application operating systems necessitate rigorous engineering practices. The character of such systems entails the interfacing of varied hardware components in such a way that they satisfy safety and performance specifications. As indicated, innovation in the railway system has precipitated the evolution of Automatic Train Operation (ATO) systems, which utilize a hardware/software Vital Control Module (VCM) architecture governed by a reliable hard RTOS. This VCM framework is central to extending control functions, improving train safety, and facilitating automated performance without human monitoring. By handling real-time information and processing tasks with minimal latency, the VCM greatly enhances response time towards unsafe conditions, thereby fulfilling the essential requirements of safety in autonomous transport systems (Amendola et al., 2023). In addition, apart from the everyday computing, operating system use is extended to more complicated control systems, which have to process nonlinear scalar equations efficiently. Studies have proven new methods towards solving such equations, pointing to their utilization in designing sophisticated automatic control systems. Such technologies are crucial in enhancing the performance of real-time systems, particularly when it becomes necessary to guarantee an optimal rate of convergence of solutions to guarantee effectiveness in use. For instance, improved methods can result in more effective algorithms in an operating system to enable the successful application of technology across sectors, including manufacturing and transportation. As developers seek more efficiency and safety in automated systems, fast and precise mathematical solution skills will contribute to system reliability and operation success (Maistrenko et al., 2021).

Definition and Purpose of Operating Systems

The description of what an operating system (OS) is critical to understanding its critical role in computing, particularly in real-time systems. Basically, an OS is a user interface to the computer hardware, managing resources and providing a friendly interface. This involves coordinating hardware and software components to facilitate efficient interaction and program execution. Operating systems utilize several methods of scheduling processes, allocating memory, and managing I/O devices to ensure maximum system performance. In real-time systems, the OS must see to it that certain requirements of timing are met, thus systems schedule tasks according to priority. The ability to respond in a consistent way within time constraints of a limited nature is essential, particularly in applications such as embedded systems and industrial control systems, where delay could have grave consequences. The function of an operating system is more than just resource management; it plays a critical function in offering system stability and security, particularly in advanced applications such as cyber-physical systems. The integration of interconnected and heterogeneous control systems, typically referred to as Federated Embedded Systems, introduces new challenges to OS design. They depend on proper coordination of multiple processes and therefore require an OS that can handle the device heterogeneity in different frameworks. Security emphasis in such contexts is paramount because exploitations are resulting in disastrous failures or compromise in safety-critical usage (Bakirtzis et al., 2018) (Figure 2.1).

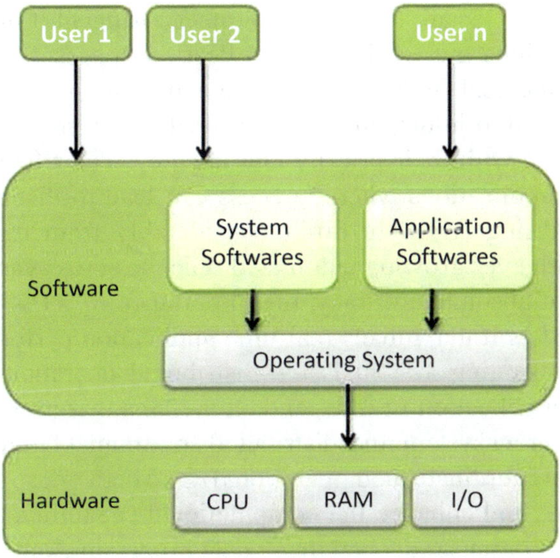

Figure 2.1. Architecture diagram of an operating system.

Source: https://www.tutorialspoint.com/operating_system/os_overview.htm.

An effective operating system must not only address performance requirements but also anticipate and handle security vulnerabilities throughout its life cycle. In addition, operating system development has created new paradigms that advance their performance in real-time applications even further. The advent of concepts like the Internet of Things (IoT) and multi-agent systems reveals the need for modern-day operating systems to cater to the complexity of networked machines and autonomous decision processes. These trends require OS infrastructures to be more flexible and robust so that they can handle diverse workloads without losing real-time operational capabilities. As systems become increasingly complex, understanding the characteristics of good operating systems will be critical in mapping potential vulnerabilities and building effective mitigation plans (Axelsson et al., 2012). The continued advancement of OS technologies is thus a fundamental research and development field in real-time applications, necessitating comprehensive assessments and innovative designs.

Types of Operating Systems

The OS ecosystem is diverse and ranges across forms, with each supporting a singular usage scenario and application environment. RTOS are vital for applications that require precise timing and extremely predictable behavior. In contrast to general-purpose operating systems, which emphasize throughput and user delay, RTOS are designed to meet stringent timing constraints, and their applications are evident in application spaces such as aerospace, automotive, and medical devices. Their architecture often incorporates priority-based scheduling algorithms, in which critical tasks are ensured processor time in accordance with their priority and urgency. Their focus on timeliness is significant in applications where lateness can lead to disastrous crashes or safety issues, causing RTOS to differ considerably from their conventional counterparts. With ever-growing automated reliance across various sectors and response times of absolute accuracy, the importance of RTOS has never been more pronounced as it maximizes real-time application performance. Another sole-proprietor operating system is the distributed operating system (DOS), which manages a collection of independent systems that user's approach as if from a single coherent system. In a distributed environment, multiple computers communicate and coordinate their operations over a network so that they are able to share resources and enhance the computational capability. Synchronization is essential for operations requiring much data processing and storage capacity, as witnessed in cloud computing scenarios. However, the complexity of synchronization and consistency poses the DOS-specific challenges. Remote procedure calls and distributed file systems are employed as methods for handling node communication and data integrity. As cloud-based infrastructure is becoming increasingly prevalent, it is essential to comprehend the behavior and nuances of distributed operating systems when designing scalable and efficient systems for real-time operations. Lastly, the advent of mobile operating systems has revolutionized the computing landscape by offering specialized solutions for handheld computers. Unlike traditional desktop operating systems, mobile OS are optimized to be battery-efficient, touch-based, and wireless. Mobile operating system architectures also prefer lean performance with robust security features in order to protect user data. With the adoption of smartphones and tablets everywhere, mobile OS have incorporated functionalities that enable real-time interaction and communication, such as applications for social networking, navigation, and instant messaging. Moreover, mobile technology evolution dictates that these operating systems have to evolve constantly to accommodate newer hardware features and software platforms. The more mobile phones integrate into everyday life, the more their operating systems are held accountable for real-time apps improving user experience along with functionality in an ever-changing digital landscape (Figure 2.2).

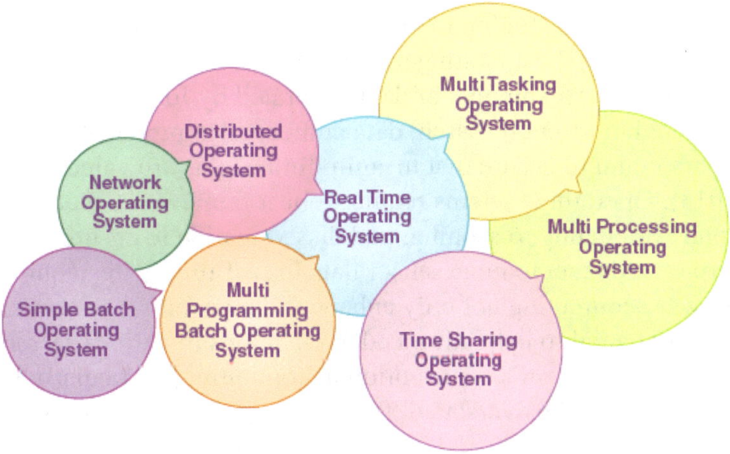

Figure 2.2. Types of operating systems.

Source: https://cdn1.byjus.com/wp-content/uploads/2022/08/word-image.png.

Importance of Operating Systems in Computing

Operating systems play a fundamental role in computing as an intermediary between the software programs and the hardware. They manage the computer resources like the CPU, memory, and I/O devices to efficiently utilize and allocate these resources. In the case of real-time applications, the performance of the operating systems is even more important since timely response of tasks is of utmost significance. When systems grow more sophisticated, an operating system must ensure not just that resources are allocated fairly but that significant activities have their deadlines met. This is particularly the case in situations where devices must answer quickly to inputs or adhere to tight schedules, such as in industrial automation and control systems. Growth in wireless technologies has also influenced operating system functionality and design to a great degree, given the growth of IoT applications at a rapid pace. Based on current publications, traditional wired communication systems have failed to cope with the dynamic process of contemporary industrial applications, and the call is therefore made for adaptive and responsive operating systems (Berge et al., 2012). Operating systems are presently needed to include protocols for smooth communication that accommodate reliable wireless connectivity in dealing with huge volumes of data created through numerous sensors. This complexity compels operating systems to exceed normal functions to become context-specific, enabling them to prioritize tasks based on real-time inputs from various sensors involved in the IoT system. These advancements are crucial in the implementation of efficient monitoring and control systems in industries. Besides, the operating system's context-awareness is paramount in ensuring that the vast amounts of data generated by IoT devices are managed. As highlighted in recent research, data contextual comprehension and processing are paramount to ensure that meaningful insights are gained (Zaslavsky et al., 2013). Operating systems require robust frameworks that facilitate data capture, modeling, reasoning, and dissemination to ensure that programs can interpret and react to huge sensor data in real-time. This requirement for context-aware computing not only enhances the operating system's efficiency but also its potential to help advanced applications in various sectors. To sum up, the operating system's contribution in computing, particularly in real-time applications, cannot be overstated; they are responsible for ensuring that systems respond appropriately and in a timely manner to evolving requirements and situations.

2.1. SCHEDULING ALGORITHMS IN REAL-TIME OPERATING SYSTEMS (RTOS)

The choice of scheduling algorithms in RTOS is fundamental to meeting the strict timing demands prevalent in real-time systems. Real-time systems are charged with ensuring critical tasks completion of their run within specified time limits, typically irreplaceable for proper operation in industries like automotive, telecommunications, and healthcare. Two broad categories of scheduling algorithms are widely referenced: fixed-priority and dynamic-priority scheduling. Fixed-priority scheduling, like the Rate Monotonic Scheduling (RMS) algorithm, assigns priorities based on task periodicity—lower periods are assigned higher priority. Dynamic-priority algorithms like Earliest Deadline First (EDF), however, dynamically change priorities in real-time as deadlines approach, thereby optimizing resource utilization and response times. With careful consideration between them, the performance and reliability of an RTOS can largely rely upon time-critical environments. Adding to the challenge of employing effective scheduling is task execution time variability and potential resource contention. Real-time tasks could exhibit erratic behavior with influences such as varying input conditions or system load change, thus making it challenging to adhere to rigid predefined schedules. Researchers have proposed hybrid scheduling techniques that combine the strengths of fixed and dynamic-priority methods to combat such issues. These hybrids are able to efficiently manage resources while also providing for the dynamic nature of real workloads. Moreover, the use of sophisticated techniques such as time-slicing and priority inheritance can also dampen the effects of resource contention, preventing higher-priority tasks from being unnecessarily preempted by lower-priority tasks. Properly handling these complexities can go a long way to improve system responsiveness and reliability, leading to overall enhanced quality of service in real-time applications. Where downtime causes significant cost overruns or compromised safety, the reliability of scheduling schemes is critical. Adaptive scheduling mechanisms that learn to adjust from experience in the form of feedback on system performance have grown in popularity as a topic of future research interest. For instance, scheduling policies can be trained using past data with machine learning algorithms so that they adapt dynamically to conditions in order to perform more efficiently. Such adaptive algorithms can also capitalize on large datasets, such as are present in semiconductor manufacturing processes where the scheduling is extremely intricate to manage complex workflows efficiently (Si et al., 2000). Through the offering of real-time flexibility in altering priorities and execution paths on the basis of system status, such advanced scheduling tools can ensure the reliability and efficacy of time-constrained applications. As the industries need more and more from their systems, scheduling algorithm development in RTOS will play a vital role in building the next-generation operation capabilities.

2.1.1. Rate Monotonic Scheduling (RMS)

Rate monotonic scheduling (RMS) is one of the most popular priority scheduling algorithms, especially designed for real-time systems. The concept behind RMS is based on the utilization of static priorities given to tasks based on their periodicity; therefore, tasks with shorter periods are given higher priority. This feature is specifically designed to support the demands of hard real-time systems, wherein it is crucial to satisfy critical deadlines. RMS favors independent and periodic tasks to make full utilization of CPU resources. Its mathematical foundation, i.e., the schedulability test, indicates that a system is schedulable if the utilization factor does not exceed a certain point of about 69%. This feature underscores the need for detailed system modeling and analysis to ensure that all tasks are run within their time budget schedules so that a reliable and predictable environment capable of supporting real-time applications is provided. Real-life application of RMS is more than theoretical concepts, demonstrating how viable it can be in reality, particularly in embedded systems where precision is of the highest priority. A good example can be found in multimedia applications—such as those using the MPlayer framework—where real-time requirements greatly affect user experience. With the adaptation of RMS as well as the exception-based programming paradigm, such changes can cause such applications to run better, thus making them run smoothly despite competing synthetic real-time workloads (Figure 2.3).

Process	Execution time	Period
P1	1	4
P2	2	6
P3	3	12

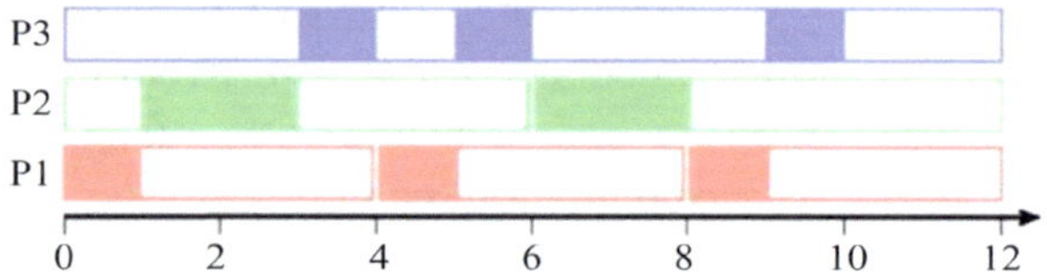

Figure 2.3. Rate monotonic scheduling example.

Source: https://external-content.duckduckgo.com/iu/?u=https%3A%2F%2Ftse2.mm.bing.net%2Fth%2Fid%2FOIP.fU4nVPuivwsa1ev1Lp1HSQHaFj%3Fr%3D0-%26pid%3DApi&f=1&ipt=350c1f929907bfd6573180333e8458b230efc9e6104f58cff9a009c2e59d3452.

Here, RMS can guarantee timely execution of high-priority tasks such as audio and video processing while maintaining the overall system responsiveness. In cases where the adoption of various scheduling policies is becoming unavoidable, RMS can complement deadline-based scheduling approaches with a hybrid approach utilizing the best of both worlds. This demonstrates that RMS is not only a theoretical model but also a functional solution to today's real-time system issues. Apart from its systematic priority, RMS also allows for the integration of advanced tuning methods that can adapt to varied operation requirements. Although traditional RMS implementations are focused on static priority configurations, recent systems benefit more from dynamic tuning systems. The use of smart PID control in real-time systems is a sample indicating relevance, where tuning algorithms change task priorities to get the best performance for most situations. Tuning techniques allow trade-offs between conflicting goals, such as reducing delay with an objective of maximizing throughput and stability. As complexity grows in real-time applications, the need for robust management tools to enhance RMS systems will increase. Library and software module construction to facilitate auto-tuning operations will significantly increase the efficiency of such scheduling algorithms, ultimately leading to improved productivity and reduced maintenance requirements in dynamic systems (Ang et al., 2005; Cucinotta et al., 2012).

2.1.2. Earliest Deadline First (EDF) Scheduling

Earliest deadline first (EDF) scheduling is a dynamic priority scheduling algorithm that forms the core of the study of RTOS. Based on the deadline of tasks and not fixed factors, EDF priorities are used to ensure that the task nearest the deadline is given priority for execution. This method is well suited to applications where task completion in a timely manner is most critical, like in embedded systems, industrial automation, and multimedia. The real-time feature of EDF supports more response times and makes it possible to satisfy the soft and hard real-time constraints, satisfying various requirements of various applications. Through this dynamic reordering of tasks, EDF enables optimal utilization of CPU resources, hence optimal system-wide performance in real-time systems. Another key advantage of EDF is that it is optimal while providing schedulability guarantees in certain situations. In an autonomous task system with known execution times, EDF can theoretically ensure that a given set of periodic tasks meet their deadlines if the total CPU utilization does not exceed 100%. This is a property that differentiates EDF from other scheduling algorithms because it is able to efficiently manage resource allocation even under varying workload conditions (Figure 2.4).

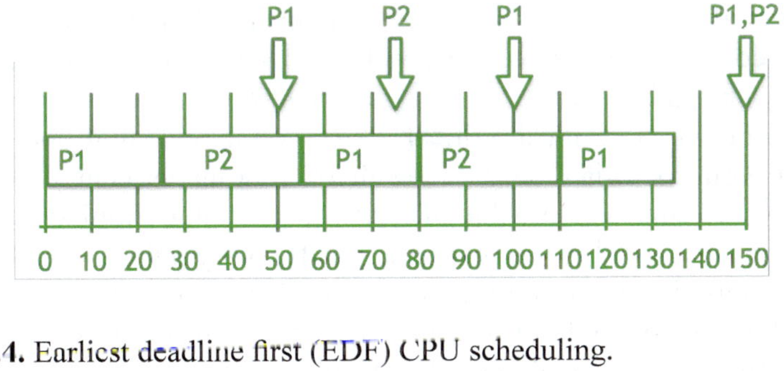

Figure 2.4. Earliest deadline first (EDF) CPU scheduling.

Source: https://media.geeksforgeeks.org/wp-content/uploads/20191227020034/gfg_earliest_deadline_first.png.

Moreover, as Cucinotta et al. (2017) underscores, the use of EDF in conjunction with strong temporal isolation guarantees from the operating system can effectively eliminate interference among co-located services, resulting in higher Quality of Service (QoS) levels for real-time applications. This effectiveness and optimality render EDF a working solution for developers who wish to optimize response times for mission-critical systems. However, aside from its positive consideration, EDF has issues of its own. For instance, it can become susceptible to scheduling anomalies such as priority inversion and the missed deadline problem. Due to workload or contention for resources situations, lower-priority tasks can hold higher-priority tasks in a standstill, leading to eventual deadline misses. Also, context switch handling in EDF can be expensive, particularly when there are numerous tasks in the system. Nonetheless, some amendments and enhancements have been proposed to address these limitations so that EDF remains relevant in RTOS. For example, adaptive scheduling algorithms with QoS guarantees, as discussed by Chowdhury et al. (2010), can provide greater throughput and delay guarantees, facilitating EDFs sustained use in contemporary real-time systems.

2.1.3. Least Laxity First (LLF) Scheduling

In RTOS, scheduling of tasks is important with regard to ensuring timely response and responsiveness of the system. Least Laxity First (LLF) scheduling is an appealing strategy when the system is dealing with periodic tasks having rigid timing constraints. The algorithm schedules the tasks based on their laxity, i.e., the difference between the time remaining until a task's deadline and its remaining execution time. By consistently choosing the task with the minimum laxity, LLF effectively prevents deadline misses, thereby maintaining real-time performance integrity. This specific advantage stresses the importance of LLF in safety-critical systems, e.g., embedded systems used in medical devices and automotive control systems, where timely task execution is crucial to both functionality and safety. Least Laxity First scheduling has a specific drawback in implementation. The most critical issue is the potential for excessive overhead in context switching as a result of continuous context switching, especially in systems where a lot of tasks are running simultaneously. The algorithms intrinsic need to compare and verify laxity values very frequently can lead to inefficiencies in high task contention systems. Additionally, LLF can be challenged to handle a dynamic system where the type of tasks can change during execution, making the scheduling process even more difficult. Moreover, as noted by some research, the algorithm can be affected by scheduling anomalies, where the decrease in a task's execution requirement might inadvertently cause a deadline to be missed, stressing the need for much consideration to be given to the operating environment during the execution of this strategy (Fauberteau et al., 2012) (Figure 2.5).

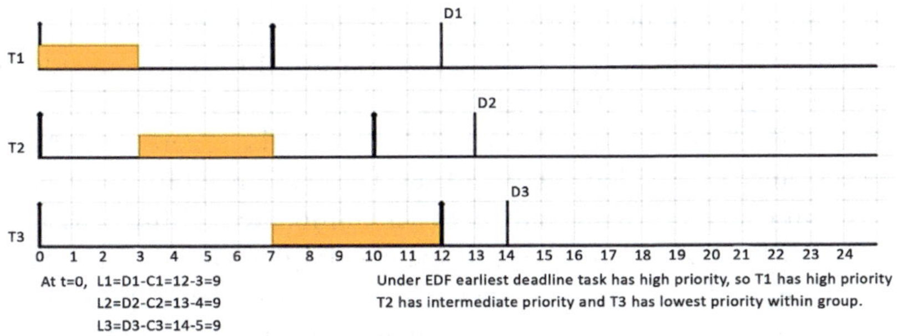

Figure 2.5. LLF scheduling algorithm.

Source: https://microcontrollerslab.com/wp-content/uploads/2018/06/Enhanced-Least-Laxity-first-LLF-example.jpg.

While it has its disadvantages, LLF scheduling provides the considerable advantage for systems that must support dynamic task involvement. Noted in recent empirical studies, this type of scheduling can be effectively integrated with incentive-based schemes, such as ones that encourage electricity customers to participate in demand response tasks (Alizadeh et al., 2013). These systems rely on real-time scheduling algorithms to accomplish the objective of customer participation that matches operations requirements such that resources can be well utilized without frequent interruption. Operators can optimize resource utilization and system performance through the use of LLF for dynamically scheduling the execution of tasks based on participation rates and real-time parameters. Therefore, LLF becomes an essential scheduling policy in the overall scenario of real-time systems, offering theoretical as well as practical methods for systemizing systems to make them more reliable and efficient in different applications.

2.2. RESOURCE MANAGEMENT IN REAL-TIME SYSTEMS

In real-time systems, resource management has to be efficient in order to achieve deterministic performance and meet stringent timing constraints. The interaction between hardware and OS is particular because real-time programs are often executed within memory-constrained environments. Typically, the advent of purpose-designed hardware solutions, such as system-on-chip design, enabled more efficient processing of tasks particular to real-time applications. But with only advanced hardware, it invites the deployment of RTOS that can allocate resources dynamically. Compared to general-purpose systems like Linux that can bring about uncertainty, RTOSs are designed with the objective of providing low-latency responses and are optimized for both embedded and safety-critical applications. Thus, as complexity in applications rises, so does the method of dealing with resources and delivering the reliability expected of real-time systems (Eiroa-Lledo et al., 2021). There is a need for frameworks to support dynamic resource management to accommodate real-time environment complexities. Effective scheduling mechanism implementation that is meant to deal with multiple concurrent tasks without sacrificing quality of service (QoS) is one of the frameworks. In particular, as machine learning algorithms are applied to increasing amounts of real-time applications, there is a strong need for scheduling methods that can suit their unique resource demands. Constructing tailored CPU brokers, for example, allows real-time processes to take precedence over resource allocations with dynamically compensating for changing system conditions. Such agility is crucial because real-time systems are prone to unpredictable events that may compromise resource availability. With effective incorporation of such brokers in existing RTOS capabilities, systems are made possible to maintain peak performance, thereby supporting new and existing applications in a unified architecture (Eide et al., 2004) (Figure 2.6).

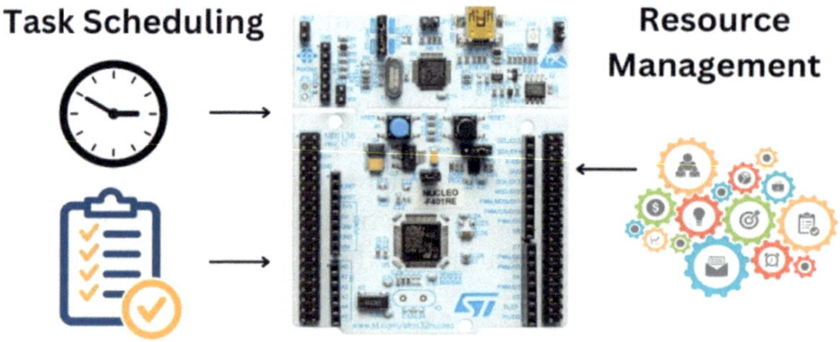

Figure 2.6. Function of real-time operating systems (RTOS).

Source: https://external-content.duckduckgo.com/iu/?u=https%3A%2F%2Fembeddedthere.com%2Fwp-content%2Fuploads%2F2023%2F05%2FReal-Time-Operation-System-RTOS-min-1024x576.webp&f=1&nofb=1&ipt=dd92fd580073b40fb67834ffa05179826770b05bcb283d63f1b7cb6a655944e3.

Furthermore, the interplay between feedback control and resource management mechanisms has the further advantage of enhancing system reliability in general. Having feedback incorporated in the resource provision process provides the possibility of continuous tuning under real-time scenarios, hence shielding QoS even in fluctuating workloads. This non-intrusive approach makes it possible for seamless integration of resource management policies with existing middleware support, resulting in a more robust working environment. For instance, resource contention among multiple applications can be effectively mitigated through the utilization of a feedback-based CPU broker that monitors constantly and allocates resources to ensure that critical real-time workloads are given the needed support. With mounting performance demands of distributed real-time embedded systems, such advanced resource management solutions will be essential in facilitating operational efficiency and adherence to the quality levels necessary for high-end real-time applications (Eide et al., 2004) (Figure 2.7).

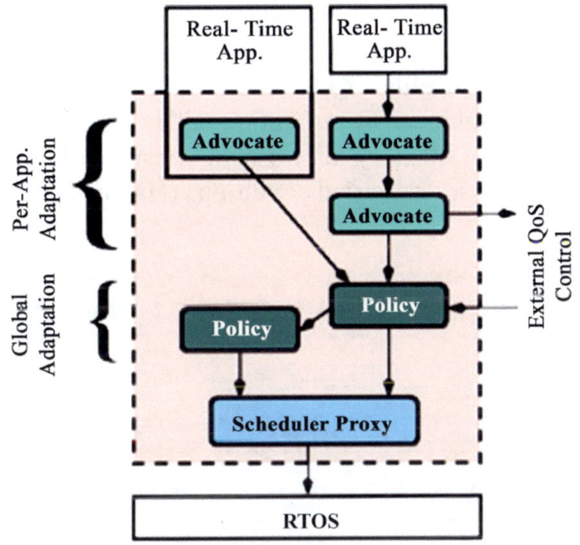

Figure 2.7. *CPU broker.*

Source: https://external-content.duckduckgo.com/iu/?u=https%3A%2F%2Fwww-old.cs.utah.edu%2Fflux%2Falchemy%2Fcpubroker-small.png&f=1&nofb=1&ipt=e2f98fdad57ad22bc3333790e03a7e94000fef22f363dcca76221d2f98788849f.

2.2.1. Memory Management Techniques

Memory management techniques are the most essential for operating systems, particularly under real-time systems where predictability is imperative. Efficient memory utilization implies that system resources are utilized efficiently, avoiding unnecessary waits which can jeopardize time-sensitive operations. Segmentation and paging techniques allow systems to allocate memory in a more adaptable way, enabling the resources to be assigned to various processes efficiently based on their real-time requirements. Besides, these approaches help in the efficient fetching of data, which is crucial in guaranteeing the responsiveness of real-time systems. The intricacies in memory management also involve managing shared resources and inter-process communication, which must be carefully managed to prevent bottlenecks that lead to catastrophic failure in real-time applications. Real-time system structures typically possess specific memory optimization techniques to meet real-time and performance needs. For instance, memory hierarchies with high-speed cache memories have the potential to drastically reduce critical task access delays. In addition, real-time constraint-specific resource allocation policies, such as priority scheduling of memory access, can enhance reliability and performance in systems. Notably, using locality of reference-exploiting methods, as has been testified in techniques embraced by current portable computer designs, provides a way of energy-efficient memory access with consistent high performance in multimedia applications across varied conditions (Havinga et al., 2000) (Figure 2.8).

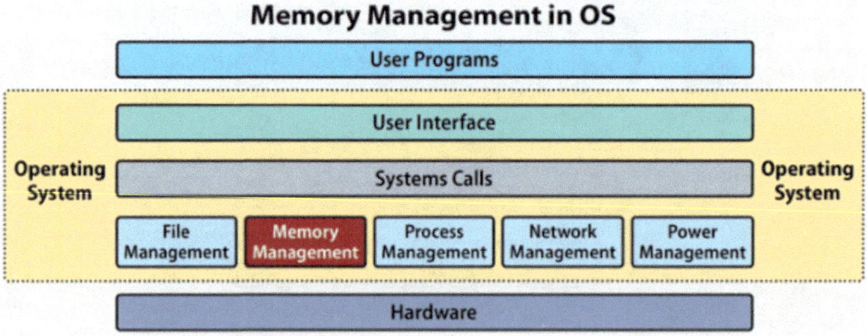

Figure 2.8. Memory management techniques.

Source: https://external-content.duckduckgo.com/iu/?u=https%3A%2F%2Fwww.enterprisestorageforum.com%2Fwp-content%2Fuploads%2F2021%2F02%2Fdata-storage-memory-management-optimizing-computer-memory_6019c48f54470.png&f=1&nofb=1&ipt=31d5251cd4cab1dff4a1e914e7d20da5d74f3de2d145b43165764d1e5c5b7b48.

This is particularly important for systems that are required to support sustained operating capacity despite fluctuating processing needs. An increasingly important part of real-time memory management is the use of Quality of Service (QoS) protocols to offer sufficient guarantees in terms of access time as well as availability of resources. The High-Level Architecture (HLA) standard, originally designed for simulation systems, is being adapted to address real-time needs that contribute significantly to distributed system memory management. Current research seeks to create schedulers that can compute Worst Case Transit Time (WCTT) and pre-allocate memory to remove runtime overheads (Adelantado et al., 2010). These advancements not only aspire to optimize the efficiency of memory use but also aspire to enhance the reliability and constancy required in real-time systems so that memory management structures can smoothly integrate into the challenging running demands of modern computing environments.

2.2.2. Process Synchronization Mechanisms

On the topic of operating systems, synchronization primitives for processes are highly critical, especially for real-time systems, where timely and predictable scheduling of tasks takes precedence. Synchronization prevents different processes from interfering with each other when they are accessing shared resources, avoiding data inconsistency and race conditions. Fundamental synchronization techniques are mutexes, semaphores, and monitors, each with its own strengths and operational complexities. For instance, mutexes facilitate single-process access to shared resources such that only one can modify a resource at any given moment in time, whereas semaphores are more flexible in that multiple processes can share a few resources at a time. Synchronization facility determination has a gigantic effect on system performance and response times, proving to be crucial in real-time application environments with timely decision-making and action. The advent of edge computing, which recent advances have pushed to the forefront, opens new challenges and opportunities for process synchronization in real-time systems. Edge computing makes data processing local to where it is produced, minimizing latency and fastening response time. This approach is beneficial in Internet of Things (IoT) contexts, where numerous devices synchronize to enable efficient processing and response to streams of data. Through the application of robust synchronization protocols, edge devices are able to function harmoniously with no need to compromise data integrity, hence supporting the need for immediate decision-making characteristic of real-time applications. The agility and responsiveness that this synchronization mechanisms offer facilitate edge computing to respond to various environments, from smart home environments to city infrastructure management, hence rendering them extremely valuable in the extension of contemporary technology solutions within real-time environments (Shi et al., 2016) (Figure 2.9).

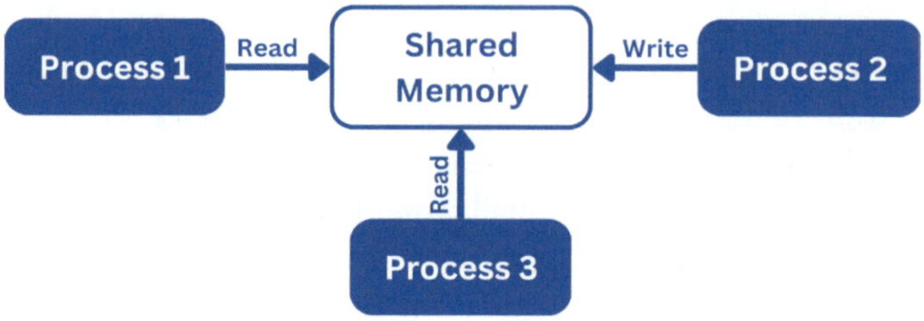

Figure 2.9. Process synchronization.

Source: https://external-content.duckduckgo.com/iu/?u=https%3A%2F %2Flearn-loner.com%2Fwp-content%2Fuploads%2F2023%2F05%2FProcess-Synchronization.png&f=1&nofb=1&ipt=b4ca787633153eafd4e93de2ff460d4098aff7c6fc9e9422f875eb89733ffbec.

Besides, with the advent of the Internet of Things (IoT), the requirements for synchronization process mechanisms are more stringent. The advent of networked devices demands seamless communication and synchronization in order to allow smart decision-making processes independently. In such a context, synchronization solutions are required to address the distinct characteristics of IoT devices and their distinct operating environments. Facilitating technologies such as RFID, smart sensors, and higher-level communication protocols accentuate synchronization mechanisms as crucial elements in effective management of the complexities of IoT systems. By interconnection of diverse technologies, such mechanisms, apart from enhancing data processing power, tackle issues of bandwidth, latency, and data privacy to emerge as pillars in the global arena of real-time applications with a focus on performance and reliability (Al-Fuqaha et al., 2015).

2.2.3. I/O Management Strategies

Good input/output (I/O) management techniques are critical in RTOS to ensure that applications attain their performance goals without any compromise. I/O operations have a tendency to be a bottleneck in most situations, limiting the responsiveness of a system. Good I/O management technique applies buffering, caching, and spooling to increase the efficiency of a system. Buffering allows holding of data temporarily during transfer, reducing peripheral device waiting times. For comparison, caching keeps frequently accessed data in faster storage, immensely speeding up the readability. These methods play a very important role in real-time systems where timely processing of the data is the deciding factor for functionality and user satisfaction. Therefore, applying these I/O management methods efficiently, operating systems can significantly increase their throughput and offer the consistent performance required in real-time systems. The I/O management architecture is generally layered in nature, separating the complexities of device operations from higher-level application requirements. In the hardware layer, there are device controllers to handle communication between the CPU and peripheral devices, whereas the operating system layer provides standard APIs for efficient data transfer. This decoupling facilitates independent development of modules as well as easier addition of new devices. In addition, in real-time systems, priority I/O request scheduling is commonly used to meet stringent timing demands. This may be facilitated through the integration of algorithms that order data transactions based on priority and urgency. By applying hierarchical I/O management strategies, operating systems not only maximize device communication but also ensure timely processing of high-priority tasks necessary for efficient real-time processing. With regard to the development of energy-efficient technology, there has been greater interest in incorporating advanced I/O management methods for maximizing performance across various applications, particularly in intelligent building systems. For instance, radiant heating and cooling systems must efficiently manage I/O for balancing system energy consumption and occupant comfort and, therefore, efficient I/O is vital in achieving significant energy savings as well as environmentally friendly system operation. I/O innovations can involve the installation of sensor networks, which dynamically adapt operation parameters with real-time inputs to improve system responsiveness. Using these sophisticated I/O management approaches can enable system efficiency improvement. Such measures highlight the significance of continuous research and adaptability of I/O management systems to facilitate meeting the new challenges of integrating emerging technologies, as highlighted in the CPUC's Energy Efficiency Strategic Plan. The integration of such measures eventually leads to the creation of smart environments with the ability to coexist harmoniously and provide optimal energy efficiency (Bauman et al., 2019; Briscoe et al., 2011).

2.3. CHALLENGES IN REAL-TIME OPERATING SYSTEMS (RTOS)

In RTOS context, managing time constraints is most likely the biggest challenge. Programs usually depend on hard temporal constraints not only specifying the data rate of processing but also predictability of task execution. For instance, latency in applications such as disaster warning systems, live broadcasting, and audio/video conferencing is quite crucial. Achieving successful time management is a critical inspection of such boundaries, followed by designing and integrating various aspects of the system. Furthermore, the computation and communication scheduling process is necessitated. As highlighted by Prodan et al. (2020), the complexity associated with developing time-critical applications typically makes projects take a lot of time as well as money, which underscores the necessity to effectively manage resources in real-time environments. Moreover, software-defined infrastructure has introduced additional complexities in managing real-time applications. While technologies such as Cloud, Fog, and Edge computing introduce better control over resources and virtualization, they also introduce system engineering and dynamic control issues associated with time-critical applications.

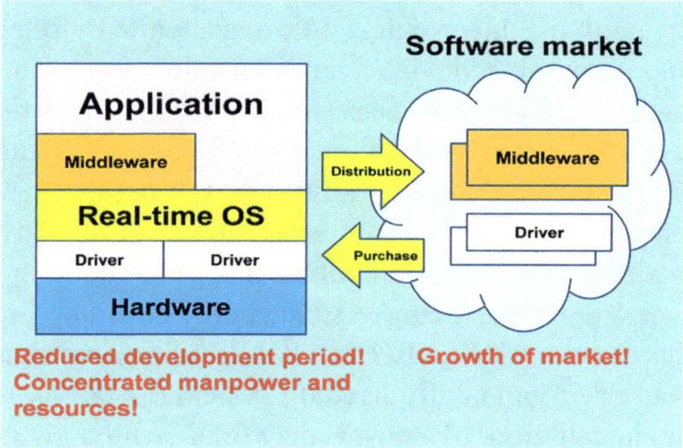

Figure 2.10. Pros and cons of real-time operating systems.

Source: https://itrelease.com/2014/07/advantages-disadvantages-real-time-operating-systems/#google_vignette.

Convergence of various virtualization technologies, from application-level Java Virtual Machines to operating system-level Docker containers, necessitates careful consideration to enable isolation as well as performance. An effective RTOS must be able to leverage these advanced features without compromising the timeliness required for successful operation. This balancing act of leveraging advanced infrastructure and maintaining real-time performance is critical, as observed by Prodan et al. (2020), demonstrating the urgent requirement for design and operation innovation. In addition, challenges extend into fields such as medical imaging, where RTOS become the focal point in the area of surgery. Intraoperative imaging technology needs precise tracking of instruments, real-time image matching, and reliable guidance to achieve successful surgical outcomes. Satisfying these requirements is not simple; long-standing issues with accuracy, ease of use, and system constraints remain prevalent with current applications. Contrasts may be felt in between high-image quality requirements and the urgent time constraints that come with surgery. Research in figure out that advanced techniques, such as automatic motion compensation and advanced image-fusion systems, play a decisive role in overcoming such challenges and ensuring successful intraoperative navigation. The requirement of addressing such technical challenges further highlights the complexity and importance of RTOS in life-or-death situations (Figure 2.10).

2.3.1. Timing Constraints and Their Implications

In real-time systems, timing constraints are critical parameters that define how well the system performs and how reliable it is. Timing constraints ensure that processes complete their tasks within predetermined deadlines, which is of utmost importance for applications where failure to meet such deadlines can be catastrophic. A case in point is in automotive systems utilizing real-time data for safety mechanisms like anti-lock braking, where a timing failure can be calamitous in its effects. Operating systems designed for real-time applications have to, hence, utilize scheduling algorithms that can execute tasks based on their urgency as well as their completion times, and thus highlight the delicate balance between resource allocation and deadline sensitivity. By not optimizing these systems, the performance is affected but, worse still, user trust is lost and even lives lost. The implications of timing constraints are not limited to the short-term system performance; they also affect the design and scalability of RTOS. As the applications grow and need more computational power, the time-related demands themselves can cause conflicts in resource allocation and may result in increased latency issues. Systems have to be prudent when dealing with resources in order to provide time-critical processes the priority they need, as well as providing resources for less critical jobs. For instance, in a multi-threaded environment, irresponsible sharing of resources would lead to bottlenecks that would significantly impact completion times of tasks. Thus, operating systems not just have to be cognizant of the reality that timing constraints do exist but also have to establish environments that anticipate and address potential conflicts of schedules so that the system remains stable under varying loads. Moreover, the implications of timing become increasingly relevant in the case of future technologies such as Fog computing, where the development of real-time features occurs further by having the computational operations closer to the source of the data. This kind of architecture presents the potential for improved responsiveness and reduced latency, chief characteristics for applications of the Internet of Things (IoT) and 5G networks. Still, the allocation of functions among different nodes has to be given a lot of thought with respect to timing restrictions to prevent introducing inconsistencies in system performance. While the demand for real-time data processing continues to grow, operating systems have to improvise by streamlining their scheduling algorithms and exploiting the benefits provided by distributed architectures. Hence, timing constraints are not mere peripheral concerns but at the very heart of fundamental design principles that govern the effectiveness and reliability of modern real-time systems, as highlighted in the midst of 21st-century energy transition issues and system infrastructure reinforcement as evidenced by Gielen et al. (2019) and Chiang et al. (2016) (Figure 2.11).

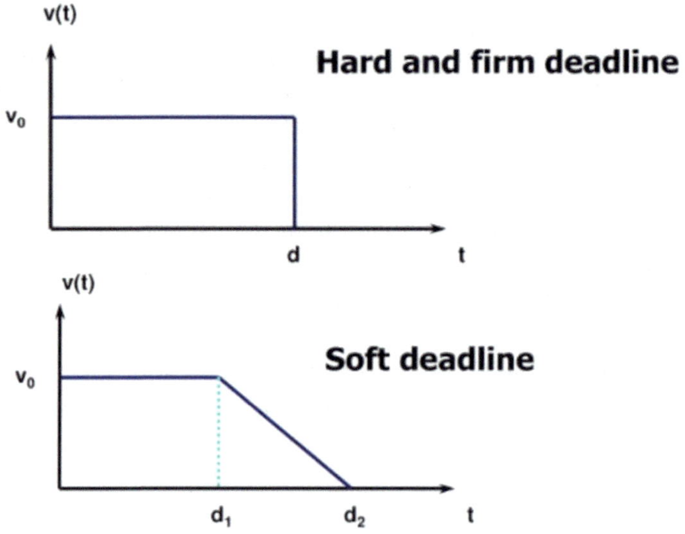

Figure 2.11. Timing constraints.

Source: https://external-content.duckduckgo.com/iu/?u=https%3A%2F%2Fimage.slideserve.com%2F211386%2Ftime-constraints-l.jpg&f=1&nofb=1&ipt=398dc78e234274e88c517ffa1b9bf0ab61336928aa41427a1c242cba9a0ef9e2.

2.3.2. Resource Contention Issues

Resource contention issues are significant issues in RTOS administration, particularly as the sophistication of computing environments keeps growing. Real-time programs generally demand strict adherence to deadlines, and it is therefore important that system resources such as CPU time and memory are available where and when needed. When multiple tasks vie for these shared resources, contention is more likely and may result in delays and violations of timing constraints. The contention could become further strengthened in systems implementing traditional wired communication technologies, which might be found to lack the needed flexibility in changing industrial scenarios.

Even though the traditionally wired systems have been providing reliability, their rigidity could hamper responsiveness for real-time execution and therefore make resource contention harder to manage (Berge et al., 2012). Technology progress in wireless systems offers a good alternative to help circumvent the obstacles of resource contention, particularly for industrial monitoring and control. Unlike the case of wired systems, wireless technologies are more scalable and flexible, and they support more dynamic resource management strategies. However, wireless solutions are also plagued by their own problems, especially related to real-time dependability and quality of service. Data latency and packet loss problems can be among the sources of contention problems that affect the performance of real-time applications. Researchers are researching straight ways of enhancing wireless network deployment for industrial application by proposing mechanisms to enhance responsiveness and dependability required for successful operation (Berge et al., 2012). Overcoming these vulnerabilities is crucial for ensuring that real-time systems can successfully operate in systems with uneven resource availability. Besides, with the growth in the volume and complexity of information processed in distributed systems, predictive resource modeling is crucial in solving contention issues. Predictive performance modeling (PPM) offers a framework for measuring task performance by studying historical latency trends in order to forecast future resource demands. PPM is an intrusive method that can help enable better scheduling and resource allocation that can minimize contention by pre-allocation of resources for priority tasks. By considering the intrinsic variability of computational loads, PPM can allow system administrators to more effectively optimize resource allocation, hence improving the performance of real-time applications. The identification and utilization of such predictive techniques will be crucial as the era of operating systems transitions towards accommodating increasing demands in terms of performance for real-time applications.

2.3.3. Scalability and Performance Trade-Offs

Scalability and performance trade-offs concepts are important in the design and management of operating system real-time applications. Since the demand for improved performance continues to rise, system architects are faced with the challenge of meeting the demand for scalability while restricting the power consumption and resource usage. Scalability is the ability of a system to process an increasing volume of work, or the ability to be expanded to meet that increase. Performance, on the other hand, tends to focus on speed and efficiency of activity. The drive for improved performance can manifest as an increase in power requirements, for example, in modern digital circuits where aggressive voltage scaling is implemented to save energy while still performing well (Le,

2019). Thus, performance optimization can unknowingly bring complexity and bottlenecks that counter system scalability, particularly for applications with multiple processes and threads. Further, the design compromises of dealing with system design intensify with architectures converging toward multiple cores and heterogeneous processors. Asynchronous design paradigms, unlike synchronous design methodology, provide a promising path to address the issue of scalability. By circumventing global clock distribution bottlenecks, asynchronous methods encourage greater modularity and reduced power dissipation, which are critical to the development of scalable systems (Singh et al., 2011). The model supports more flexibility in task scheduling and responding to fluctuating loads. With increasing applications in terms of complexity, say those using gesture recognition for smart phones, systems must scale perfectly without sacrificing overall performance. In our case, the employment of local handshake communication ensures that performance does not degrade significantly as system complexity increases. Finally, awareness of these trade-offs is essential for the support of real-time performance in applications requiring immediate response, e.g., industrial automation or autonomous vehicles. Real-time systems are usually needed to operate deterministically, and scalability, particularly with increasing workloads and process complexity, poses a threat. As the demand for low-power solutions increases, new methods—like low-power FF design—have emerged to address the need to balance energy efficiency without compromising the performance (Le, 2019). These methods show the delicate balance between the consumption of power and overall digital system potential in real-time applications. Hence, continued research into scalability and performance trade-offs not only invites improved system design but also inspires innovation in operating systems for real-time systems, and the doors are opened to responsive and sustainable technology.

2.4. CASE STUDIES OF REAL-TIME OPERATING SYSTEMS (RTOS)

Analysis of RTOS case studies gives a valuable description of their use and performance in the real world across various sectors. One such example is seen in the industrial sector, wherein RTOS are employed to operate advanced control systems for manufacturing processes. These require precise timing and dependability to ensure operation without shutdown. For instance, advanced RTOS platforms have been employed to sense and control robot assembly lines in a way that the activity can be real-time tuned as procedure fluctuations arise. The applications evidently demonstrate the important role played by power-saving technologies, as described by Fisher et al. (2011), in improving system performance while conserving resources. Consequently, RTOS case studies within industries form part of a broader trend toward harmonizing efficiency and reliability, underlining growing convergence between technological innovation and operational effectiveness. Another compelling case includes the convergence of RTOS in embedded systems with the healthcare sector, demonstrating their indispensable importance in life-critical applications. Such systems are required to adhere to demanding safety regulations and deadlines, and the use of RTOS is thus extremely important for successful implementation. For example, surgical robots utilize RTOS to interpret sensor information for carrying out movements with extremely high precision, thereby ensuring much higher safety and effectiveness of procedures. As research has demonstrated, the dependability of RTOS in performing multiple tasks simultaneously ensures medical personnel are able to interact with complex devices efficiently and thereby achieve better patient care outcomes. The intersection of RTOS technology and healthcare is a sign of the on-going trend towards real-time usage as the demand for high-tech medical devices accelerates, necessitating focus on system integrity as well as performance according to the educational advancements by Barletta et al. (2012). Moreover, the transport sector increasingly relies on RTOS to enhance safety as well as efficacy. Intelligent transportation systems (ITS) apply RTOS to provide real-time data to control traffic and manage vehicles, indicative of their usefulness in modern infrastructures. For instance, RTOS-based solutions in autonomous vehicles require rapid processing of diversified sensor data to make decisions in split seconds. This usefulness has significant implications in the reduction of traffic flow and accident avoidance on the road. The connection of RTOS to other ITS technologies identify the importance of real-time applications in various domains and indicates convergence of engineering work and innovative solutions. The study in question evidently demonstrates how real-time responsiveness as the focus contributes not just to technological advancement but also to social benefits, complementing critical evaluation laid out by Barletta et al. (2012).

2.4.1. VxWorks: Features and Applications

VxWorks, a leading wind river systems RTOS, is highly renowned for its performance and reliability in embedded systems. Being designed specifically for applications requiring high determinism and responsiveness levels, VxWorks finds applications across aerospace, automotive, telecommunications, and industrial automation industries. It features modular architecture, under which developers can customize the kernel and other components of the system according to their respective application requirements. This flexibility allows VxWorks to maintain the strict timing requirements necessary in real-time applications and make it the preferred choice where failure is not an option. Furthermore, VxWorks also supports advanced scheduling algorithms, memory management techniques, and inter-process communication mechanisms that enhance its effectiveness in handling complex tasks. One of the main advantages of VxWorks is that it has the ability to support different connectivity options and protocols, a parameter that is most important in current applications. Particularly, the embedding of networking stacks ensures seamless communication between widespread systems, and therefore, VxWorks is adaptive to the evolving demands of Industry 4.0 and IoT initiatives. With industrial networks carrying increasingly heterogeneous types of data with varied levels of criticality, VxWorks supports real-time data exchange that is necessary for automation process and control traffic, hence enhancing system flexibility and reliability. Such flexibility becomes relevant with the dynamism that is associated with changing industrial landscapes, particularly with the advent of IIoT applications—where fast, secure communication is critical in order to ensure operational efficiency and safety (Behnke et al., 2023) (Figure 2.12).

Figure 2.12. VxWorks.

Source: https://cdn-optimized.imweb.me/upload/S20230524c739889383882/ed-d27705b52b0.png?w=500.

Apart from that, VxWorks has gained traction in emerging markets such as autonomous driving and connected vehicles. As the auto sector is under pressure to innovate at speed, VxWorks provides a robust platform for implementing advanced ADAS capabilities that enable features like collision avoidance and lane-keep assist.

The real-time performance of the operating systems plays a critical role in handling multiple sensor data and decision-making in milliseconds. This responsiveness is also important in situations in which safety is not merely desirable but imperative, as evidenced with VxWorks application to scenarios that require judicious handling of real-time constraints (Chen et al., 2023). With continued innovation in autonomous vehicle technology research, the role of VxWorks in safe operation is bound to grow, and thus it becomes a basis for future vehicular technology breakthroughs.

2.4.2. QNX: Architecture and Use Cases

QNX's architecture is basically designed to accommodate real-time applications, a very critical aspect in most industries such as automotive systems, telecommunications, and industrial automation. In essence, QNX adopts a microkernel architecture, which operates on the principle of limiting the amount of code executed in kernel mode. This design maximizes the security and reliability of the systems as it keeps the required services in user space, which is autonomous and can be designed and delivered independently. Consequently, failures in one service will not endanger bringing down the whole operating system. This organization also improves real-time performance immediately in that it facilitates quicker context switching and fewer overheads than monolithic kernels. This organization qualifies QNX as a top contender for systems that must respond timely to external events in order to operate. The applications of QNX in the real world are varied and far-reaching, impacting several key industries where performance and reliability are paramount. In cars, for instance, QNX enables many next-gen driver assistance systems (ADAS) with quick processing of data from sensors and cameras. Its real-time performance ensures that such systems act with immediacy to changes in the driving environment, significantly enhancing safety. Similarly, in telecommunications, QNX supports the infrastructure that drives network operation, providing responsiveness necessary for voice and data communication essential to modern networks of communication (Figure 2.13).

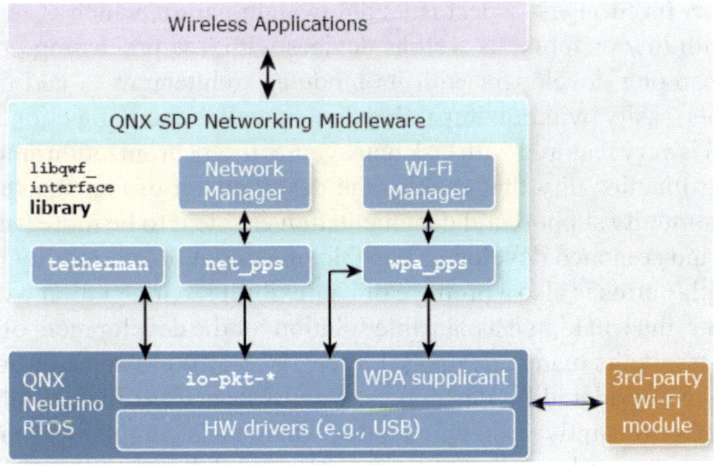

Figure 2.13. The architecture of QNX.

Source: https://www.qnx.com/developers/docs/7.1/com.qnx.doc.qwf.overview/images/qwf_arch.png.

The flexibility of the architectures makes it possible to optimize it for specific usage cases and make QNX a feasible option where there are strict time and safety requirements in various industries. The real-time performance of QNX can be tested using various performance metrics that highlight QNX's advantages over other operating systems. Taking advantage of a microkernel design, QNX has a minimal footprint that minimizes the scheduling latency of processes and inter-process communication. This optimization is particularly valuable when high throughput and low response times are crucial, for instance in robotics and automation. Additionally, with ITS increasingly being deployed, QNX has evolved as a key enabler of coordinated management of distributed smart environments. Tests have demonstrated that middleware systems using QNX can efficiently manage the communications between ITS components with good system performance and minimum computation overhead (Barrero et al., 2013). In addition, comparison studies between QNX and alternative real-time extensions to general-purpose operating systems confirm the real-time operation advantage that is inherent in its design (Radder et al., 2015). These findings continue to establish QNXs position as an advance operating system for real-time applications.

2.4.3. FreeRTOS: Advantages and Limitations

FreeRTOS, an open-source RTOS widely used, offers numerous strengths that qualify it for embedded systems and applications where resources and timing are an issue. Its strongest aspect is its lightweight nature, which is essential for devices with low memory, as well as devices with low processing power. It is a favorite among developers with its modular architecture to add or remove components easily without impacting the overall system function. Besides, FreeRTOS is very featured with task management, synchronization among tasks, and timing functionality that enables the development of responsive systems. Heavy community support and documentation enable it to be more usable, with both new and seasoned developers capable of using it. Its portability to various hardware platforms is also a promise of its flexibility in integration with diverse applications, thus making it a plausible solution for the development of real-time systems. Despite its many advantages, FreeRTOS also has some disadvantages that must be considered by developers. One of its serious disadvantages is its adoption of a preemptive schedule model, which adds complexity in managing task interactions and resource sharing. This model can pose challenges in maintaining system stability, especially where tasks vie for limited resources. Additionally, while FreeRTOS is designed to be lightweight, task organization and task priority can impact performance and create opportunities for timing issues if not carefully controlled. In addition, FreeRTOS lacks some of the premium features and existing support contained within more comprehensive operating systems, which will likely need additional development effort for certain applications. Thus, programmers will have to thoroughly weigh these limitations when deciding whether FreeRTOS is suitable for their specific application (Figure 2.14).

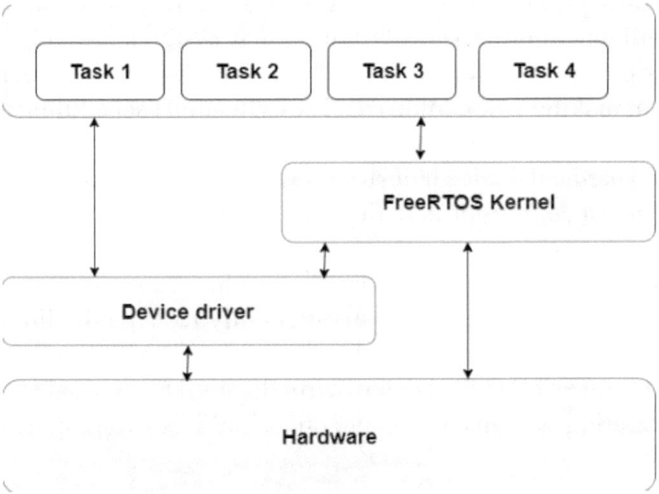

Figure 2.14. The architecture of FreeRTOS.

Source: https://www.researchgate.net/profile/Mahmoud-Qutqut/publication/328031606/figure/fig7/AS:677403684773888@1538517032028/The-Architecture-of-FreeRTOS-reproduced-from-80.jpg.

The increasing relevance of real-time applications, especially when dealing with the Internet of Things (IoT), emphasizes the need for secure protocols along with good performance measurements (Tariq et al., 2023). While FreeRTOS is effective in resource management and scheduling, its security environment may not be as comprehensive as other more secure operating systems. This constraint is of concern, especially against the backdrop of vulnerable IoT devices that are largely subject to malicious attacks. It thus becomes necessary to apply FreeRTOS alongside other security features to circumvent possible vulnerabilities and maintain the integrity of connected systems. In addition, as technologies such as virtual reality and augmented reality expand, the needs for operating systems also evolve in the process with the need for FreeRTOS to cope with new security and performance issues (Arena et al., 2022). In this atmosphere, some balance of benefits versus limitations will be the deciding factor in determining the future of FreeRTOS in real-time application development.

2.5. FUTURE TRENDS IN REAL-TIME OPERATING SYSTEMS (RTOS)

The landscape of RTOS is evolving at breakneck speed, in response to advances in both compute capability and app requirements from various industries. Among the most prominent trends is the integration of machine learning and artificial intelligence into RTOS design so that systems are able to learn and enhance their performance in real-time. These intelligent RTOS can learn from operating data, making autonomous decisions to adjust scheduling and resource allocation and thereby enhance responsiveness and efficiency. As automotive, aerospace, and medical device industries require higher-order and more general-purpose performance, the introduction of such intelligent features signals the future of more autonomous systems capable of handling more complex and dynamic conditions. Further, with the increasing demand for accuracy and dependability, such advancements can potentially reshape the limits of system design and operating effectiveness in real-time areas. The other vital trend reshaping the future of RTOS is that of virtualization technologies, which allow numerous operating systems to execute on a single hardware platform.

Figure 2.15. *Future trends in real-time operating systems.*

Source: https://fidus.com/wp-content/uploads/RTOS-Blog-3-1024x1024.png.

This shift to virtualization not only improves the utilization of resources but also enhances system reliability and fault tolerance, which are paramount in safety-related situations. Virtualization separates various applications into distinct environments, providing a safety buffer for the vulnerabilities of single-point failure. Virtualization also allows innovators to innovate and experiment with numerous applications in parallel, significantly accelerating development and deployment cycles. As organizations pursue increased efficiency and cost reduction with stringent safety standards being maintained, the use of virtualization in RTOS environments will become increasingly popular, addressing many problems across areas such as embedded systems, telecommunications, and intelligent infrastructure. In addition, the merging of IoT with RTOS is creating new avenues for future innovation. As billions of devices become connected, there will be a requirement for robust RTOS that can sustain the real-time processing and communication needs of these devices. RTOS deployed in IoT-based applications will require improved energy efficiency and low-latency support to handle the massive data being generated. The use of edge computing in this context further expands the scope of RTOS to enable closer data processing to the source and avoid latency inherent in cloud-based technology. Developments in RTOS, driven by burgeoning interconnectivity of devices, societal demands for smart technologies, and needs for real-time response, mark a revolutionary phase. These developments will introduce prospects of greater automation and data analysis in real-time processes that will ultimately find their way to various industries, including transportation, healthcare, and industrial automation (Figure 2.15).

2.5.1. Integration with IoT and Edge Computing

The internet of things (IoT) has revolutionized the manner in which devices communicate and converse with one another, particularly at network topology peripheries. Seamless connection to edge computing is crucial for efficient processing of the large volumes of data generated by various IoT devices. Extending computing resources to the edge where data is generated reduces latency, conserves bandwidth, and speeds up the processing rate of data. Hence, uses like real-time applications in industrial automation and healthcare are greatly useful. For instance, as noted by Akrivopoulos et al. (2017), new applications like automated healthcare monitoring platforms apply edge computing to support immediate processing of information, enabling timely medical intervention as well as patient independence in monitoring health condition. Hence, architectural harmonization between edge computing and IoT is a central element in facilitating real-time operational functions. In addition to increasing speed and efficiency, the combination of IoT with edge computing alleviates the inherent problem that arises from resource constraints in wireless sensor networks (WSNs). Since most WSN devices run on low power and processing, there is a need to create communication protocols that reduce overhead and optimize energy usage. To effectively manage these limitations, one typically needs to utilize an integrated network infrastructure that accommodates heterogeneous WSN applications. According to Leung et al. (2015), a cross-layer design employing lightweight, cloud-based RESTful web services can improve the operational management of such devices. Such methodologies describe real-time applications as capable of sustaining their functionality in the face of resource-limited situations, making the design need in OS for real-time applications so pertinent. The implications of IoT and edge computing integration are not necessarily technical but also alter business models across industries. By developing a robust ecosystem in which devices are able to pass and exchange data in a simple, seamless form, organizations can sharpen decision-making and promote innovation. IoT ability to produce exponential volumes of data opens up opportunities for advanced analytics, while edge computing opens up instant insight into hitherto inaccessible data. This shift is particularly evident in sectors like smart cities and health, where response systems are able to react to real-time events. Through real-time data administration and analysis, the integration of these technologies can enable more efficient operations and system overall resilience and thereby illustrate the need to incorporate smart operating system principles in order to support such evolving applications.

2.5.2. Advances in Scheduling Algorithms

The evolution of scheduling algorithms has been instrumental in driving the advancement of RTOS features, particularly with more demanding timing requirements given by applications to meet. Traditional approaches to scheduling, such as Rate Monotonic Scheduling (RMS) and Earliest Deadline First (EDF), form rudimentary models of task prioritization based on periodicity and deadlines. However, the dynamic nature of modern systems, characterized by varying task loads and real-time constraints, demands more sophisticated mechanisms. The most recent advancements include the integration of adaptive and hybrid scheduling algorithms with the capacity to adjust task priorities and resources allocation adaptively as a function of system status. This is extremely important for applications in embedded systems and IoT environments, where low latency has to be guaranteed and deadlines respected in order to ensure functionality and reliability. Furthermore, advances in embedding machine learning techniques into scheduling algorithms hold promise to optimize resource utilization in real-time systems. Predictive analytics can help the algorithms anticipate peak loads and adjust scheduling accordingly to meet real-time demands, making the system responsive and improving overall throughput. Energy efficiency is another area of thrust, particularly in battery-operated equipment. Research suggests intelligent scheduling can lower energy consumption while maintaining performance levels significantly. This dual emphasis on performance and energy efficiency is fulfilled in the paradigm cited in current research, with its emphasis on the crucial role of scheduling in optimizing the use of constrained resource systems, such as IoT devices in which both computing power and energy resources are limited (Biason et al., 2017). In addition, the application of the High-Level Architecture (HLA) standard in real-time systems has facilitated advancements in developing resilient scheduling algorithms appropriate for intricate federations. Because the current HLA standard fails to effectively address real-time constraints, scholars have attempted to develop techniques that bridge these protocols with hard real-time requirements. Using a bottom-up approach that integrates hardware demands with software characteristics, scheduling could be made simpler to achieve deadlines consistently as well as tackle the intricacies of distributed real-time simulations. This shift represents a widening insight that achieving efficiency in real-time computing relies not only on the algorithms themselves but also on their ideal union with the infrastructure of the supporting system (Adelantado et al., 2011). As such ideas come in abundance, they create doors for later developments in scheduling that will certainly make RTOS much more reliable and performant.

2.5.3. Impact of Machine Learning on Real-Time Systems

The addition of machine learning (ML) to real-time systems is a groundbreaking achievement in the field of operating systems. Real-time systems are characterized by their ability to process data and respond quickly to stimuli, a feature that is important in such fields as automotive control, aerospace, and telecommunications. Machine learning enhances this by enabling systems to adapt from previous patterns and make rational forecasts of impending states. This predictive capability not only increases system efficiency but also allows for adaptive responses, making it possible for real-time systems to optimize their operation dynamically. For example, the addition of Massive MIMO technology in 5G networks is a case in point for this combination of machine learning and real-time computing, where enhanced signal processing allows for record spectral efficiency and spatial processing capabilities, transforming the mechanisms for data transmission in modern communication networks (Björnson et al., 2019). While machine learning algorithms are being developed further, so do the challenges for real-time systems. A key challenge is the computational resource requirement, as most ML models are computationally resource-intensive and may not be capable of meeting the stringent timing constraints of real-time systems. The addition of ML therefore needs to be handled well so that the fundamental reliability and determinism of real-time systems are preserved. Besides, how machine learning can be used in automation varies from application to application. For instance, the efficiency of automation in use cases such as NASAs aviation operations demonstrates the revolutionizing potential of ML-driven decision-making in real-time, emphasizing the need for a baseline understanding of levels of automation across various environments (Kopardekar et al., 2025). This nearly invisible overlap of resource demands and operational effectiveness makes effective strategies for optimizing machine learning algorithms in real-time systems an imperative. The ongoing innovation in machine learning algorithms specifically for use in real-time systems is rich with promise for innovation. As researchers start exploring new ways to accelerate response times and resource utilization, the deployment of lean and effective ML models becomes the focal point. Edge computing and distributed ML frameworks are endeavors that can enhance real-time processing to a large extent, providing computational resources closer to where data is generated. Further, network communication advancements, like those that come with the deployment of Massive MIMO systems, are capable of leveraging machine learning to improve data transfer efficiency to an extent that yields low-latency responses essential to real-time applications (Björnson et al., 2019). By combining the predictive power of ML with the origins of real-time systems, engineers are able to design intelligent architectures that, in addition to optimizing performance, also provide opportunities for applications in the future across a broad spectrum of areas (Figure 2.16).

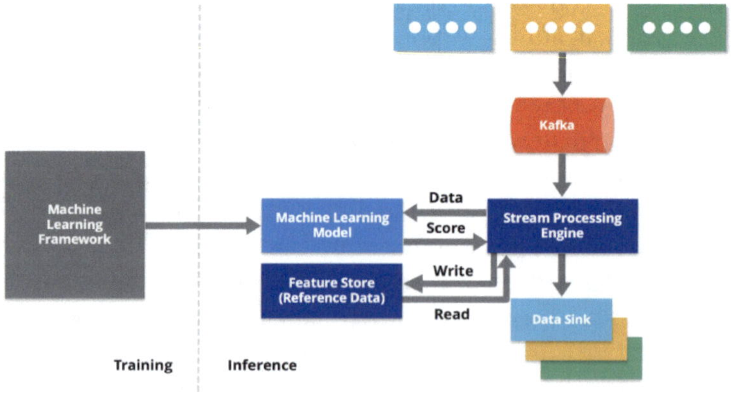

Figure 2.16. The integration of machine learning (ML) into real-time systems.

Source: https://hazelcast.com/wp-content/uploads/2021/12/real-time-machine-learning-diagram.png.

SUMMARY

The intrinsic intricacies of real-time applications accentuate the necessity of operating systems that can cope with stringent timing requirements. Not only do these systems need to control the resources effectively, but they must also ensure that the tasks are executed within the stipulated timelines. With applications in sectors such as healthcare, transportation, and telecommunications relying increasingly on correct timing and dependability, the demand for dependable operating systems is increasing. Managing these challenges efficiently necessitates the application of advanced scheduling algorithms and methods of resource management that can adapt dynamically to different workloads. Through this, operating systems can greatly enhance performance and reliability in delivering real-time functionality. Furthermore, since current methods provide many solutions for controlling resources in real-time systems, still there are broad gaps to be filled. Software aging is a unique challenge were running continuously causes degradation and premature failure. Proactive techniques such as software rejuvenation, say the literature, offer a persuasive means of mitigating this issue, particularly for long-lived applications in mission-critical scenarios (Raju et al., 2012). The use of rejuvenation schedules unique to the system's performance metrics ensures applications are consistent over their lifetime of operation. These approaches highlight constant improvement in operating system design in meeting evolving needs. Furthermore, enhancing better-balanced algorithms for resource allocation is critical to enabling heterogeneous quality of service (QoS) requirements among real-time applications. The conventional plans fail to serve particular needs of various users under unique utility requirements, leading to inefficient usage of resources (Low et al., 2006). Breakthroughs in distributed flow control algorithms encourage a vision where bandwidth can be allocated more uniformly and efficiently, thereby catering to the individual needs of real-time applications. With interdisciplinary research continuing to push the frontiers of operating systems, the creation of these systems will play a crucial role in shaping the future of real-time applications in every sector.

In the area of real-time applications, there cannot be too much stress on operating systems. Operating systems in the area are designed with particular focus on managing hardware resources and executing tasks under strict timing requirements, such that processes are ensured to meet their deadlines. The performance of RTOS relies mostly on their scheduling policies, which dictate how tasks are scheduled and executed. Particularly, ability to manage multi-core architectures effectively is critical, as increasing pressures on processing capacity demand parallel execution paradigms. This is addressed by the inclusion of sophisticated scheduling techniques that can address the unique requirements posed by real-time features and thus enhance performance without sacrificing responsiveness during time-critical scenarios. Software framework developments such as OpenMP significantly enhance the ability of RTOS. Although it possesses a significant superiority over other techniques of concurrency management using parallel processing, the standard OpenMP lacks inherent support for temporal guarantees necessary within real-time systems. Such a limitation necessitates the development of specific frameworks like OpenMP-RT. By the provision of specialized constructs in real-time task scheduling as well as in communication protocol, which are crucial in system reliability, OpenMP-RT enhances the expressiveness of programming languages when used in real-time systems. Its use ensures increased accuracy and predictability, drawing attention to a hybrid model to overcome the challenges of concurrent processing within environments where time constraints are of utmost importance. Further, innovative approaches such as real-time recognition of hand movements point to the synergy of deep learning techniques and real-time environments. Employing Long Short-Term Memory (LSTM) networks, the solution detects and assesses hand movements in real-time to translate gestures into voice or written text. With exceptional accuracy rates of 99.6%, the technology is a means of communication, particularly for deaf and mute children. The integration of machine learning and RTOS presents evidence of the possibility of creating responsive applications that do not only deliver performance requirements but also allow for social connectivity and accessibility. With real-time applications continuing to expand, the interplay between operating systems, advanced programming environments, and new technologies will undoubtedly shape the future dynamics of computational effectiveness and efficiency.

REFERENCES

1. Adelantado, M., Chaudron, J. B., & Siron, P. (2010). Towards an HLA run-time infrastructure with hard real-time capabilities. https://core.ac.uk/download/12042130.pdf (accessed on 29th September 2025).
2. Adelantado, M., Chaudron, J. B., Noulard, E., Siron, P., et al. (2011). HLA high performance and real-time simulation studies with CERTI. https://core.ac.uk/download/12042649.pdf (accessed on 29th September 2025).
3. Akrivopoulos, O., Antoniou, A., Chatzigiannakis, I., Tselios, C., et al. (2017). On the deployment of healthcare applications over fog computing infrastructure. https://core.ac.uk/download/98343526.pdf (accessed on 29th September 2025).
4. Al-Fuqaha, A., Guizani, M., Mohammadi, M., Aledhari, M., & Ayyash, M. (2015). Internet of Things: A survey on enabling technologies, protocols, and applications. *IEEE Communications Surveys & Tutorials, 17*, 2347–2376. https://doi.org/10.1109/comst.2015.2444095 (accessed on 29th September 2025).
5. Alizadeh, M., Scaglione, A., van der Schaar, M., Xiao, L., et al. (2013). Incentive design for direct load control programs. http://arxiv.org/abs/1310.0402 (accessed on 29th September 2025).
6. Amendola, A., Barbareschi, M., De Simone, S., Mezzina, G., Moriconi, A., Saragaglia, C. L., Serra, D., et al. (2023). A real-time vital control module to increase capabilities of railway control systems in highly automated train operations. *Real-Time Systems, 59*, 636–661. https://www.semanticscholar.org/paper/944389a5107f56dcc6301b9fa644cd2c4ff30566 (accessed on 29th September 2025).
7. Ang, K. H., Chong, G. C. Y., & Li, Y. (2005). PID control system analysis, design, and technology. https://core.ac.uk/download/1394222.pdf (accessed on 29th September 2025).
8. Arena, F., Collotta, M., Pau, G., & Termine, F. (2022). An overview of augmented reality. *Computers, 11*, 28–28. https://doi.org/10.3390/computers11020028 (accessed on 29th September 2025).
9. Axelsson, J., & Kobetski, A. (2012). Federated embedded systems–A review of the literature in related fields. https://core.ac.uk/download/11434985.pdf (accessed on 29th September 2025).
10. Bakirtzis, G., Carter, B. T., Elks, C. R., Fleming, C., et al. (2018). A model-based approach to security analysis for cyber-physical systems. http://arxiv.org/abs/1710.11442 (accessed on 29th September 2025).

11. Barletta, W. A., Chattopadhyay, S., & Seryi, A. (2012). Educating and training accelerator scientists and technologists for tomorrow. http://arxiv.org/abs/1207.3065 (accessed on 29th September 2025).
12. Barrero, F., Cortés, F., Recalde, G., Derlis, D., Toral, S., et al. (2013). Analysis of embedded CORBA middleware performance on urban distributed transportation equipment's. https://core.ac.uk/download/51403424.pdf (accessed on 29th September 2025).
13. Bauman, F., Carbonnier, K., Cheng, H., Dawe, M., et al. (2019). Optimizing radiant systems for energy efficiency and comfort. https://core.ac.uk/download/322493983.pdf (accessed on 29th September 2025).
14. Behnke, I., & Austad, H. (2023). Real-time performance of industrial IoT communication technologies: A review. *IEEE Internet of Things Journal, 11*, 7399–7410. https://doi.org/10.1109/jiot.2023.3332507 (accessed on 29th September 2025).
15. Berge, J., Ganesan, S., Goldsmith, M., Gungor, V., Hong, Y., Matsuda, T., Scheible, G., et al. (2012). Wireless industrial monitoring and control networks: The journey so far and the road ahead. https://core.ac.uk/download/pdf/11484488.pdf (accessed on 29th September 2025).
16. Biason, A., Kelly, M., Pielli, C., Rossi, M., et al. (2017). EC-CENTRIC: An energy- and context-centric perspective on IoT systems and protocol design. https://core.ac.uk/download/84922330.pdf (accessed on 29th September 2025).
17. Björnson, E., Hoydis, J., Marzetta, T. L., Sanguinetti, L., et al. (2019). Massive MIMO is a reality–What is next? Five promising research directions for antenna arrays. http://arxiv.org/abs/1902.07678 (accessed on 29th September 2025).
18. Briscoe, G., De Wilde, P., & Sadedin, S. (2011). Digital ecosystems: Ecosystem-oriented architectures. http://arxiv.org/abs/1112.0204 (accessed on 29th September 2025).
19. Bux, M., Gusew, W., Leser, U., Witt, C., et al. (2018). Predictive performance modeling for distributed computing using black-box monitoring and machine learning. http://arxiv.org/abs/1805.11877 (accessed on 29th September 2025).
20. Chen, L., Li, Y., Huang, C., Xing, Y., Tian, D., Li, L., Hu, Z., et al. (2023). Milestones in autonomous driving and intelligent vehicles—Part I: Control, computing system design, communication, HD map, testing, and human behaviors. *IEEE Transactions on Systems, Man, and Cybernetics: Systems, 53*, 5831–5847. https://doi.org/10.1109/tsmc.2023.3276218 (accessed on 29th September 2025).

21. Chiang, M., & Zhang, T. (2016). Fog and IoT: An overview of research opportunities. *IEEE Internet of Things Journal, 3*, 854–864. https://doi.org/10.1109/jiot.2016.2584538 (accessed on 29th September 2025).

22. Chowdhury, P., & Misra, I. S. (2010). A fair and efficient packet scheduling scheme for IEEE 802.16 broadband wireless access systems. http://arxiv.org/abs/1009.6091 (accessed on 29th September 2025).

23. Cramer, C. J., Dongarra, J., Dror, R. O., Goldberg, D., Hager, G., Haoqiang, J., Hennessy, J. L., et al. (2012). A review of high-performance computing foundations for scientists. http://arxiv.org/abs/1205.5177 (accessed on 29th September 2025).

24. Cucinotta, T., & Faggioli, D. (2012). Handling timing constraints violations in soft real-time applications as exceptions. https://core.ac.uk/download/pdf/54933053.pdf (accessed on 29th September 2025).

25. Cucinotta, T., Marinoni, M., Melani, A., Parri, A., et al. (2017). Temporal isolation among LTE/5G network functions by real-time scheduling. https://core.ac.uk/download/pdf/84495671.pdf (accessed on 29th September 2025).

26. Eide, E. N., & Stack, T. (2004). Dynamic CPU management for real-time, middleware-based systems. https://core.ac.uk/download/276284192.pdf (accessed on 29th September 2025).

27. Eiroa-Lledo, E., Linstead, E., Springer, T., Stevens, A., et al. (2021). On-device deep learning inference for system-on-chip (SoC) architectures. https://core.ac.uk/download/392381428.pdf (accessed on 29th September 2025).

28. Fauberteau, F., & Midonnet, S. (2012). Sustainability in static-priority restricted-migration scheduling. https://core.ac.uk/download/48333646.pdf (accessed on 29th September 2025).

29. Fisher, D., Hand, J., Liesen, R., Wilson, E., et al. (2011). Screening of energy efficient technologies for industrial buildings' retrofit. https://core.ac.uk/download/9033399.pdf (accessed on 29th September 2025).

30. Gielen, D., Boshell, F., Saygin, D., Bazilian, M., Wagner, N., & Gorini, R. (2019). The role of renewable energy in the global energy transformation. *Energy Strategy Reviews, 24*, 38–50. https://doi.org/10.1016/j.esr.2019.01.006 (accessed on 29th September 2025).

31. Gurrala, V., Talasila, S., Vaishnavi, R., Shruthi, J., & Supreeth, J. (2025). Real time hand gesture recognition using LSTM based deep learning. *2025 8th International Conference on Electronics, Materials Engineering & Nano-Technology (IEMENTech)*. https://www.semanticscholar.org/paper/279ab055a0504de6f1ff7ef106c4efd3562c1c3d (accessed on 29th September 2025).

32. Harris, R., Millman, K. J., van der Walt, S., Gommers, R., Virtanen, P., Cournapeau, D., Wieser, E., et al. (2020). Array programming with NumPy. *Nature, 585*, 357–362. https://doi.org/10.1038/s41586-020-2649-2 (accessed on 29th September 2025).

33. Havinga, P. J. M. (2000). The design of a system architecture for mobile multimedia computers. https://core.ac.uk/download/pdf/11460964.pdf (accessed on 29th September 2025).

34. Kopardekar, P. H., & Sridhar, B. (2025). Towards autonomous aviation operations: What can we learn from other areas of automation? https://core.ac.uk/download/pdf/286393131.pdf (accessed on 29th September 2025).

35. Le, V. L. (2019). Ultra-low power digital integrated circuit design. https://www.semanticscholar.org/paper/f6798405decea53d8a6f28bd891938d181788ba4 (accessed on 29th September 2025).

36. León, A. E. (2015). Integration of DFIG-based wind farms into series-compensated transmission systems. *IEEE Transactions on Sustainable Energy, 7*, 451–460. https://doi.org/10.1109/tste.2015.2498312 (accessed on 29th September 2025).

37. Leung, V. C. M., Mahapatra, C., Sheng, Z., Zhu, Q., et al. (2015). Recent advances in industrial wireless sensor networks towards efficient management in IoT. https://core.ac.uk/download/30611701.pdf (accessed on 29th September 2025).

38. Low, S. H., Palaniswami, M., & Wang, W. H. (2006). Application-oriented flow control: Fundamentals, algorithms and fairness. https://core.ac.uk/download/4875885.pdf (accessed on 29th September 2025).

39. Maistrenko, A., Maistrenko, K., & Svetlakov, A. (2021). Dichotomy. Dichotomy? Dichotomy! A modified method of dichotomy for solution of nonlinear scalar equations and some results of its investigation. https://www.semanticscholar.org/paper/7cfd9df9070c4051c0aefcfb4063f3b170b40629 (accessed on 29th September 2025).

40. McDonald, B., & Mueller, F. (2024). OpenMP-RT: Native pragma support for real-time tasks and synchronization with LLVM under Linux. *Proceedings of the 25th ACM SIGPLAN/SIGBED International Conference on Languages, Compilers, and Tools for Embedded Systems*. https://www.semanticscholar.org/paper/51c19139fe90a3db47ec0253691652504552c6f2 (accessed on 29th September 2025).

41. Prodan, R., Taylor, I., & Zhao, Z. (2020). Editorial for FGCS special issue on “Time-critical applications on software-defined infrastructures.”

https://core.ac.uk/download/489777707.pdf (accessed on 29th September 2025).

42. Radder, D. (2015). Hard real-time Linux for off-the-shelf multicore architectures. https://core.ac.uk/download/46920332.pdf (accessed on 29th September 2025).
43. Raju, R., & Sumathi, G. (2012). Software aging analysis of web server using neural networks. http://arxiv.org/abs/1206.1534 (accessed on 29th September 2025).
44. Schiappacasse, A. (2018). Intraoperative navigation systems for image-guided surgery. https://core.ac.uk/download/162442361.pdf (accessed on 29th September 2025).
45. Shi, W., Cao, J., Zhang, Q., Li, Y., & Xu, L. (2016). Edge computing: Vision and challenges. *IEEE Internet of Things Journal, 3*, 637–646. https://doi.org/10.1109/jiot.2016.2579198 (accessed on 29th September 2025).
46. Si, J., Hoppensteadt, F., Golshani, F., Collins, D. W., Ringhofer, C., & Tsakalis, K. (2000). Interdisciplinary research on modeling and scheduling of semiconductor manufacturing operations. https://www.semanticscholar.org/paper/3262ffcdc6c0d216f2fc6afe6928ad2b35d20407 (accessed on 29th September 2025).
47. Singh, M., & Nowick, S. (2011). Introduction to special issue: Asynchrony in system design. *ACM Journal on Emerging Technologies in Computing Systems, 7*, 14:1–14:2. https://www.semanticscholar.org/paper/9df526b7af72d82d63ed7bc8c8535f3133cc0d2a (accessed on 29th September 2025).
48. Tariq, U., Ahmed, I., Bashir, A. K., & Shaukat, K. (2023). A critical cybersecurity analysis and future research directions for the Internet of Things: A comprehensive review. *Sensors, 23*, 4117–4117. https://doi.org/10.3390/s23084117 (accessed on 29th September 2025).
49. Turner, J. (2002). Terabit burst switching final report. https://www.semanticscholar.org/paper/a2d249aa452025cca1d3dbafb2f7b470f84755e4 (accessed on 29th September 2025).
50. Zaslavsky, A., Perera, C., Georgakopoulos, D., & Christen, P. (2013). Context aware computing for the Internet of Things: A survey. https://core.ac.uk/download/327950084.pdf (accessed on 29th September 2025).

CHAPTER 3

RTOS ARCHITECTURE AND COMPONENTS

Contents

INTRODUCTION

The explanation of real-time operating systems (RTOS) architecture and composition is pivotal in understanding the complex working and design relationships that are typical of them. RTOS is intended to manage hardware and software resources in such a way that real-time data processing and responsiveness are enabled, which is integral in applications ranging as widely as embedded systems and critical infrastructure. This first analysis will outline the fundamental principles behind RTOS design, with emphasis on the importance of efficient resource management, low latency, and high reliability. Simple notions of task scheduling, inter-process communication, and interrupt handling will also be addressed, providing a simple framework upon which to explore more advanced RTOS features. With the emergence of mobile and multimedia applications, the investigation of these elements becomes more pertinent because they are a convergence of computational requirements and operational limitations that the RTOS architecture has to successfully traverse. A relevant case can be pointed out in the revolutionary design of the Mobile Digital Companion, which shows how the teachings of RTOS are applied. This structure emphasizes energy efficiency to enhance battery life while maintaining usability across environments. By employing system decomposition at various levels and fusion of optimized modules, the Mobile Digital Companion is a natural case study illustrating how RTOS performance can be optimized while minimizing energy consumption. This system demonstrates the effect of specialized functionalities and energy-saving techniques at every level of structure. The approach used for the Mobile Digital Companion is characteristic of a general trend in RTOS design, with flexibility and flexibility being critical on the basis of limitations from battery life and operating environment, emphasizing the value of advanced design methodologies for next-generation computing environments (Havinga et al., 2000). Secondly, with advancements in technology, the challenges associated with multimedia and mobile computing necessitate a reexamination of dominant paradigms. Personal mobile computing, for instance, is an essential area that requires architectural innovation in research because desktop models are unsuitable to meet the requirements of such emerging applications. RTOS architectures must cope with restricted power from batteries and diversity of data types in operating in conditions of uncertainty. A self-chasing, reconfigurable module-based method with modules plugged into a reconfigurable communication network switch is a contemporary approach of overcoming these issues. By efficient processing of data and prevention of wastage of resources, like in the Octopus communication system, RTOS structures can ensure remarkable mobile device performance and responsiveness (Havinga et al., 1999). This dynamic environment demands the investigation of the unique features and architectural models that characterize RTOS, setting the stage for further research in the subsequent sections of this chapter.

Definition of Real-Time Operating Systems (RTOS)

Real-time operating systems (RTOS) are operating systems whose primary function is to manage hardware resources and execute tasks with strict timing deadlines. This feature distinguishes RTOS from most operating systems, which focus on throughput and general-purpose task scheduling. An RTOS promises critical tasks the earliest service relative to certain deadlines, such as in applications where timely decision needs to be taken, like in industrial automation or embedded systems. The design of an RTOS typically encompasses building blocks like a kernel responsible for task scheduling, an inter-process communication mechanism, and timing-optimized device drivers. With this specific consideration, the likelihood of consistent operation of systems where missing the delivery of the timing constraint can result in catastrophe is made possible. For RTOS, structure and building blocks are designed in coordination to ensure predictable performance.

Figure 3.1. The basics of real-time operating systems.

Source: https://cdn.educba.com/academy/wp-content/uploads/2024/02/Real-Time-Operating-System.jpg.

The kernel, often the core of RTOS, employs priority-based scheduling algorithms to schedule tasks by urgency and priority. An example is the uRT51 processor, specifically designed for embedded applications in real-time control. It illustrates how hardware-level incorporation of RTOS capabilities can significantly enhance performance and reliability in time-sensitive applications (Alimenti et al., 2007). Additionally, event-driven architecture commonly employed enables the system to react swiftly to the external world, hence improving resource optimization and best task management. It is this built-in coordination between architecture and components that causes RTOS to deliver at its optimal best in cases where timing is everything. In addition, reliability in RTOS entails complex design elements that cater to various levels of operation complexity. For example, the provision of redundant channels in high-reliability systems illustrates how RTOS may be implemented to enhance fault tolerance and deliver seamless operation in failure conditions (Burns et al., 2010). In such a system, one channel can be optimized for high reliability, and another one could use static analysis to establish error-free performance. This multi-layered approach to system design not only minimizes risks of hardware failure but also facilitates trust in the achievement of mission-critical deadlines. The development of dependable RTOS architecture thus integrates advanced task management techniques along with an understanding of the nuanced needs for reliability and performance in mission-critical systems (Figure 3.1).

Importance of RTOS in Embedded Systems

The prevalence of embedded systems in present-day technology underscores the imperative necessity for RTOS in ensuring their proper operation. Unlike conventional software systems, embedded systems often operate under tight real-time constraints, which demand a system that can execute tasks with high determinism and low latency. An RTOS fulfills these needs by synchronizing the execution of the various tasks and the management of resources in an optimal way, thus enabling the system to respond in real-time to external stimuli. The increasing complexity of embedded environments with the enhancement of hardware capabilities and application features further necessitates the use of an RTOS. Cardoso et al. (2014) emphasizes that with growing complexity in embedded systems, the employment of an RTOS becomes necessary not only for managing complex hardware but also for providing runtime services critical to system functions. Besides meeting deterministic responses and latency, RTOS environments are directly involved in determining the safety and security of embedded systems, especially in safety-critical applications such as transportation, healthcare, and aerospace. These sectors require robust systems that can react to failures and cyber-attacks in a timely fashion. RTOS's purpose shifts into various phases of the lifecycle, from design to deployment, and is aimed at identifying potential vulnerabilities in advance. By developing a highly structured model that captures key system properties, developers can undertake thorough vulnerability analysis before deployment. Bakirtzis et al. (2018) illustrates how creating an enhanced taxonomy of system characteristics facilitates preemption of attack vectors and architectural defenses development during design time, thus enhancing overall security and reliability. Besides, intermixing hardware acceleration with RTOS can enhance system performance in embedded systems to a large degree. With the appearance of high-end hardware platforms, such as field-programmable gate arrays (FPGAs), developers can naturally port important RTOS runtime services to the hardware platform. This combined-based solution not only saves computational overhead on the processor but also improves system latency and predictability, concerns that are important for real-time applications. According to Cardoso et al. (2014), hardware accelerators can transform the way systems execute concurrent jobs and manage resources, leading to application innovation that demands high performance and reliability. This mutual dependence between RTOS and hardware advancements speaks volumes about the continuous evolution in embedded systems and underscores their relevance in various industries.

3.1. KEY CHARACTERISTICS OF RTOS

Among the fundamental characteristics that distinguish RTOS in embedded systems is determinism, that is, in meeting execution time deadlines. Determinism applies to those applications requiring providing a consistent level of performance under varying amounts of computation. Such is accomplished by an RTOS through advanced scheduling algorithms that give priority to time-critical functions. Through controlling resources in an efficient way, these systems ensure that critical processes are provided with the necessary CPU time within their designated deadlines.

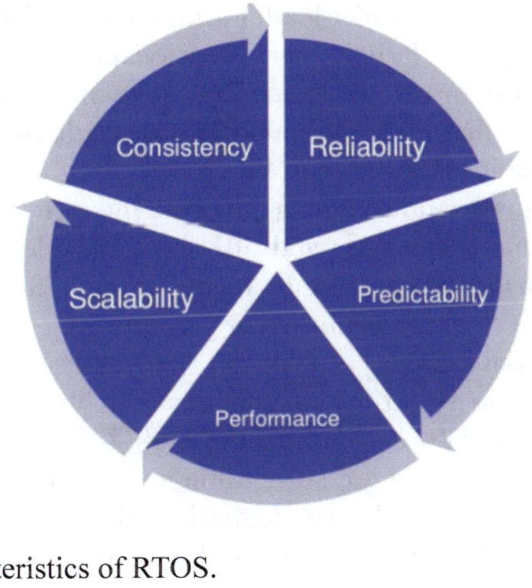

Figure 3.2. Characteristics of RTOS.

Source: https://media.licdn.com/dms/image/v2/C4D12AQHEi26HVjqbbQ/article-cover_image-shrink_720_1280/article-cover_image-shrink_720_1280/0/1640275652889?e=2147483647&v=beta&t=nRrK64M2QU3TEByHblubqnPsLfiO9_ZsnKk39zjQfMc.

These kinds of scheduling mechanisms are extremely important in applications dealing with robotics and telecommunication where minute delay can lead to complete system failure or be a safety hazard. Moreover, an RTOS usually includes a periodic interrupt service, which provides precise time handling, thus increasing overall system reliability and efficiency. The ability to handle varying workloads along with tight timing constraints makes RTOS an essential element of much technologically advanced application. Resource management functions of the RTOS are yet another crucial element of the system, which lies at the heart of the systems performance and reliability. It encompasses allocating system resources such as memory and processing capability in a manner that promotes timely execution of critical tasks. In contrast with general-purpose operating systems, RTOS optimize throughput and minimize latency through a specialized framework. This characteristic is optimized by facilities such as semaphores governing shared access to resources and priority inheritance, preventing issues such as priority inversion. For instance, with real-time kernels such as Xenomai on Linux operating systems, these resource management methods can be supported by offloading time management to dedicated hardware, thereby freeing the CPU, and improving overall efficiency (Boukhobza et al., 2012) (Figure 3.2). As such, efficient management of resources not only ensures prompt performance of work but also plays a critical role in system stability while under load. Furthermore, reliability is an inherent RTOS characteristic, particularly in high integrity applications. The majority of real-time systems must ensure the execution of essential functions flawlessly, with the consequence that there is redundancy in deployment of systems and diverse channels. Their reliability can be enhanced by employing techniques explained in recent publications, which advocate independent channel systems maintaining functional correctness and offering fault tolerance. As explained in recent publications, one channel may be operating with high dependability, while the other utilizes static analysis for guaranteeing deadline satisfaction irrespective of potential defects (Burns et al., 2010). This two-channel approach facilitates systematic treatment of uncertainties which may arise in operations and therefore encourages the development of highly reliable real-time systems. In general, the incorporation of solid time management, efficient use of resources, and fault tolerance designs underlines the central role of reliability in RTOS structure, making them an integral part of contemporary embedded systems.

3.1.1. Determinism and Predictability

In RTOS life, determinism and predictability are basic premises that control system efficiency and dependability. Determinism refers to the ability of the system to provide the same output every time under the same conditions, while predictability is the ability of the systems to control such outputs' timing. These are most essential in embedded systems, where processes need to adhere to a specific time limit to correctly perform. As the level of complexity of embedded applications rises, the demand for effective RTOS solutions that can comfortably execute the time-critical tasks also increases. Determinism makes it possible for developers to predict the system response under various conditions and hence enhance the overall reliability and effectiveness of hardware and software in embedded systems. Incorporation of hardware components into RTOS architectures is now the primary method towards improving determinism and predictability. For instance, offloading runtime services required by the system to hardware components improves the performance of the system by reducing latency and improving response times. The hybrid method has been illustrated on FreeRTOS whereby transferring critical services to hardware reduces the computational burden on the CPU. Such designs utilize field-programmable gate arrays (FPGAs) to incorporate hardware accelerators that optimize operations and enable control of timing precisely. As a result, this not only improves the efficiency of the systems but also strengthens determinism, making it a necessity in situations where timing is of high importance and predictability matters most (Cardoso et al., 2014). Additionally, time management capability strongly affects the functionality of an RTOS. With stringent hard real-time needs, advanced kernel environments such as Xenomai have been used to provide better timing precision for embedded systems. Deterministic task scheduling in such an environment relies on effective interrupt service routines processing time critical events. However, precision against system overload is a subtle balance since growing interrupts can strain CPU resources, thus affecting overall efficiency. To address this challenge, time management service movement to configurable hardware blocks provides relief of resources, thereby attaining optimality in performance terms without sacrificing determinism. These advancements in RTOS structure reveal the common endeavor for higher predictability, enhancing the convergent link between hardware efficiency and software dependability in embedded systems (Boukhobza et al., 2012).

3.1.2. Multitasking Capabilities

The architecture design of a RTOS is inherently tied to multitasking feature, which allows for efficient execution of different processes simultaneously. Multitasking in systems in general is basically attained through the use of time-slicing or thread management methods, allowing the CPU to switch immediately between tasks. However, in the case of embedded systems, particularly those employed in safety-critical applications, the need for multitasking is further limited by the need for guaranteeing system reliability and performance. Embedded systems often have well-specified tasks and tight timing constraints, which further underscores the need for proper design of multitasking mechanisms. The availability of configurable high-density field devices, as noted by Bria et al. (2003), enables embedding specialized multitasking operating systems, which can handle numerous processor cores without degrading task performance to fulfill some requirements of an application. Moreover, the multitasking aspect of an RTOS significantly enhances the capacity of the systems to handle real-time events and maintain operations efficiently (Figure 3.3).

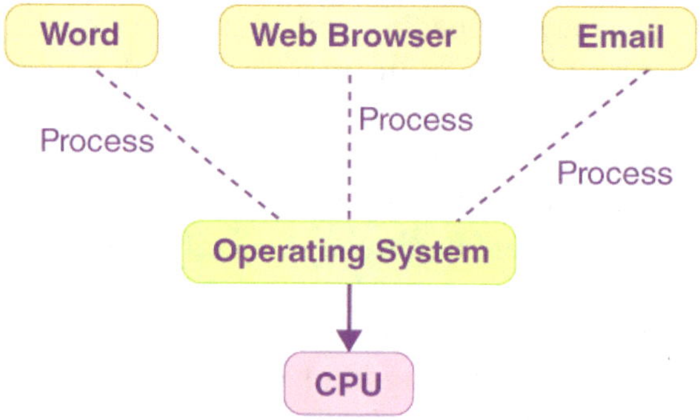

Figure 3.3. Multitasking operating system.

Source: https://cdn1.byjus.com/wp-content/uploads/2022/06/multitasking-operating-system.png.

Unlike traditional general-purpose multitasking systems, whose applications can be accommodated in the design process, multitasking in an SOPC context is preselected. This allows for the optimized hardware and software configuration to meet the applications requirements. The embedded processors efficiently manage several tasks simultaneously through the utilization of a hardware task manager or scheduler to ensure timely handling. This architecture minimizes latency and maximizes throughput; the performance paradigms needed in safety-critical systems where responsiveness to multitasking is a luxury. The formal approach outlined by Abdi et al. (2017), employing certified software to handle faults without sacrificing performance, also illustrates the necessity of robust multitasking support in modern RTOS designs (Figure 3.4). The seamless integration of multitasking in RTOS systems not only promotes efficiency but also ensures compliance with safety standards that are paramount in various industries, including automotive and aerospace industries. Because tasks execute concurrently, it is important to monitor not only the execution of each task but also the impact of failure and recovery processes on the system as a whole. With advanced scheduling models, as revealed by Abdi et al. (2017), the developers can achieve fault tolerance in close timing constraints of safety-critical applications. Consequently, the future of embedded systems demands continuous optimization of multitasking architectures to maintain performance as well as safety. Thus, the knowledge and documentation of multitasking capabilities in RTOS architecture become essential to further develop reliable and efficient embedded solutions in a fast growing technologically complexifying environment.

Figure 3.4. SOPC (system on a programmable chip).

Source: https://www.ariat-tech.com/upfile/images/14/20240724113822602.jpg.

3.1.3. Resource Management and Scheduling

Effective scheduling and resource management are essential in the case of RTOS as they ensure that tasks are executed under strict timing limits while achieving optimal system performance. RTOS architectures allow for multitasking, requiring sophisticated scheduling algorithms that schedule tasks based on the priority of their urgency and resource need. One common supervisor approach is the application of priority scheduling, where high-priority tasks override lower-priority ones to meet hard deadlines. Design becomes crucial in situations where the timely execution of tasks directly impacts system dependability and performance, notably in industrial and automotive applications where safety is of utmost concern. By exercising proper control over system resources, RTOS allows optimal task scheduling, minimizes delay, and supports a uniform operating environment required in real-time systems. Besides the basic scheduling methods, integration with more advanced approaches such as dynamic resource allocation elevates the capabilities of RTOS architectures.

Dynamic allocation allows the system to respond suitably to changing workloads while maintaining required quality of service (QoS). For instance, if there are a number of high-priority tasks reaching at one point in time, the scheduler must allocate CPU time and memory resources with finesse so that all tasks are accomplished within their deadline. As mentioned in recent literature, adding real-time capabilities to distributed systems—particularly for the High-Level Architecture (HLA) framework—is a complicated endeavor (Figure 3.5).

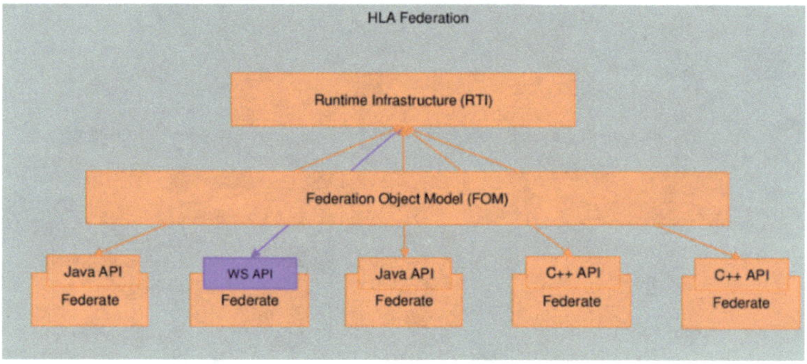

Figure 3.5. High-level architecture (HLA).

Source: https://www.researchgate.net/profile/Jo-Hannay/publication/283725455/figure/fig9/AS:667865275453455@1536242898966/High-Level-Architecture-HLA.png.

The need for Worst Case Transit Time (WCTT) guarantees and best scheduling services clearly indicates the complexity of resource management in such applications. Its solution is crucial in constructing efficient and robust real-time systems that are capable of responding to diverse needs in various applications (Adelantado et al., 2010). Additionally, the application of hardware schedulers in RTOS has a revolutionary impact on system performance and efficiency. Traditional software-based scheduling is often beset by overhead that can lead to increased latency and decreased responsiveness. Hardware schedulers, however, have already been used to greatly decrease scheduling overhead via, for instance, recent breakthroughs resulting in decreases in scheduling overhead of over 1,000 clock cycles. Such improvements highlight the benefits of using reprogrammable FPGA-based systems that can offer flexibility and substantial performance improvement without requiring unconscionable resource demands. Accompanying various scheduling algorithms, like Earliest Deadline First (EDF) and Least Slack Time (LST), these hardware solutions enable system performance to be fine-tuned. The potential for achieving a decrease in scheduling jitter, from several 100 clock cycles to just a few, points towards the critical function that proper management of resources and scheduling perform in making RTOS capable of fulfilling severe timing requirements effectively (Bergmann et al., 2015).

3.2. RTOS ARCHITECTURE OVERVIEW

The architecture of a RTOS is essentially designed to support the concurrent execution of tasks and rapid response to events. The architecture is characterized by a set of well-defined components, including the kernel, scheduler, and inter-process communication facilities. The kernel is the fundamental building component of the RTOS, serving as a resource manager and providing basic services such as task management, timing, and synchronization. The scheduler schedules tasks along with their respective timing constraints, thus guaranteeing high-priority tasks the CPU usage necessary to meet deadlines. These interactions make it possible for an RTOS to successfully run where timing is a requirement, e.g., embedded systems in automobile or aerospace companies, paving the way for successful real-time execution. In more recent trends, some architectures have emerged as having potential to advance the performance of RTOS implementations. For instance, the uRT51 processor architecture integrates basic real-time functions directly into its hardware platform. By integrating task management, timing functions, and prioritization directly into the processor, the uRT51 architecture spotlights the possibility of optimizing performance in real-time control applications. In comparison, studies have demonstrated that the use of such a real-time-specialized processor can lead to better scheduling behavior than traditional RTOS-based systems, as indicated in experiments on control applications. This hardware integration of features tailored for real-time execution is one of the predominant trends in RTOS design, where efficiency and reliability can be increased considerably by astute design choices (Alimenti et al., 2007). Another noteworthy approach to enriching RTOS architecture is that of employing the TASTE toolset, which was developed from research activities aimed at simplifying real-time embedded system software design. The toolset centers on the heterogeneous nature of such systems and strives to bridge across technologies like established languages and tools such as Simulink and C. By making multiple technologies available to use rather than requiring one language, TASTE promotes more flexible and robust system design. By more heavily relying on this flexibility, developers reduce the chances of parts failing to interoperate in the RTOS architecture. The future potential of TASTE and other similar frameworks not only makes the design easier but also provides a foundation for future embedded system software developments, pointing towards an embedded system future where the RTOS architectures are becoming more integrated and flexible (Conquet et al., 2010) (Figure 3.6).

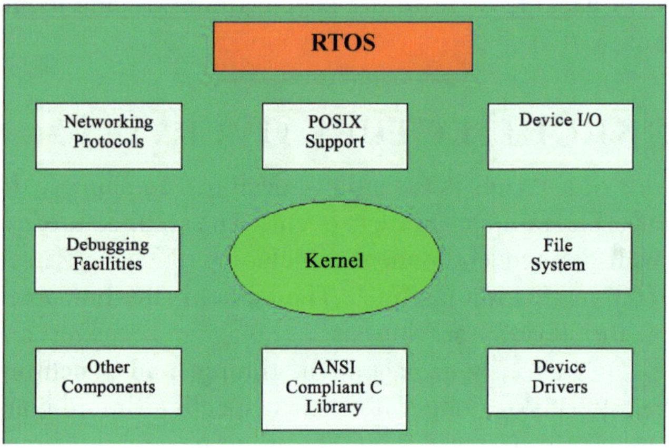

Figure 3.6. General architecture of RTOS.

Source: https://www.researchgate.net/profile/Swapan-Debbarma-Phd/publication/315645980/figure/fig2/AS:476092936003585@1490520809316/General-Architecture-of-RTOS.png.

3.2.1. Layered Architecture Model

The layered architecture model is a critical framework in RTOS development, providing an orderly way of differentiating different functionalities and components. Separating the software into a variety of layers allows developers to manage complexity, enhance modularity, and simplify embedded system maintenance. Each layer performs a distinct function, such as the hardware abstraction layer (HAL), which gives a generic interface to the hardware. Such separation offers hardware flexibility in the selection of hardware since, as seen with the Zerynth Virtual Machine (Zerynth, 2025), the HAL separates the hardware features of microcontrollers such that developers can develop on the application layer without requiring a lot of hardware experience, thus simplifying the development (Ahmad et al., 2017). Therefore, this model is optimally suited for environments that require quick adaptability and scalability, necessary to apply in the field of the Internet of Things (IoT). The layered architecture also facilitates an independence between various components to some degree, which is particularly helpful when using multiple RTOS in combination. This module-based architecture allows programmers to port their applications across different environments with ease; an illustration is the way Zerynth VM can transition from Chibi2 OS to FreeRTOS while still being compatible with a range of hardware platforms (Ahmad et al., 2017) (Figure 3.7).

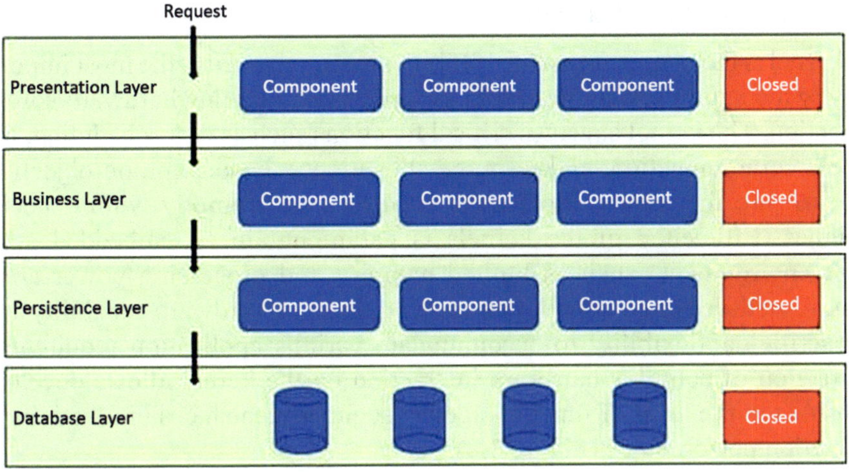

Figure 3.7. Layered architecture.

Source: https://external-content.duckduckgo.com/iu/?u=https%3A%2F%2Fcdn.educba.com%2Facademy%2Fwp-content%2Fuploads%2F2020%2F09%2FLayered-Architecture.jpg&f=1&nofb=1&ipt=6430dace65c8d4b165119ec9148f903b757c9bfc29a575e5448430ad84aa860b.

The layering also allows each team or developer to create individual components of the project, which makes it easier to collaborate and be productive. Such a feature is most important in complex systems, where other teams might be able to optimize certain layers for performance, security, or reliability without having a direct impact on other components.

By reducing interdependencies, the model of layered architecture supports the design of robust and efficient embedded systems. Moreover, layered architecture is of major benefit to resource-limited embedded systems, which has been evidenced by the PECOS component model. The system employs a graphical notation in component definitions with the benefit of generating efficient code for small microcontrollers and reducing runtime support needs. As resource constraints are typical in embedded systems, such a model facilitates neat separation of application logic and system-level considerations, promoting an abstraction that is suited to the aspects of component-based software engineering. Using such architectures, developers can ensure solutions are optimal in performance and retainability, irrespective of shifting requirements. Overall, layered architecture model is crucial in developing RTOS that not only have the capability of meeting existing system demands but also be able to adapt with future technological evolutions.

3.2.2. Kernel and Its Role

The kernel is the core component of RTOS structure, and it is the most important entity in managing system resources as well as coordinating hardware-software interaction. The kernel executes critical functions such as task scheduling, inter-process communication, and resource allocation, whose common objective is to make sure that time-critical tasks are executed promptly within specified deadlines. Efficiency of the kernels is paramount in an embedded system where environments such as limited memory and processing power are the norm. A well-designed kernel maximizes the use of hardware capability while not sacrificing flexibility to accommodate various application requirements. Abstraction of complex hardware interaction by the kernel allows developers to abstract at the level of function and consequently enhances productivity and application performance (Figure 3.8).

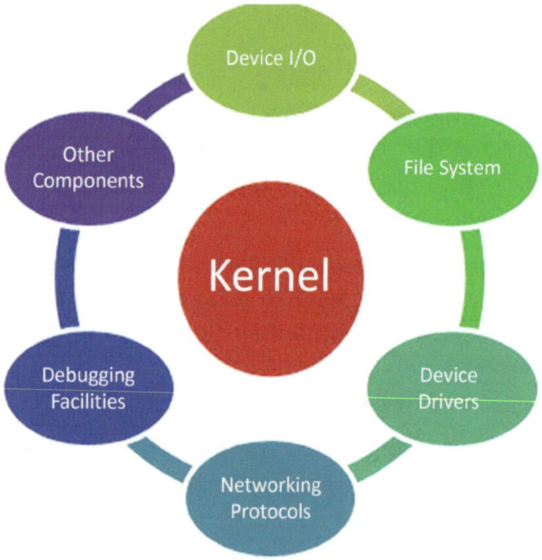

Figure 3.8. The kernel plays a pivotal role in the architecture of real-time operating systems (RTOS).

Source: https://external-content.duckduckgo.com/iu/?u=https%3A%2F%2Fwww.engineersgarage.com%2Fwp-content%2Fuploads%2F2019%2F07%2FA-Figure-Illustrating-General-Architecture-RTOS.jpg&f=1&nofb=1&ipt=a081559c41ec70e9efe9afc482fb35643c0d52425789b9fb47181c8eca088bd6.

Synchronization is another important aspect of the kernel's functionality, particularly for RTOS. The kernel provides facilities to enable multiple tasks or threads to run concurrently without permitting conflicts and data corruption.

This is of utmost significance in real-time systems that run on systems with limited resources, where timing and accuracy of operations are of utmost importance. For instance, like in RTOS implementations that interact with hardware systems such as the DLR LWR-III robot, synchronized control ensures that control algorithms tightly synchronize with hardware units. This is crucial, especially when hard real-time constraints are being kept, where even minimal latency may lead to system breakdown or suboptimal performance (Burger et al., 2010). Hence, the function of kernels in synchronizing control has a direct impact on the reliability and efficiency of real-time programs. The evolution of software architecture, particularly the application of component-based software engineering (CBSE), further highlights the significance of kernels. By facilitating modularity in design, CBSE enables the design of versatile programs that are capable of adapting to the ever-evolving requirements of embedded systems. However, it is essential that the low-level services provided by the kernel be as efficient as possible and cheap enough with regards to system resources. Component-based design can strike a balance between the need for flexibility and the constraints of embedded environments, such as the size of the memory and the power consumption (Greenfield et al., 2009). As a result, the kernel has to develop in parallel with these architectural changes so that it can continue to support strong and responsive real-time applications across various fields.

3.2.3. User Interface and Application Layer

User interface (UI) is a critical component of the application layer in RTOS, interfacing the user with the underlying systems functionality. A satisfactory UI encourages usability and productivity, allowing users to easily interact with embedded applications. Since RTOS is increasingly used in quite a variety of industries such as aerospace and automotive, the UI not only needs to be intuitive but also responsive to any action on the part of the user with immediacy. This need is underlined even more strongly by the requirement of the RTOS to meet stringent timing requirements for task execution, which necessitates that the UI design be optimized for performance. Since modularity and responsiveness are characteristics of systems like Embedded Linux, an organized UI can enhance the total user experience and operational reliability of working applications built over an RTOS and subsequently the systems responsiveness and effectiveness in mission-critical contexts (Boukhobza et al., 2012). The application layer of an RTOS is comprised of different software components that play mutual interactions with the user interface and make functional applications work best. Developers can construct top-level services based on the application layer that address the subtleties of real-time operations, prioritizing critical functions while maintaining non-critical processes responsive. Furthermore, as observed in multicore architectures developed under the High-Performance Spacecraft Computing (HPSC) program, application layers are capable of facilitating sophisticated computational tasks and applications and still guarantee user interactivity. The adoption of adaptive middleware in this context supports an adaptive platform with the potential to adapt to varying working requirements, balancing performance, and power management in a best-suited manner (Cudmore et al., 2025) (Figure 3.9).

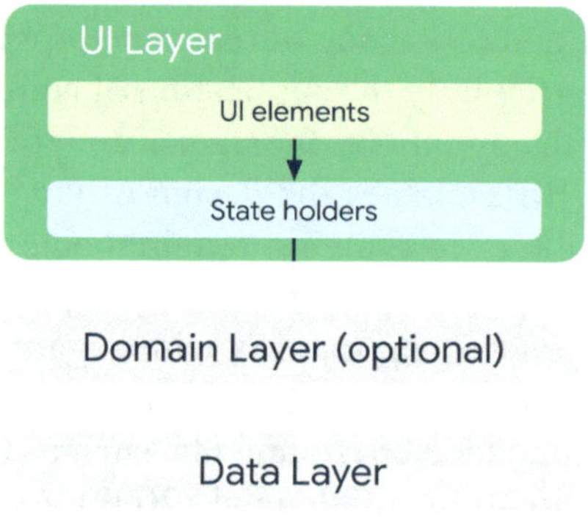

Figure 3.9. The user interface (UI) serves as a critical component of the application layer within real-time operating systems (RTOS).

Source: https://external-content.duckduckgo.com/iu/?u=https%3A%2F% 2Fdeveloper.android.com%2Fstatic%2Ftopic%2Flibraries%2Farchitecture%2Fimages%2Fmad-arch-ui-overview.png&f=1&nofb=1&ipt=7148ffd08d82219882aa07c03b45a6a8a9654dc8ef8cd57944b1ce10b5f74fad.

These technological improvements in the application layer enable software developers to unlock the full potential of the hardware, significantly impacting the UIs effectiveness. Moreover, the inclusion of robust user interfaces in the application layer enables the management of the diverse functionalities that modern embedded systems entail. With usability emphasized, the UI must be both user-friendly for inexperienced and experienced users and offer various modes of interaction to cater to various users' needs. This has been particularly relevant in fields such as aerospace, where user applications must impart important information without intimidating operators with complexity. An effective UI here not only enhances user productivity but also to the reliability and safety of the entire system. As RTOS evolve further, emphasis on designing user-centered interfaces will be even greater and the application layer will be essential in facilitating the human machine and machine communication to be smooth, efficient, and responsive to the real-time demands placed upon embedded systems (Boukhobza et al., 2012).

3.3. TYPES OF RTOS

The classification of RTOS is the essence of understanding their extensive range of functionalities and applications in embedded systems. Primarily, RTOS is classified into two broad categories: hard real-time and soft real-time systems. Hard real-time systems are applied in systems where very tight timing is required, where missing a deadline can result in catastrophe, particularly in safety-critical systems such as medical devices or automotive systems. In contrast, soft real-time systems are more flexible, where occasional deadlines missed will not toss system performance or safety into free fall.

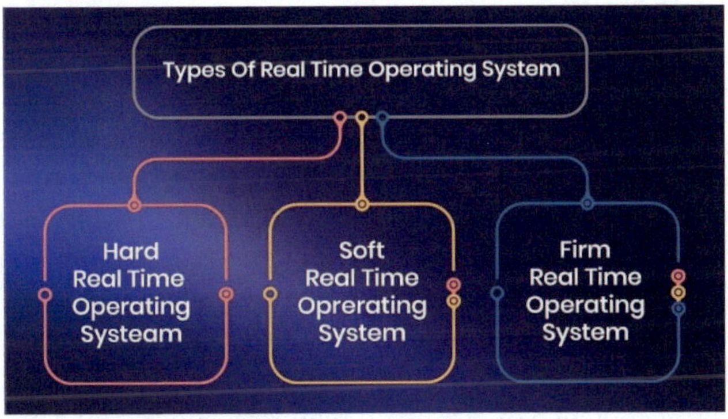

Figure 3.10. Types of RTOS.

Source: https://media.excellentwebworld.com/wp-content/uploads/2024/05/29044544/types-of-RTOS.webp.

This differentiation leads to the necessity of application-specific RTOS solutions that tailor solutions to meet special requirements in achieving reliability and efficiency in a defined paradigm of functions and limitations. Proceeding further to cover types of RTOS, one important variation is the embedded RTOS that is applied in resource-poor environments. These systems usually execute on microcontrollers and are designed to consume minimal resources with guaranteed performance. Architectural patterns such as the PECOS component model are such examples and present a disciplined method for software development which is particularly useful for the creation of embedded real-time systems such as those needed for autonomous robots. This model enhances efficiency through the use of graphical representations for elements and thus results in optimized code generation with minimal runtime support, making it suitable for devices with limited processing capabilities (Jawawi et al., 2006). Another important classification of RTOS is general-purpose RTOS, which, unlike its embedded versions, supports a broader range of applications. These systems are hosted on normal computers and are distinguished by the ability to sustain variable system loads and processes. General-purpose RTOSs are more likely to include common characteristics of regular operating systems, such as multitasking and user interfaces, thus being generic in most domains, such as telecommunication and multimedia applications. Thirdly, fault-tolerant support implemented in RTOS is also critical, especially with respect to safety-critical applications where system reliability becomes a priority. Techniques using established software components and fault detection that is robust, as proposed in most design methods, can uphold the functionality and integrity of real-time systems despite the occurrence of unexpected challenges (Abdi et al., 2017) (Figure 3.10).

3.3.1. Hard Real-Time Systems

Hard real-time systems are designed to ensure that significant tasks are finished within bounded time limits, which are most vital to the system's performance overall. These systems are typically used in systems in which failure to meet deadlines would lead to catastrophic consequences, e.g., in aerospace control systems, medical devices, and factory automation. The implementation of hard RTOS must be such that deterministic behavior is ensured in order to guarantee the performance within specified time intervals. As advancements were made in such systems, acceptance of advanced features such as real-time kernels such as Xenomai emerged as means to enhance the timing precision and reliability. The integration of such kernels signifies the resolve to achieve higher levels of performance and handling of resources, a necessity for the support of operation integrity of hard real-time applications, particularly in embedded systems (Boukhobza et al., 2012). Proper time management is crucial in hard real-time systems due to its direct impact on the reliability and predictability of the execution of tasks. A high-performance RTOS must employ specific scheduling algorithms in order to allocate CPU resources in the right way to ensure timely service to high-priority tasks. Further, periodic interrupt service routines play a specific role to maintain correct timing to allow proper observation and control of task execution. However, the irony is that the issue comes in finding a balance between honoring high precision requirements without adding unnecessary overhead to the CPU. Methods such as offloading time management onto special hardware devices, as implemented in platforms like Field Programmable Gate Arrays (FPGAs), have been found to effectively curb CPU load without sacrificing tight timing guarantees. This kind of technology contributes significantly to the operation of hard real-time systems with ease in their high-performance environments (Boukhobza et al., 2012). In real-world utilization, specifications of hard real-time systems in most instances are more than just simple execution and scheduling; they must handle data-intensive processes and extraneous environmental influences from the outside world. For instance, systems performing under hazardous conditions, such as nuclear plant inspection, must handle high levels of data and extremely high-performance specifications. Having a hardware/software platform on which to take in and process data at rates consistently maintained translates to the system being capable of running reliably, even under load. This deterministic throughput with high-performance processing aligns to the fundamental requirements of hard real-time applications—where timing and data integrity are not optional. With growing maturity in real-time applications, the integration of cutting-edge technology to overcome such challenges not only enhances performance but even enhances the safety and effectiveness of hard real-time systems in mission-critical contexts.

3.3.2. Soft Real-Time Systems

Soft real-time systems are essential in a wide range of applications, mostly because they can cater to tasks whose deadlines matter but are not crucially important. Unlike hard real-time systems, which require strict compliance with timing requirements, soft real-time systems can tolerate some misses without disastrous consequences. That makes them best for multimedia applications, telecommunication, and interactive systems where user satisfaction is the priority. The architecture of soft real-time systems typically incorporates sophisticated scheduling algorithms and multitasking facilities provided in RTOS that allow effective synchronization of concurrent tasks with acceptable performance levels. The support for quality of service (QoS) in soft real-time environments enhances system dependability and user satisfaction, giving them a prominent place in modern computing scenarios. While designing soft real-time systems, the developers are often faced with unique challenges that set them apart from general computer systems. The emphasis on responsiveness and timely processing of tasks involves incorporating advanced resource management and scheduling algorithms. In this regard, some of the techniques such as priority-based scheduling and time-slicing play a fundamental role in optimizing task execution and meeting deadlines as near as possible. As illustrated by current studies, the application of multitasking paradigms in embedded systems can enhance system performance and responsiveness significantly. But with their enhancement are their trade-offs, such as in experimental comparison of RTOS over rudimentary interrupt handling techniques where RTOS has achieved higher precision in task completion and even a broader variance in performance values. These results reinforce the need for ongoing research into balance between responsiveness and reliability in soft real-time systems. Soft real-time systems are also implicated by being part of distributed computing environments, where tasks can be split across several processors or nodes. As the High-Level Architecture (HLA) standards state, successful implementation of real-time capabilities in such federated systems is achieved by maintaining careful focus on constraints of real-time computing. Work towards enhancing Run-Time Infrastructures (RTI) has a tendency to focus on key factors like the Worst-Case Transit Time (WCTT) and quality of service guarantees, whereby the resulting system is able to meet soft real-time constraints even if there are complicated distributed communications. The ongoing innovation of formal models and bottom-up solutions in the development of RTI validates the importance of theoretical and experience-based innovations in efforts to promote higher efficiency and consistency in soft real-time applications. Ongoing evolution confirms the significance of adaptive solutions that are in the position to address the particular requirements of unique soft real-time cases to make them compatible with modern technological standards (Figure 3.11).

Characteristics	Hard RTS	Soft RTS
• Response Time	Hard-required	Soft-required
• Peak load performance	Predictable	Degraded
• Controlled by	Environment	Computer
• Safety	Critical	Non-critical
• Size of data	Small	Large

Figure 3.11. Hard RTS and soft RTS.

Source: https://images.theengineeringprojects.com/image/main/2021/06/Hard-RTS-vs-Soft-RTS.png.

3.3.3. Firm Real-Time Systems

Firm real-time system design is essential when there is a need for deadline satisfaction in applications where deadline failure is tolerated to some extent without catastrophic consequences. Although hard real-time systems are tasked with the requirement of rigid enforcement of timing constraints, firm real-time systems allow some occasional slippage. Such flexibility is particularly valuable in workloads that are subject to varying levels and availability of resources and workloads. The operating requirements in these systems are generally such that they require high-level management techniques in order to optimize utilization of resources with acceptable performance. Such systems are executed by intensive integration of real-time scheduling algorithms and fault-tolerant communication protocols that ensure timely data processing and response, thus fulfilling the needs of diverse applications in industrial automation and automobile engineering. With growing requirements for firm real-time systems, especially in advanced applications such as distributed control systems, the difficulties involved in implementing and designing them have expanded. Dependence on spatially distributed sensors and actuators requires impeccable coordination and synchronization in order to prevent premature processing-induced faults. To compound such difficulties, the systems must be capable of supporting the parallelism that lies in their hardware design while ensuring safe multithreading and efficient resource use. Real-time scheduling is of prime concern in this sense, ensuring efficient management of system resources to provide deterministic response. Besides, the ability to support sophisticated fault tolerance methodologies has become increasingly important, allowing systems to support online reconfiguration and recovery upon failure without penalty to performance. This intersection of control and computer science compounds the difficulties that come with firm real-time system development (Broenink et al., 2003). In addition to traditional firmware, application of container-based virtualization technologies is a very promising area in the area of firm real-time systems. The new approach enables one to deploy isolated application environments capable of coexisting on a single host, using all available resources and flexibility. Given the unique requirements of domains such as automotive and aviation, where collocated mixed criticality applications are possible, the challenge is to make container-based virtualization work effectively with real-time behavior. Even with existing solutions, they have laid some groundwork for constructing real-time characteristics into containers, but there are still fundamental gaps to fill. As the research community embarks on these new frontiers, the continued development of methodologies to transcend the natural limitations of container-based virtualization will be key to being able to run firm real-time systems in environments with limited resources (Ashjaei et al., 2020).

3.4. RTOS COMPONENTS

The design of a RTOS is deeply involved in handling system resources optimally to realize task completion within a timely manner. The very core of an RTOS are its most vital building blocks, the scheduler being one of them that allocates the sequence of task execution as a function of priority and timing requirements. This timing mechanism is important for real-time applications where immediate responses are a bare necessity, particularly in industries like automotive and aerospace where safety is of utmost importance. With the evolution of these systems, using Commercial Off the Shelf (COTS) components has become a widespread practice to counter costs and development time. However, this approach also calls for a robust framework to harmonize safety requirements and system development processes, hence the necessity of a complete integrated safety life cycle for contemporary RTOS design, as highlighted in current literature on high-integrity systems and their complexity (Caseley et al., 2017). Inter-process communication (IPC) is another crucial component of an RTOS, allowing tasks to communicate. IPC facilities such as message queues, semaphores, and shared memory allow tasks to be synchronized and to communicate with one another without interfering with each other, which is crucial in a multitasking environment. These facilities must be implemented efficiently and with speed, respecting the stringent timing requirements of real-time systems.

Figure 3.12. RTOS components.

Source: https://www.guru99.com/images/1/121119_0515_Realtimeope1.png.

Low-latency, dependable communication is currently emphasized as essential to allow high-integrity systems. By employing heterogenous replicated channels for meaningful computations, RTOS can ensure reliability and insulate against threats to task failure. Such a heterogenous approach not only supports operational consistency but is also safety-conformant, upholding the relation between communication infrastructures and overall system reliability (Burns et al., 2010). The necessity of memory management in RTOS architecture cannot be overemphasized. Compared to general-purpose operating systems, which tend to allocate memory more loosely, RTOS must be capable of providing deterministic memory access patterns to prevent the spikes of latency. This is critical in those applications where execution predictability is absolutely essential. Memory management under RTOS tends to include static allocation methods that circumvent as much dynamic resource allocation at runtime as possible, reducing the possibility of fragmentation and ensuring that tasks are always capable of accessing the resources they need. Since COTS elements are increasingly being utilized in systems, the issue of integrating the disparate components such that memory integrity can be guaranteed becomes pertinent. Developing a well-structured resource allocation policy that guarantees reliability is important in constructing high-integrity real-time systems. The ongoing discussion in the literature evidences a commitment to further refine such techniques against the backdrop of the complexity of current usage, pointing to the increasingly vital role played by memory management in RTOS design (Burns et al., 2010; Caseley et al., 2017) (Figure 3.12).

3.4.1. Task Management

One of the most critical aspects of RTOS is task management, which directly reflects in the ability of the systems to satisfy stringent timing requirements. Task management has the basic function in an RTOS of creating, scheduling, and removing tasks optimally while ensuring deadlines are met. An optimally structured task management allows for dynamic task priorities based on urgency and significance. This scheduling is particularly critical in environments where several tasks compete for the use of the CPU, since it avoids having high-priority operations get queued behind low-priority processes. Additionally, effective task management employs preemptive multitasking, which allows high-priority tasks to interrupt or preempt low-priority tasks, thus maximizing the responsiveness of real-time applications and improving system performance under stress conditions. The challenge of managing tasks is also heightened in the case of hard real-time systems, where missing deadlines would be catastrophic. A key characteristic of an RTOS is that it will run tasks deterministically so that the task execution time can be anticipated. The foundation for this determinism is the time management system of the RTOSs, and it consists of establishing periodic interrupt service routines controlled by a software time manager. As revealed by current research, such as that encompassing inserting real-time kernels into embedded systems, the efficiency of time management is most critical to ensure in order to achieve execution deadlines. With this, advances like bringing time management services to configurable hardware modules, as discussed by Boukhobza et al. (2012), are examined as a way of minimizing CPU overhead and significantly enhancing accuracy and responsiveness required for execution of real-time tasks. Further, management of tasks in RTOS implementations is intrinsically integrated with larger systems, such as ones employing the High-Level Architecture (HLA) standards. The support for real-time is a requirement in such systems, especially when simulating real-world events with multiple federated objects distributed across multiple platforms. The existing HLA standards have been demonstrated to be lacking in fulfilling real-time systems' specific requirements, thereby necessitating further efforts in enhancing RTI frameworks. Substantial work focuses on the deployment of Quality of Service (QoS) warranties and the development of scheduling algorithms that harmonize well with the host operating systems, as in attempts towards providing real-time capability for HLA federations on single machines within Linux-based environments (Adelantado et al., 2010). Ultimately, advances in task management practice increase the efficiency of single real-time activities and also increase the robustness of complicated, distributed systems.

3.4.2. Inter-Process Communication (IPC)

Inter-process communication (IPC) is a fundamental mechanism used in RTOS, through which processes can exchange data and coordinate their activities with good efficiency. Within the RTOS domain, where timely and efficient execution is important, IPC ensures that there is a balance between task communication without degrading performance or system integrity. The various IPC methods, such as message queues, semaphores, and shared memory, offer varying strengths based on the specific needs of embedded systems. For instance, message queues provide a sequential approach of passing messages between tasks and is highly beneficial in systems where there are processes of various rates. Not only does this sequential approach to communication simplify sending of data, but system resilience is also enhanced since sender and receiver processes are decoupled from one another, hence reducing potential bottlenecks and race conditions of direct data sharing. More advanced IPC methods can be incorporated to further enhance the performance of RTOS-based embedded systems. For example, when advanced IPC methods with high precision, e.g., those provided by Xenomai real-time kernel, are incorporated in embedded Linux systems, they achieve quicker response and determinism in task completion. At the heart of this enhancement is the ability of the device to regulate timing and processing precedence, hence allowing vital tasks to recover from their execution deadlines regularly (Figure 3.13).

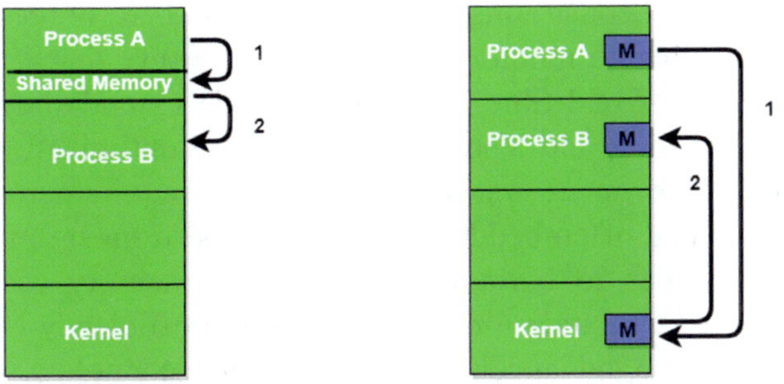

Figure 3.13. Shared memory and message passing.

Source: https://media.geeksforgeeks.org/wp-content/uploads/1-76.png.

The modular nature of embedded Linux, typically integrated with IPC frameworks, facilitates integration and allows programmers to develop highly reactive, application-specific systems. Ensuring that the IPC mechanisms are efficient and sufficient, engineers are able to reduce the overhead usually seen in traditional RTOS configurations to ensure high performance while working on multiple tasks at a time. uRT51 processor architecture provides a good illustration of the ways in which hardware-based IPC solutions can help towards improved performance in control applications embedded. By utilizing certain hardware features that are optimized for real-time operations, the uRT51 optimizes the performance of IPC methods. The tasks are scheduled and prioritized more rigorously compared to conventional RTOS configurations with the consequences being fewer latencies and higher throughput. The experimental tests indicate that, in applications where rapid response times and simultaneous execution of multiple tasks are called for, the hardware-based approach of the uRT51 significantly outperforms traditional software-based IPC implementations. Consequently, the incorporation of IPC within RTOS designs not merely draws attention to the importance of inter-process communication, but also emphasizes the innovative potential for merging hardware power with traditional IPC methods towards creating advanced embedded solutions that prioritize performance and reliability over other considerations, such as in the instance of the uRT51 architecture (Alimenti et al., 2007; Boukhobza et al., 2012).

3.4.3. Memory Management

Memory management is a critical component within the RTOS design, with a direct influence on system performance and reliability. Effective memory management is extremely crucial in embedded systems since they operate under stringent time constraints and with limited resources. An RTOS must manage and allocate memory effectively to ensure that it can meet the timing requirements of real-time applications. This extends beyond memory size and access handling and also encompasses the optimization of memory allocation policies to meet various application requirements. Moreover, with the extensive use of embedded Linux systems in most applications, the inclusion of RTOS has to harmoniously manage memory resources while catering to increased demands for determinism and efficiency (Boukhobza et al., 2012). Furthermore, advancements in multicore technology are central in modern memory management in RTOS. As in the case of projects like High Performance Spacecraft Computing (HPSC), multicore processor utilization has transformed memory resources allocation and management. Dynamic computational performance reconfiguration and energy management are facilitated by the HPSC architecture, freeing memory resources on demand for real-time processing. Such adaptability is paramount during space missions, where limitations of regular memory management can interfere with the execution of tasks as well as system dependability. With such advancements, RTOS can handle computationally intensive tasks with greater efficiency and provide efficient memory allocation to ensure adherence to execution deadlines, which is paramount to mission success (Cudmore et al., 2025). Besides technology advancement, memory management strategies in RTOS must also incorporate various memory allocation schemes—static, dynamic, and stack-based. Each has its advantages and limitations, particularly with regard to speed, fragmentation, and predictability. Static memory allocation facilitates predictable performance, which is critical for real-time applications, but is not programmable. Dynamic memory allocation, however, is programmable but it involves overhead and potential unpredictability that can degrade time-sensitive applications. Effective memory management in an RTOS must therefore strike a balance between these conflicting demands at times by employing hybrid methodologies to optimize performance and dependability concurrently. Lastly, RTOS structure complexity justifies the necessity of sophisticated memory management mechanisms to enhance stability and efficiency on a wide range of embedded applications (Boukhobza et al., 2012).

3.5. APPLICATIONS OF RTOS

The applications of RTOS are diverse and manifold, to mention but a few fields such as automotive, telecommunication, and automation industry. In automotive use, for instance, increasing sophistication of electronic control units necessitates timely and precise timing, where RTOS is able to highly enhance the systems' performance by ensuring that crucial operations are fulfilled within stringent deadlines. The automotive industry employs RTOS to synchronize functions such as anti-lock braking systems and adaptive cruise control that are paramount for safety and operational effectiveness. Additionally, the modularity and efficiency of RTOS solutions, particularly with embedded Linux and real-time kernels such as Xenomai, exemplify their applicability in enhancing performance across a variety of embedded applications, symbolizing the dynamic nature of modern automotive technology (Boukhobza et al., 2012). RTOS in telecommunication is crucial in order to manage more than one process while maintaining the flow of real-time traffic data and guaranteeing service quality. RTOS supports the ability of task prioritization, which enables smooth handling of voice over IP (VoIP) calls and real-time video processing where delay can cause substantial user dissatisfaction. The deterministic nature of RTOS gives assurance that packets of data are transmitted with minimal latency, which is imperative in guaranteeing the integrity of communications in high-speed networks. Furthermore, as technology in telecommunications advances, innovative RTOS implementations keep arising that accommodate more intricate networking protocols and allow robust, responsive communication networks. The reliability and efficiency of such systems require precise scheduling and ongoing service, underscoring the intrinsic relevance of RTOS in this sector (Boukhobza et al., 2012). Industrial automation is another critical area where RTOS applications are founded upon, providing the basis for sophisticated control systems that drive manufacturing processes. In the manufacturing context, RTOS is employed to facilitate real-time operation of equipment in order to provide seamless operation within contexts that require high response rates and disciplined coordination of numerous devices. The uRT51 processor demonstrates how hardware implementation provides significant enhancement of real-time capability beyond traditional RTOS-based systems utilizing optimized scheduling capabilities. As industries increasingly adopt automation technologies, demand for reliable and efficient RTOS integrations will rise, with the capacity to handle gigabytes of data while maintaining time-sensitive standards for critical manufacturing activities. Adoption of RTOS in industrial use, therefore, is an innovative means of enhancing productivity and reliability in today's manufacturing environments.

3.5.1. Automotive Systems

Automotive control systems are becoming more dependent on RTOS to address complex functionality and provide safety in a vehicle. The need for performance and reliability grows as these systems develop, which highlights the importance of stable RTOS architectures that are capable of supporting multiple components, including sensor integration and data processing. Timing accuracy is highly essential in automotive use, so cache performance is an important factor to consider. The caching integration, although positive to improve performance, makes timing analysis more complex since caches are probabilistic. In particular, the realization of architectures such as Random Modulo (RM) cache presents favorable benefits through minimizing the worst-case execution time (WCET) calculations, thus enabling improved timing guarantees for automotive software systems. This synchronization with conventional performance standards is necessary to ensure integrity and responsiveness needed for contemporary vehicles. The safety-criticality of automotive systems puts strong emphasis on the verification processes of embedded software components. Contemporary vehicles rely on a multitude of embedded systems, which not only add value to user experience but also uphold important safety levels. But garnering verified safety assurance is often extremely expensive and time-consuming. To offset this challenge, cutting-edge design methodologies must be utilized to gain from RTOS without sacrificing safety (Figure 3.14).

Figure 3.14. Automotive systems are increasingly reliant on real-time operating systems (RTOS) to manage complex functionalities and ensure safety in vehicles.

Source: https://media.licdn.com/dms/image/v2/D5612AQGwR1to5wOgDA/article-cover_image-shrink_720_1280/article-cover_image-shrink_720_1280/0/1735648396769?e=2147483647&v=beta&t=109quhMjqrf7jR0L9L5MyXDdKlMasoFc6ui3VUa3BTM.

One of the possible solutions is to utilize a small number of proven software that manages faults and coordinates recovery functions in an effective manner. These strategies can aid to support the critical safety requirements of the automotive systems even while there is a growth of advanced functions and performance needs. Such a forward-looking design practice is the foundation of RTOS automotive architecture, emphasizing safety as well as performance in concert. In addition, use of schedulability analysis is an essential role in ensuring that safety-critical tasks of automotive systems meet their timing constraints, especially during faults. New methods facilitate fault detection by keeping application timing under close observation to guarantee that the recovery process is efficient and rapid. This becomes the case considering the desire for protecting integrity upon potential failure. Techniques involving full restarts of the platform enable immediate modification in system operation, yielding fault-tolerance robustness. Through schedulability results for restart-tolerant models of tasks, car systems can be able to handle faults efficiently while maintaining stability in their performance. This enhances the reliability of RTOS in the automotive industry as well as adheres to regulatory needs, allowing for future prospects of development in the industry and minimizing failure risks in safety-critical applications (Abdi et al., 2017; Ferrer et al., 2016).

3.5.2. Industrial Automation

The industrial automation field has seen dramatic changes with the introduction of RTOS, making the process more efficient and reliable in manufacturing. As industries take a strong approach towards automation to achieve maximum productivity, the incorporation of RTOS has made multitasking operations essential to ensure uninterrupted workflow. RTOS architecture enables deterministic task scheduling, making sure time-dependent operations are performed within deadlines required for them. Such a quality is most important in industries where precision is paramount, such as automotive manufacturing and aviation. Also, the ability to prioritize well is aligned with growing demand for reactive and adaptive automations that can handle varied loads as well as operational uncertainty, resulting in improved overall system performance and reduced downtime. The synergy of industrial automation and containerized virtualization offers new prospects for resource optimization of use and application development. Containerization delivers the potential to deploy self-contained application pieces on shared physical infrastructure without overhead compared with traditional virtualization. This way, industrial automation platforms can leverage containerized applications to enhance flexibility and scalability. Notwithstanding this, problems remain insofar as real-time activity within such platforms, as exemplified by the ongoing research into the integration of real-time functionality within container-based systems. The needs of mission-critical applications within industrial settings, where multitasking among diverse components may be at play, necessitate a careful virtualization approach, one that respects the timing limits imposed by the operational model of RTOS environments (Ashjaei et al., 2020). In addition, the comparison of the performance of RTOS and primitive interrupt techniques has shown some important implications for use in industrial automation. Studies have found that RTOS consistently surpasses primitive methods in precision while performing simultaneous tasks, which is a very important aspect to consider for high-reliability processes like sensor monitoring and control systems. However, variability of information being observed in primitive methods means that while less intricate, RTOS implementations may have to be tuned more to adjust performance on diverse operational benchmarks. With further growth of industries into advanced automation, RTOS architecture will thus be the backbone of systems demanding accuracy and responsibility, thus enabling advanced multitasking functionality that caters to diverse needs of today's industrial environments (Alhamidi et al., 2015).

3.5.3. Telecommunications

The integration of telecommunication systems in RTOS architecture is key to enhancing the performance and reliability of many applications, particularly in space-based environments. As telecommunication demand increases, especially in NASA missions, architectures like the Space Telecommunications Radio System (STRS) are being established to enable efficient communication between various platforms. The STRS model focuses on a primary method of the management of space-based software-defined radios, requiring flexibility and adaptability in processing resources since they are usually constrained in such settings. In its focus on a systematic design that characterizes the interactions of software components with the execution platform, the STRS architecture attempts to enhance the operating abilities of telecommunications within the environment of RTOS systems so that they meet the rigid demands of real-time tasks and make space for future evolution (Briones et al., 2025). In examining the components of RTOS architecture, it is critical to examine the role of software-defined radios in current telecommunication. The STRS architecture is a testament to this evolution where transceiver operation is primarily defined by software, allowing for enormous flexibility in communication processes. Such a structure makes it possible to update radios and upgrade them with the same ease that software gets updated, minimizing the need for hardware updates and keeping old systems functional for longer. Such flexibility is essential in a field with cutting-edge technology, where new standards and communication protocols emerge on a daily basis. Moreover, the common waveform software interfaces that the standardization provides foster interoperability between various hardware and software products, hence reducing operational risks and telecommunications costs in RTOS environments (Hall et al., 2025). An effective RTOS architecture calls for consideration to be taken in abstracting application software from hardware. This idea not only makes the development easier but also enhances the overall integrity of telecommunications systems. By supporting independent update at both hardware and software levels, organizations can apply advanced technological solutions without replacing current infrastructure. The STRS program, through its emphasis on common interfaces and operational testing practices, is a telecommunications industry best practice. With all these developments in place, they provide a basis to foster innovation and bolster the capabilities of RTOS architectures. The ongoing dialogue about telecommunications standards, like those used by NASA, will ensure that the future of RTOS continues to be an advancement in the direction of an efficiency, flexibility, and reliability orientation of communication systems (Briones et al., 2025).

SUMMARY

In general, the study of RTOS and their architecture highlights the increasing role of sound architecture in designing embedded systems, particularly in safety-critical contexts. As systems become more advanced and high-performance, assured safety guarantees become the primary concern. With the assistance of a sound RTOS architecture, designers can ensure that timing constraints are always met, which is critical to application reliability and safety. This research attests that design methodologies encompassing fault tolerance and scheduling efficiency, i.e., utilizing minimal verified software, are significant in guaranteeing system integrity during the occurrence of faults, thus improving total safety levels in embedded system design (Abdi et al., 2017). Furthermore, application of Commercial Off the Shelf (COTS) components in safety-critical systems has benefits as well as challenges. Though COTS application will reduce the time and cost of development, it is risky in terms of verification of safety and compliance with extremely tight standards. A life cycle that facilitates an integrated safety approach incorporating safety considerations into the design and development process is extremely important in verifying possible risks from these components. The emerging consensus regarding the application of such methodologies underscores their importance in guiding engineering decisions since systems become ever more reliant upon complex supply chains. Consequently, it is apparent that an active safety engineering strategy needs to be compatible with new components and architectures typical of modern RTOS (Caseley et al., 2017). Lastly, ongoing studies and field implementation point towards a shift towards overall safety engineering practices offering concrete benefits within real-life settings. From case studies of industrial projects, the feasibility of integrated safety measures in solution to the intricacies associated with COTS components can be estimated. These studies not only assure the requirement of robust evidence generation for safety cases but also keep the door ajar to novel solutions for solving safety problems. Lastly, the conclusion derived from the study of RTOS architecture and components highlights the critical interaction amongst safety, performance, and efficiency. While seeing to it that the dependability of embedded systems is not sacrificed, the sector can continue to evolve by aligning design practices with exacting safety standards (Caseley et al., 2017). The RTOS design with asynchronous characteristics is marked by its concern with the timely execution of tasks and resource management, which are essential for tasks that require consistent performance levels. One aspect to note here is the application of task scheduling algorithms in RTOS design. These algorithms determine the task prioritization and execution methodology, which dramatically affects the responsiveness of the system. While general-purpose operating systems may focus on optimizing multitasking as well as user interface, RTOS is more interested in guaranteeing that mission-critical activities are accomplished within deadlines. This is particularly observed in applications applied under the Internet of Things (IoT) scenario, where efficient processing power management equates to better energy consumption and performance. With the integration of these scheduling methods, RTOS can supply the devices with wider capability while ensuring real-time characteristics that ensure efficient operation even in resource-constrained situations (Roussel et al., 2015). Inter-task communication mechanisms are yet another core component of RTOS architecture. The mechanisms enable data exchange among tasks and enable synchronization in order to prevent shared-resource conflicts. There are various implementations, such as message queues, semaphores, and event flags, which act to make activities run in synchronization without compromising system integrity. Moreover, such communication approaches play a significant role in software applications that need real-time coordination, for instance, in embedded systems. Proper management of interactions leads to greater reliability and stability of applications ranging from industrial automation to telecommunication systems. The integration of these components in this context not only contributes resilience from the performance perspective but also gives the assurance required that the entire design be capable of providing complex operation specifications with real-time response (Walter et al., 2007). Lastly, the kernel of an RTOS is its central component that provides minimal services such as task management, timing, and interrupt handling. This kernel is designed to be lightweight in terms of weight, so it can operate in a more effective way under systems with limited resources. The architecture typically consists of a microkernel, which can have added services depending on the needs of individual applications. With modular development support, the RTOS can be customized to suit different applications, particularly relevant when using IoT, where devices have specific needs in terms of their operations. The ability to use a number of hardware timers, which is offered by advanced RTOS like RIOT OS, underscores the potential to facilitate innovative solutions in real-time applications. Such capabilities demonstrate the diversity and power of RTOS design to tackle diverse technological challenges (Roussel et al., 2015).

REFERENCES

1. Abdi, F., Caccamo, M., Mancuso, R., Tabish, R., et al. (2017). Restart-based fault-tolerance: System design and schedulable analysis. http://arxiv.org/abs/1705.02412 (accessed on 29th September 2025).
2. Abella Ferrer, J., Andersson, J., Cazorla Almeida, F. J., Gianarro, C., et al. (2016). Random Modulo: A new processor cache design for real-time critical systems. https://core.ac.uk/download/81571672.pdf (accessed on 29th September 2025).
3. Adelantado, M., Chaudron, J. B., & Siron, P. (2010). Towards an HLA run-time infrastructure with hard real-time capabilities. https://core.ac.uk/download/12042130.pdf (accessed on 29th September 2025).
4. Ahmad, N. (2017). Porting of FreeRTOS on a Python virtual machine for embedded and IoT devices. https://core.ac.uk/download/79623606.pdf (accessed on 29th September 2025).
5. Alhamidi, M. R. (Machmud), Habibie, N. (Novian), Hardjono, B. (Benny), Jati, H., et al. (2015). Comparative study of RTOS and primitive interrupt in embedded system. https://core.ac.uk/download/296598900.pdf (accessed on 29th September 2025).
6. Alimenti, O., Cayssials, R. L., Duval, M., et al. (2007). uRT51: An embedded real-time processor implemented on FPGA devices. https://core.ac.uk/download/323211451.pdf (accessed on 29th September 2025).
7. Ashjaei, M., Behnam, M., & Papadopoulos, A. V. (2020). Real-time containers: A survey. https://core.ac.uk/download/296708949.pdf (accessed on 29th September 2025).
8. Bakirtzis, G., Carter, B. T., Elks, C. R., Fleming, C., et al. (2018). A model-based approach to security analysis for cyber-physical systems. http://arxiv.org/abs/1710.11442 (accessed on 29th September 2025).
9. Bergmann, N. W., & Tang, Y. (2015). A hardware scheduler based on task queues for FPGA-based embedded real-time systems. https://core.ac.uk/download/43368987.pdf (accessed on 29th September 2025).
10. Bhat, B., Ferdinand, C., Lee, C. G., Maiza, C., Dasari, D., et al. (2017). An extensible framework for multicore response time analysis. https://core.ac.uk/download/84338821.pdf (accessed on 29th September 2025).
11. Boukhobza, J., & Olivier, P. (2012). A hardware time manager implementation for the Xenomai real-time kernel of embedded Linux. http://arxiv.org/abs/1208.6428 (accessed on 29th September 2025).
12. Bria, O. N., De Giusti, M. R., Jaquenod, G. A., Villagarcía Wanza, D., et al. (2003). Adapting an IP MC6805 core for multiprocessing and

multitasking. https://core.ac.uk/download/153565669.pdf (accessed on 29th September 2025).

13. Briones, J., Hall, C. S., Handler, L. M., Kacpura, T. J., et al. (2025). Updates to the NASA space telecommunications radio system (STRS) architecture. https://core.ac.uk/download/pdf/10542737.pdf (accessed on 29th September 2025).
14. Broenink, J. F., & Orlic, B. (2003). Real-time and fault tolerance in distributed control software. https://core.ac.uk/download/pdf/11458244.pdf (accessed on 29th September 2025).
15. Burger, R., Haddadin, S., Hirzinger, G., Parusel, S., et al. (2010). The driver concept for the DLR Lightweight Robot III. https://core.ac.uk/download/11144335.pdf (accessed on 29th September 2025).
16. Burns, A., & Littlewood, B. (2010). Reasoning about the reliability of multi-version, diverse real-time systems. https://core.ac.uk/download/9559398.pdf (accessed on 29th September 2025).
17. Cardoso, N., Cardoso, P., Gomes, T., Mendes, R., et al. (2014). Co-designed FreeRTOS deployed on FPGA. https://core.ac.uk/download/55637223.pdf (accessed on 29th September 2025).
18. Caseley, F., Hall, H., Jackson, P., Hall, J. G., et al. (2017). Safety engineering with COTS components. https://core.ac.uk/download/82983623.pdf (accessed on 29th September 2025).
19. Conde, J. F., García-Martínez, A., & Viña, Á. (1996). Implementation of a hardware/software platform for real-time data-intensive applications in hazardous environments. https://core.ac.uk/download/29399336.pdf (accessed on 29th September 2025).
20. Conquet, E., Dissaux, P., Hugues, J., Perrotin, M., et al. (2010). The TASTE toolset: Turning human-designed heterogeneous systems into computer-built homogeneous software. https://core.ac.uk/download/12041536.pdf (accessed on 29th September 2025).
21. Cudmore, A. (2025). High performance spacecraft computing (HPSC) middleware update. https://core.ac.uk/download/pdf/286393153.pdf (accessed on 29th September 2025).
22. Greenfield, A., Massa, A., Angelov, C., Szypersky, C., Heiser, G., Buttazzo, G. C., Kopetz, H., et al. (2009). Component-based real-time operating system for embedded applications. https://core.ac.uk/download/50126191.pdf (accessed on 29th September 2025).
23. Hall, C. S., Johnson, S. K., Kacpura, T. J., Liebetreu, K., et al. (2025). Open architecture standard for NASA's software-defined space

telecommunications radio systems. https://core.ac.uk/download/pdf/10543929.pdf (accessed on 29th September 2025).

24. Havinga, P. J. M. (2000). *The Design of a System Architecture for Mobile Multimedia Computers*. https://core.ac.uk/download/pdf/11460964.pdf (accessed on 29th September 2025).
25. Havinga, P. J. M., & Smit, G. J. M. (1999). Octopus–An energy-efficient architecture for wireless multimedia systems. https://core.ac.uk/download/pdf/11454381.pdf (accessed on 29th September 2025).
26. Jawawi, D. N., Deris, S., & Mamat, R. (2006). A component-oriented programming framework for developing embedded mobile robot software using PECOS model. https://core.ac.uk/download/11777296.pdf (accessed on 29th September 2025).
27. Norwood, D. E. (2011). Hardware thread management modeling for precision timed processors. https://core.ac.uk/download/51197010.pdf (accessed on 29th September 2025).
28. Roussel, K., Song, Y. Q., & Zendra, O. (2015). RIOT OS paves the way for implementation of high-performance MAC protocols. https://core.ac.uk/download/49532959.pdf (accessed on 29th September 2025).
29. Sinha, S. (2018). Scheduling policies and system software architectures for mixed-criticality computing. https://core.ac.uk/download/304658766.pdf (accessed on 29th September 2025).
30. Walter, N. J., & Zahra, A. L. (2007). *The Waikato Region: Major Tourism Issues and Opportunities to Facilitate Tourism Development: Public summary*. https://core.ac.uk/download/29194698.pdf (accessed on 29th September 2025).

CHAPTER 4

TASK SCHEDULING IN REAL-TIME SYSTEMS

Contents

INTRODUCTION

As the world is progressing towards being more technology-dependent, the significance of scheduling tasks in real-time systems cannot be overstressed. Real-time systems are designed to process data and respond to events within a certain time frame, and thus scheduling becomes a critical factor in meeting these deadlines. Scheduling tasks properly ensures high-priority tasks have access to the resources they need at the appropriate time while simultaneously processing lower-priority tasks without impacting the system's overall performance. The problem is to meet such conflicting demands without taking into account resource constraints and potential flaws. By comprehending the fundamental principles of task scheduling, developers and engineers can construct systems that are both reliable and efficient, which are critical in applications ranging from medical devices to automotive systems. Task scheduling techniques must be modified to suit varied operating environments and architectures, particularly when integrating heterogeneous components. For instance, the majority of real-time systems use condition-responsive scheduling algorithms, which demand a dynamic approach to managing tasks. The application of the High-Level Architecture (HLA) standard to real-time systems demonstrates the efforts aimed at developing a platform that enables synchronized management of distributed tasks.

Figure 4.1. *Task scheduling in real-time systems.*

Source: https://files.codingninjas.in/article_images/tasks-in-real-time-system-2-1643134678.jpg.

However, issues still arise as the HLA standard disregards some constraints in real-time computation. Solving these issues is crucial to building resilient distributed systems, with the ability to accomplish jobs in an organized and effective way (Adelantado et al., 2010). With ongoing research, it is clear that novel techniques are needed to increase adaptability and robustness of scheduling mechanisms employed in such environments. In addition, advancements in task scheduling techniques are still driven by demands for improved fault tolerance and performance in diversified operational environments. The existing advances reflect a growing focus on fault-tolerant systems that can overcome barriers such as component failure without incurring a degradation in performance. For instance, development of general-purpose real-time fault-tolerant systems signifies an important shift towards constructing more fault-immune structures. These models offer justification for the comprehension of scheduling dynamics like pinwheel task systems that guarantee real-time under even potential fault scenarios (Baruah et al., 1996). With the demand for complicated real-time applications growing by the day, the demand to enhance task scheduling techniques is ever more pertinent, forming a foundation for high-risk applications where reliability is crucial (Figure 4.1).

Importance of Task Scheduling

The significance of task scheduling within real-time systems cannot be overestimated as it holds the key to the running and viability of applications in the majority of essential environments. Due to its significance, adequate scheduling of tasks ensures that processes that depend on time are assigned adequate processing capacity to operate successfully, ensuring system accuracy and reliability. In processes such as automated manufacturing, in which procedures rely on precise timing and synchronization, a good scheduling system can simplify production procedures and the use of resources. Good scheduling of activities within environments that are prone to variation and uncertainty is of utmost importance; otherwise, delays in working procedures can lead to decreased productivity and increased operational expense. In addition, the intersection of increasing task management complexity necessitates new scheduling techniques to manage multiple and simultaneous tasks, and hence underscoring the critical role played by advanced scheduling algorithms in modern real-time systems (Barbosa et al., 2017). With the increasing usage of multiprocessor architectures in real-time systems, the importance of task scheduling is even more significant. These systems typically consist of mixed-criticality tasks, i.e., programs with different levels of importance and urgency. Understanding how to schedule these tasks within a common resource environment has a significant impact on system performance as well as safety. Current research focuses on new scheduling theories specific for such an environment that facilitate more efficient management of tasks with varying criticality levels. For instance, mixed-criticality systems are improved by specific scheduling tests and heuristics that make efficient partitioning and task allocation across processors. This development not only improves task schedulability but also safety-critical application reliability, proving the significance of effective task scheduling frameworks within modern technological settings (Lautenbach et al., 2014). Lastly, efficient task scheduling in real-time systems is most closely associated with the capability of the system to fulfill performance requirements without sacrificing possible risks. The employment of trustworthy scheduling approaches allows the proper utilization of system resources, which is particularly crucial in applications where responsiveness and safety are considered paramount. In addition, newer algorithms such as genetic algorithms have emerged as effective tools for addressing the natural challenges of scheduling in flexible manufacturing systems. Genetic algorithms optimize the use of resources through learning to meet changing demands of tasks, improving the performance of real-time systems. With the changing face of technology, the long-term importance of task scheduling is apparent; it forms the foundation for the success and efficiency of real-time applications across numerous fields, where timing and accuracy are paramount (Barbosa et al., 2017).

4.1. TASK SCHEDULING ALGORITHMS

Effective task scheduling in real-time systems is crucial to ensure that applications with strict timing constraints meet their deadlines. The majority of real-time operating systems (RTOS) offer rudimentary task control services that facilitate the execution of applications that have fixed and invariant deadlines. However, task synchronization issues and varying execution rates might necessitate the application of other extra scheduling algorithms in addition to those offered by the RTOS. Task scheduling algorithms need to consider diverse requirements like priority levels, task workloads, and deadlines. Hence, employing a scheduling algorithm that is specially designed to handle a set of synchronized, time-critical tasks becomes increasingly important in preventing missed deadlines and system integrity (Eckhardt et al., 2025). The advent of task scheduling algorithms introduced new methods, particularly for complex applications with parallel tasks. In most instances, parallel task jobs are formulated as directed acyclic graphs (DAGs), providing an understanding of task dependence and execution. Traditional methods traditionally employed scheduling algorithms based on decomposition that partitioned tasks along their DAG structure. But newer advancements now introduce a federated method to scheduling that complements the traditional framework. For instance, the reservation-based scheme proposed guarantees improved performance over other federated scheduling systems by effectively executing parallel tasks while maintaining important system constraints (Agrawal et al., 2017). The technique not only ensures efficient execution of collections of DAG tasks but also facilitates interoperation among other schedulers to maintain the needed flexibility for real-time systems. The significance of scheduling algorithms for tasks goes beyond mere deadline satisfaction; it has system performance and resource consumption implications in real-time systems. With increased complexity in systems, the interaction among concurrent tasks calls for new scheduling methods with the capability of supporting concurrent execution. Reservation-based federated scheduling presents new demands for fault-tolerant frameworks with the capability of handling arbitrary deadlines and optimizing performance. These improvements address the challenge of having a uniform speedup factor as opposed to optimal scheduling methods and thus address the particular requirements of modern real-time systems. By optimizing task scheduling methods, researchers and implementers can enhance the reliability and efficiency of real-time systems, ultimately aiming to ensure that they run optimally under fluctuating conditions (Figure 4.2).

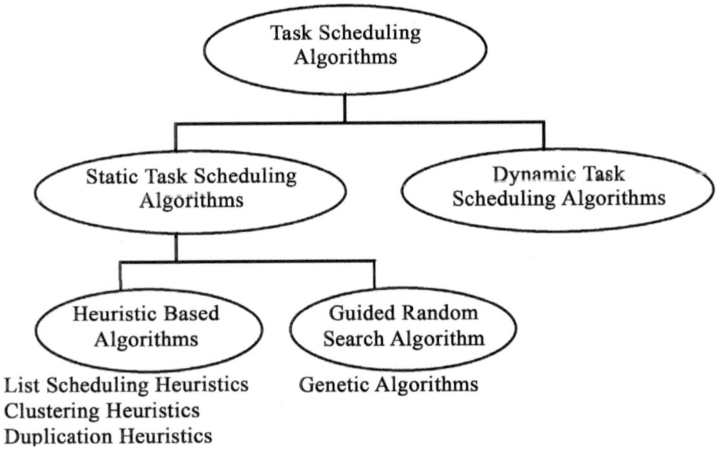

Figure 4.2. *Classification of task scheduling algorithm.*

Source: https://www.researchgate.net/profile/Vikas-Kumar-82/publication/269757446/figure/fig1/AS:305067052814336@1449745061642/Classification-of-task-scheduling-algorithm.png.

4.1.1. Rate Monotonic Scheduling (RMS)

The nomenclature employed when explaining Rate Monotonic Scheduling (RMS) also underscores its role as a pioneering fixed-priority scheduling algorithm for real-time systems. RMS is based on the assignment of priority to tasks according to their periodicity, where lower periods have higher priority. This feature aligns it with the need of hard real-time systems in which timely execution takes precedence. Most prominently, RMS provides for guaranteed schedulability of a set of tasks, thereby permitting system designers to ensure that important tasks always get executed within deadlines. Algorithmic efficiency finds particular demonstration in uniprocessor systems, where it has been universally preferred due to its determinism and mathematically proven capacity for guaranteeing accomplishment of tasks, providing for an assured environment for real-time systems. However, the limitations of RMS surface when investigating mixed-criticality systems, where tasks are distinguished on their relative criticality and importance. Such situations call for the need to determine that tasks with higher criticality are provided guaranteed resources as well as maximizing the utilization of resources in less demanding situations. This is challenging to the scheduling paradigm because the conventional RMS design may not be sufficient for such systems that require real-time dynamic adaptation as well as isolation between tasks. Above all, the mixed-criticality task model provides a solution through the separation of tasks based on their criticality, thereby adapting to varying resource availability and system robustness. The combination of RMS with mixed-criticality models is more and more being explored, pushing the debate regarding the application of traditional scheduling theories to adapt to the dynamic nature of real-time computing (Sinha et al., 2018) (Figure 4.3).

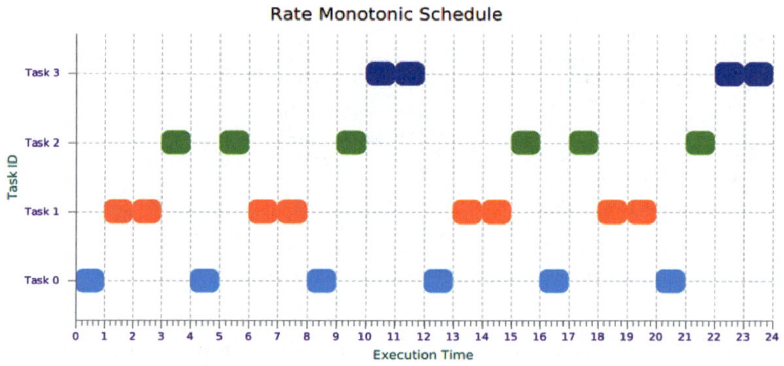

Figure 4.3. *Rate monotonic scheduling (RMS).*

Source: https://imgur.com/rms-2-NRLwZT3.

In the discussion of the intersection of RMS and next-generation runtime environments, the imperatives of today often surpass the conventional. Examples of these include implementations in complex simulation platforms, particularly those modeled on the High-Level Architecture (HLA) standards, where more and more attention to deadlines, quality of service (QoS), and scheduling services is required. Both of these aspects are of monumental significance in ensuring that real-time simulations yield timely and accurate responses. Developing new methods for achieving hard real-time properties—such as those expounded in recent studies in enhancing runtime environments—is therefore reflective of the need for innovation in scheduling techniques. This necessity to connect RMS with requirements of contemporary times not just indicates the algorithms historical significance but also highlights its potential adaptability in meeting present real-time systems challenges (Adelantado et al., 2010).

4.1.2. Earliest Deadline First (EDF)

In real-time systems, the Earliest Deadline First scheduling algorithm is an algorithm that schedules tasks dynamically based on priorities allocated according to deadlines. Unlike static scheduling methods in which priorities are predetermined during design time, EDF allows real-time decision-making by dynamically modifying the priority of tasks with approaching deadlines. This flexibility renders EDF to be used in many different applications, from embedded systems of automotive technology to multimedia processing, where rapid execution is the priority. The optimality of the algorithm for scheduling preemptive periodic tasks emphasizes its efficacy in such a way that given a group of tasks to be executed within a specified time, EDF will discover an existence schedule for them, enhancing therefore the reliability of real-time systems. However, using EDF in systems with resource constraints can be tricky. Current Hard Real-Time (HRT) kernels, as they ensure timely behavior, are based on restrictive policies for resource usage. Restrictiveness generally keeps them from being used in multimedia systems where resource utilization policy flexibility is very important. As suggested, the lack of such flexibility can stifle the possibility of performance enhancement in systems that need efficiency along with stringent timing. Thus, improving EDF scheduling mechanisms in order to support multimedia applications has been an area of study. By developing more adaptive frameworks, such as employing real-time transactions (RTT), we are able to improve the adaptability as well as effectiveness of real-time systems that operate under intricate constraints and perhaps even alter the method in which EDF is applied in real-world applications (Jansen et al., 1998, 1999) (Figure 4.4).

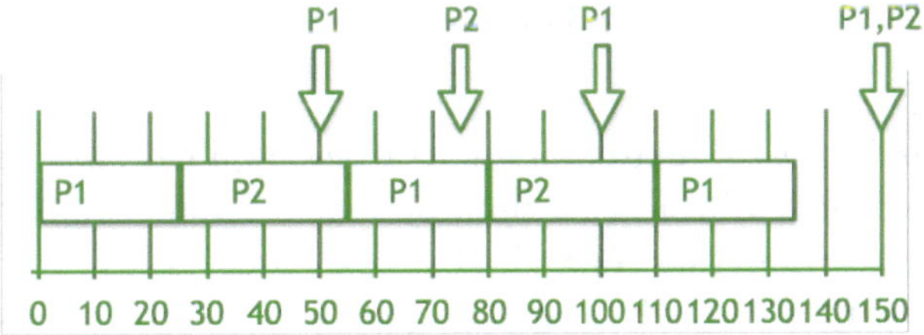

Figure 4.4. *Earliest deadline first (EDF) algorithm.*

Source: https://www.geeksforgeeks.org/operating-systems/earliest-deadline-first-edf-cpu-scheduling-algorithm/.

One of the most important considerations in enhancing EDF is re-examining resource management in real-time systems. The inclusion of such concepts as Deadline Inheritance allows the tasks to inherit greater priorities temporarily under certain conditions, thereby reducing blocking when lower-priority jobs are executing. This is particularly helpful in systems where tasks may compete for shared resources as it helps in the reduction of response time for critical processes. Moreover, as multimedia applications have emerged, there has been increasing need for effective schedulability analysis that necessitates the use of special scheduling algorithms to meet both timing promises and resource utilization. These improvements in EDF not only broaden its applicability to more advanced environments but also enable more sophisticated real-time task scheduling in systems where meeting deadlines is critical.

4.1.3. Least Laxity First (LLF)

Least laxity first (LLF) scheduling algorithm is a new technique for real-time task scheduling that can reduce task lateness and achieve timely task completion. Tasks in the LLF algorithm are scheduled based on their laxity, or the time left to complete a tasks deadline minus its remaining processing time. The smaller the laxity, the higher the priority given to that task so that LLF can easily schedule tasks with tight deadlines.

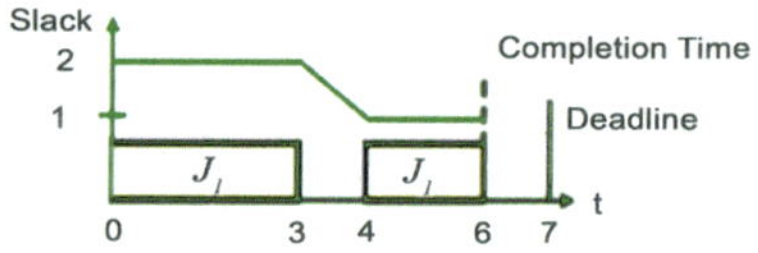

Figure 4.5. *Least slack time (LST) scheduling algorithm.*

Source: https://media.geeksforgeeks.org/wp-content/uploads/20191228172730/gfg_lst.png.

This feature makes LLF extremely useful in applications where deadline compliance is critical, like in real-time applications and embedded systems. By continuously evaluating task laxity, LLF reacts to the time-varying character of actual workloads and thus provides a dynamic and adaptable scheduling policy that caters to time-varying system loads. However, while LLF has plenty to provide, it is not problem-free. Computational overhead in continuously monitoring and recalculation of task priorities as a function of laxity is excessive in systems supporting numerous concurrently running tasks. Furthermore, LLF can help introduce complexities when incorporated in multiprocessor environments where jobs can be executed parallel to one another. Such complexities need an effective implementation strategy so that the advantages of LLFs, i.e., proactive deadline handling, are realized without draining system resources. Simulation implementation, such as the real-time multiprocessor scheduler YARTISS, provides valuable insight into the behavior and performance of LLFs under any circumstance, allowing researchers to enhance their approach and tailor real-time task management strategies (Chandarli et al., 2012) (Figure 4.5). Moreover, the application of LLF in buildings with sophisticated event management systems such as those implemented in the event managing and coordinating system (RT-EMaCS) model is an example of its potential paradigm. By coordinating events more effectively between organizers and coordinators, RT-EMaCS utilizes LLF to enhance the effectiveness of scheduling and reduce latency when handling real-time events. These systems demonstrate the ability of LLF not only to ensure timely completion of tasks but also to make interactions within multi-agent systems simpler. Lastly, incorporating LLF into real-time scheduling software demonstrates its adaptability and effectiveness across various applications, reinforcing its significance in ensuring improved performance of real-time systems (Minj et al., 2013).

4.2. FACTORS INFLUENCING TASK SCHEDULING

The intricacies of scheduling tasks in real-time systems are controlled by a number of factors that play a huge role in efficiency and performance. At the top of them is choosing the algorithm for scheduling, which determines the way tasks are prioritized and executed. Different algorithms affect latency, responsiveness, and resource utilization in different ways. For instance, fixed-priority scheduling methodologies are extremely common due to their support for determinable task control, which is essential in meeting stringent timing requirements. The support of approaches like k2U illustrates the potential for enhanced scheduling performance in various models of tasks since it reinforces the fact that there is an optimal schedulability test to make the scheduling easier, especially in multiple processor-dominated systems and heterogenous task demands (Chen et al., 2015). Thus, those fundamental principles that dictate the selection of scheduling techniques are paramount to determining system success. The nature and characteristics of the tasks themselves, including their periodicity, execution time, and need for a deadline, are also crucial considerations for task scheduling. Real-time systems generally have difficulty with tasks that must not only meet functional requirements but meet them within defined temporal limits for the integrity of the system. The decision-making process for task allocation becomes even more challenging given the fact that scheduling periodic tasks has been proven to be NP-complete in the strong sense (Bansal et al., 2018). Given the natural limitations of ensuring deadline satisfaction in the presence of changing task priorities, various methodologies have been investigated, including partitioned scheduling, which statically assigns tasks to processors in order to preserve timing specifications. This complexity requires the development of approximation algorithms, which enhance efficiency in terms of satisfying performance requirements. Also, conditions of deployment critically affect task scheduling decisions since real-time systems typically operate under diverse operating conditions. Reliability of the system, the speed of the processor, and resource constraints are some factors to be appropriately managed. The recent work in resource augmentation by increasing the number of processors provides credence to the potential of improving the quality of scheduling under some cases of inputs, in corresponding relation between performance gains and task parameters like the period-to-deadline ratio (Bansal et al., 2018). The above observations affirm the relevance of shaping the scheduling methods to special demands of the operating environment. In general, the ubiquitous nature of real-time task scheduling embodies the interaction of algorithm selection, task characteristic, and environmental factor, each independently impacting system performance and reliability.

4.2.1. Task Characteristics

Characterization of tasks is critical in real-time system implementation and design because it has a direct effect on scheduling efficiency as well as system performance. Real-time tasks are generally classified according to their timing constraints, resource requirements, as well as impact of faults. Timing constraints provide deadlines that must be met in order for the system to remain intact, with hard real-time tasks necessitating strict compliance. The nature of resource demand determines how work is coordinated within a processing environment, requiring coordination to minimize resource contention. There is also the requirement to understand the fault-tolerance characteristics of work due to its role in ensuring the system remains stable and timing constraints in the event of failure. Hence, understanding such inherent task characteristics is crucial to designing an effective scheduling technique that meets system performance specifications and ensures timely task completion (Chen et al., 1998). Apart from timing and resource considerations, task execution variability also plays a major role in determining the performance of real-time systems. Variability arises due to many sources, such as changing system loads, availability of resources, and non-deterministic execution durations. To address this, researchers have adopted predictive performance modeling (PPM) techniques that draw upon previous performance measurements in making projections of future task behavior. Such methods enable system designers to better anticipate variability in task execution and allocate resources accordingly. With the application of non-intrusive PPM solutions, it is possible to optimize scheduling without direct modifications to the actual workload management, thus ensuring flexibility in dynamic systems. The ability to make predictions regarding the performance parameters like running time enhances the robustness of real-time scheduling and aids in maintaining necessary timing constraints and resource utilization (Bux et al., 2018) (Figure 4.6).

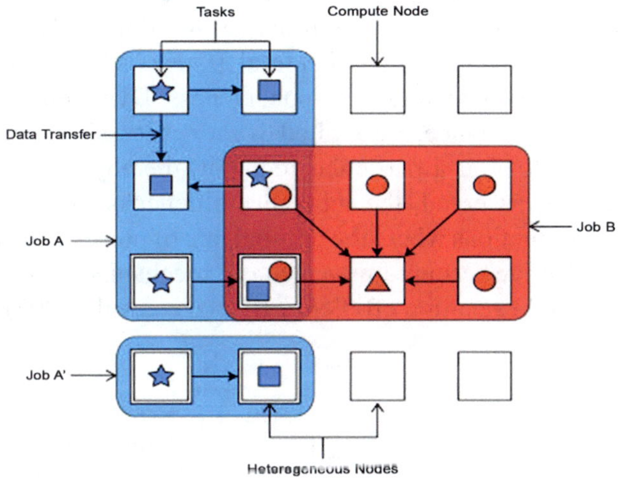

Figure 4.6. *Predictive performance modeling (PPM).*

Source: https://www.sciencedirect.com/topics/computer-science/predictive-performance.

Furthermore, the relationship between task characteristics and scheduling strategy is crucial to designing an efficient real-time system. Selecting the right scheduling policy—such as rate-monotonic or earliest deadline first—is critically dependent on the nature of the tasks being scheduled. For instance, tasks with hard timing constraints may prefer preemptive priority-based scheduling so that missing deadlines can be avoided. Further, with a satisfactory knowledge base on task properties, sophisticated resource control protocols can be derived so that stability in the system can be maintained while task variability is accommodated. Task execution time and resource knowledge can also be blended further to provide improved scheduling algorithms, with a formal framework for managing performance as well as reliability. Accordingly, the alignment of task characteristics with scheduling methods results in the development of more robust real-time systems that are able to handle sophisticated operational demands successfully (Chen et al., 1998).

4.2.2. System Resources

In task scheduling in real-time systems, efficient management of system resources is an integral component that enhances total performance and reliability. CPU cycles, memory, and I/O capacity are some of the resources to be managed strategically such that they meet stringent time limits found in real-time systems. The challenge gets amplified given that such resources have discrete levels and typically get shared across multiple tasks. This resource allocation process thus requires architectural frameworks that not only save resources but also maximize system responsiveness. Dynamic Voltage Scaling (DVS) techniques, for instance, are applied to vary processing speeds in relation to demands of workload at a particular moment, thereby maximizing energy efficiency. However, as noted, the inherent bottlenecks of DVS can lead to underutilization in situations where the optimal rate of processing is not feasible, requiring more adaptive resource management mechanisms to facilitate peak task prioritization and execution efficiency (Buttazzo et al., 2007) (Figure 4.7).

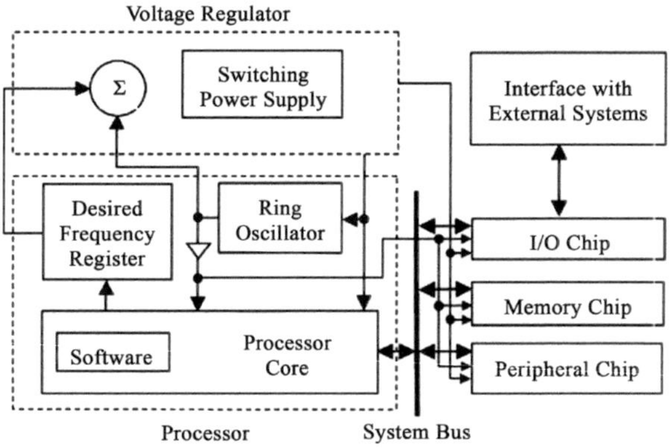

Figure 4.7. *Dynamic voltage scaling (DVS) architecture.*

Source: https://www.researchgate.net/profile/Dr-Tomar/publication/331063720/figure/fig15/AS:725774713778183@1550049584429/A-dynamic-voltage-scaling-DVS-architecture.ppm.

Besides, successful scheduling of tasks in real-time systems necessitates consideration of the varying system resource behavior at runtime. The recent advances in hierarchical scheduling architectures hold promise for harmonious coexistence between various elements in a system, yet with independent design and evolution and maintaining required temporal decoupling. The method utilizes processor reservation methods to assign computation resources effectively, along with managing the complexities arising due to contending resource access requirements. The issue is dynamically adapting resource mappings to components, as mode changes need to be handled effectively by systems. Implication from recent advances identifies efficient timer management, particularly through facilities like Relative Timed Event Queues, which allow low-overhead, modular designs that deliver effective resource allocation for periodic tasks (Holenderski et al., 2012). Flexibility of resource use is also provided by maturing protocols addressing multitasking and parallel processing in real-time systems. Deployment of sound, modular scheduling algorithms such as Parallel-SRP articulates the ability of modern systems to support multiple resources in parallel under demanding real-time requirements. Such models not only facilitate higher parallelism but also guarantee deadlock-free execution and correct schedulability analysis. These innovations are particularly tailored to meet situations where there is multimedia processing involved, and where varying priority assignments between tasks produce better operational performance. Lastly, the ongoing evolution of mechanisms for controlling system resources will reshape paradigms in task scheduling that will provide a firm foundation for the development of responsive and sustainable real-time systems that are able to address contemporary demands for efficiency as well as reliability (Holenderski et al., 2012).

4.2.3. Timing Constraints

For the field of real-time systems, timing constraints play a significant role that has a very direct influence on task scheduling and task completion. The fundamental intention of such systems is to ensure that timely missions are completed reliably and efficiently within previously defined timing constraints. Timing constraints are not only required for the operational functionality of the system but also for achieving predictable response to external stimuli. An in-depth examination of these limitations allows for effective scheduling algorithms that guarantee deadline meets are always realized. Various scheduling methods, such as rate-monotonic and earliest deadline first, have been proposed to guarantee schedulability under these constraints. Lastly, the effectiveness of real-time systems depends on reconciling resource allocation and the precision of timing, hence enhancing overall system performance and reliability within a dynamic environment (Chen et al., 1998). Timing constraints and the interaction between systems architecture are also important, particularly in mixed-criticality systems, where tasks with varying levels of criticality coexist. In such designs, treatment of timing constraints is further improved, with the system having to ensure critical tasks take priority while not sacrificing performance for low-criticality tasks. Temporal and spatial isolation mechanisms are also present in such structures to prevent low-criticality tasks from interfering with high-criticality tasks. This not only maintains the integrity of critical tasks but also allows for improved resource utilization during normal operation. By deploying proper virtualization techniques, designers can further enhance the ability of the system to manage timing constraints well and thus reach a more robust task scheduling paradigm supporting different operational needs at the cost of satisfying strict timing constraints (Sinha et al., 2018). To further enhance the effectiveness of real-time scheduling, including fault tolerance in consideration along with timing constraints is very important. The ability of a system to ensure operational stability despite failures adds additional challenges to scheduling algorithms. More specifically, work on preemptive priority-based scheduling methods is especially crucial to enable tasks with both resource and fault-tolerance needs. Such scheduling systems need to incorporate additional constraints to enable potential failures while ensuring that all timing commitments still remain supported. Techniques such as priority-based protocols and Markov chain models have been examined to balance these opposing requirements, highlighting the subtle interplay between fault tolerance and timing requirements. Through proper integration of these variables, researchers and engineers can come up with more reliable real-time systems that can accomplish critical activities even in the presence of unexpected challenges (Chen et al., 1998).

4.3. PERFORMANCE METRICS

In real-time systems, performance metrics are of extreme importance to determine task scheduling efficiency and system reliability. Such metrics as execution time, resource usage, and response time provide insight into the performance of a system under different loads and configurations. Since the character of computational workloads becomes increasingly advanced with the expansion of data and parallel processing needs, the precise measurement of performance metrics is essential. For instance, predictive performance modeling (PPM) techniques utilize historical performance information so that projected task behavior can be approximated and scheduling choices optimized. This nonintrusive solution enhances the total management system without necessitating changes to existing workload, addressing the problems of performance for most real-time systems nowadays (Bux et al., 2018). Another critical thing about performance measures for task scheduling is derived from embedding statistical models with predictive power for outcomes of tasks in dynamic environments. Predictive task execution complexity in cloud computing, since resource configurations can change at any time, becomes paramount. For instance, predictive models have proved to be extremely accurate and recall their tasks when making failure predictions, allowing preemptive rescheduling before even actual failures occur. Such strategic anticipation not only boosts the efficiency of task execution but significantly boosts resource utilization as well. When applied in this predictive model, performance measurements provide a vehicle to significantly improve the throughput of real-time systems through corresponding adaptations of scheduling techniques (Khomh et al., 2015). Additionally, the implications of using predictive performance metrics go beyond merely task completion ratios. They also make tangible reductions in operational overhead, for instance, in studies that show a dramatic reduction in the job failure rate when better scheduling algorithms are used. Through optimizing the scheduling process on performance measures, systems can diminish delays and optimize resource utilization, which is essential to maintaining integrity of time-critical applications. Thus, by means of high-performance metrics, not just can a scheduling context be made more responsive, but resource handling can also be synchronized with varying demands of real-time systems, ultimately resulting in system reliability and efficiency (Bux et al., 2018; Khomh et al., 2015) (Figure 4.8).

Figure 4.8. *Performance tracking tool displaying real-time data.*

Source: https://external-content.duckduckgo.com/iu/?u=https%3A%2F%2Fimg.freepik.com%2Fpremium-photo%2Fvisual-performance-tracking-tool-displaying-realtime-data-live-metrics_1327465-30854.jpg&f=1&nofb=1&ipt=37c2082e907d58a2a95ea60a041ec245c8653658a40e5a1ed409258fb1d77a1a.

4.3.1. Response Time

Response time is a critical parameter in the context of real-time systems, particularly for task scheduling. Practically speaking, response time is the amount of time between submitting a task and it is ending, with a direct influence on systems' perceived efficiency and reliability. In the context of embedded systems such as those used in autonomous cars or health devices, meeting strict response time constraints is necessary for safety and operation. According to definitions in research, response time improvement can be achieved using various scheduling techniques that optimize real-time task priority without compromising system performance. As tasks become more complex and parallelizable, responsive scheduling algorithms have to be included in a system in an effort to meet deadline without major resource utilization or latency (Fahmida et al., 2020). Moreover, the improvement in response time also parallels that of improving energy efficiency within real-time systems.

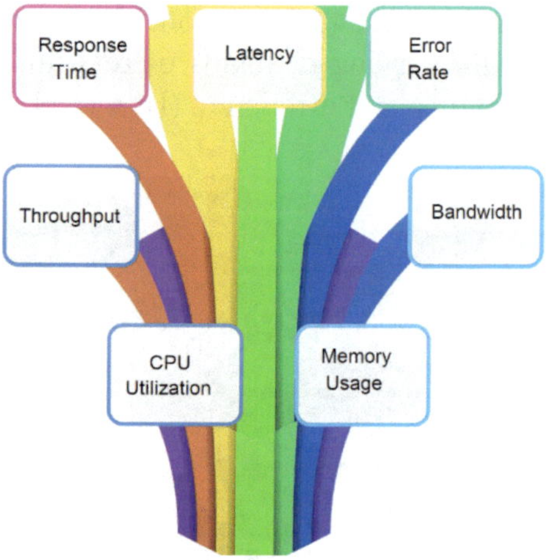

Figure 4.9. Performance indicator.

Source: https://softwareg.com.au/cdn/shop/articles/performance-testing1.png?crop=center&height=2048&v=1707786438&width=2048.

The multi-core processors have been the catalyst for this enhancement with the capability to execute several tasks concurrently while meeting their respective deadlines. For instance, new scheduling methods have been proposed considering various elements like interdependencies of tasks and execution rates, which play an important role in reducing response time as well as energy usage. This improvement is particularly relevant in distributed systems, where balancing resources and loads among servers supports adaptive task scheduling to fulfill hard real-time requirements on time. Utilizing dynamic voltage and frequency scaling (DVFS) techniques along with traditional scheduling algorithms, scholars have been able to make significant energy conservation and response time performance improvements (Fahmida et al., 2020). Finally, the new-age rapidly evolving technology of edge computing and cloud computing gives rise to newer problems in maintaining optimal response times for scheduling tasks. There exists an increased necessity of intelligent scheduling algorithms to handle a heterogeneous collection of tasks and ensure high-quality service delivery. In addition to reducing response times, intelligent scheduling algorithms also handle the heterogeneity in task arrival rates and availability of resources, as evident in current research. As highlighted in recent work, the best task scheduling in cloud data centers is finding a balance between profit maximization and reduced energy costs with response times that are acceptable. These approaches are able to distribute tasks over a number of computing resources dynamically, ensuring each task meets its delay requirement even in changing conditions. Overall, the synergy between response time and efficient task scheduling strategies remains a central focus of real-time system optimization (Figure 4.9).

4.3.2. CPU Utilization

Effective utilization of the CPU is a major issue in planning and execution of scheduling activities in real-time systems. Since they operate under stringent time conditions, effective use of the CPU has a direct impact on their ability to deliver within deadlines and maintain system stability. This problem is even more important in systems with dynamic workloads and limited resources, where poorly scheduled tasks can introduce more latency and even system failures. Methods like optimal feedback scheduling strive to enhance the overall control performance by learning task distribution with available CPU resources. The complexity of these algorithms, however, produces a huge computational overhead, making them less relevant in real-world scenarios. This balancing of performance and efficiency highlights the importance of achieving high CPU utilization for real-time systems without compromising operational integrity (Dong et al., 2007). In order to increase CPU utilization, particularly in multitasking environments, new methods have emerged that exploit state-of-the-art computational techniques. As one example, predictive performance modeling (PPM) helps systems forecast how tasks will be run at various levels of load based on historic data. By employing non-intrusive analysis that observes system behavior without altering workload, these techniques can predict values like execution time and resource demands. This predictive insight supports task optimization as it avoids bottlenecks or resource shortcomings by anticipating them in advance and adjusting accordingly to enhance CPU utilization. The integration of such prediction techniques into task scheduling models not only contributes to optimizing the real-time responsiveness of systems but also assists in sustaining high levels of CPU efficiency notwithstanding the growing complexity of workload management (Bux et al., 2018). Concomitantly, the need for adaptability in CPU policy usage within real-time systems highlights the role played by intelligent scheduling algorithms. These algorithms must be in a position to respond to task property changes as well as changes in computational resources and dynamically adjust to varying performance demands. Adaptive-based feedback scheduling, for instance, can properly scale concurrent task scheduling in real-time. By employing algorithmic learning from past experience in task execution to tailor scheduling on the basis of actual-time data, the systems achieve optimal CPU usage with minimal overhead. Adaptive feedback schemes built-in to achieve optimal provisioning of computational resources also enhance system dependability and responsiveness, key considerations in operating in real-time environments (Dong et al., 2007).

4.3.3. Jitter

In task scheduling for real-time systems, jitter is a factor that determines the adverse impact it may have on the timely delivery of tasks and brings about poor performance in high-reliability requirement environments. Jitter is a variation in time for sending data packets or executing tasks that may occur as an outcome due to different processing times or network latency. In real-time environments, such as those employed in medicine or automation, regular timing is important to guarantee deadlines and system performance are optimized. The effect of jitter not only affects control quality in real-time systems but also raises significant challenges in maintaining the Quality of Service (QoS) demands anticipated in modern computing systems (Barzegaran et al., 2020). To mitigate the adverse effects of jitter, various scheduling techniques have been developed to maximize the execution of tasks within stringent timing constraints. For instance, the implementation of Gate Control List (GCL) in Time Sensitive Networking (TSN) offers enhanced predictability when sending time-sensitive information using effective bandwidth management and minimizing contention between tasks. By synthesizing GCLs for messages in a network topology, researchers have made it possible to have better control quality with the guarantee that deadlines will always be honored (Barzegaran et al., 2020). Scheduling paradigms seek to balance efficiency and reliability and eventually try to counteract the impacts of jitter on system performance, which is particularly important for real-time control schemes. Moreover, jitter's impact also extends to outside classical computer networks to high-stakes fields such as healthcare, where the passing of accurate and timely data can be a question of life and death. Research into e-health applications has developed new paradigms for scheduling tasks to focus on data from sensors monitoring vital signs, thereby solving jitter problems. For instance, Priority Based-Fair Queuing (PFQ) technique has been shown to significantly reduce delay and jitter in emergency applications and shows a substantial improvement over traditional queuing models such as First in First Out (FIFO) and Weight Fair Queuing (WFQ). By allocating the resources in the ratio of the priority of the data they are carrying, such new scheduling techniques not only enhance the overall efficiency of real-time systems but also facilitate the dependability required in mission-critical systems where time is of the essence (Figure 4.10).

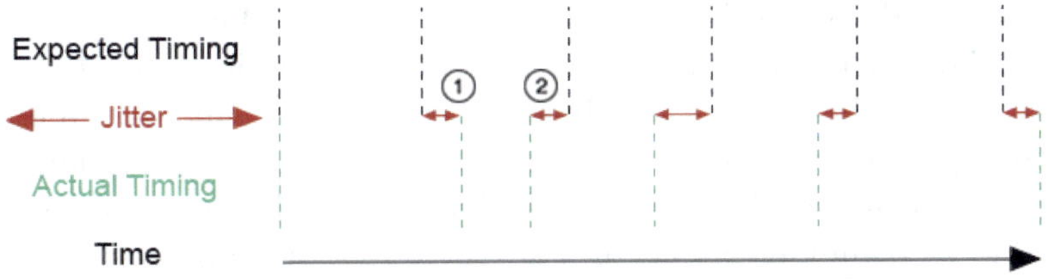

Figure 4.10. *Jitter in a real-time system.*

Source: https://www.ni.com/docs/en-US/bundle/labview-nxg-rt-module-programming-with-rt-target/page/determinism-real-time.html?srsltid=AfmBOooZl96K4RLIRzRrDwkGhdYEaM__99gjLOaE3PVLVv9aGfA1dgKN.

4.4. CHALLENGES IN TASK SCHEDULING

Real-time system task scheduling brings in the entire gamut of issues that stem from the very basic necessity to ensure that critical tasks adhere to their timing constraints. One of the primary difficulties arises from the dynamic nature of such a system, where the execution time and availability of resources can alter randomly. This unpredictability renders it hard to create static scheduling algorithms, which subsequently can lead to poor performance. Asynchronous multi-core architectures add extra layers of complexity since tasks need to be distributed across varying core capacities in a way that optimizes utilization of resources. Responsive task allocation strategies that optimize in real time have become essential as performance and energy efficiency demands rise in high-performance computing scenarios. Innovative scheduling techniques, as discussed in recent research, focus on dynamic task management capable of significantly reducing execution time without requiring extensive offline analysis—an important advancement in addressing inherent challenges in task scheduling (Ayguadé et al., 2017). One particular issue in real-time task scheduling is various levels of criticality associated with tasks, particularly salient in safety-critical applications such as autonomous vehicles. Mixed-criticality scheduling techniques must be implemented to ensure high-priority tasks are allocated the necessary resources and processing time needed to meet critical deadlines, while simultaneously addressing lower-priority tasks that are possibly less time-sensitive. Balancing both needs is crucial to system stability as well as reliability, especially where modes of failure can have catastrophic effects. The integration of such methods within frameworks like ROS2 is important, as it reflects the complexity of task scheduling and the influence of scheduling. Specifically, compromises between different scheduling policies—fixed-priority and earliest-deadline-first—reflect the need for tailored solutions that serve the specific needs of real-time systems within a mixed-criticality environment (Bhaskar et al., 2024). In addition, the communication middleware of real-time systems, particularly for context-aware applications like autonomous cars, introduces an extra layer of complexity in task scheduling effectively. As data need to be communicated across different system components efficiently, communication overhead may influence the timing of task completion. The scheduling schemes for real-time tasks must cope with such communication latency, where the transfer of vital sensor information and decision-making is carried out effectively. The synchronization among the systems scheduling capabilities and its underlying communication infrastructure is especially vital to address latency issues that can eventually undermine system performance. Strategies that enhance the middleware real-time capabilities and strengthen inter-task communication channels are imperative. This communication is a reflection of the multi-sided richness of task scheduling problems that demand holistic solutions beyond mere computational efficiency to also highlight robust communication mechanisms in order to meet deadlines for complex and autonomous systems (Bhaskar et al., 2024).

4.4.1. Resource Contention

Resource contention remains a prevalent problem in the realm of real-time task scheduling, particularly with systems heading towards multicore processors. The very nature of multicore processors offers the possibility of having more than one task executed at the same time, enhancing performance exponentially. However, such concurrent execution is likely to result in shared hardware resource contention, such as caches, memory, and communication bandwidth. Such contention can adversely affect the deterministic timing required by real-time applications to make meeting deadlines a challenging task. As noted, certification standards have traditionally focused on single-core architectures and hence leave a void in guidelines that apply to multicore systems. The CAST-32A is born with the aim to meet these requirements by specifying a mode for planning, creating, and validating the software that runs on multicore platforms, even though there are staggering obstacles in synchronizing these standards with current Commercial Off-The-Shelf (COTS) multicore architectures (Ferrer et al., 2017). The impact of resource contention in real-time systems also complicates task scheduling dynamics by causing uncertainty in the execution of high-priority tasks. In the event that tasks are competing for shared resources, the temporal guarantee that specific tasks will complete within specific time constraints can be greatly eroded. This necessitates new scheduling algorithms that can efficiently allocate resources without generating considerable contention effects. Methods like priority ceiling protocols, which temporarily raise the priority of tasks competing for shared resources, have been suggested to reduce contention effects. Nevertheless, such solutions tend to create extra overhead that can counter timing predictability, adding other challenges in real-world applications. Hence, a balanced perspective on both the theoretical environment of resource contention and the practical effectiveness of various scheduling algorithms remains crucial in the design of real-time systems (Berge et al., 2012). Additionally, the introduction of wireless technology in industrial monitoring and control networks adds a multi-faceted dimension to the issue of resource contention. As industries increasingly adopt wireless substitutes for the traditional wired infrastructure, the flexibility and scalability of wireless communications systems introduce new possibilities for resource sharing. The systems themselves pose their own challenges, particularly in the areas of real-time performance and reliable data communication in the presence of concurrent communications. Wireless nodes can compete, resulting in delay and packet loss that disrupts the real-time demands of real-time applications. Recent research focuses on enhancing wireless communication techniques to address such issues, particularly for high-priority applications whose real-time performance should be guaranteed. Here, the necessity of good task scheduling mechanisms that are competent to effectively solve resource contention along with the unique character of wireless networks becomes ever more evident (Berge et al., 2012).

4.4.2. Scalability Issues

The growing complexity of task scheduling in real-time systems does point out the most important scalability issues that need to be addressed in order to deliver performance and efficiency. With systems tending to be multi-core and multi-processor in nature, the classical von Neumann programming model struggles to effectively allocate resources. Particularly, the multicore/multi-processor system-on-chip (MPSoC) architecture software challenges need to deviate from the conventional sequential programming models, for which there is great focus on designing new software models and tools that can effectively exploit parallelism and enable tasks to execute without errors. The effective incorporation of heterogeneous embedded MPSoC systems relies upon the balance between this emerging programming paradigm and the wide legacy of certified sequential code, making it challenging to transition towards more scalable alternatives (Bekooij et al., 2009). Furthermore, the rapid dissemination of data-intensive applications adds additional scalability issues into real-time task scheduling. As such systems involve processing a lot of data, data distribution, co-placement, and scheduling of data besides computing resources is a concern. For instance, comparison of high-performance computing systems and models like Apache Hadoop was employed to identify unique ecosystem characteristics that affect the schedule of jobs. The latter depicts a batch-oriented model of distribution, which is quite different from the strict timing constraints of real-time systems. This contrast underscores the need for methods that exploit insights from both paradigms and map them to real-time environments, where latency and predictability are best (Fox et al., 2014). Finally, the confrontation between new paradigms, also referred to as Big Data Ogres, brings another level of scalability issues that influence scheduling performance in real-time systems. These Ogres, or proxy application workloads based on both high-performance computing and Apache-Hadoop paradigms, are not only employed as performance measures but also indicators where classic models of real-time scheduling fall short. The underlying architectures of the paradigms are similar but differ with regard to the implementation, especially when viewed in terms of efficiency of scheduling and management of resources. As the necessity for systems with high workloads increases to allow for higher complexity, the intersection of approaches from various paradigms becomes necessary in addressing the inherent scalability issues faced in real-time task scheduling (Fox et al., 2014).

4.4.3. Predictability

In the scenario of scheduling tasks for real-time systems, predictability emerges as one of the most important properties that defines the ability of a system to run under strict timing requirements. Real-time systems are likely to require deterministic execution, where tasks must complete within guaranteed deadlines for functionality and safety reasons. Predictability of task execution time and utilization of resources is thus very important. Predictability allows system designers to properly model timing behavior, thereby enabling resource allocation and avoiding tasks from interfering with one another's execution. As systems become increasingly complex, with numerous tasks often executing concurrently, predictability is an issue that calls for sophisticated scheduling algorithms and methods. Predictability in task scheduling is the research topic that affects several design choices in real-time systems. More recent research has identified the deficiencies of standard scheduling techniques, particularly in distributed systems where different nodes have to coordinate nicely among themselves. A perfect example is the application of the High-Level Architecture (HLA) standard, which, while the foundation for modeling concurrent systems, has a tendency to overlook provisions for the fine-grained requirements of hard real-time operation. As noted in earlier literature, improvement in real-time in HLA federations has centered primarily on QoS guarantees and acquiring insight into worst-case transit times (Adelantado et al., 2010). Such improvements are required for the delivery of a predictable system where one can anticipate reliable performance of real-time tasks. Moreover, some scheduling paradigms have proven to be more predictable than others, hence guiding the selection of scheduling techniques in real-time systems. For instance, studies of periodic and parallel rigid tasks have offered precise schedulability tests for sub-classes of Fixed Task Priority (FTP) Gang schedulers (Berten et al., 2010). This research indicates that while some scheduling methods, such as Gang FJP schedulers, lose their accuracy in predictability, others can be effectively designed to enhance predictability. This is extremely crucial as it enables designers to select appropriate schedulers that not only meet deadline requirements but also guarantee an executable schedule in system behavior. Thus, incorporating predictability in scheduling schemes forms the basis of dependable real-time system design.

4.5. APPLICATIONS OF REAL-TIME TASK SCHEDULING

Real-time task scheduling has general use in most fields, primarily due to its critical role in ensuring timely processing and system reliability. In industrial automation, for instance, manufacturing systems employ real-time scheduling to schedule tasks to interact with machines and robots. Such systems must run periodic tasks with some deadlines to avoid malfunctioning or production delays. Increasing use of advanced scheduling algorithms makes the functionality of RTOS such that they can support several synchronized tasks, which may operate at different rates. This functionality becomes extremely critical with the increasing complexity of industrial applications in recent times, which need sophisticated scheduling schemes that can efficiently schedule resources and maintain system efficiency (Eckhardt et al., 2025). Another significant application domain is automotive systems, where scheduling tasks in real-time is critical in ensuring both performance and safety. Modern cars possess many control systems with plenty of sensors and actuators that must work in concert with each other to deliver responsive and safe performance. The scheduling of these tasks not only encompasses timely finishing more importantly, but it also encompasses handling interdependencies in the best possible way so that the risk of failure occurrence due to conflicting tasks or delays is reduced to the maximum level. Studies as at REACTION 2014 indicate that with vehicles becoming more and more interconnected, the need for efficient scheduling policies that can cope with sophisticated task interdependencies is of maximum priority. This is an emphasis of the necessity of vehicle systems to utilize robust real-time scheduling paradigms for enhancement in safety and functionality (Chen et al., 2014). In telecommunications, real-time scheduling of tasks is also imperative in data traffic management and ensuring access to bandwidth for high-priority communication tasks. With the networks fluctuating with traffic and demand, good scheduling algorithms are required in maintaining Quality of Service (QoS) levels. Real-time task scheduling enables networks to assign high priority to high-priority communications, i.e., emergency alerts or time-sensitive data transfers, to ensure that such tasks are allocated resources even in heavy-hyped environments. Further, research emphasizes deploying scheduling schemes that can evenly distribute loads across multiple network nodes to achieve maximum system performance overall. By making use of effective scheduling techniques, telecommunication operators can enhance their infrastructures reactivity and thereby meet the growing requirements of real-time applications in an increasingly connected world (Eckhardt et al., 2025).

4.5.1. Embedded Systems

Embedded systems form the cornerstone of many real-time applications across industries spanning from cars to telecommunication. These systems have the tendency to perform specific tasks within limited time frames where predictability and task scheduling reliability take precedence. Task scheduling becomes a matter of extreme priority when dealing with real-time systems since it decides in which order and when the tasks should be executed. Good scheduling algorithms, regardless of fixed-priority or dynamic-priority schemes, must guarantee the processing of all tasks within their individual deadlines to ensure system stability. Embedded system performance thus relies on the ability to dynamically schedule tasks, adjusting not only to the workload's immediate needs but also taking into account the added complexities in multi-core processors and parallel processes in the system architecture. Task model development iteratively has been instrumental in dealing with multiple workloads in real-time embedded systems. Researchers have come up with expressive task models of various categories, each of which has been developed for handling some application needs and fostering schedulability analysis. The k2U framework is a fine representation of this advancement that enables the testing of various task models under various fixed-priority scheduling policies and thereby provides a comprehensive approach to schedulability testing. One of the framework's key strengths is its k-point effective schedulability test, which acts as a black-box interface for analyzing task performance. Promising new and improved tests resembling state-of-the-art solutions, the k2U framework builds upon the knowledge of task scheduling in embedded systems, additionally emphasizing the importance of adaptive scheduling techniques to meet the high requirements of real-time applications (Chen et al., 2015) (Figure 4.11).

Figure 4.11. *Embedded systems.*

Source: https://datascientest.com/en/files/2024/06/Embedded-systems-datascientest-1024x585.jpg.

Although improvements in processor performance are tremendous, they raise system dependability concerns, particularly in embedded systems faced with radiation-induced transient faults as well as power densities. The implications of technology scaling intersect with task scheduling such that fault-tolerance techniques must be integrated within a system to ensure system reliability. However, integrating these techniques makes it cumbersome to maintain timing constraints critical in real-time scenarios. As outlined by recent studies, novel task mapping and scheduling policies have emerged to balance the requirements of fault tolerance with the need to maintain reliability as well as timing constraints. On top of this, thermal elevation mitigation inherent in fault-tolerance designs has also been the focal point of studies, leading to a new scheduling approach optimizing for power and temperature with deadline guarantees (Ansari et al., 2022).

4.5.2. Robotics

The combination of robotics and real-time task scheduling has groundbreaking implications across many sectors. With enhanced task complexity resulting from robotics advancements, efficient use of computational resources is imperative. Conventional centralized approaches used to solve RAPs offer a structured means of managing these complexities but with drawbacks, particularly in dynamic environments. Unlike market-based methods, which have been seen as a viable substitute, mainly due to the evolving environment of information and communication technologies (ICT) (Al-Yafi et al., 2009), this trend is concurrent with a growing appreciative awareness of uncertainty on resource availability and the emphasis on the unique challenge found in mobile task allocation problems where variables constantly change. The need for advanced scheduling mechanisms increases even more when the computational effort involved in handling intricate robotic systems is considered. Agent coordination to achieve a series of interdependent tasks involves handling advanced temporal and resource requirements and calls for a masterful understanding of both tasks and environment. Human scheduling professionals typically handle such complex scheduling scenarios through accumulated experience over time, which points to the possible reward in transcribing this experiential wisdom into computational systems. However, it is equally difficult to capture the nuance of decision-making by such experts, and therefore, innovative approaches are needed to successfully codify their heuristics (Golen et al., 2018) (Figure 4.12).

Figure 4.12. *The intersection of robotics and task scheduling within real-time systems offers transformative potential across various industries.*

Source: https://external-content.duckduckgo.com/iu/?u=https%3A%2F%2Fimg.freepik.com%2Fpremium-photo%2Fsmart-factory-robots-coordinating-realtime-manufacturing-tasks_198067-1166047.jpg&f=1&nofb=1&ipt=62442e234af4656 9eae038ce06eea87316dc7dd5eb141be8ffae75357e3685e0.

These processes can enhance robotic responsiveness and efficiency in real-time systems, accelerating the development of intelligent robots that can autonomously perform tasks. Additionally, the simultaneous optimization of human and machine performance is a significant advancement in robotics. Using apprenticeship learning in order to learn from demonstrations by experts can significantly enhance task scheduling efficiencies, as proven in a number of case studies. For instance, human-scheduling-example-based scheduling methodologies preferred solving regular optimization techniques with a positive predisposition, showing excellent speed and accuracy in high-level tasks like weapon-to-target assignment. Human-machine integration not only enhances operation efficiency but also invites working out increasingly complicated scheduling problems that could possibly go beyond the level of human capacity alone. As the future of robotics unfolds, sophisticated methods of task scheduling are going to play a vital role in making optimal use of real-time systems as well as the maximum potential of robot technologies.

SUMMARY

In reviewing the discussion of task scheduling within real-time systems, it is important to take into consideration the central position scheduling algorithms maintain in ensuring system reliability and operation. Choice of scheduling technique has a direct bearing on real-time system performance, particularly in safety-related applications where meeting rigid deadlines is not a possibility. As can be seen through this essay, the effectiveness of scheduling algorithms such as Rate Monotonic Scheduling (RMS) and Earliest Deadline First (EDF) dictates the success of system operations. Complete information regarding these algorithms leads to optimal loading of system loads and resource allocation and enhances overall performance as well as dependability in situations where timely execution is very crucial. Also, new technology in scheduling illustrates that there is also ongoing development of paradigms that are being adapted to address emerging computational models. Integrating parallel processing with real-time systems is also a clear indication of the movement towards utilizing multi-core architectures to maximize efficiency. Static scheduling methods, brought forth in recent work, e.g., the OpenMP-compliant ones, demonstrate the move away from the conventional dynamic methods to more predictable allocation strategies for safety-critical systems (Bertogna et al., 2017). Not only does such an approach provide high predictability, but it also plays a key role in the increasing complexity of tasks that need to be run in real-time. These developments represent fundamental paradigm shifts in how we proceed with designing and implementing trustworthy task scheduling frameworks. Furthermore, the implications for verifying and analyzing the behavior of such scheduling systems cannot be overstated. Using formal techniques—for example, the real-time semantics derived from modeling languages such as Creol—gives programmers a means to rigorously analyze process schedulability and their ability to meet deadlines (Chothia et al., 2010). This ensures that theoretical concepts correspond to actual applications and, ultimately, improve the development of systems efficient but also reliable. In our further immersion in an era increasingly based on embedded systems and networked devices, the principles outlined in this essay will continue to direct future research and application in task scheduling in real-time systems, ensuring optimal performance and safety in high-stakes operation domains.

Task scheduling is an important feature in the realm of real-time systems, whereby tasks are scheduled to execute with very tight deadlines. Real-time systems must deal with varied workloads and applications that require efficient task schedulers. Various task models provide distinct demands, and as a result of these differences, researchers have considered how to develop schedule-dependent schedulability tests with various complexity and performance measures. These advances in scheduling techniques are an ongoing effort to overcome the challenge posed by uniprocessor and multiprocessor computer architectures in minimizing the entire system reliability and efficiency. It becomes necessary in guaranteeing application integrity where time becomes as crucial as task success itself, thereby underlining the observation that correct task model knowledge becomes critical in enhancing task scheduling methodologies in real-time systems. At the forefront of ongoing research is that of k2U framework, advocated to provide a systematic approach to schedulability analysis of numerous task models of fixed-priority scheduling algorithms. Central to this framework are the k-point effective schedulability tests, which provide a black-box interface. The innovative approach enables automatic derivation of sufficient utilization-based tests, hence making the process of analysis simpler in various architectures. These advances emphasize the value of flexibility in task scheduling, allowing researchers and practitioners to utilize methodologies that are applicable broadly regardless of system specifics. In facilitating this degree of generalizability, the k2U framework assists with advancing the understanding and utilization of real-time task scheduling, which becomes increasingly significant as demands from applications become more intricate. Apart from that, task scheduling research is also extended to future technologies such as Knowledge-Defined Networking (KDN), which has been gaining momentum recently for its capability to enhance computational performance in regard to smart predictions. The use of systems based on machine learning frameworks puts systems in a place to optimize task offloading decisions based on historical performances. By the generation of a hyperprofile over boundary nodes and employing k-Nearest Neighbor (kNN) queries, the utilization efficiency of the resources can be significantly improved, aligned with the goals of reducing total network utilization while meeting stringent processing needs.

These advancements support the function of adding new approaches in the area of real-time systems because they provide not only enhancing performance but also coping with the sophisticated challenge posed by the dynamic workloads in modern technological settings (Calyam et al., 2017; Chen et al., 2015).

REFERENCES

1. Abella Ferrer, J., Agirre, I., Azkarate-Askasua, M., Cazorla, F. J., et al. (2017). On the tailoring of CAST-32A certification guidance to real COTS multicore architectures. https://core.ac.uk/download/157811610.pdf (accessed on 29th September 2025).
2. Adelantado, M., Chaudron, J. B., & Siron, P. (2010). Towards an HLA run-time infrastructure with hard real-time capabilities. https://core.ac.uk/download/12042130.pdf (accessed on 29th September 2025).
3. Agrawal, K., Chen, J. J., Li, J., Ueter, M., et al. (2017). Reservation-based federated scheduling for parallel real-time tasks. http://arxiv.org/abs/1712.05040 (accessed on 29th September 2025).
4. Ahrendts, L., Boroske, T., Ernst, R., Quinton, S., et al. (2018). Verifying weakly-hard real-time properties of traffic streams in switched networks. https://core.ac.uk/download/159309611.pdf (accessed on 29th September 2025).
5. Alnusairi, T. S., Daadaa, Y., & Shahin, A. A. (2018). Binary PSOGSA for load balancing task scheduling in cloud environment. http://arxiv.org/abs/1806.00329 (accessed on 29th September 2025).
6. Al-Yafi, K., & Lee, H. (2009). Centralized versus market-based approaches to mobile task allocation problem: State-of-the-art. https://core.ac.uk/download/336587.pdf (accessed on 29th September 2025).
7. Ansari, M., Ejlali, A., Henkel, J., Hessabi, S., et al. (2022). A survey of fault-tolerance techniques for embedded systems from the perspective of power, energy, and thermal issues. https://core.ac.uk/download/521173291.pdf (accessed on 29th September 2025).
8. Audsley, N., Baruah, S., Burns, A., & Punnekkat, S. (2019). A lazy bailout approach for dual-criticality systems on uniprocessor platforms. https://core.ac.uk/download/287581442.pdf (accessed on 29th September 2025).
9. Audsley, N., Chiodo, M., Demmeler, T., Eles, P., Gonzaléz Harbour, M., González Harbour, M., Gu, Z., et al. (2006). Analysis and optimization of distributed real-time embedded systems. https://core.ac.uk/download/13721535.pdf (accessed on 29th September 2025).
10. Ayguadé Parra, E., Badia Sala, R. M., Casas, M., Chronaki, K., et al. (2017). Task scheduling techniques for asymmetric multi-core systems. https://core.ac.uk/download/87650226.pdf (accessed on 29th September 2025).
11. Bana, S., & Bana, S. (2020). A priority-based fair queuing (PFQ) model for wireless healthcare system. https://core.ac.uk/download/293755073.pdf (accessed on 29th September 2025).

12. Bansal, N., Chakraborty, S., Chen, J. J., von der Brüggen, G., et al. (2018). Packing sporadic real-time tasks on identical multiprocessor systems. https://core.ac.uk/download/301650244.pdf (accessed on 29th September 2025).
13. Barbosa, J., Ferreira, A., Leitão, P., Lima, R., et al. (2017). A genetic algorithm approach for the scheduling in a robotic-centric flexible manufacturing system. https://core.ac.uk/download/153416959.pdf (accessed on 29th September 2025).
14. Baruah, S., & Bestavros, A. (1996). Pinwheel scheduling for fault-tolerant broadcast disks in real-time database systems. https://open.bu.edu/bitstream/2144/1599/1/1996-023-pinwheel-bdisks.pdf (accessed on 29th September 2025).
15. Barzegaran, M., Pop, P., & Zarrin, B. (2020). Quality-of-control-aware scheduling of communication in TSN-based fog computing platforms using constraint programming. https://core.ac.uk/download/296708937.pdf (accessed on 29th September 2025).
16. Bekooij, M., Domer, R., Leupers, R., Nohl, A., et al. (2009). Programming MPSoC platforms: Road works ahead. https://core.ac.uk/download/pdf/11473351.pdf (accessed on 29th September 2025).
17. Berge, J., Ganesan, S., Goldsmith, M., Gungor, V., Hong, Y., Matsuda, T., Scheible, G., et al. (2012). Wireless industrial monitoring and control networks: The journey so far and the road ahead. https://core.ac.uk/download/pdf/11484488.pdf (accessed on 29th September 2025).
18. Berten, V., & Goossens, J. (2010). Gang FTP scheduling of periodic and parallel rigid real-time tasks. http://arxiv.org/abs/1006.2617 (accessed on 29th September 2025).
19. Bertogna, M., Buttazzo, G., Cerutti, I., Melani, A., et al. (2017). A static scheduling approach to enable safety-critical OpenMP applications. https://core.ac.uk/download/81582027.pdf (accessed on 29th September 2025).
20. Bhaskar, S. V., & Gupta, V. (2024). Mixed-criticality scheduling in ROS2 for autonomous vehicles. https://core.ac.uk/download/645941848.pdf (accessed on 29th September 2025).
21. Broenink, J. F., & Orlic, B. (2003). Real-time and fault tolerance in distributed control software. https://core.ac.uk/download/pdf/11458244.pdf (accessed on 29th September 2025).
22. Buttazzo, G., & Marinoni, M. (2007). Elastic DVS management in processors with discrete voltage/frequency modes. https://core.ac.uk/download/pdf/54929054.pdf (accessed on 29th September 2025).

23. Bux, M., Gusew, W., Leser, U., Witt, C., et al. (2018). Predictive performance modeling for distributed computing using black-box monitoring and machine learning. http://arxiv.org/abs/1805.11877 (accessed on 29th September 2025).
24. Calyam, P., Coleman, K., Crutcher, A., Esposito, F., et al. (2017). Hyper profile-based computation offloading for mobile edge networks. http://arxiv.org/abs/1707.09422 (accessed on 29th September 2025).
25. Chandarli, Y., Fauberteau, F., Masson, D., Midonnet, S., et al. (2012). YARTISS: A tool to visualize, test, compare and evaluate real-time scheduling algorithms. https://core.ac.uk/download/48341300.pdf (accessed on 29th September 2025).
26. Chen, C. M. (1998). Scheduling issues in real-time systems. https://core.ac.uk/download/56097665.pdf (accessed on 29th September 2025).
27. Chen, J. J., & Freier, M. (2014). Time-triggered scheduling analysis for real-time applications on multicore platforms. https://core.ac.uk/download/29406317.pdf (accessed on 29th September 2025).
28. Chen, J. J., Huang, W. H., & Liu, C. (2015). k2U: A general framework from k-point effective schedulability analysis to utilization-based tests. http://arxiv.org/abs/1501.07084 (accessed on 29th September 2025).
29. Chothia, T., & Jaghoori, M. M. (2010). Timed automata semantics for analyzing Creol. http://arxiv.org/abs/1007.5095 (accessed on 29th September 2025).
30. Dede, C. J., Scace, J. R., & Sullivan, T. R. (2025). Factors shaping the evolution of electronic documentation systems. https://core.ac.uk/download/pdf/42820992.pdf (accessed on 29th September 2025).
31. Dong, J., Sun, Y., Tian, Y. C., Xia, F., et al. (2007). Neural feedback scheduling of real-time control tasks. http://arxiv.org/abs/0805.3062 (accessed on 29th September 2025).
32. Eckhardt, D. E., Jr. (2025). Time-critical multirate scheduling using contemporary real-time operating system services. https://core.ac.uk/download/pdf/42851133.pdf (accessed on 29th September 2025).
33. Fahmida, S., Fisher, N., Guo, Z., Modekurthy, V., et al. (2020). CPU energy-aware parallel real-time scheduling. https://core.ac.uk/download/343692383.pdf (accessed on 29th September 2025).
34. Fox, G. C., Jha, S., Luckow, A., Mantha, P., et al. (2014). A tale of two data-intensive paradigms: Applications, abstractions, and architectures. http://arxiv.org/abs/1403.1528 (accessed on 29th September 2025).

35. Golen, T., Gombolay, M., Jensen, R., Shah, J., et al. (2018). Human-machine collaborative optimization via apprenticeship scheduling. http://arxiv.org/abs/1805.04220 (accessed on 29th September 2025).
36. Goossens, J., & Nelis, V. (2009). MORA: An energy-aware slack reclamation scheme for scheduling sporadic real-time tasks upon multiprocessor platforms. http://arxiv.org/abs/0906.0268 (accessed on 29th September 2025).
37. Hahn, S., Reineke, J., & Shah, D. (2018). Experimental evaluation of cache-related preemption delays aware timing analysis. https://core.ac.uk/download/161409479.pdf (accessed on 29th September 2025).
38. He, B., Li, M., & Lu, Y. (2013). Collaborative signal and information processing for target detection with heterogeneous sensor networks. https://core.ac.uk/download/19118173.pdf (accessed on 29th September 2025).
39. Holenderski, M. J. (2012). Multi-resource management in embedded real-time systems. https://core.ac.uk/download/576992280.pdf (accessed on 29th September 2025).
40. Jansen, P. G., & Laan, R. (1999). The stack resource protocol based on real-time transactions. https://core.ac.uk/download/pdf/11454259.pdf (accessed on 29th September 2025).
41. Jansen, P. G., Laan, R., & Scholten, H. (1998). Flexible scheduling in multimedia kernels: An overview. https://core.ac.uk/download/pdf/11454423.pdf (accessed on 29th September 2025).
42. Kempf, J. F., Lebeltel, O., & Maler, O. (2014). Formal and informal methods for multi-core design space exploration. http://arxiv.org/abs/1406.2071 (accessed on 29th September 2025).
43. Khomh, F., Soualhia, M., & Tahar, S. (2015). Predicting scheduling failures in the cloud. http://arxiv.org/abs/1507.03562 (accessed on 29th September 2025).
44. Lautenbach, A. (2014). Partitioned fixed-priority multiprocessor scheduling for mixed-criticality real-time systems. https://core.ac.uk/download/622425448.pdf (accessed on 29th September 2025).
45. Minj, I. (2013). Real time event management and coordinating system. https://core.ac.uk/download/53189841.pdf (accessed on 29th September 2025).
46. Ramalhinho-Lourenço, H. (2025). Supply chain management: An opportunity for metaheuristics. https://core.ac.uk/download/pdf/6475386.pdf (accessed on 29th September 2025).

47. Sinha, S. (2018). Scheduling policies and system software architectures for mixed-criticality computing. https://core.ac.uk/download/304658766.pdf (accessed on 29th September 2025).
48. Xhafa, F. (2007). A hyper-heuristic for adaptive scheduling in computational grids. https://core.ac.uk/download/187768787.pdf (accessed on 29th September 2025).
49. Yuan, H. (2020). Energy and performance-optimized scheduling of tasks in distributed cloud and edge computing systems. https://core.ac.uk/download/352837574.pdf (accessed on 29th September 2025).

CHAPTER 5

INTER-TASK COMMUNICATION AND SYNCHRONIZATION IN RTOS

Contents

INTRODUCTION

The advent of real-time operating systems (RTOS) has transformed the area of embedded systems by emphasizing the compelling need of real-time and reliable handling of tasks. With applications demanding immediate response, particularly in domains like automotive control and industrial automation, becoming the standard, understanding inter-task communication and synchronization has become a matter of utmost priority. This urgency is also paralleled by the broader technological context, represented by waves towards intelligent manufacturing in Industry 4.0. In all such scenarios, flexibility and capability to produce customized products quickly command effective inter-task mechanisms. By establishing strong communication protocols and synchronization methods, RTOS enables system developers to create systems capable of handling the subtleties of real-time demands without compromising reliability or performance.

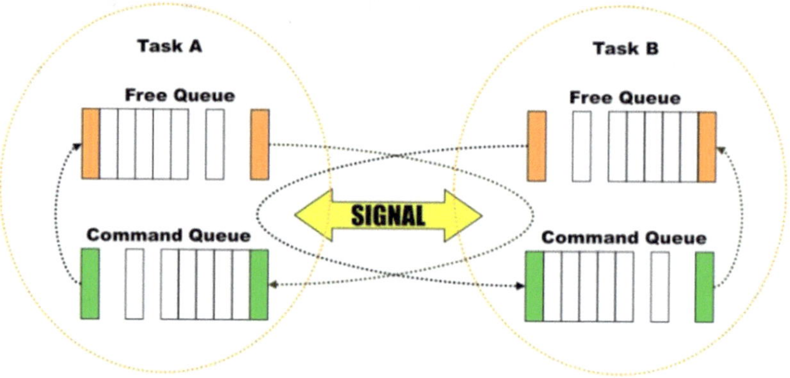

Figure 5.1. Inter-task communication.

Source: https://external-content.duckduckgo.com/iu/?u=https%3A%2F%2Fimage.slideserve.com%2F482237%2Finter-task-communication15-l.jpg&f=1&nofb=1&ipt=3b6e7664c4e8f9484a910a3507b725f7440049f957384c5d214dd3ffc7fdbc87.

These advancements not only support existing technologies but also provide for future innovation in automation and computing. As the world is becoming increasingly networked, the integration of technologies such as the Internet of Things (IoT) and mobile edge computing (MEC) has further increased pressure on the requirement for sophisticated communication infrastructures in RTOS environments. As attention turns to lowering latency and enhancing computational efficiency, inter-task communication must change to support apps that require speedy data exchange and processing at the network edge. This can be accomplished by developers with RTOS, which ensures the most important tasks cooperate perfectly with one another, exchanging data and following the stringent timing requirements of various apps. Such synchronization of more than one task enables unbreakable operations, providing the extent of toughness required in an era where cloud and edge computing technologies prevail, the convergence of such technologies being a focal area for future research and development in RTOS. It is also important to study inter-task communication and synchronization procedures in RTOS not only from the perspective of theoretical development but also for practical applications. Resource management difficulties, task ordering, and exception handling are directly related to the efficiency of such communication mechanisms. With research continuing to refine such systems, the inference made has the potential to lead innovations that transcend infancy challenges, such as scalability and compatibilities with next-generation technologies. The evolution of MEC, for instance, is a mirror image of the imperative to harmonize wireless and mobile computing efficiencies to new standards for synchronizing tasks in RTOS. Thereby, the impacts of efficient task management extend beyond immediate applications, providing enhancement that can transform operational paradigms for industrial and technology domains alike, hence realizing the vision of a whole actualized networked ecosystem (Figure 5.1).

Importance of Inter-Task Communication

Effective inter-task communication is essential in RTOS so that synchronization and efficient sharing of resources among concurrent tasks are ensured. The possibility of resource contention is higher when several tasks are executed concurrently, necessitating efficient methods for communication in an effort not to interfere and ensure predictable action. Without communication, tasks are able to utilize out-of-date or inconsistent data and generate erroneous results or bring about system failure. Thus, an explicit communication scheme among the tasks enhances the system's performance and reliability overall. These schemes not only maximize resource allocation but also offer a path for every task to suitably notify others in state transitions or access critical data, enhancing a culture of collaboration and efficiency within the RTOS environment. Secondly, the need for inter-task communication is also common in application development, particularly when developing complex systems that demand real-time performance. With changing applications that span heterogeneous functionalities, from wireless sensor networks (WSNs) to industrial automation, the inter-task dependency rises. Developers are hence forced to employ sophisticated communication means to keep things in sync and satisfy Quality of Service (QoS) constraints. It is important to apply these techniques, however, especially when operations are responsible for critical functions and performance metrics such as latency and reliability. The use of simulated environments, such as seen in the work on tools such as RTNS, is beneficial in exploring and ensuring communication policies. These simulations give an entire overview of how communication influences system performance and make sure that design choices are consistent with working requirements of modern applications, thus enhancing the importance of inter-task communication in the RTOS model. Finally, the relationship between inter-task communication and system efficiency is emphasized by pressure that modern applications impose to attain a trade-off between computation and communication. With systems imposing higher computation loads, communication overhead must be controlled closely in order not to introduce bottlenecks, thus degrading real-time responsiveness. Constructing robust frameworks to facilitate inter-task coordination is not only beneficial but critical to achieving the best performance of the system. It has been proven through research that simulation of task interaction can help simplify the influence of communication delays as well as timing mismatches on overall QoS. By examining these factors, developers can design improved resource management policies with the capability to address the intricate demands of today's programs. This holistic practice then accentuates the way inter-task communication lies at the heart of task synchronization, hence solidifying its critical place in the effective operation of RTOS environments (Chitnis et al., 2009; N/A, 2025).

Overview of Synchronization Mechanisms

Synchronization of tasks in an RTOS is an important means of maintaining consistency of the data and proper time execution of operations. Various synchronization primitives, including mutexes, semaphores, and condition variables, are employed to manage interactions between multiple tasks that execute concurrently. Mutexes, for instance, are employed to support mutual exclusion, through which a single task can run with a specified shared resource at a time. This guarantees the prevention of race conditions, whereby multiple or more than one task attempt to modify the same variable simultaneously, with unpredictable consequences. Semaphores, aside from synchronizing access to resources, also give notifications of task preparedness and ensure improved interaction between tasks. Both processes are important in guaranteeing deterministic execution typical in RTOS environments and thus enabling inter-task communication that is dependable for embedded systems. A second important aspect of synchronization methods in RTOS is how they impact system performance and resource management. Based on ongoing research, though common, software solutions for synchronization are generally accompanied by overheads that decrease system efficiency. Implementing hardware-based solutions offers a feasible means to aid in alleviating such inefficiencies. For instance, the use of Field Programmable Gate Arrays (FPGAs) decreases CPU load through time management function delegation, hence enhancing RTOS performance. The introduction of a configurable hardware component enhances the determinism of time management services without loss of flexibility, a critical expectation for real-time systems. Systems achieve higher timing precision without CPU overhead through this hardware assistance, as underscored in relevant literature. The transition to hardware-assisted synchronization methods is a paradigm shift in RTOS design, especially for embedded systems. Furthermore, the architecture technology of synchronization mechanisms continues to develop to overcome real-time scheduling issues. Advanced hardware schedulers with the capacity to use a variety of algorithms, i.e., time-sliced priority scheduling or Earliest Deadline First, has emerged to enhance real-time performance in soft-core processor systems. The flexibility to configure these schedulers provides tailored solutions in terms of an application's unique needs, enhancing the overall system utilization. As suggested, this hardware-assisted approach possesses the potential for decreasing scheduling overhead significantly, thereby facilitating quicker context switching and lower scheduling jitter. These improvements position synchronization mechanisms not only as task coordination devices but as performance-impactful and reliability-affecting key components of embedded systems. Therefore, studying these new kinds of synchronization techniques is valuable for RTOS development in its ability to handle the needs of today's applications.

5.1. TYPES OF INTER-TASK COMMUNICATION

In real-time operating systems (RTOS), inter-task communication is essential to ensured efficient synchronization and data transfer of concurrent tasks. The most basic type of inter-task communication is message passing, where tasks communicate with one another by sending and receiving messages. This can provide decoupled and unambiguous communication, which is so crucial in systems where tasks could be executed at different priorities or timing. Using message queues allows tasks to be sent asynchronously, and therefore there is more flexibility and less latency. Additionally, this method reduces the dangers of shared data, as it isolates tasks from accessing another task's space of memory directly. Consequently, message passing enhances system modularity in design as well as adheres to modern methods of controlling complex applications, as experienced in methods discussed in the literature addressing overall communication mechanisms (N/A, 2025). Another major technique for inter-task communication involves shared memory, where tasks share and communicate within a common memory segment for data sharing. This method is very effective due to its low latency and high throughput, allowing multiple tasks to communicate simultaneously without the overhead of passing messages. For ensuring data integrity and synchrony, mechanisms like semaphores and mutexes are used to prevent race conditions as well as access control to shared resources. The impact of these synchronization primitives is important, especially for systems where responsiveness and timing are essential, such as in-flight control systems. For instance, NASAs Space Shuttle Cockpit Avionics Upgrade project utilized cutting-edge hardware and software design, showcasing the importance of real-time synchronization in conjunction with shared memory architectures to provide better situational awareness and reduce workload in high-risk environments (Ferguson et al., 2025). In addition to shared memory and message passing, event-driven communication is an essential inter-task communication mechanism. It employs events or signals upon which tasks listen and respond, allowing for a more dynamic model of interaction. This mechanism finds optimal use in scenarios where task execution time depends on external input or conditions. For example, an interrupt may signal the occurrence of an event to be processed by a task, which will call for handling data immediately or making decisions. The event-driven method ensures efficient use of resources as tasks are able to remain inactive until they are called upon, conserving processing power and maximizing efficiency in a system. Enriched through the design application strategy presented in earlier case studies, the method of communication used here is an indicator of a strong tide towards responsiveness and flexibility in real-time systems that finds resonance with contemporary design practices in RTOS (N/A, 2025).

5.1.1. Message Passing

Message passing in RTOS is a native synchronization and inter-task communication mechanism. Message passing offers a means of sending messages among tasks in such a way that they can communicate with each other and synchronize their operations effectively. Since real-time applications are timed quite closely, message passing is utilized in lieu of shared memory since it has the potential to reduce chances for data inconsistency as well as race conditions. All tasks can send and receive messages asynchronously, making the communication patterns more flexible. Decoupling tasks enables the system to be responsive and meet timing constraints in spite of changing demands placed on the system. The use of message passing hence is critical to the robustness and efficiency of RTOS in managing concurrent processes and resource conflicts. The design of message passing protocols of RTOS must also deal with performance challenges typical of distributed applications. As documented in the literature, these challenges interact with one another in complex ways, such that the components of communication infrastructure—such as channel bandwidth and congestion—have an effect on application-level performance. More precisely, message passing execution can be affected by protocol processing activities, including connection management, overhead of message handling, and error detection procedures. In addition, issues concerning the general operating system architecture are capable of offering bottlenecks that affect maximum performance. For instance, context switching delay as well as memory access can hinder vital inter-task communications, breaking timing guarantees offered by RTOS. As a result, these factors must be known to design adequate message passing schemes that are compatible with real-time demands (Schmidt et al., 1992) (Figure 5.2).

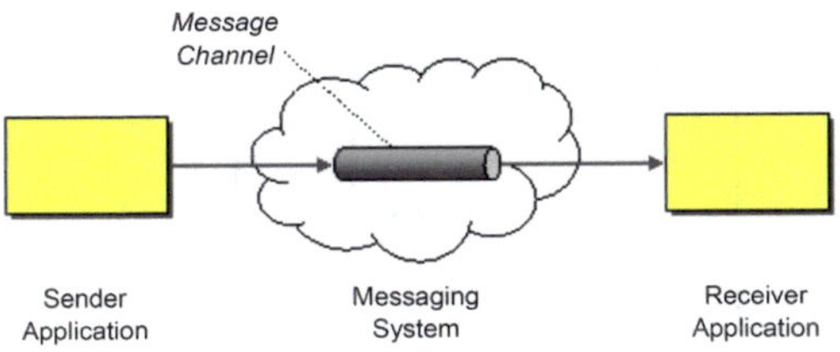

Figure 5.2. *Message passing serves as a fundamental mechanism for inter-task communication.*

Source: https://library.fiveable.me/embedded-systems-design/unit-9/inter-task-communication-synchronization/study-guide/UdiPgKSptW2AiOYi.

Furthermore, the design of a dependable message passing system must incorporate fault tolerance and reliability aspects. In an RTOS environment, the tasks must remain functional even under faulty or unexpected states. This requirement for reliability can be augmented through designing specific protocols that ensure messages are passed securely and uncorrupted. For example, split token usage, as introduced in distributed computing systems, facilitates both message passing and functional computation but lowers the possibility of message collision (Bolotin et al., 1990). Through such mechanisms, RTOS can achieve substantial fault tolerance, where message passing is not merely a means of information but also an aspect of maintaining system operations' integrity and functionality. Thus, making mechanisms for message passing more reliable is paramount to ensuring that real-time applications are able to meet strict operational requirements.

5.1.2. Shared Memory

The Shared Memory idea is key to synchronization and inter-task communication in RTOS. Such a system facilitates a number of tasks to share a common memory space, thereby facilitating efficient sharing of data and parallel execution. Unlike message-passing systems where performance is reduced by overhead taken for copying and queuing, shared memory offers direct access that can optimize performance, especially in time-critical systems. As operations in an RTOS are usually of varying priorities and urgency of execution, the utilization of shared memory has the benefit of encouraging responsiveness and reduced latency, critical features in real-time systems. Its utilization, however, has to utilize highly disciplined synchronization techniques to preclude race conditions and corruption of data, which undermine system reliability. Shared memory has special advantages but also excels when it comes to synchronization and conflicts of resources.

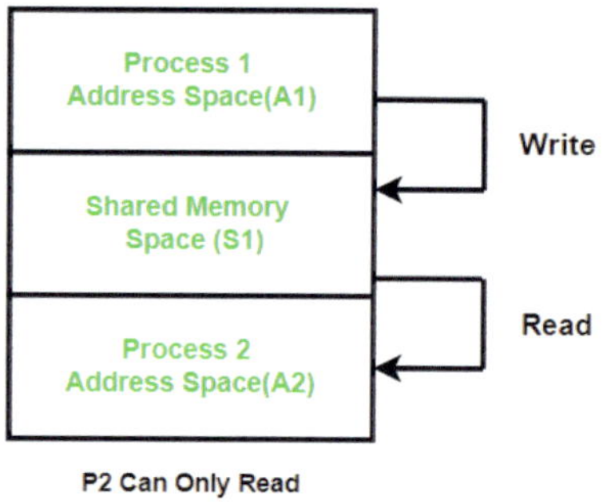

Figure 5.3. *Working of shared memory.*

Source: https://www.geeksforgeeks.org/computer-organization-architecture/what-is-a-shared-memory/.

Timing analysis is made difficult in multicore processor systems by the potential for interference across cores due to multiple cores sharing resources. That makes access harder and requires the presence of sophisticated arbitration policies and scheduling procedures to enable access elegantly without jeopardizing system performance. It is necessary to develop middleware frameworks that will offer predictability and timeliness for high-integrity systems, particularly those with high real-time demands (Alfaro et al., 2008). Good synchronization mechanisms, such as semaphores and mutexes, must be utilized together with shared memory to avoid concurrent access in order to safeguard the data consistency and system behavior. Besides, hardware architectures also play a significant role in deploying shared memory paradigms in RTOS. Increased use of multicore processors has led to new approaches, such as software-based Time Division Multiple Access (TDMA) arbitration, which can effectively control access to common memory resources. These approaches aim to control inter-core interference through the introduction of strict timing constraints and hence enhance overall system performance (Cornaglia et al., 2015). As shared memory schemes are augmented by better arbitration techniques, they can cope with the growing demands of safety-critical systems—providing simultaneous execution for high-priority tasks and ensuring uniform access to shared data. Thus, utilizing shared memory in the case of an RTOS needs ongoing research and development to balance performance gain with the inherent intricacies of synchronization and resource management (Figure 5.3).

5.1.3. Signals and Events

In RTOS, handling of event and signal is paramount to offering effective inter-task communication and synchronization. Signals serve as events that notify particular events or state changes to tasks, while events regulate how multiple tasks are executed concurrently. This practice is particularly crucial in those applications where prompt reaction is important, such as wireless sensor networks (WSN). Through the use of such synchronization methods, tasks can be kept responsive and share resources effectively, ensuring the highest performance as well as the lowest latency. Proper handling of events and signals dramatically lessens the difficulty of creating real-time applications and offers a systematic method of task management that meets the rigorous demands of RTOS environments (Ulianko et al., 2012). Furthermore, events and signals enable asynchronous inter-task communication, in which tasks can run without blocking one another. The system enables various tasks to process data or perform computations concurrently, therefore improving throughput and resource usage efficiency. For example, in wireless sensor networks for the Internet of Things (IoT), tasks mostly need to communicate with various actuators and sensors. The ability to notify an event in advance allows the system to initiate the necessary response in a different task so that the data transfer is synchronized and smooth. This capability is particularly beneficial in real-time data analysis-based applications and decision-making with immediate responses, where uncoordinated behavior can generate performance bottlenecks or data loss during mission-critical operations (Roussel et al., 2015). Employing powerful signaling mechanisms in RTOS environments allows more efficiency and reliability in task-to-task communication. Employing characteristics such as priority signaling, which ensures critical priorities to be addressed right away, minimizing response times for mission-critical systems. Further, more recent RTOS feature other functionalities like the use of multiple hardware timers concurrently, which further enhance the synchronization among tasks in application-intensive programs. This is particularly important in application with precise timing, e.g., multi-sensor applications in a wireless communication environment. By investing in such sophisticated signaling and event management techniques, developers are able to create more resilient and dynamic systems capable of coping with the challenges posed by the dynamic nature of the environments encountered in IoT systems (Roussel et al., 2015; Ulianko et al., 2012).

5.2. SYNCHRONIZATION MECHANISMS

Effective synchronization facilities are needed in RTOS to ensure smooth operation of tasks without data inconsistency or conflicts. Synchronization facilities ensure orderly access to common resources, which is crucial in a scenario where multiple tasks execute concurrently. Some of the old mechanisms of synchronization are binary semaphores, mutexes, and message queues, and they offer control over access and communication between tasks. Semaphores, for instance, are utilized to signal task readiness or resource availability such that race conditions cannot lead to uncontrollable action.

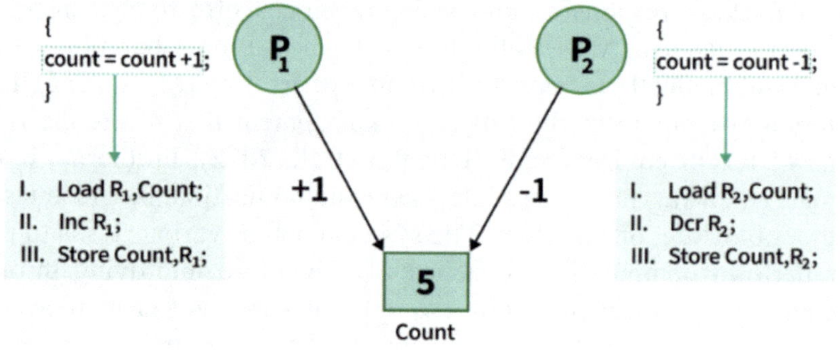

Figure 5.4. *Process synchronization.*

Source: https://www.geeksforgeeks.org/operating-systems/introduction-of-process-synchronization/.

In these cases, employing effective synchronization is of paramount importance to guarantee system responsiveness and reliability, particularly where tasks must have strict timing common with real-time applications. Additionally, synchronization mechanisms' design must consider distributed systems complexities observed in various operating systems. Inefficient synchronization protocols cause bottlenecks in performance by impeding effective inter-task communication. The Operating System Transport System Architecture (OSTSA) therefore provides an important framework for grouping synchronization components and their roles in distributed applications. By examining communication infrastructure considerations and computing infrastructure considerations, programmers are able to maximize the use of RTOS synchronization mechanisms. For instance, utilizing the OSTSA taxonomy, systems are able to ensure protocol processing tasks such as flow control and error detection are accomplished efficiently, thus optimizing real-time application performance across varying networking environments

(Schmidt et al., 1992) (Figure 5.4). In addition to traditional synchronization services, advanced capabilities such as process migration and checkpointing can be quite effective in enhancing the performance and reliability of RTOS. This can be seen in an example distributed operating system such as Amoeba, which offers a limited repertoire of kernel operations to support process management for process migration and state representation. Such an ability can guarantee tasks are capable of experiencing continuity as they are transferred from one computational environment to another. These features highlight the necessity of exact synchronization policy design to enable diverse operational needs while maximizing computational efficiency. As the nature of distributed systems continues to evolve, the incorporation of tunable synchronization tools will be critical to enable robust inter-task communication and to guarantee that the intricacies of real-time applications are addressed adequately (Mullender et al., 1987).

5.2.1. Mutexes

In RTOS, coordination of tasks is a must for the stability and performance of the system. Mutexes or mutual exclusions are one of the fundamental synchronization primitives constructed to synchronize concurrent access to common resources by different tasks. Mutexes prevent race conditions because they permit access to a shared resource by only one task at any given time, thus preventing the risk of corruption of data and unpredictability in task execution. These mechanisms are particularly critical in highly inter-task communicating systems, where multiple concurrent access to shared data structures can lead to inconsistencies. Adept utilization of mutexes can thus render RTOS applications more predictable and reliable, allowing system designers to develop responsive and fault-tolerant systems. While applying mutexes within an RTOS, the developers must make various compromises between performance and complexity. Although mutexes are a necessary protection against data corruption, using mutexes can add overhead and affect system responsiveness (Figure 5.5).

Also, improper use of mutexes can lead to priority inversion, where lower-priority tasks are holding a mutex belonging to higher-priority tasks and hence causing latency and missed deadlines. To counter such issues, advanced mechanisms like priority inheritance algorithms can be employed, where the priority of the task that is holding the mutex is increased temporarily until release, thereby reducing the likelihood of priority-related issues. Such strategies highlight the importance of efficient design and analysis while applying mutexes in an RTOS, leading to successful inter-task communication and synchronization patterns. Moreover, practice in mutex management in RTOS has changed with growing embedded system complexity, particularly in wireless sensor network application. As with the examples of such frameworks as EnergyMicro Gecko, which target minimizing low-energy usage but allowing sophisticated inter-task communications, efficient mutex usage assumes priority. In application environments where tasks are likely to communicate with one another through shared data structures or remote procedure calls, system throughput and reliability may depend upon the performance of mutexes. Thus, the integration of robust mutex strategies, along with techniques for measuring system performance metrics, allows developers to create RTOS that not only can be effective but also can meet the rigorous demands of current applications, ensuring consistent performance efficiency under various conditions (Ulianko et al., 2012; Yan et al., 2017).

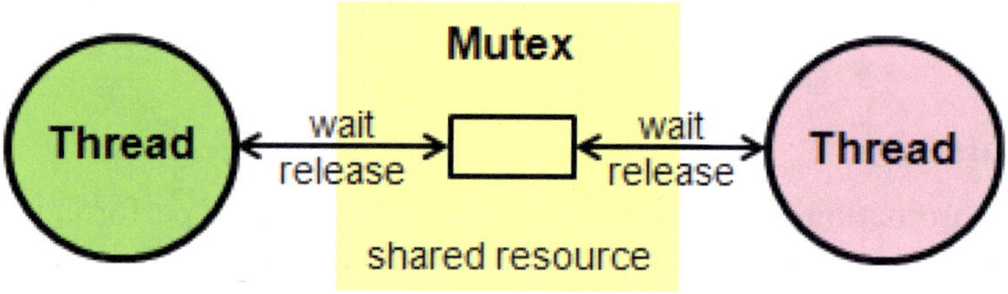

Figure 5.5. *Mutex is used to synchronize the execution of threads.*

Source: https://os.mbed.com/handbook/RTOS.

5.2.2. Semaphores

In the case of RTOS, semaphores play a key role in inter-task communication and synchronization. Inter-task synchronization facilities are essential to provide control over access to shared resources among concurrent tasks in a multitasking system. Basically, semaphores are signaling devices through which tasks can signal their status—availability or non-availability of a resource or occurrence of an event. By utilizing semaphores, system designers can prevent race conditions and have only a single task, at any time, executing in pieces of critical code. This type of control not only enhances the dependability of the systems but also ensures maximum performance through avoiding resource contention. Semaphores are realized ranging from basic binary ones to complex counting semaphores based on the usage scenario demanded by specific systems. Besides, the efficiency of semaphores in an RTOS environment can be increased even more by the presence of an Operating System Abstraction Layer (OSAL). This will make it easier to integrate semaphores on different RTOS platforms, with the outcome being increased portability and flexibility.

For instance, as identified in recent research, an execution environment can employ semaphores portable across OSes, e.g., Free RTOS or Zephyros, without binding the semaphore logic to the host OS. Not only does this abstraction ease the development process but also assist with clean separation between system and application-level implementations (Figure 5.6).

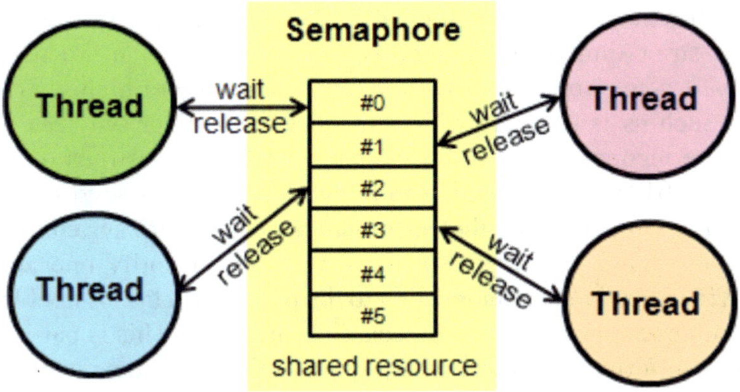

Figure 5.6. *Semaphores play a pivotal role in facilitating inter-task communication and synchronization.*

Source: https://os.mbed.com/handbook/RTOS.

Hence, developers can focus on the optimization of the application's performance while gaining the benefit of robust synchronization primitives provided by the RTOS. In practice, the deployment of semaphores in reality involves careful consideration of their binary or counting types based on the needs of the tasks at hand. For example, in an event-driven OS-based wireless sensor network, semaphores can effectively minimize energy consumption without disrupting concurrent data transmission. Selecting the appropriate semaphore type may directly impact the efficiency of application execution in systems operating under strict energy constraints, such as with EnergyMicro Gecko microcontrollers integration. With task efficient yielding and accessing shared resources via semaphores, developers can significantly improve overall system response and performance. Such meticulous design features underscore the central importance of semaphores in driving inter-task synchronization and communication in RTOS designs (Chalokh et al., 2018; Ulianko et al., 2012).

5.2.3. Monitors

Application of monitors in RTOS is critical in ensuring efficient synchronization as well as inter-task communication. A monitor is a synchronization primitive at the high level that encapsulates shared data and procedures that operate on it, allowing safer access to resources by concurrent tasks. Not only does this design pattern organize access to shared information but also makes multi-threading easier through abstraction of the complexity associated with locking. When RTOS tasks talk to one another, monitors allow the coordination necessary to prevent race conditions and create mutual exclusion, particularly where there must be very strict timing and reliability. These functions make monitors an essential part when coming up with systems that require highly stringent performance, such as is the case with embedded systems or wireless sensor networks, where inconsistency within the data can have disastrous outcomes (Ulianko et al., 2012). Besides acting to regulate access to shared resources, monitors also help in enhancing the performance of the entire system through minimizing block time for tasks. By allowing tasks to notify one another, monitors provide effective communication to the point that a task is not blocked for longer than necessary in hopes of resource availability. This is particularly important in event-driven systems, where good timing and context switching are of the most critical importance. Optimization of task execution and use of resources are extremely valuable benefits of monitors, particularly when applications get more complex. For example, in wireless sensor networks based on RTOS, monitors can assist in controlling data processing and collection operations between groups of sensors, leading to improved system efficiency and responsiveness in general (Li et al., 2013) (Figure 5.7).

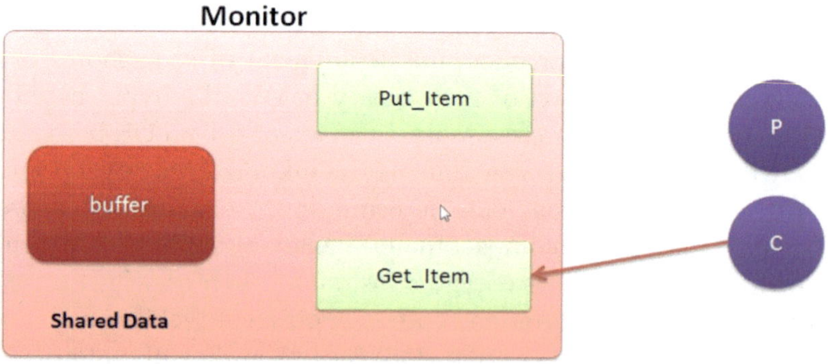

Figure 5.7. *Monitors in synchronization.*

Source: https://i.ytimg.com/vi/_5sbBARRpws/maxresdefault.jpg.

Further, the utilization of monitors in an RTOS environment has the potential to heavily influence the systems design choices, especially regarding reliability and safety. As has briefly been discussed in the case of systems like Quest-V, task partitioning, and their interactions through monitored channels of communication facilitate greater fault tolerance. Each task can run in its own personal environment and be able to synchronize and communicate effectively with others without a good opportunity for adverse effects as a result of single points of failure. Monitors help in defining clear interfaces and protocols for task communication, a necessary feature in real-time systems where timing and sequence of execution are of utmost significance. As the demand for more powerful and sophisticated real-time applications grows, the advantages offered by using monitor-based synchronization methods will become more prominent in contributing to more stable and effective RTOS architectures (Li et al., 2013).

5.3. CHALLENGES IN INTER-TASK COMMUNICATION

The domain of RTOS is burdened with specific challenges for inter-task communication, especially when tasks are subject to precise synchronization and coordination. This is typically added to by ensuring performance within the system and preventing communication bottlenecks. Since tasks in an RTOS environment are executed in parallel, the effectiveness of communication protocols is paramount to the overall system effectiveness. Inadequate design of inter-task communication channels may lead to latency and therefore missed deadlines and ineffective use of resources. Effective methods to counteract communication overhead, such as effective scheduling algorithms, are essential in minimizing response times but at the same time may lead to variability of access times and risk of race conditions between tasks, contributing to the intricacies of reliability for real-time. In addition, compromise between communication between tasks and resource allocation is increasingly becoming essential. On the one hand, methods for minimizing the overhead of scheduling, for example, via the utilization of hardware schedulers, can significantly reduce the overhead of scheduling, as noted in the achievements outlined by Bergmann et al. (2015). These resource solutions, while effective in minimizing delays, also lead to increased usage of resources, thus indirectly elevating the complexity of handling sparse system resources in an embedded system. Therefore, attaining this balance requires sophisticated resource management policies that extend to both computational as well as communication resources and meet real-time constraints for the system without compromising performance. For more advanced applications, say those that span Wireless Sensor Networks (WSNs), the need for effective inter-task communication grows. Quality of service and real-time applications possess rigorous resource management mechanisms that account for both communication needs and computational complexity. According to Chitnis et al. (2009), the application of simulation tools will assist in checking designs for conformance to real-time specifications. Such models are capable of representing the complexities of inter-task communications so that potential performance bottlenecks can be identified before deployment. Inter-task communication problems hence necessitate a multi-faceted insight into resource management, multitasking ability, and the inherent limitations of real-time requirements to be successful in RTOS environments.

5.3.1. Deadlock Situations

In RTOS, deadlock conditions bring a lot of trouble to inter-task communication and synchronization. Deadlock occurs when a group of tasks has come to a state of indefinite waiting for resources owned by one another, leading to system hang, ultimately paralyzing computational effectiveness. The nature of such deadlocks is higher in RTOS environments with tight timing and scarcity of resources. Tasks compete for limited resources, and therefore effective resource allocation policies are necessary. When a task is unable to proceed due to unavailable resources, it not only fails to execute but can also trigger cascading effects that lead to more pervasive system failures, degrading overall system performance in a ripple-like manner.

Additionally, the process of deadlock scenarios is more comprehensible if one explores the techniques followed for the synchronization of tasks in RTOS. Various mechanisms, such as priority-based scheduling and lock mechanisms, can be employed to avoid the occurrence of deadlocks. Such approaches involve inter-task communication protocols to refrain from allowing tasks to access a common resource in a way that would leave them in a deadlock state. CSP (communicating sequential processes) algebra lies at the core of modeling interactions like this, allowing communication and synchronization issues in distributed systems to be easier to solve (Broenink et al., 2002).

By employing CSP-based libraries, interactions between tasks can be more clearly defined, allowing for smoother execution paths and fewer instances of deadlocks. In addition to preventing deadlock situations, advances in programming paradigms bring forth new ideas that are thread safe and efficient. Models of execution like SCOOP (simple concurrent object-oriented programming) are brought forth to help developers by implementing data race freedom with concurrent execution. These advancements not only facilitate novel syntax and semantics leading to improved coding standards but significantly enhance performance, at times even 15-fold improvement compared to traditional models. Further, by removing certain types of deadlocks through the application of structured programming methods, such solutions pave the way for more robust inter-task communication and synchronization in RTOS (Meyer et al., 2015). These innovations assist in guaranteeing that systems requiring responses in real-time continue to improve without allowing the complexities caused by potential deadlock conditions (Figure 5.8).

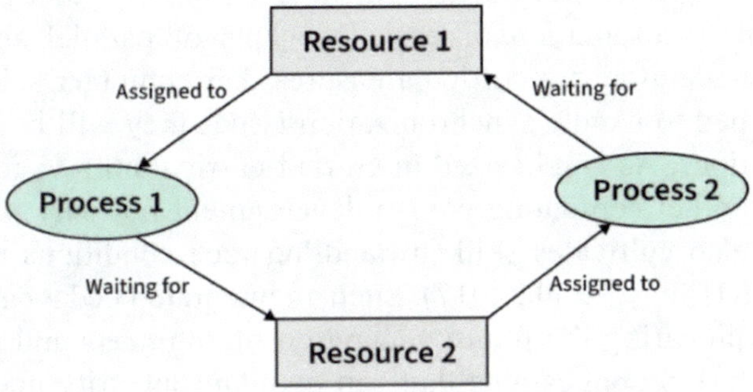

Figure 5.8. *Deadlock occurs in the operating system.*

Source: https://www.geeksforgeeks.org/operating-systems/introduction-of-deadlock-in-operating-system/.

5.3.2. Race Conditions

Race conditions are a principal area of concern in the case of RTOS, particularly in terms of synchronization and inter-task communication. A race condition arises when more than one task acts upon a shared resource in a concurrent manner, leading to non-deterministic behavior in terms of the timing of their incidence. In an RTOS, wherein tasks are usually prioritized based upon timing-critical requirements, the possibility for race conditions grows exponentially. Thus, this indeterminacy can undermine system stability and performance and result in functionalities that can behave in a bizarre manner. The nuances of race conditions need to be appreciated, since developers have to implement strong synchronization methodologies so that such issues do not lose focus on overall system integrity. Race conditions can be alleviated by applying proper synchronization techniques that enable tasks to access common resources in a controlled manner. Techniques such as mutexes, semaphores, and message queues are applied in implementing exclusivity and managing the access timing correctly. For example, using mutexes, a task could acquire a resource under lock while it is being used so that other tasks cannot use the resource simultaneously. This aligns with principles in the backdrop of parallel and distributed computing, in which systems are designed so that distributed components have equal communications and interactions, as reported in the progress of the PRISM C++ library (Al-Nayeem et al., 2011). Therefore, effective synchronization techniques are not merely theoretical ideas; they are tangible necessities of real-world implementation within the arena of RTOS. A sound comprehension of race conditions and their potential effects encourage more resilient system design. Training and curriculum development on this front becomes very important. Incorporation of basic concepts of parallel and distributed computing in undergraduate curricula ensures that computer science students are well-equipped to handle synchronization issues they will be working with in real applications. As emphasized in current curriculum revisions, computer systems and parallel computing course development not only provides depth in theory but also cultivates skill in handling race conditions and inter-task communication (Danner et al., 2017). Such an integrated pedagogical approach is essential in preparing the future generation of engineers and developers to design robust RTOS applications that can maintain integrity upon concurrent execution (Figure 5.9).

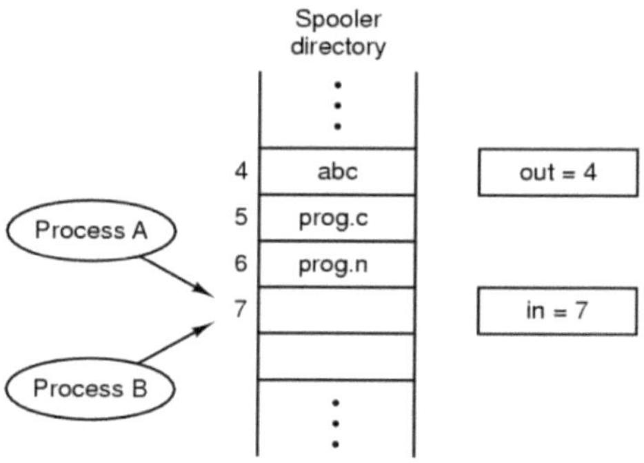

Figure 5.9. *Race conditions.*

Source: https://external-content.duckduckgo.com/iu/?u=https%3A%2F %2Fimage3.slideserve.com%2F5709752%2Finterprocess-communication-race-conditions-l.jpg&f=1&nofb=1&ipt=b5edec2255aad432dbc7db213af593a40649ec113302c51b678088a617ec909a.

5.3.3. Priority Inversion

Within the context of RTOS, the problem of priority inversion is a significant bottleneck to inter-task communication and synchronization. Priority inversion happens when a low-priority task gains access to a resource utilized by a high-priority task, causing the latter to yield to intermediate-priority tasks, thereby increasing response times. The situation can significantly disrupt the deterministic nature common in real-time systems, thereby undermining their dependability. Because real-time tasks are generally employed for important operations—e.g., in automotive or aircraft environments—reducing the dangers of priority inversion is essential in system integrity maintenance and timely task completion. Solutions like priority inheritance protocols have been proposed to address this issue, where a lower-priority task assumes temporarily the higher priority of the served task, thus providing greater system responsiveness. The integration of priority inversion with the facilities for inter-task communication further complicates the design of RTOS. Inter-task communication is typically managed by shared resources, which are typically guarded by locks or semaphores. A scenario where a high-priority task must wait for the shared resources held by a low-priority task can lead to a domino effect of inefficiencies.

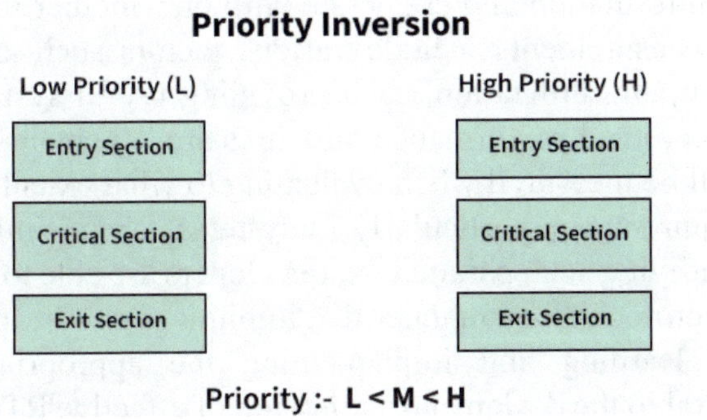

Figure 5.10. *Priority inversion.*

Source: https://media.geeksforgeeks.org/wp-content/uploads/20250113144309727353/priority_inversion.webp.

This not only results in poor system performance but may also jeopardize timely completion of critical operations. In these systems, there is a need to use robust synchronization mechanisms. For example, the use of real-time communication middleware, specifically designed for high-integrity systems, can assist in ensuring more predictable message passing, thereby reducing the likelihood of priority inversion conditions. While systems become more complex in their design to live up to Industry 4.0 standards, addressing these communication-dependent problems will be crucial to ensuring operational dependability and performance. Successful solutions to deal with priority inversion must be devised and deployed based on comprehending the particular requirements of real-time applications. A multidisciplinary solution incorporating input from scheduling theory as well as high-integrity system design needs to be ensured to develop a model for dealing with this prevalent issue. The improvement of communication protocols that support timely completion of tasks along with advanced resource management techniques has a dramatic decrease in the impact of priority inversion. Moreover, as outlined in communication paradigms for safety-critical systems research, middleware with predictability and timeliness is essential when implementing system robustness in priority inversion adversity (Alfaro et al., 2008). With sophisticated software architectures emerging, e.g., those of products like Zerynth VM, developing flexible RTOS configurations can assist in injecting the degree of flexibility needed in order to address evolving market needs as well as address the core problem of priority inversion (Figure 5.10).

5.4. PERFORMANCE METRICS

For RTOS, performance measurements are critical measures of how efficiently tasks exchange information and cooperate with one another in a multi-tasking system. These measurements include various factors such as task run time, delay, throughput, and utilization, each providing useful system performance information. Theoretical performance measures are benchmarks against which performance will be measured when evaluating to what extent an RTOS meets its real-time requirements, particularly in systems where timing is extremely critical. By quantifying such parameters, developers are able to adjust inter-task communication protocols in a manner that minimizes overhead and maximizes efficacy. Thus, learning and implementing the appropriate performance measures is central to the design and evaluation of effective RTOS applications, striking a balance between response requirements and computation requirements within varying environments (N/A, 2025). Complementing the intricacy of performance measures in RTOS is the need to make real-time systems comply with Quality of Service (QoS) parameters, which mandate predictable performance across varied operating conditions. As new-age applications like Wireless Sensor Networks (WSNs), where communication and computation are integrated, arise, it becomes absolutely essential to employ extensive resource management methods. This is an acknowledgment of the significance of performance metrics to not only monitor communication efficiency but also to quantify the computational load that the system is subject to. The relevant research indicates that tools such as RTNS for simulation possess the potential to unearth such performance parameters by simulating both the communication and CPU operations within the framework of the RTOS paradigm (Chitnis et al., 2009). As a result, utilizing these measures more effectively facilitates an understanding of system dynamics to enable developers to better coordinate inter-task communication with real-time requirements. Additionally, the use of good performance measures can lead to significant improvements to system reliability and responsiveness. In applications requiring timely decision, such as industrial automation or process control, performance measures can become important in predicting and avoiding possible bottlenecks before their exacerbation to catastrophic failure. With continuous observation of task execution and communication intervals, developers can provide timely corrections to task scheduling and allocation. These pre-emptive steps are especially important in concurrent tasks where synchronization failures can lead to propagating failures. The ongoing monitoring of these metrics facilitates iterative design that not only improves task interaction but also maximizes the overall system robustness in real-time systems, thus underlining the pivotal role played by performance metrics in effective operation of RTOS (N/A, 2025).

5.4.1. Latency

In RTOS, inter-task communication and synchronization are determined by latency. Latency, which is the duration between initiating a command and its execution, directly affects an RTOSs ability to meet hard timing requirements. Latency may result from task scheduling overhead, context switching, as well as data transfer duration between tasks. Therefore, reducing latency is critical in applications where response time is critical, e.g., in wireless sensor networks or embedded systems. By properly controlling latency, RTOS can provide for tasks being carried out in a predictable and consistent manner, thereby providing synchronization between parallel processes, and enhancing the general performance of the system. One of the current challenges in overcoming latency within an RTOS context is to balance accuracy with effectiveness. As noted in current debate, the precision of time management directly relates to an RTOSs ability to handle determinism for embedded systems. The higher the precision timing devices, such as periodic interrupt services, the more responsive the RTOS becomes but loads the CPU heavily, thus reducing system performance as a whole. This is a paradox where the need for rapid task execution has to be balanced against the resources available. It is important that developers use a strategic approach in developing systems with minimum latency while being meticulous in taking resource constraint and overall system throughput into consideration, in order to obtain the optimal balance such that the demands of RT applications are met. Software and hardware advancements have attempted to address the latency problems in RTOS. Use of a real-time kernel, such as Xenomai, combined with enhanced time management by using hardware alternatives can take the latency down significantly. New research indicates the usage of Field Programmable Gate Arrays (FPGAs) to shift time management tasks away from the CPU and decrease processor overload and enhance latency outcomes. Such platforms support more efficient processing ability allocation, allowing critical functions to execute with lesser delays, thus enhancing inter-task communication integrity. These developments indicate a promising way forward for future research into RTOS design, eventually producing more fault-tolerant systems that are capable of fulfilling the stringent demands of real-time applications (Boukhobza et al., 2012; Ulianko et al., 2012) (Figure 5.11).

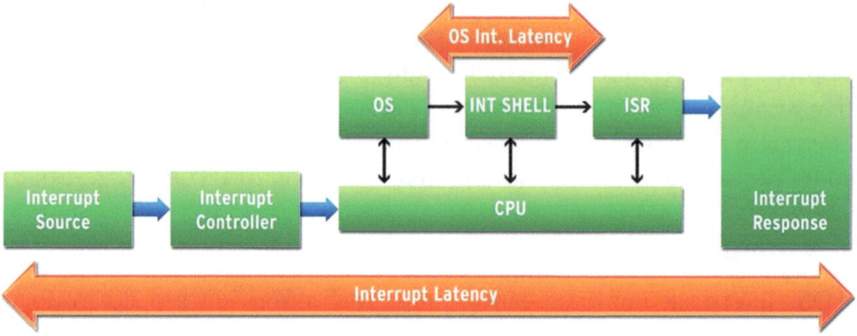

Figure 5.11. *Measuring interrupt latency.*

Source: https://blogs.sw.siemens.com/wp-content/uploads/sites/51/2012/06/il.jpg.

5.4.2. Throughput

Throughput, a highly critical metric in the evaluation of RTOS, is the amount of work performed in an interval of time. This performance measure is crucial to understanding mechanisms of inter-task communication and task management effectiveness in an RTOS. High throughput is particularly of topmost concern in cases where tasks are competing for limited processing resources since it ultimately determines the capability of the systems to meet real-time deadlines. As complexity of tasks increases, best throughput demands an extremely strong synchronization policy that can overcome contention and latency between competing tasks. Emphasizing throughput guarantees that the system would be capable of sustaining variability in applications from light control processes to heavy computations, highlighting the primary aim of efficient inter-task communication in system performance. Between throughput and synchronization policies, things are complicated in an RTOS environment. For instance, excessive reliance on locking can lead to bottlenecks that severely degrade throughput. Designers therefore have to meticulously choose the primitives employed for synchronization within the system. Techniques such as message passing, semaphores, and event flags can enhance throughput by restricting the duration tasks spend waiting for access to shared resources. Moreover, the use of advanced techniques such as Heterogeneous Transactional Memory (HeTM) can mask and encapsulate the memory management complexities and minimize intra- and inter-device synchronization delays, thus allowing for greater throughput in heterogeneous systems (Castro et al., 2019) (Figure 5.12).

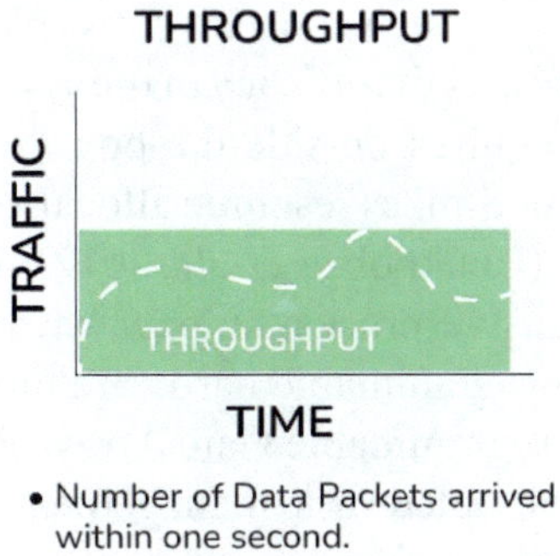

Figure 5.12. *High throughput is particularly crucial in scenarios in which multiple tasks vie for limited processing resources.*

*Source:*https://media.geeksforgeeks.org/wp-content/uploads/20240205152604/Throughput-vs-Latency.webp.

Optimization of such synchronization techniques is essential to generating scenarios under which tasks can be executed simultaneously without hindering each other's performance. In military and critical applications, in which high throughput is a requirement as well as hard real-time performance, specific architectures have been developed to optimize these attributes. The Army Fault Tolerant Architecture (AFTA) is one such initiative, as it is specifically designed to meet stringent computational throughput and input/output requirements (Alger et al., 2025). AFTAs modular design supports dependable and effective inter-task communication, which is critical for the successful execution of integrated mission systems. Throughput versus reliability optimization in such designs enables the hard real-time requirements of various applications to be satisfied without degrading performance or system integrity. As environments grow more complex with the advent of new computing technologies, throughput continues to be at the forefront of developing and verifying efficient RTOS designs.

5.4.3. Resource Utilization

Efficient use of resources in RTOS is essential in order to maintain performance and meet hard timing constraints in embedded applications. CPU scheduling and resource optimization becomes essential under hard real-time conditions. The efficiency and modularity of embedded operating systems such as Embedded Linux with real-time kernel such as Xenomai support the high deterministic response needed for safety-critical applications. Better time precision, driven by timely interrupt services from software, is critical to improving the overall responsiveness of the system. Such constant stress placed on the CPU, however, incurs overhead and diminishes the efficacy of the system by default. Overcoming challenges of this type requires outside-the-box thinking that maximizes the capacity of hardware and optimizes resource allocation while ensuring deadlines reliably and at little cost (Boukhobza et al., 2012). In the interest of reducing dependency on CPU-intensive processes, new advances suggest shifting time management services to programmable hardware modules. Incorporating these capabilities into a Field Programmable Gate Array (FPGA) not only eases CPU load but also offers unparalleled task management flexibility. This hardware approach ensures that timing-critical services do not compromise processing efficiency but instead enhance it by partitioning tasks across dedicated channels.

Through leveraging FPGA technologies, RTOS becomes more precise and contains less scheduling overhead such that it allows the central processor to focus its time on time-critical processes while it performs other operations better. This architectural shift is an essential one in real-time systems to improve resource usage optimization, thus leading to improved overall system performance in embedded environments (Boukhobza et al., 2012). Furthermore, the availability of hardware schedulers has been demonstrated to raise the resource management capabilities of soft-core processor systems considerably. Through such schedulers, many scheduling algorithms such as time-sliced priority scheduling and Least Slack Time, can be supported that offer increasingly sophisticated levels of control of task execution.

By supporting very low-overhead scheduling more than 1,000 clock cycles in some instances, these hardware solutions actually increase system utilization limits by up to 19.2%. In addition, hardware transitions from software scheduling decrease operation jitter by orders of magnitude, making task execution more predictable. Through the inclusion of such hardware solutions in RTOS implementations, developers are able to find a fine balance between resource allocation, scheduling of tasks, and performance demands and thereby create an ecosystem where resource usage is optimized without any compromise on system reliability.

5.5. TOOLS AND TECHNIQUES FOR IMPLEMENTATION

Inter-task communication and synchronization as applied in RTOS demand the utilization of robust tools and methods that guarantee coherence of concurrent activities. Among the most significant innovations in this area is the TASTE toolset, a spin-off of issues that accompany real-time software development. TASTE was originally designed to address satellite flight software but has since found applications in other embedded systems with similar characteristics. Its design process takes into consideration the heterogeneity of real-time systems and encourages an approach that integrates existing technologies, such as Simulink, SDL, and Ada. The confluence enables developers to generate homogeneous software architectures that can be executed directly on physical targets, simplifying the implementation step in an RTOS environment (Conquet et al., 2010). Another essential field in the tools and techniques of implementation is the management of mixed-criticality tasks in real-time systems. The mixed-criticality computation model is gaining broader application due to its potential to hold critical tasks to their functional integrity without sacrificing the consumption of resources. The model needs rigorous design methods where task isolation on both temporal and spatial domains becomes imperative to avoid potential failures. Fixed-priority algorithms are typically used under this model to schedule the order of execution of tasks based on their criticality level. Virtualization techniques have evolved as a cornerstone for building software architectures for implementing this model with improved isolation and dependable management of tasks. Hence, such methods offer an all-embracing perspective towards the implementation of effective communication and synchronization in RTOS environments (Gupta et al., 2018). The integration of advanced tools for task communication and synchronization is crucial in a bid to enhance the execution effectiveness of RTOS. The integration of tools such as the TASTE toolset, in conjunction with methodologies for mixed-criticality systems, not only eases the development process but also addresses resource allocation as well as task-priority issues. The structured implementation of these tools guarantees enhanced coordination of tasks, leading to enhanced performance of real-time systems. Besides, with increasing complexity of embedded systems, the necessity for such tools takes on increasingly supreme status. With a combination of tried methodology and new tools, programmers can ensure that inter-task communication and synchronization are implemented correctly, paving the way for efficient and dependable real-time systems that meet stringent operational needs (Conquet et al., 2010; Sinha et al., 2018).

5.5.1. RTOS Development Environments

The development of RTOS is increasingly influenced by the needs of modern applications, particularly in the context of Internet of Things (IoT) and Industry 4.0. RTOS operating environments must provide robust inter-task communication and synchronization services that are instrumental in handling the complexity associated with the concurrent execution of tasks. With increasing intelligent and networked objects with advancements in systems, the demand for high performance, flexibility, and low latency is necessitated. Creative solutions from platforms and tools, such as Zerynth, meet these needs. By leveraging the capability of layering architecture, Zerynth facilitates seamless integration into various hardware platforms and RTOS, thereby supporting interoperability and scalability demanded by current development environments (Ahmad et al., 2017). Thus, these environments not only enable development with rapid execution cycles but also allow developers to focus more on functionality and less on underlying subtleties. The most characteristic aspect of RTOS development environments is that they can abstract the dependency on hardware, thereby allowing developers to develop applications more easily without deep system-specific issues. Hardware Abstraction Layer (HAL) in platforms like Zerynth provides essential channels of communication with different microcontroller units (MCUs) while maintaining the independence of the RTOS.

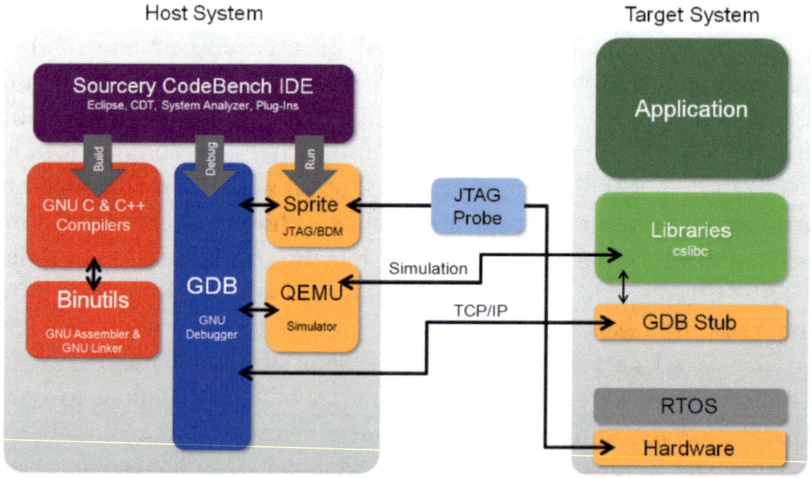

Figure 5.13. *Embedded software development tools.*

Source: https://blogs.sw.siemens.com/wp-content/uploads/sites/51/2015/03/Bare-Metal-development-environment.png?ste_sid=505ecd94885893262f5cb6d27f91d2cf.

Abstraction enables the programmers to concentrate on application layer components, employing languages like Python or hybrid C/Python that do not imply lengthy handling of the RTOSs functioning principles. Consequently, developers can rapidly prototype and configure IoT applications, drastically reducing time-to-market. This layered software architecture significantly increases productivity and enhances the performance of inter-task communication and synchronization across various RTOS environments (N/A, 2025). With the drive of industries towards automation, these flexible environments will play a vital role in the success of embedded systems. In general, the evolution of RTOS development environments illustrates the all-crucial intersection of technological advancements and efficient programming methods. With the capacity to modularize behavior through abstraction layers, these platforms are tailored to meet the demands of modern applications, specifically in how they communicate and synchronize between tasks. The introduction of frameworks like the Zerynth Virtual Machine allows developers to enjoy the flexibility they require to transcend the conventional constraints of hardware variability and software interoperability. By enabling seamless portability between various RTOS choices, such as FreeRTOS, it is simpler to add application features while optimizing performance (Ahmad et al., 2017). Overall, as the programmers struggle through the intricacies of RTOS systems, adopting such cutting-edge environments can greatly improve the reliability and performance of their applications, particularly in more integrated ecosystems (Figure 5.13).

5.5.2. Debugging Tools

In RTOS, effective debuggers are pillar components that ensure robust inter-task synchronization and communication. They facilitate the identification and repair of errors in complex, concurrent environments where multiple tasks execute together in parallel. For the programmer battling with the complexity of RTOS, nondeterminism in task interaction introduces the challenges, making bugs hard to pursue. Good debuggers provide essential features such as real-time observation, logging, and visualization support that enhance task state understanding as well as knowledge about their transitions. Using these facilities, developers are able to diagnose synchronization errors, find race conditions, and analyze communication failures among tasks and hence result in a fault-tolerant application design later on. Moreover, debugging operations are facilitated more effectively by the inclusion of persistent checkpoints to allow developers to transfer sensor network applications from simulated testbeds to real testbeds. This recursive method alleviates the usual challenges of using the transition from simulation to testbed, such as application failure demanding massive debugging operations. Through the use of debug tools with features of checkpointing, engineers can replicate settings of high fidelity, thereby conserve iterative and time-intensive effort, and enhance the reliability of programs in the real world. This technology bridges the gap between the nonintrusiveness of simulations and the realism of physical debugging environments, offering a balance between simulated precision and real-world conditions (Dunkels et al., 2009) (Figure 5.14).

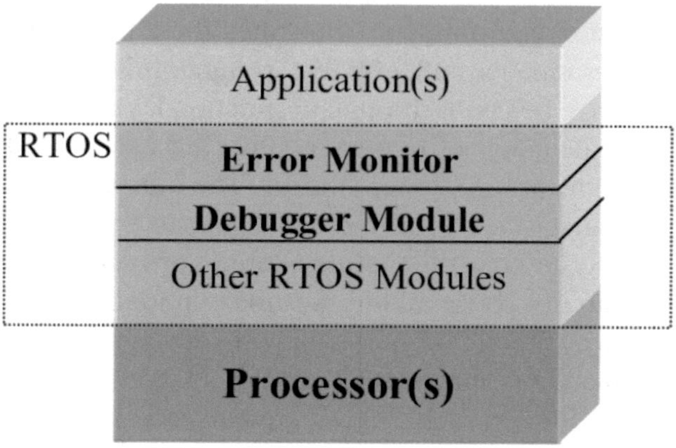

Figure 5.14. *The debugger RTOS structure and the application(s) reside on the target system. The debugger software is entirely within the RTOS code and runs on the target processor.*

Source: https://www.researchgate.net/figure/Debugger-RTOS-structure-and-the-applications-reside-on-the-target-system-The-debugger_fig2_3916166.

The ongoing transition to multicore and MPSoC system architecture underscores the relevance of sophisticated debugging aids that are tailored to deal with software parallelism. The traditional programming models that are rooted in sequential processing become increasingly less appropriate given the sophistication and performance requirements of modern embedded systems. Their task now requires them to adopt new methods that not only maximize the use of available hardware resources but also ensure parallel software fault-free construction. With the discussion around MPSoC programming challenges still refining, it can clearly be seen that debugging tools applied must also enhance to provide frameworks with the capability to deal with new concurrent programming models (Bekooij et al., 2009). This shift targets a software development methodology that is based on pragmatism, where existing certified code deployed can be adapted in phases to meet increasing architectural demands. The future of debugging tools finally becomes critical to the realization of the full capabilities of RTOS environments.

5.5.3. Performance Analysis Tools

In the optimization of inter-task communication and synchronization in RTOS, the inclusion of performance analysis tools is immensely crucial. These enable developers to grasp how a system behaves under varying levels of workload, which is crucial to ensuring that tasks will achieve their timing requirements without compromising the overall effectiveness of a system. Through latency, throughput, and CPU utilization measurement, performance analysis tools enable engineers to adjust scheduling policy or task priority dynamically. This flexibility ensures that high-priority tasks receive the number of resources needed to maintain real-time execution. Because RTOS programs have increasingly sophisticated interdependencies, performance analysis tools become even more important to detect bottlenecks and inefficiencies that could lead to delays in tasks or system failure. Hybrid simulation methodologies have emerged as a powerful tool for performance analysis in RTOS, particularly when dealing with the intricacies of task synchronization and communication. The capability to simulate various interactions through a combination of simulation technologies enables more comprehension of the way tasks interact with each other in real-time reality. This approach dissects challenging situations into an easily managed collection of components that can be examined individually prior to being combined. As with hybrid simulation software applied in the creation of Internet of Things ecosystems, such programs could be a vital component of comprehending completely how things co-act within a diverse task environment. The deployment of such simulations facilitates the strong performance analysis that can accommodate the dynamic nature of task interactions to provide enhanced resource management and scheduling efficiency of tasks in RTOS systems (D'Angelo et al., 2017). Furthermore, thc use of analytic models tailored for performance analysis is pivotal to guaranteeing reliable RTOS applications. AFTAs approach to performance analysis, for example, applies measures such as reliability, availability, and life cycle cost in attempting to create a general impression of system pcrformance (Alger et al., 2025). By employing such analytical models, developers can anticipate likely failure points and counteract inter-task communication and synchronization threats. Such proactive performance management enhances system reliability by analyzing common mode failures and identifying dependencies that may cause synchronization issues. In doing so, performance analysis software not only assists the existing task run time statistics but also directs long-term design decisions that ensure system stability and performance in real-time systems.

SUMMARY

In conclusion of the talk of inter-task communication and synchronization in RTOS, the role played by such operating systems in the proper execution of time-critical tasks is evident. Synchronization methods of an RTOS ensure that multiple tasks execute in a healthy manner without interfering with each other, thus maintaining the integrity as well as the reliability of real-time critical applications. By enabling inter-task communication, RTOS architectures permit real-time response necessary in such applications as automobile control or medical devices were speed and accuracy matter most. Not only does this performance-critical feature of RTOS, but it also enables scalability and flexibility required nowadays in embedded systems. In addition, the proper choice of an RTOS will have a staggering effect on inter-task communication efficiency. As put forward in recent discussions on wireless sensor networks, the selection of an RTOS would best be done according to the requirements of the target application, particularly in terms of energy efficiency and processing performance (Ulianko et al., 2012). As a case, low-power implementations of RTOS ensure longer device operation in far-flung locations, as well as appropriate communication protocols between distributed sensor nodes. The intrinsic advantages of using an RTOS in such applications bring into focus the importance of careful consideration when embedding such systems into embedded projects. Furthermore, advances in RTOS architecture, such as the utilization of real-time kernels, have shown a vast enhancement in handling time sensitivity as well as task execution predictability (Boukhobza et al., 2012). This innovation not only addresses the issue of timing constraints problems but also facilitates the design of systems that are more responsive and efficient in their nature. As the domain of embedded systems continues to expand, embracing the power of RTOS for inter-task communication will remain necessary. Eventually, the integration of solid task synchronization and sound communication protocols forms the cornerstone of revolutionary applications, guiding the real-time system capabilities into an increasingly complex technological landscape.

The intricate topology of communication and synchronization among tasks in RTOS is driven by different vital factors that enable consistent and effective operations. Underlying this dynamic is the need to observe strict adherence to functional requirements, as these define the operational parameters for communications systems in high-frequency environments. Analysis of the like requirements illustrates that effective communication protocols form the pillar of the RTOS, and the ability to execute tasks in parallel while meeting the stipulated deadlines. The ability to analyze in-depth conceptual design results in best proposals for improving communication effectiveness as well as minimizing latency in the system. Understanding these building blocks is crucial for the design of a sound RTOS that can deal with the complexities of several running processes with stringent timing constraints, in line with the need for preemptive response and sound design practice (Al-Kinani et al., 2025). One of the important aspects of inter-task synchronization is the organization of the RTOS, which must offer effective communication structures between tasks. The Quest-V infrastructure is a model of a modern means of achieving this goal with its new style of design as a chip-based distributed system. It is implemented through a number of sandbox kernels that operate in isolation, offering separate domains of processing without failure in one of the kernels impacting others. To this level of partitioning is essential for maintaining system integrity, for enabling real-time applications to continue operating uninterrupted because of failures in non-system components. Shared memory channels, properly managed by system monitors, facilitate efficient communication between sandboxes. This approach reveals the need for accurate planning and design while synchronizing task communication to avoid bottlenecks, hence providing optimal system performance in the context of an RTOS environment (Li et al., 2013). Also, synchronization among tasks in an RTOS relies on how the RTOS can effectively manage timing in different processing cores. In such environments as Quest-V, each sandbox executes with its own physical clocks independent of the others, highlighting the decentralized nature of event times. This property allows non-interdependent sandboxes to schedule and perform I/O independently of central hypervisor reliance, improving efficiency and responsiveness. Such strategies highlight the need for inter-task interaction not to interfere, hence maintaining system integrity. When it comes to inter-task communication, one finds that precise boundaries on interactions, without a global scheduler, need to be set so that predictable performance can be achieved All these findings in combination illustrate that a thorough understanding of synchronization approaches is central in realizing the full potential for RTOS in modern computer systems (Li et al., 2013).

REFERENCES

1. Adelantado, M., Chaudron, J. B., Noulard, E., et al. (2011). HLA high performance and real-time simulation studies with CERTI. https://core.ac.uk/download/12042649.pdf (accessed on 29th September 2025).
2. Ahmad, N. (2017). Porting of FreeRTOS on a Python virtual machine for embedded and IoT devices. https://core.ac.uk/download/79623606.pdf (accessed on 29th September 2025).
3. Alger, L. S., Babikyan, C. A., Butler, B. P., et al. (2025). Advanced information processing system: The Army fault tolerant architecture conceptual study. Volume 1: Army fault tolerant architecture overview. https://core.ac.uk/download/pdf/42811478.pdf (accessed on 29th September 2025).
4. Alger, L. S., Babikyan, C. A., Butler, B. P., et al. (2025). Advanced information processing system: The Army fault tolerant architecture conceptual study. Volume 2: Army fault tolerant architecture design and analysis. https://core.ac.uk/download/pdf/42811477.pdf (accessed on 29th September 2025).
5. Al-Kinani, G., Frankfort, M., Kaushal, D., et al. (2025). Planning assistance for the 30/20 GHz program, Volume 1. https://core.ac.uk/download/pdf/42851563.pdf (accessed on 29th September 2025).
6. Al-Nayeem, A., Kim, C., Sha, L., et al. (2011). PALS/PRISM software design description (SDD): Ver. 0.51. https://core.ac.uk/download/4833878.pdf (accessed on 29th September 2025).
7. Bekooij, M., Domer, R., Leupers, R., et al. (2009). Programming MPSoC platforms: Road works ahead. https://core.ac.uk/download/pdf/11473351.pdf (accessed on 29th September 2025).
8. Berge, G., Ganesan, R., Goldsmith, D., Gungor, V., Hong, Y., Matsuda, T., et al. (2012). Wireless industrial monitoring and control networks: The journey so far and the road ahead. https://core.ac.uk/download/pdf/11484488.pdf (accessed on 29th September 2025).
9. Bergmann, N. W., & Tang, Y. (2015). A hardware scheduler based on task queues for FPGA-based embedded real-time systems. https://core.ac.uk/download/43368987.pdf (accessed on 29th September 2025).
10. Bolotin, G. S., Lewis, B. F., Manning, R. M., et al. (1990). Distributed computing system with dual independent communications paths between computers and employing split tokens. https://core.ac.uk/download/pdf/10427529.pdf (accessed on 29th September 2025).

11. Boukhobza, J., & Olivier, P. (2012). A hardware time manager implementation for the Xenomai real-time kernel of embedded Linux. http://arxiv.org/abs/1208.6428 (accessed on 29th September 2025).
12. Broenink, J. F., & Orlic, B. (2002). CSP channels for CAN-bus connected embedded control systems. https://core.ac.uk/download/pdf/11457907.pdf (accessed on 29th September 2025).
13. Caldwell, D. G., Gray, J. O., Petrone, M., et al. (2006). A haptic-enabled multimodal interface for the planning of hip arthroplasty. https://core.ac.uk/download/104526.pdf (accessed on 29th September 2025).
14. Castro, D., Ilic, A., Khan, A. M., et al. (2019). HeTM: Transactional memory for heterogeneous systems. http://arxiv.org/abs/1905.00661 (accessed on 29th September 2025).
15. Chalokh, S., & Rieder, M. (2018). XF operating system. https://core.ac.uk/download/157831670.pdf (accessed on 29th September 2025).
16. Chitnis, M., Liang, Y., Lipari, G., et al. (2009). Simulating real-time aspects of wireless sensor networks. https://core.ac.uk/download/pdf/54936513.pdf (accessed on 29th September 2025).
17. Conquet, E., Dissaux, P., Hugues, J., et al. (2010). The TASTE Toolset: Turning human-designed heterogeneous systems into computer-built homogeneous software. https://core.ac.uk/download/12041536.pdf (accessed on 29th September 2025).
18. Cornaglia, A., Mezzetti, E., Vardanega, T., et al. (2015). Software-enforced interconnect arbitration for COTS multicores. https://core.ac.uk/download/62920115.pdf (accessed on 29th September 2025).
19. D'Angelo, G., Ferretti, S., & Ghini, V. (2017). Distributed hybrid simulation of the Internet of Things and smart territories. http://arxiv.org/abs/1710.04252 (accessed on 29th September 2025).
20. Danner, A., Newhall, T., & Webb, K. (2017). Pervasive parallel and distributed computing in a liberal arts college curriculum. https://core.ac.uk/download/76223480.pdf (accessed on 29th September 2025).
21. De Poorter, E., Famaey, J., Hoebeke, J., et al. (2020). Survey on wireless technology trade-offs for the industrial internet of things. https://core.ac.uk/download/299792107.pdf (accessed on 29th September 2025).
22. Dunkels, A., Eriksson, J., Finne, N., et al. (2009). Sensor net checkpointing: Enabling repeatability in testbeds and realism in simulations. https://core.ac.uk/download/11434667.pdf (accessed on 29th September 2025).
23. Ferguson, R. C., & Thompson, H. C. (2025). Case study of the Space Shuttle cockpit avionics upgrade software. https://core.ac.uk/download/pdf/10536784.pdf (accessed on 29th September 2025).

24. Goldberg, J., Green, M. W., Kautz, W. H., et al. (2025). Development and analysis of the Software Implemented Fault-Tolerance (SIFT) computer. https://core.ac.uk/download/pdf/42849796.pdf (accessed on 29th September 2025).

25. Hu, S. M., Hu, X. Q., Manocha, D., et al. (2020). TZC: Efficient inter-process communication for robotics middleware with partial serialization. http://arxiv.org/abs/1810.00556 (accessed on 29th September 2025).

26. Korf, F., Meyer, P., Schmidt, T. C., et al. (2018). Simulation of mixed critical in-vehicular networks. http://arxiv.org/abs/1808.03081 (accessed on 29th September 2025).

27. Li, Y., Missimer, E., & West, R. (2013). Predictable migration and communication in the Quest-V multikernal. https://open.bu.edu/bitstream/2144/11425/1/2013-017-quest-mig-ipc.pdf (accessed on 29th September 2025).

28. Mao, Y., You, C., Zhang, J., Huang, K., & Letaief, K. B. (2017). A survey on mobile edge computing: The communication perspective. *IEEE Communications Surveys & Tutorials, 19*, 2322–2358. https://doi.org/10.1109/comst.2017.2745201 (accessed on 29th September 2025).

29. Meyer, B., Nanz, S., & West, S. (2015). Efficient and reasonable object-oriented concurrency. http://arxiv.org/abs/1405.7153 (accessed on 29th September 2025).

30. Mullender, S. J. (1987). Process management in distributed operating systems. https://core.ac.uk/download/pdf/11460997.pdf (accessed on 29th September 2025).

31. Puente Alfaro, J. A. de la, Pulido Pavón, J. A., Urueña Pascual, S., et al. (2008). Communication paradigms for high-integrity distributed systems with hard real-time requirements. https://core.ac.uk/download/148655143.pdf (accessed on 29th September 2025).

32. Roussel, K., Song, Y. Q., & Zendra, O. (2015). RIOT OS paves the way for implementation of high-performance MAC protocols. https://core.ac.uk/download/49532959.pdf (accessed on 29th September 2025).

33. Schmidt, D. C., & Suda, T. (1992). Computing infrastructure issues in distributed communications systems: A survey of operating system transport system architectures. https://core.ac.uk/download/287622717.pdf (accessed on 29th September 2025).

34. Sinha, S. (2018). Scheduling policies and system software architectures for mixed-criticality computing. https://core.ac.uk/download/304658766.pdf (accessed on 29th September 2025).

35. Ulianko, M. (2012). Implementation of RTOS to the WSN node. https://core.ac.uk/download/30281552.pdf (accessed on 29th September 2025).
36. Yan, S., Sebesta, S., Sha, L., Buttazzo, G., Lampson, K., et al. (2017). Improving responsiveness of time-sensitive applications by exploiting dynamic task dependencies. https://core.ac.uk/download/pdf/132328503.pdf (accessed on 29th September 2025).
37. Zhong, R. Y., Xu, X., Klotz, E., & Newman, S. T. (2017). Intelligent manufacturing in the context of Industry 4.0: A review. *Engineering, 3*, 616–630. https://doi.org/10.1016/j.eng.2017.05.015 (accessed on 29th September 2025).

CHAPTER 6

TIME MANAGEMENT IN RTOS

Contents

INTRODUCTION

With the fast-paced technological era of the modern world, in which computing needs are constantly on the rise, real-time operating systems (RTOS) have become a core area of study and application. With their ability to execute information and tasks within close time windows, RTOS systems form a core aspect of aviation to healthcare industries. Good time management in such systems becomes the top priority, with a straight bearing on the responsiveness and reliability of programs that require instant, deterministic responses. By extension, the success of an RTOS relies not only on its support for multitasking but also on how it executes scheduling and task prioritization efficiently. It is therefore crucial for developers and researchers aiming to improve real-time performance for various applications to appreciate the complexities involved in time management in RTOS environments. Scheduling tasks is one of the pillars of time management in RTOS, which affects the sequence of task execution as well as the use of resources. The inherent complexity arises due to satisfying multiple requirements, including task priority, their processing time, and system responsiveness. Advanced scheduling algorithms, like Rate Monotonic Scheduling (RMS) and Earliest Deadline First (EDF), are employed on a large scale to address these complexities. These algorithms guarantee that time-critical tasks are provided with the resources to satisfy their deadlines, thereby improving overall system dependability. Therefore, a careful study of these algorithms provides valuable insights into maximizing RTOS performance. Besides, the inclusion of Quality of Service (QoS) guarantees makes it more complicated, as the developers need to consider both temporal limits and user requirements in their task management methods, further highlighting the essence of good time management in RTOS applications (Adelantado et al., 2010). Moreover, the development of sophisticated software structures, i.e., networked IP-based ones such as those for live video database management systems, has also brought into focus the importance of time management in RTOS platforms. Such systems lay the ground for the real-time demands of modern software with the requirement for data to be sorted together harmoniously from varied sources to enable timely responses for applications ranging from public safety to medical monitoring (Alex et al., 2025). With advancements in technology, the need for robust methods to manage time in RTOS increases. This need surpasses mere task scheduling to reach levels requiring continuous data management and real-time network responses, hence enlarging the traditional time management techniques' scope. Hence, thorough analysis of time management in RTOS should be paired with adaptive scheduling algorithms and new architectural designs to address the intricate nature of real-time computation fully.

Importance of Time Management in RTOS

Effective time management in RTOS is crucial to meet tight deadlines and respond promptly to systems. RTOS must schedule the tasks based on their time requirements for predictability and reliability in the operation. This is particularly critical in embedded systems, where the failure to meet timing requirements may turn out to be catastrophic. By using task scheduling algorithms that schedule tasks based on priority, programmers can guarantee that important operations are performed in a timely manner. Time management techniques, like RMS and EDF, are good examples of this procedure that enables systems to dynamically assign resources while still supporting deterministic execution. Hence, time management ability is the foundation of reliable RTOS design that is essential not only for system performance but also for mission-critical safety. Time management is also useful for resource allocation, particularly in the face of contemporary challenges of cloud computing. As systems evolve towards supporting sophisticated applications that entail coordination and cooperation, effective time management becomes essential in ensuring resource allocation aligns with user service level expectations. The bring-up of cloud services involves not only optimization of internal resources by RTOS but also optimization of external loads and changing workloads. This accompanies conclusions emphasizing the need to come up with SLA-based resource management frameworks that address the unique challenges in cloud environments (Buyya et al., 2011). With more dynamic demands for resources, the development of robust scheduling and resource management tools in RTOS can maximize optimal utilization of resources and therefore overall service quality and system performance. Furthermore, the role of time management in RTOS goes beyond mere task execution; strategic decision-making that is critical for cooperative and coordinated design processes is included. Where tasks are executed simultaneously and there is cooperation between several systems, well-structured time management approaches ensure that design requirements are met while minimizing the risks. Research indicates that incorporating domain-independent coordination mechanisms can lead to better decision-making in RTOS design but also indicates a requirement for some domain adaptations in order to capitalize on these benefits to the fullest (Coates et al., 2000). Using effective decision management frameworks for considering time constraints and cooperation, RTOS can improve coordination and workflow management. This impact results in a more efficient system that effectively provides for the timeliness required for complex applications, thereby emphasizing the fundamental role of time management within the framework of RTOS.

6.1. CHARACTERISTICS OF RTOS

Real-time operating systems (RTOS) are distinct because they possess certain special characteristics differentiating them from normal operating systems to a large extent via their focus on time management and determinism. Having the capability to meet hard execution time deadlines is one of the inherent qualities of an RTOS, and it is a must in many embedded applications like industrial automation and robotic control. This becomes achievable to a large degree with the presence of a time manager, which schedules interval interrupt services in order to cater to tasks that get performed within their respective time slots. A precise time management mechanism allows an RTOS to meet the needs of real-time tasks with a balance that is just right between precision and CPU utilization needed to preserve efficiency for the system overall. As has been noted, the efficacy of an RTOS is irrevocably linked to its ability to manage such time constraints and is thus of overriding importance that developers recognize and utilize effective timing strategies within their systems (Boukhobza et al., 2012). Another key aspect of RTOS is the use of scheduling algorithms that program tasks according to urgency and length.

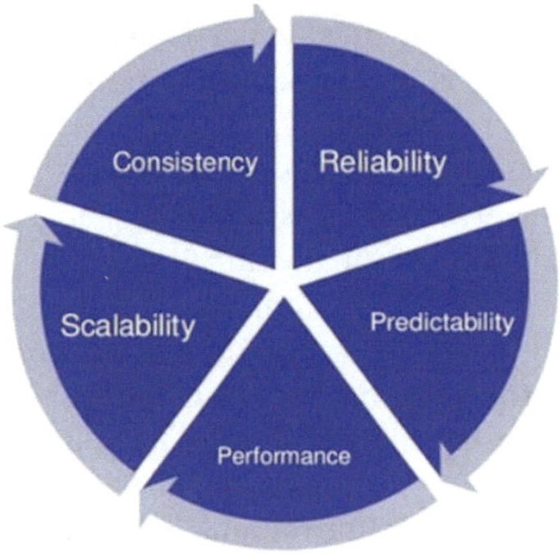

Figure 6.1. Characteristics of RTOS.

Source: https://external-content.duckduckgo.com/iu/?u=https%3A%2F%2Fwww.founderjar.com%2Fwp-content%2Fuploads%2F2023%2F06%2FCharacteristics-of-RTOS.jpeg&f=1&nofb=1&ipt=23130a71ad1d3578c36a419ea73a46a350f7881852842a198c4b77995ea00edc.

The Rate Monotonic Scheduling (RMS) algorithm is a classic example, where tasks are given priorities based on their periodicity. The tasks needing execution more frequently are given higher priorities so that the critical tasks are given the required CPU time without delay. This action is critical, particularly in systems consisting of multiple concurrent tasks, where the issue at hand is to maintain a sense of harmony between system resources and real-time requirements. As proof indicates, some workloads can be more complex in scheduling, particularly where the involved tasks are harmonically non-similar, periodic tasks. The ability of an RTOS to manage such heterogeneous workloads efficiently is crucial for ensuring system performance is optimal even with changes in conditions and configurations (Churnetski et al., 2006). In addition, the modularity and flexibility of RTOS are of critical advantages in the field of time management. The flexibility of these systems allows developers to customize them to particular applications by setting up the underlying hardware and software modules. For example, moving the time management services into configurable hardware modules, e.g., Field Programmable Gate Arrays (FPGAs), can considerably decrease CPU overhead, making the system more responsive and efficient. This modular architecture not only allows optimization of processing time but also improves reliability by moving time-critical operations away from the CPU and allowing critical functions to be performed uninterrupted. Thus, the continued advancement of RTOS, particularly the integration of advanced time management solutions, points to the growing criticality of real-time functionality in an increasingly interconnected world (Boukhobza et al., 2012) (Figure 6.1).

6.1.1. Determinism and Predictability

On the subject of RTOS, determinism and predictability are essential to ensure that tasks complete within deadlines and operate as expected under varied environments. Determinism refers to the ability of a system to produce the same output under the same initial conditions, which is essential for systems where reliability is not negotiable. Predictability does imply making promises about system behavior, so that developers can make predictions about the system's behavior under certain inputs or conditions. These are interconnected concepts, because a deterministic system is by definition predictable, and this enables developers to accurately measure their application's timing characteristics. The determinism and predictability implications are especially strong for multi-core systems, where contention for shared resources can cause unanticipated behavior. In such systems, ensuring timing correctness is problematic because there may be interference between tasks across different cores. Solutions to these issues, as the literature suggests, lie in four broad categories: full integration, temporal isolation, inclusion of interference effects in schedulability analysis, and mapping and allocation. Each method has certain strengths and limitations in ensuring Real-Time Systems can operate reliably under concurrent loads, ultimately affecting the performance and usability of the overall system (Ma et al., 2019). Furthermore, with the ongoing demands of real-time applications, particularly with the emergence of mixed criticality computing, there is ever-greater demand for reliable software platforms. The Linux kernel can be originally designed as a general operating system, but it is more widely used in real-time applications because it caters to hardware and peripheral features. The PREEMPT_RT patch implements changes designed to enhance the predictability and reduce the latency of the Linux kernel. The patch comes with inherent challenges but also offers the potential for better management of time within real-time systems via minimizing interrupt and scheduling latencies (Reghenzani et al., 2019). Addressing these challenges is crucial in developing reliable real-time systems that can fulfill strict timing constraints within heterogeneous operating environments.

6.1.2. Resource Management

Good resource management is very important in RTOS not only for optimal performance but also for ensuring system reliability under conditions of constraint. The performance of an RTOS largely depends on the efficient use of both system resources and human resources, hence determining its performance integrity. Resource management entails a set of activities such as scheduling, prioritization, and effective utilization of hardware and software resources. While organizations strive to meet stringent real-time needs, the potential to use resources in a fruitful way is realized, facilitating improved responsiveness, decreased latency, and improved user experience. SHRM-based strategies are especially essential in establishing a climate where employees contribute positively toward organizational goals aimed at RTOS, thereby enhancing overall system reliability and performance (Dyer et al., 2004). Under the conditions of RTOS, the fast pace of technological evolution requires a shift towards newer, more flexible paradigms of resource management. The increased complexity of real-time applications demands re-examination within organizations of their paradigms of resource utilization. This dynamic setup requires the adoption of a reliability-enhancing human resource strategy (REHRS) that makes clear the capacity of staff versus project and new industry demands. By effective human resource management, companies can create a workforce capable of adapting to the demands of real-time environments and thus improve system reliability in chaotic operating regimes. In addition, understanding key people issues in workload distribution and performance measurement can provide insights that can lead to streamlining operations and maximizing efficiency, in harmony with research findings that point to agile and responsive action in resource management (Dyer et al., 1999). As RTOS further development continues to gain momentum, the integration of robust resource management policies is an absolute requirement if competitiveness is to be maintained. The forces of upcoming markets and the need for timely innovation compel firms to attract and keep high-class talent—a prerequisite underscored by the urgency in the human resource discussion today. Placing strategies focused on developing core organizational competencies in position can enhance technology deployment effectiveness in RTOS. Care in how human practices impact operating reliability, along with a keen awareness of external competition dynamics, can stimulate sustainable performance increases. Organizations that become proactive at constantly improving their practices of resource management position themselves to not just respond to existing conditions but also be pioneers in an era of irrepressible competition and complexity (Dyer et al., 1999, 2004).

6.1.3. Multitasking Capabilities

Good multitasking capability is essential within an RTOS to allow that multiple tasks be run concurrently without sacrificing system performance. Real-time systems are typically employed where time precision matters, requiring a robust environment that ensures task priority according to urgency and deadline. One of the ways through which effective multitasking can be achieved is by using priority-based scheduling algorithms like Rate-Monotonic Scheduling (RMS) and Earliest Deadline First (EDF). RMS, for instance, gives a higher priority to tasks whose periods are shorter. Not only does this make it easy to schedule the tasks, but also reduces overhead, ultimately making the whole system respond faster. Using these advanced scheduling techniques, an RTOS can multitask efficiently to cater to time-critical working needs of different applications like industrial automation and medical devices. Furthermore, the multitasking capability of an RTOS relates very much to system resource handling concerning CPU time and memory. An efficient resource management framework prevents task contention and ensures multiple tasks access to the available resources to complete in their allocated time slots. This can involve partitioning memory space and implementing solutions like dynamic allocation to achieve peak application performance. Implementing efficient error handling methods, like those specified in recent enhancements to 32-bit RV32I processors, can also enhance multitasking performance. For example, the Interrupt Error Checker (IEC) ensures that tasks can be interrupted and resumed without violation of data integrity. As such, multitasking is facilitated with added reliability, complemented by multi-layered error handling and resource management, which is critical in mission-critical applications (Niadu et al., 2025). Compatibility with high-end features specifically tailored for RTOS support to enhance multitasking ability is equally important. Atomic operations and hardware task management enable a smoother multitasking environment with no unnecessary delays in context switching between tasks. Second, priority-based interrupt handling aids deterministic execution by giving urgent tasks immediate response times. All these RTOS-dependent factors, coupled with efficient scheduling algorithms, are behind a robust multitasking environment that is suitable for the stringent requirements of real-time operation. Also, synchronization mechanisms play an important role here as they prevent conflicts and open shared resources for access in a predictable way. Therefore, by improving multitasking performance through a combined set of features and methods, RTOS can achieve optimal performance in resource-constrained real-time applications, resulting in improved system reliability and user satisfaction (Sultana, 2023) (Figure 6.2).

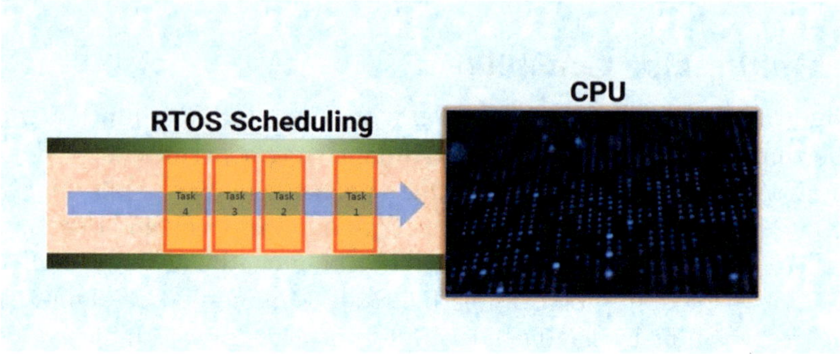

Figure 6.2. *Real-time operating system (RTOS) multitasking and scheduling.*

Source: https://external-content.duckduckgo.com/iu/?u=https%3A%2F%2Fi.ytimg.com%2Fvi%2F6L5DjHHHi-U%2Fmaxresdefault.jpg&f=1&nofb=1&ipt=a9a654bea817d03dba73d1c5c3a05658feebed576a0dbf4c7483deb167b882a9.

6.2. TIME MANAGEMENT TECHNIQUES

Effective time management techniques are critical to the smooth functioning of RTOS in cases where precise timing and response are required. In cases where operations are precisely time-bound, such as with video-on-demand systems, proper time distribution guarantees smooth functioning. Techniques like task prioritization, where higher-priority tasks are executed initially, can be particularly effective in enhancing system efficiency. The capacity for parallelizing work, as pointed out by García-Martínez et al. (1996), not only enhances efficiency but also maximizes the use of resources. Through the utilization of multithreading, RTOS can achieve a guarantee that processes for input/output do not hinder the execution of the main task, thereby keeping the system consistent in terms of timing and responsiveness. By incorporating such methods, reliability as well as a very strong structure that meets the strict demands of real-time applications is developed. In addition to prioritization, integration of measures that quantify performance in time management for RTOS systems is essential. Typical performance measures are general and not appropriate for the effective assessment of the performance of time allocation and task execution. The integration of robust measures addressing responses to external events, intertask synchronization, and data transfer can greatly enhance the assessment of an RTOS's capabilities. As underscored by Conde et al. (1996), the application of these fine-grained metrics allows for a better understanding of how time is managed in the system. This not only assists developers in optimizing their coding style but also supports ongoing development of high-reliability and high-performance real-time systems. By focusing the limelight on such measures, time management skills can be evolved so that they ensure deterministic outcomes, which are of paramount importance in real-time computing. Naturally, the instructional aspect of implementing effective time management skills into reality cannot be overlooked either. People dealing with RTOS must acquire strong time management skills, which are further complemented with training and practical exposure. Techniques such as time blocking, where sometimes are allocated for activity, can be particularly useful in guaranteeing concentration and productivity. Moreover, the awareness of recognizing and avoiding time-consuming activities helps maintain systems performance integrity in heavy loads. Through the adoption of systematic approaches to allocating time, as cited in previously discussed techniques, developers improve both individual efficiency and the overall performance of the RTOS environment. Integrating these learning programs with solid performance measures provides for continuous improvement in time management planning, which is imperative for the dynamic nature of real-time systems.

6.2.1. Time Slicing

In the context of RTOS, time slicing is a fundamental scheme for managing the execution of processes over limited CPU resources. By dividing available processor time into smaller, fixed slices known as quantum, an RTOS can offer CPU cycles effectively to numerous processes. Multitasking according to this mechanism enhances system responsiveness and ensures that high-priority processes receive adequate attention. However, effective time slicing requires accuracy in the calibration of the quantum duration; allocating tasks too small an amount can cause average performance degradation as a result of context-switching overhead. It is therefore necessary to find a balance that is tolerable under system performance criteria without compromising real-time needs, guaranteeing predictability and stability for various applications in embedded systems. The use of time slicing in multicore processor environments also comes with additional complexities that must be handled in order to maximize performance. Whereas single-core environments do not present the idca of shared resources, multicore environments add the notion of shared resources like cache, which can add unpredictability in scheduling and executing tasks. The unpredictability can complicate accurate estimation of Worst-Case Execution Time (WCET) for tasks, an important need in real-time systems where guarantees of timing are essential. Mitigation of these kinds of problems often involves sophisticated cache management techniques with the aim of maximizing the allocation of resources among simultaneous processes. This approach plays a pivotal role in ensuring determinism within the system so that time slicing can be effective without affecting the performance demanded in real-time applications. With multicore architectures gaining popularity in the realm of embedded systems, this focus on time slicing becomes increasingly pivotal (Alhammad et al., 2015) (Figure 6.3).

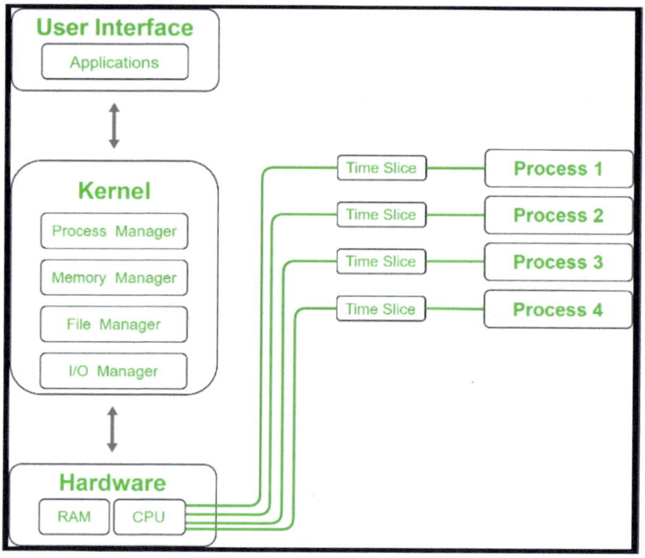

Figure 6.3. *Time slicing.*

Source: https://media.geeksforgeeks.org/wp-content/uploads/20200822112752/timeslice1bg.jpg.

Research exploring the intersection of time slicing, multicore processors, and real-time systems has had significant advances with them but so come the dominant problems. For instance, research programs have examined the impact of various cache management techniques on the predictability of time-sliced applications. The approach is aimed at maximizing predictability without resulting in excessive side effects due to resource conflicts. Further, WCET computation is a more intricate task in the multicore setup because of the requirement of a high-level understanding of interaction and synchronization between tasks. The analysis must also take into account task communication patterns and their impact on execution time in an attempt to utilize the parallel processing capabilities of the multicore structure. With the provided technology, further studies in such fields will be required to better fine-tune time management methods within RTOS environments to be in a position to meet the tight demands of today's embedded software applications (Bonenfant et al., 2010).

6.2.2. Priority Inversion Handling

Priority inversion is an issue in RTOS and represents a significant challenge that can undermine time management and system performance. Priority inversion occurs when a lower-priority task is holding a resource required by a higher-priority task and causes the latter to wait as it completes. This can lead to nondeterministic delays, essentially compromising the determinism which is critical for real-time applications. Resolution of priority inversion is important to ensure that high-priority tasks are within their deadlines and system reliability is maintained. By rigorous solution of priority inversion, RTOS implementers can thoroughly improve the overall timing profile of embedded systems and make them more resilient to failure caused by latency. A number of techniques have been proposed to overcome the effects of priority inversion, among the most effective being dynamic priority adjustment. If the blocking task is lower priority than that of the blocked task, RTOS can incrementally increase the priority of the blocking task temporarily so it can run more rapidly. This strategy makes the higher-priority task receive CPU time without being significantly delayed. Proper resource sharing and synchronization methods must also be needed to minimize interference resulting from priority inversion. By employing these techniques, developers are able to establish a more predictable environment for task execution, thereby satisfying basic performance constraints, such as determinism and latency, which are characteristics of real-time systems (Conde et al., 1996) (Figure 6.4).

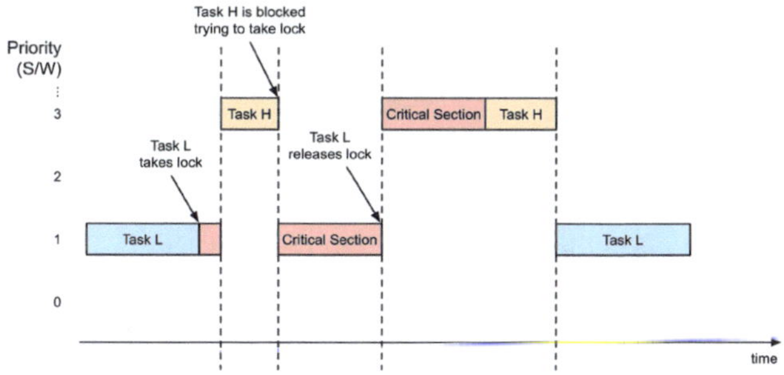

Figure 6.4. *Priority inversion.*

Source: https://www.digikey.in/en/maker/projects/introduction-to-rtos-solution-to-part-11-priority-inversion/abf4b8f7cd4a4c70bece35678d178321.

Support for hardware can also enhance management of priority inversion in RTOS platforms. Hardware implementations such as specialized accelerators or specific protocol designs are able to offload part of the runtime services and thus reduce the computational load for the processor. A good example is a hybrid hardware/software solution that helps manage resource scheduling and synchronization operations with better efficiency, thus preventing priority inversion scenarios in complex embedded systems. These advancements are particularly beneficial in latency-critical systems, where timely execution of critical tasks becomes the most sought aspect. Such technology enables RTOS to support more efficient handling of time, enabling an environment where timely response to external events is attained even with the constraint of priority inversion (Cardoso et al., 2014).

6.2.3. Time Partitioning

In RTOS, time partitioning is a significant method for managing the allocation of processor time between multiple concurrent tasks. Time partitioning enhances system predictability and reliability by dividing the processors time into distinct chunks of time, each for different tasks.

Figure 6.5. *Programmable logic in-the-middle (PLIM).*

Source: https://cpslab.bu.edu/wp-content/uploads/2023/03/plim_zcu102-evaluation-board-w.jpg.

This becomes particularly significant in environments where deadlines need to be complied with, say, in embedded systems used in the automotive or aerospace sectors. This structured partitioning allows RTOS to allocate high-priority activities computational resources necessary so that latency is minimized and the overall response of the system is enhanced. Last but not least, accurate time partitioning not only optimizes the use of resources but also strengthens the system design towards fault tolerance, thus providing uninterrupted operation irrespective of potential task overloads. Moreover, the correct application of time partitioning also requires a strict scheduling algorithm that is effective enough to deal with varying workloads while respecting reserved time slots. Classical scheduling methods may fail to offer determinism, especially in multi-core processors where contention for hardware resources might lead to unforeseen delays. Newer approaches, such as those embracing the concept of Programmable Logic In-the-Middle (PLIM), are potential remedies for the shortcomings of classical methods. PLIM includes the additional benefit of an intermediate component that manages memory transactions, thereby reducing unpredictability from shared resource references. By applying such advanced methods, time partitioning can be optimized to ensure that programs are capable of functioning effectively within their allowed time periods without compromising real-time guarantees (Mancuso et al., 2020) (Figure 6.5). Thus, the harmony between cutting-edge scheduling algorithms and time partitioning is at the heart of optimal performance in RTOS systems of great complexity. The implications of effective time partitioning also extend beyond mere task scheduling; they impact also on the fields of system design as well as resource allocation. As discussed in surface habitat systems research and the requirements for real-time stable operations (Kennedy et al., 2025), time partitioning allows systems to determine their functional tasks and manage risks effectively. Through the definition of accurate time boundaries, the developers can more effectively plan for interactions between various subsystems and thereby provide smoother operations within the overall design. This is in accordance with improved operational efficiency in applications that call for open interoperability between multiple components, such as in the instance of lunar colonies or other planetary expeditions. Thus, the advantage gained from time partitioning demonstrates its significance to not only enable task efficiency but also ensure overall integrity of complex real-time systems.

6.3. CHALLENGES IN TIME MANAGEMENT

Effective time management is critical in RTOS due to the stringent demands of various applications. Systems operating under hard timing constraints must utilize resources effectively while maintaining stability of performance. Satisfying the incompatible requirements of tasks is one prevalent challenge, where deadlines can be missed if not managed appropriately. For instance, traditional scheduling methods may not be effective in situations where there is huge uncertainty of task completion times. As highlighted by existing literature, the application of advanced scheduling mechanisms can alleviate such issues. Nevertheless, this also increases system complexity, with caution exercised in the design to prevent defeating the benefit of such advanced mechanisms via the overhead (Ulianko et al., 2012). Thus, the developers need to balance adding functionality and overall responsiveness in the RTOS. Interactions between various components of the system pose another primary challenge of handling time in RTOS systems. For example, performance parameters need to consider not only the execution time of an individual task but also communication delay and I/O operations. The growing demand for high-performance, multi-core processors seen in safety-critical environments like avionics and the automotive industries added more complexity to these concerns. Such next-generation microprocessor architectures usually do not support commercial RTOS widely used in these industries strongly, which complicates real-time scheduling. In response, researchers have initiated work towards new open-source solutions like DEmOS that simulate RTOS scheduling on commercial Linux platforms. This approach not only facilitates benchmarking but also offers scope for novel scheduling algorithms because the sector calls for time management methods that are efficient yet flexible enough to fit changing hardware infrastructures (Matěj, 2021). Moreover, power consumption management while ensuring real-time constraints is a constant challenge that RTOS developers must address. Embedded systems increasingly being battery-powered for use calls for effective performance without consuming resources. The majority of real-time applications, especially those in wireless sensor networks and IoT, suffer from the dual issue of needing timely responsiveness with constrained energy budgets. The algorithmic choice has significant implications for time and power efficiency, necessitating careful trade-off consideration. Current studies indicate that choosing energy-efficient scheduling policies can achieve optimal system performance with suitable time management solutions. This, however, becomes even harder for the design options, with energy-aware scheduling algorithms that are added requiring to be dealt with without introducing too much latency, thereby maintaining the requirement of a systematic approach to time administration in RTOS systems (Matěj, 2021; Ulianko et al., 2012).

6.3.1. Jitter and Latency Issues

In RTOS, jitter and latency are two highly significant parameters whose breach can have a heavy impact on the timeliness and dependability of system behavior. Jitter refers to the variance in response time of task execution, while latency is the time interval between the request for service and the start of the actual service. Both of these can intrude into the predictability of real-time application, which exists in critical systems like industrial automation or aerospace. Resolving them effectively includes investigating scheduling techniques within the RTOS, which may relieve or exacerbate jitter and latency and impact the system responsiveness and reliability as a whole. Hence, managing these parameters is not merely a technical problem but also crucial in ensuring user confidence and system security in time-critical settings. A solution to mitigating jitter and latency is implementing a hybrid scheduling scheme based on both static and dynamic parameters.

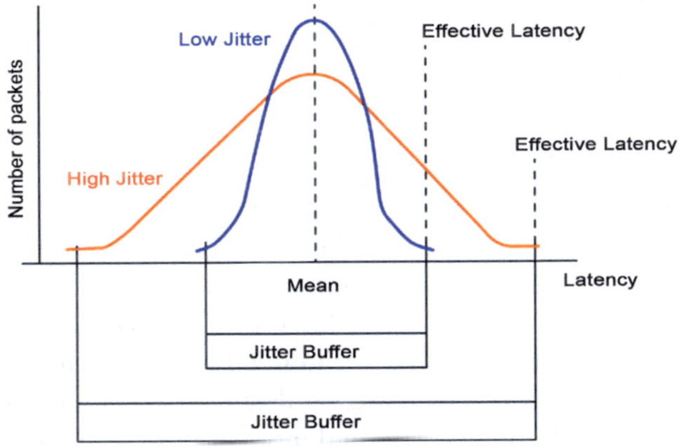

Figure 6.6. *Jitter and latency are critical parameters that can significantly affect the timeliness and reliability of system performance.*

Source: https://media.geeksforgeeks.org/wp-content/uploads/20240215111436/Difference-between-Latency-and-Jitter-in-OS.png.

Static scheduling ensures predictability by maintaining that certain tasks are meeting their timing needs based on priorities set, while dynamic scheduling allows the system to adapt based on real-time circumstances and resource availability (Gill et al., 2002). By integrating these two mechanisms, systems can achieve a balance that will maximize utilization while providing the guarantees of performance required by critical tasks. This hybrid approach enables the system to react more dynamically towards changes in workload and unexpected situations and thereby reduce both mean and peak jitter and latency. Thus, task scheduling is in large part a question of the ability of the system to maintain real-time functionality in spite of changing conditions, which is paramount when it comes to mission-critical environments. Furthermore, adaptive rescheduling enabled through middleware incorporation can also reduce latency- and jitter-induced issues. Middleware frameworks may support dynamic real-time performance tuning via dynamically varying task execution rates and resource assignments as functions of changing system states (Shea et al., 2008). They allow reflective switching among alternative scheduling heuristics so that the performance of each strategy is experimented with in real-time, and the scheduling scheme is modified accordingly. The capability of delivering real-time feedback and dynamic control minimizes disturbance in service levels so that it can comfortably manage timing-sensitive operations. As demands increase for flexible and effective real-time systems, the use of novel scheduling techniques and reactive middleware will be critical in addressing jitter as well as latency problems so that the stringent requirements of modern-day RTOS applications can be met (Figure 6.6).

6.3.2. Resource Contention

Contestation of resources in RTOS takes place when tasks compete for limited computational resources, leading to delays and potential failure in satisfying time constraints. It is particularly germane in environments where determinism is paramount, e.g., aerospace or embedded systems. The inherent design of general-purpose operating systems, including Linux, accommodates a wide range of user interactions but tends to be designed for high throughput over the strict latency requirements essential in real-time systems. As Linux is increasingly used in flight-critical applications by organizations like NASA and SpaceX, it becomes imperative to understand the implications of this resource contention in an effort to ensure timely processing of tasks and adherence to deadlines (Madden et al., 2025). The challenges of resource contention provide critical issues to managing an RTOS using strategies that will minimize the risk of performance degradation in time-critical applications. Efficient management of time using strategies is crucial in addressing resource contention under RTOS environments. These strategies are usually achieved through prioritizations according to the criticality of the tasks and scheduler algorithms designed to accommodate mixed-criticality task models. By ensuring that important tasks do not go without compute time even when the system is heavily loaded, such algorithms enhance use of resources and reduce the likelihood of deadline miss. Mixed criticality allows for no degradation in the functionality of less important tasks at the cost of prioritizing the most important tasks (Sinha et al., 2018). In addition, spatial and temporal isolation between tasks is an essential requirement in system design for the ability of multiple tasks to be present simultaneously without interference. This separation can be achieved using various virtualization techniques that divide resource usage, hence lessening contention, and system integrity in real-time systems. Moreover, the inclusion of advanced scheduling mechanisms in an RTOS can significantly lower the adverse effect of resource contention. These include fixed-priority scheduling with the mixed-criticality paradigm, whereby high-priority processes always get the necessary computational resources. This approach not only guarantees task timing but also guarantees system stability in the face of fluctuating loads. The continuous improvement of these scheduling algorithms along with advancement in virtualization techniques demonstrates a promising way to improve resource optimization in real-time systems. Last but not least, it is essential to solve resource conflict by proper time management and suitable scheduling models to make RTOS reliable and efficient based on the high demands of modern applications in various areas.

6.3.3. Scalability Concerns

Scalability is an issue in RTOS that can cause influential impacts on time management and overall system performance. The larger and more complex systems become, the more difficult it is to manage the resources in an effective way. This problem is particularly clear in distributed and multi-core systems, which require good communication and synchronization across different elements. Middleware is the solution in this instance since it can provide scalable distributed systems to be constructed through providing abstractions and communication protocols as outlined by Emmerich et al. (2000). Scalability does, however, require middleware solutions themselves to be adequate enough to handle the loads of a dynamic and resource-constrained environment typical for RTOS applications. Scalability even extends to the limitations imposed by current technology, and specifically in the case of wireless networks utilized for industrial monitoring and control. Traditional wire-based communication systems are typically non-adaptable and sensitive enough to offer the dynamism required to adapt with today's applications in real-time. As Berge et al. (2012) pointed out, although wireless technologies can mitigate these limitations, they are not yet mature in terms of reliability and real-time performance. The increasing size and complexity of industrial applications have a tendency to saturate existing wireless infrastructures, leading to time-critical operations being delayed and failing. Therefore, addressing scalability in such environments is not just a question of implementing advanced middleware but also bringing in new wireless solutions that have the ability to deal with extremely high real-time constraints. Lastly, to address scalability problems successfully, researchers and engineers must focus on developing methodologies that can be employed to systematically construct distributed systems. This means enhancing notation and means favoring modular architecture, which is simpler to scale both in hardware as well as software aspects. The steady expansion in middleware work, as identified by Emmerich et al. (2000), illustrates a movement towards adaptive and reconfigurable mechanisms that are able to handle various loads and allocations of resources without any flaw. These advancements are necessary to make RTOS continue remaining effective and reliable as they expand, and time management is still optimized even during situations of high demand. By sorting these factors out initially, the sector can enable the development of stronger and more efficient real-time systems that can succeed even within more intricate industrial settings.

6.4. TOOLS AND TECHNIQUES FOR TIME ANALYSIS

Good time analysis in RTOS is paramount to ensuring the best performance and reliability of embedded systems. A variety of tools and methodologies is employed to estimate, monitor, and analyze time consumption in the different system processes. For instance, real-time analysis tools may be incorporated within the RTOS to allow developers to learn about task execution time, inter-task communications delay, and schedule overhead. The employment of advanced software products geared towards time analysis has been found to enhance decision-making and optimally distribute resources. Beyond the support of engineers to identify task execution bottlenecks, such advancements enable sensitization of the schedule policy to align with close timing constraints in system-critical applications, thus enhancing the responsiveness and agility of the system design (Kaur et al., 2024). Grounding its design on the fundamental tools for time analysis, rate-based task scheduling is a central mechanism in effective time management under an RTOS regime. With dynamic adjustment of execution rates to suit system demand, this scheduling technique offers a good solution for meeting real-time constraints, particularly for distributed systems such as the Internet of Things (IoT). The incorporation of a rate-based scheduler in an RTOS like VxWorks has been found to provide incredible resource management enhancement, allowing tasks to handle dynamic system loads perfectly. Using tools like the Cheddar scheduling analysis tool, developers can examine the performance and deadline satisfaction of their applications in different scenarios. This adaptability is significant in intricate systems that must be adaptable as well as efficient in managing greater than one task (Springer et al., 2024). As needs in real-time systems evolve, the inclusion of new tools for time analysis will be essential in enhancing functional operations. Analytics based on artificial intelligence allow the identification of inefficiencies and unexpected issues that can undermine performance. In addition, the ability to provide real-time observations of system activity ensures that engineers can potentially respond proactively to issues as they arise. Advanced methods such as automated task prioritization based on runtime measurements facilitate a varied time management strategy. By widespread evaluations and deployments, these tools not only enhance the time management efficiency of RTOS but also provide a gateway to future system design innovation to facilitate embedded solutions to cope with the ever-increasing demands of contemporary applications (Kaur et al., 2024) (Figure 6.7).

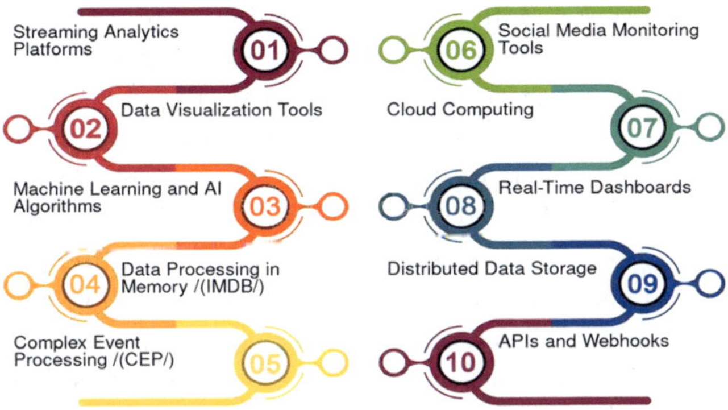

Figure 6.7. *Tools and techniques for real-time data analysis.*

Source: https://fastercapital.co/i/Instantaneous-Market-Research--Unveiling-Trends-in-the-FastMarket-update--Tools-and-Techniques-for-Real-Time-Data-Analysis.webp.

6.4.1. Simulation Tools

Application of simulation software in RTOS is an important element for enhancing time management functions. By allowing developers to simulate various system contexts, the software facilitates easier analysis of task scheduling, resource allocation, and responsiveness of the system. Simulation software enables designers to visualize their systems' behavior under different workloads and reveal bottlenecks that may not be apparent using traditional coding techniques. This is highly applicable when optimizing embedded applications' performance, particularly in safety-critical areas such as avionics and automotive systems where timing is so absolutely crucial. Overall, the use of simulation tools facilitates increased efficiency in design with improved decision-making regarding time management within RTOS environments. Besides, simulation tools integrate theoretical models with practical applications, stressing their relevance in education and research. For instance, software such as PRISE not only allows for learning of essential embedded systems but also experiments with new engineering ways of designing software functions in real-time environments. By simulating varied operation conditions, these platforms provide a secure medium for testing time management strategies by researchers and students without risking real hardware. Such experimentations are invaluable while handling concurrency and synchronization complexities in RTOS, enabling us to get a deeper insight into how varying scheduling algorithms affect the overall time management efficiency. This learning component enhances the ability of future engineers to undertake challenges posed by embedded systems in the modern world. Furthermore, as companies aim for more effective and sustainable production systems, simulation tools play a key role in the discovery of energy saving opportunities with optimized time management (Casta et al., 2019). The integration of time and energy efficiency cannot be overlooked because both minimize idle times as well as maximize resource usage. Simulation tools give manufacturers an opportunity to experiment with various management approaches, making their practicality apparent in real industrial contexts. This two-way system not only fosters the development of management and control techniques but also aligns with the general goals of Industry 4.0, which revolve around innovation and sustainability. By embracing simulation tools, organizations can ensure they are remaining competitive within an ever-evolving technology landscape and optimally leveraging time and resources within their RTOS infrastructures.

6.4.2. Profiling and Benchmarking

Profiling and benchmarking are critical techniques in the area of RTOS that enable effective time management. Profiling involves systematically collecting performance data of software components, enabling developers to identify inefficiencies and bottlenecks. By analyzing the use of RTOS tasks, such as response times and CPU usage, developers are able to pinpoint areas that require optimization. Such information is extremely valuable for improving system performance, especially in real-time applications where consistent behavior is critical. Profiling not only aids the optimization of individual parts but also allows a general understanding of how such parts interact, supporting the basis of a holistic approach to performance analysis within an RTOS context. Benchmarking is a useful compliment to profiling since it offers a comparative study against industry standard or competition. Benchmarking allows developers to measure the performance of their RTOSs relative to others of similar nature, and while doing so, they can learn lessons that will guide their improvement strategies. Benchmarking begins with profiling analysis of the strengths and weaknesses and requires close familiarity with the enterprise's operational goals. Application of benchmarking techniques helps firms observe their processes and understand their performance in relation to a broader value chain, according to the premises in the theory of benchmarking-based enterprises (BBE) (Vasilescu et al., 2025). A general overview in this manner ultimately helps RTOS developers to develop metrics that are in line with best practices and maximize system efficiency. Application of profiling and benchmarking in RTOS systems emphasizes a strategic time management process that is dynamic and iterative. As companies build their systems, repeated assessment through profiling informs adjustments necessary for attaining performance benchmarks. This loop of evaluation allows teams to refine process workflows, suggesting adjustments that are essential for efficient timing constraint management. By repeatedly referring back to performance metrics and using the lessons learned through both profiling and benchmarking, the developers are most suited to innovate and enhance their RTOS. Not only does this foresight contribute to enhancing the quality of software solutions, but it also ensures that they are in compliance with the basic requirements of real-time constraints, thus establishing the importance of these methodologies in the efficient management of time in RTOS (Vasilescu et al., 2025).

6.4.3. Real-Time Trace Analysis

Time management effectiveness in RTOS is severely dependent on the ability to perform complete Real-Time Trace Analysis. This is an analytical process involving meticulous gathering and testing time-stamped data reflecting system activity during real runtime. This type of analysis simplifies the identification of bottlenecks as well as anomalies and hence enables developers to optimize system performance and resource utilization. By observing task scheduling and the duration it takes to run them, developers can ensure deadlines are not met while ensuring system stability. Advanced trace analysis techniques enable developers to better see time-related issues and underscore the role played by these analyses in helping bring about overall performance optimization in real-world applications. An example of an application of Advanced Trace Analysis in the real world is in fault injection strategy design, which is important to guaranteeing the dependability of embedded systems in safety-critical applications. The example includes the employment of fault injection environments for carrying out systematic testing of low-cost embedded microprocessor-based boards, allowing for an analysis of their behavior in various stress conditions. Here, EXFI demonstrates the critical intersection of fault injection and trace analysis. With a software-based approach drawing on Trace Exception Mode, faults within the system that might be present are efficiently detected and removed in real-time, enhancing system resilience and reliability within real-time processing limitations (Benso et al., 1998) (Figure 6.8).

Figure 6.8. *Real-time track analysis.*

Source: https://media.geeksforgeeks.org/wp-content/uploads/20240705124654/Real-time-anallytics.webp.

Apart from this, integration of data analysis techniques into Real-Time Trace Analysis becomes increasingly important with the additional focus on big-data center infrastructures. The consolidation of several systems and parts requires a proper mechanism for analyzing the massive amounts of data generated in the process. Logging mechanisms such as BiDAl have the advantage of collecting and analyzing log data across different platforms. Applied with modern data mining technologies, data mining for this aim transforms system performance evaluation to discover previously hidden patterns and correlations that are directly applicable to practice in time management of RTOS environments. This analysis improves efficiency and lessens complexity, ultimately enhancing time management in real-time complex systems (Babaoglu et al., 2015).

SUMMARY

To sum up, proper time management for RTOS is important in the aspect of addressing the particular requirements of real-time applications. Real-time systems require operating systems to not only be capable of meeting deadlines but also to guarantee determinism, which is critical for performance and function. Analysis of some of the various RTOS features—such as reacting to external events and synchronization of tasks—takes on central significance to ensure that systems are responsive and dependable under dynamic conditions. As suggested by research, the aggregate measure of these features can provide a valuable analysis framework through which to evaluate the performance of different operating systems, ultimately helping drive developers' system architecture and design decisions (Conde et al., 1996). Furthermore, good time management is far more than just technical requirements; it affects the overall reliability and efficacy of the systems used in high-stakes applications. Time management errors can bring about disastrous system failure, particularly in such domains as healthcare, aerospace, and transport where stakes are very high. With a system that performs detailed analyses of intertask data exchanges and resource sharing, developers can identify bottlenecks and optimize system performance. This preventive solution to time management in RTOS not only keeps risks away but also optimizes the end-user experience by ensuring execution of applications as wished under various workloads (Weinmann, 2025). Given consideration to the ever-coming computing technology breakthroughs, the call for efficient management of time within RTOS will only grow stronger. With more sectors utilizing real-time data for making decisions, the operating systems have to evolve to cater to these constantly changing needs. Greater R&D in measurement of performance will keep driving this evolution, paving the way towards industry standardization. By incorporating holistic evaluation practices and an environment of continuous improvement, stakeholders have the ability to significantly enhance the reliability of real-time systems so that they are capable of keeping abreast with the increasing demands of modern-day applications (Conde et al., 1996). This feedback mechanism promotes technological advancement, while simultaneously ensuring the highest possible levels of system performance as well as reliability.

Effective use of time in RTOS is vital for the successful functioning of embedded systems. One major aspect is providing support for task scheduling and prioritizing, so that time-dependent tasks are carried out within deadlines. As applications across various domains are progressively demanding—e.g., satellite flight software applications—there certainly exists a demand for solutions supporting a variety of real-time requirements. The TASTE toolset itself exemplifies such a requirement by creating an end-to-end framework that takes existing technologies like Simulink and C and integrates them into an efficient process for generating real-time software. Not only does this make it easier to minimize the loss of complexity involved with numerous programming languages, but it also maximizes the transparent construction and verification of high-quality systems needed for applications today, particularly in high-stakes areas like aerospace and defense (Conquet et al., 2010). Moreover, the topology of IoT adds new challenges in time management for RTOS. With an increasing number of devices getting connected, synchronization of heterogeneous modules with accuracy becomes a requirement. Employing higher Media Access Control (MAC) protocols that offer real-time communication in wireless sensor networks is one way to counter such complexities. Legacy operating systems typically are not on the list, with the real-time ability necessary for secure communication among IoT devices. RIOT OS is a prime example in this space to illustrate how a well-crafted, custom-fit RTOS can have comprehensive time management features. With support of concurrent use of hardware timers and enhanced power efficiency, RIOT OS addresses the critical requirements of modern IoT applications, subsequently paving the way for improved time management solutions in embedded systems (Roussel et al., 2015). Overall, the efficient time management in RTOS is critical to enhanced performance and reliability of embedded systems in numerous industries. By employing the latest tools like TASTE and advanced operating systems like RIOT, programmers can coordinate tasks better and receive better scheduling. These steps not only improve real-time applications' responsiveness but also ensure that they remain capable of dealing with the complexities introduced by the latest technologies like IoT. The importance of such advancements cannot be exaggerated, as they provide the basis for successful and reliable systems that support our increasingly networked world. A global understanding and application of these time management strategies in RTOS will be essential to addressing the challenges of modern embedded computing environments.

REFERENCES

1. Adelantado, M., Chaudron, J. B., & Siron, P. (2010). Towards an HLA run-time infrastructure with hard real-time capabilities. https://core.ac.uk/download/12042130.pdf (accessed on 29th September 2025).
2. Alhammad, A., Fröhlich, A., Gracioli, G., et al. (2015). A survey on cache management mechanisms for real-time embedded systems. https://core.ac.uk/download/144148885.pdf (accessed on 29th September 2025).
3. Aved, A. J., Hamza-Lup, G. L., Hua, K. A., & Peng, R. (2025). An IP-based live database approach to surveillance application development. https://core.ac.uk/download/pdf/22877002.pdf (accessed on 29th September 2025).
4. Babaoglu, O., Balliu, A., Marzolla, M., et al. (2015). A big data analyzer for large trace logs. http://arxiv.org/abs/1509.00773 (accessed on 29th September 2025).
5. Benso, A., Carreira, J., Rebaudengo, M., Sonza Reorda, M., Prinetto, P., Powell, D., et al. (1998). EXFI: A low-cost fault injection system for embedded microprocessor-based boards. https://core.ac.uk/download/pdf/11373965.pdf (accessed on 29th September 2025).
6. Berge, G., Ganesan, R., Goldsmith, D., Gungor, V., Hong, Y., Matsuda, T., et al. (2012). Wireless industrial monitoring and control networks: The journey so far and the road ahead. https://core.ac.uk/download/pdf/11484488.pdf (accessed on 29th September 2025).
7. Bergmann, N. W., & Tang, Y. (2015). A hardware scheduler based on task queues for FPGA-based embedded real-time systems. https://core.ac.uk/download/43368987.pdf (accessed on 29th September 2025).
8. Bonenfant, A., Gerdes, M., Mikulu, F., et al. (2010). WCET analysis of a parallel 3D multigrid solver executed on the MERASA multi-core. https://core.ac.uk/download/62915730.pdf (accessed on 29th September 2025).
9. Boukhobza, J., & Olivier, P. (2012). A hardware time manager implementation for the Xenomai real-time kernel of embedded Linux. http://arxiv.org/abs/1208.6428 (accessed on 29th September 2025).
10. Buyya, R., Calheiros, R. N., & Garg, S. K. (2011). SLA-oriented resource provisioning for cloud computing: Challenges, architecture, and solutions. http://arxiv.org/abs/1201.4522 (accessed on 29th September 2025).
11. Cardoso, N., Cardoso, P., Gomes, T., et al. (2014). Co-designed FreeRTOS deployed on FPGA. https://core.ac.uk/download/55637223.pdf (accessed on 29th September 2025).

12. Churnetski, K. (2006). Real-time scheduling algorithms, task visualization. https://core.ac.uk/download/232137715.pdf (accessed on 29th September 2025).
13. Coates, G., Duffy, A. H. B., Hills, B., et al. (2000). Coordination approaches and systems–Part I: A strategic perspective. https://core.ac.uk/download/9019019.pdf (accessed on 29th September 2025).
14. Conde, J. F., García-Martínez, A., & Viña, Á. (1996). A comprehensive approach in performance evaluation for modern real-time operating systems. https://core.ac.uk/download/29399340.pdf (accessed on 29th September 2025).
15. Conquet, E., Dissaux, P., Hugues, J., et al. (2010). The TASTE Toolset: Turning human designed heterogeneous systems into computer built homogeneous software. https://core.ac.uk/download/12041536.pdf (accessed on 29th September 2025).
16. Díaz Castañeda, J. L., & Ocampo-Martínez, C. (2019). Energy efficiency in discrete-manufacturing systems: Insights, trends, and control strategies. https://core.ac.uk/download/288625543.pdf (accessed on 29th September 2025).
17. Díaz González, F., Gallart, R., Girbau Llistuella, F., et al. (2018). Smart grid architecture for rural distribution networks: Application to a Spanish pilot network. https://core.ac.uk/download/157811722.pdf (accessed on 29th September 2025).
18. Dyer, L., & Ericksen, J. (2004). Toward a strategic human resource management model of high reliability organization performance. https://core.ac.uk/download/5119743.pdf (accessed on 29th September 2025).
19. Dyer, L., Takla, M. G., & Wright, P. M. (1999). Execution: The critical "what's next?" in strategic human resource management. https://core.ac.uk/download/5132392.pdf (accessed on 29th September 2025).
20. Emmerich, W. (2000). Software engineering and middleware: A roadmap (Invited talk). https://core.ac.uk/download/1669452.pdf (accessed on 29th September 2025).
21. García-Martínez, A., Molano, A., & Viña, Á. (1996). The design and implementation of a multimedia storage server to support video-on-demand applications. https://core.ac.uk/download/29399342.pdf (accessed on 29th September 2025).
22. Gill, C. D. (2002). Flexible scheduling in middleware for distributed rate-based real-time applications–Doctoral dissertation, May 2002. https://core.ac.uk/download/233234588.pdf (accessed on 29th September 2025).

23. Giurca Vasilescu, L., & Sitnikov, C. (2025). A global vision over benchmarking process: Benchmarking based enterprises. https://core.ac.uk/download/pdf/7299774.pdf (accessed on 29th September 2025).
24. Hamez, A., Hugues, J., & Siron, P. (2012). PRISE: An integrated platform for research and teaching of critical embedded systems. https://core.ac.uk/download/12043826.pdf (accessed on 29th September 2025).
25. Kafka, M. (2021). Thermal and power management in avionics OS scheduler. https://core.ac.uk/download/480385479.pdf (accessed on 29th September 2025).
26. Kaur, R., Kowsalya, P., Aldehayyat, J., Rakesh, J., Dhande, J., & Singh, M. (2024). Innovations in project management: Leveraging technology for improved efficiency and performance. In *2024 International Conference on Innovative Computing, Intelligent Communication and Smart Electrical Systems (ICSES)*. https://www.semanticscholar.org/paper/37cd0b14b30f5da9536cd3c20dda21c9a473c545 (accessed on 29th September 2025).
27. Kennedy, K. J. (2025). Surface habitat systems. https://core.ac.uk/download/pdf/10547314.pdf (accessed on 29th September 2025).
28. Kihl, M., Nyberg, C., & Widell, N. (2002). Overload protection for CORBA systems with time constraints. https://core.ac.uk/download/83786423.pdf (accessed on 29th September 2025).
29. Madden, M. M. (2025). Challenges using Linux as a real-time operating system. https://core.ac.uk/download/pdf/323104037.pdf (accessed on 29th September 2025).
30. Maïza, C., Rihani, H., Rivas, J. M., Goossens, J., Altmeyer, S., & Davis, R. I. (2019). A survey of timing verification techniques for multi-core real-time systems. *ACM Computing Surveys, 52*, 1–38. https://doi.org/10.1145/3323212 (accessed on 29th September 2025).
31. Mancuso, R., & Roozkhosh, S. (2020). The potential of programmable logic in the middle: Cache bleaching. https://open.bu.edu/bitstream/2144/40671/1/PLIM_rtas20.pdf (accessed on 29th September 2025).
32. Niadu, K. V., Yamini, A., Kumar, Y. N. V. S. A., Supraja, S. S., & Sushma, G. (2025). Implementation of robust real-time RV32I processor. *International Journal of Innovative Science and Research Technology*. https://www.semanticscholar.org/paper/798ca7707c0a11594321de6dfb18aa0360f84a6e (accessed on 29th September 2025).
33. Raj, C. A. (2025). Innovations in real-time operating systems (RTOS) for safety-critical embedded systems. *Journal of Computer Science and Technology Studies*. https://www.semanticscholar.org/paper/75bda91f2aee21dcb015c79325d5aeda643e4c17 (accessed on 29th September 2025).

34. Reghenzani, F., Massari, G., & Fornaciari, W. (2019). The real-time Linux kernel. *ACM Computing Surveys, 52*, 1–36. https://doi.org/10.1145/3297714 (accessed on 29th September 2025).
35. Roussel, K., Song, Y. Q., & Zendra, O. (2015). RIOT OS paves the way for implementation of high-performance MAC protocols. https://core.ac.uk/download/49532959.pdf (accessed on 29th September 2025).
36. Shea, T. J. (2008). Control system integration. https://core.ac.uk/download/44195324.pdf (accessed on 29th September 2025).
37. Sinha, S. (2018). Scheduling policies and system software architectures for mixed-criticality computing. https://core.ac.uk/download/304658766.pdf (accessed on 29th September 2025).
38. Springer, T., & Zhao, P. (2024). Design and implementation of a real-time rate-based task scheduler for real-time operating systems: A case study with VxWorks. *Advances in Internet of Things & Embedded Systems*. https://www.semanticscholar.org/paper/fd6b0a7a1f5403d0106d488d7bbd5b1209fbd1cd (accessed on 29th September 2025).
39. Sultana, H. (2023). Real-time systems: Scheduling and resource management networking. *ShodhKosh: Journal of Visual and Performing Arts*. https://www.semanticscholar.org/paper/f282c9ab27d11e6e381a330db3f4df6bee60e56e (accessed on 29th September 2025).
40. Ulianko, M. (2012). Implementation of RTOS to the WSN node. https://core.ac.uk/download/30281552.pdf (accessed on 29th September 2025).
41. Varsha, S., Manasa, D. N., & Manvitha, H. (2024). Real-time operating system for smart home automation. In *2024 8th International Conference on Computational System and Information Technology for Sustainable Solutions (CSITSS)*. https://www.semanticscholar.org/paper/5f6af47261a4e025587a7aaaa6503b8b17e60024 (accessed on 29th September 2025).
42. Weinmann, J. (2025). Agglomerative magnets and informal regulatory networks: Electricity market design convergence in the USA and Continental Europe. https://core.ac.uk/download/pdf/7139849.pdf (accessed on 29th September 2025).

CHAPTER 7

MEMORY MANAGEMENT IN REAL-TIME SYSTEMS

Contents

INTRODUCTION

With the rapid-evolving nature of computing, effective real-time memory management has emerged as a key research topic. Because the demand for responsive and reliable programs only grows stronger, it becomes necessary to learn the dynamics of memory allocation and handling. Real-time systems, which carry out data processing and deliver output within definite time limits, have unique problems that are not consistently addressed by traditional memory handling techniques. This short memory management review highlights the requirement for maximizing performance and power efficiency, particularly as emerging technologies such as non-volatile memory revolutionize the underlying computing system building blocks. The integration of new memory technologies introduces concerns regarding methodology in use today, paving the way for improved methodology aligned with the stringent demands of real-time programs. Subtracted from the intricacy of memory management is the intensive energy usage in modern computing systems.

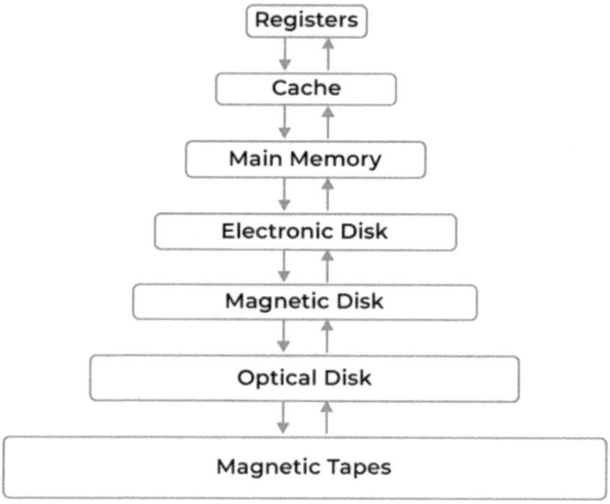

Figure 7.1. Memory management.

Source: https://www.geeksforgeeks.org/operating-systems/memory-management-in-operating-system/.

As previous studies have indicated, the majority of energy used by computing systems is for main memory access, which has triggered researchers to explore innovative solutions such as phase change memory (PCM) (Mittal et al., 2013). PCM provides unique advantages in the form of low read latency and low leakage power but is burdened by issues such as high write latency along with low write endurance. Consequently, scientists are compelled to explore architecture-level approaches intended to minimize power usage in systems based on PCM. This research is essential not only to guide the evolution of memory technology but also to establish environmentally friendly methods in developing real-time systems, whereby responsivity and power consumption have to be symbiotic. Additionally, advancements in fields like cloud computing similarly highlight the need for advanced memory management methods in real-time systems. The shift to cloud infrastructures brings new challenges as resources are often managed by ad-hoc frameworks that require manual tuning by experts (Berral et al., 2013). Efficient memory management in such a scenario necessitates sophisticated awareness of resource allocation based on information available in real-time and client requests. Machine learning and data mining techniques are being explored as alternative means of forecasting resource requirements and quality of service that have great potential to simplify memory management operations. With the integration of advanced prediction mechanisms, engineers can build stronger and more efficient real-time systems capable of handling the advanced demands of modern applications, ultimately contributing to the general objective of enhancing systemic performance in dynamic computation environments (Figure 7.1).

Definition of Real-Time Systems

Real-time systems are known for their capability to process data and respond to input within tight time constraints, a characteristic that differs from common computing systems. The systems are not only required to perform the tasks but also do them on time, and therefore, they play an important role in fields such as vehicle systems, telecommunications, and medical devices. The need for real-time arises from the risk of delayed responses leading to critical failure or danger. Thus, designing real-time systems involves giving a lot of importance to timing, reliability, and performance aspects, which are crucial to their smooth functioning in dynamic and often changing environments. Classification of real-time systems is most commonly divided into hard and soft. Hard real-time systems require mandatory observance of timing constraints, with even slight deviations potentially having catastrophic effects. Soft real-time systems tolerate some delay without serious adverse effect on operation, placing a premium upon throughput over observance of strict timing. This real-time separation affects memory management methods, as hard real-time systems need deterministic memory allocation to enable timely job execution, while soft systems may indeed utilize more lenient approaches, which will allow for optimizations in resource consumption. In both cases, efficient memory management is crucial in enabling the unique run-time needs of real-time applications. Addressing the challenges of memory management in real-time systems demands a fine understanding of their operating constraints and requirements. For instance, the incorporation of advanced behaviors, such as constraints and synchronization, is very taxing to implementers of such systems. As shown in recent studies, software component composability matters in dealing with such complexities (Aksit et al., 2000). This issue also persists even within quantum memory management, where the dependencies and operational requirements must be tactically balanced to provide performance and prevent resource bottlenecks (Amy et al., 2019).

Hence, having a clear focus on real-time system definitions and their unique resource managing needs remains instrumental in further enhancing the capabilities and reliability of such systems within an interconnected world.

Importance of Memory Management

Efficient memory management is extremely crucial in real-time systems since the system must react in a timely and deterministic manner to stimuli. Real-time systems do not have the timing constraints like regular applications; hence memory deallocation and allocation should occur predictably. Inefficient memory management may cause fragmentation in the sense that small free portions of memory will be unusable and hence slow down the processing of data. This need for efficiency is particularly applicable where dynamic systems involve component classifiers. For instance, the Geometrically Optimum and Online-Weighted Ensemble algorithm uses an effective memory management policy to achieve maximum weight distribution based on recent data points, showing the critical necessity of flexibility in memory resources in dynamically evolving systems (Bonab et al., 2017). This optimization not only improves accuracy but also optimizes memory use in terms of operation requirements, thereby demonstrating the pivotal role that effective memory management plays in ensuring the system is reliable. Even farther, memory management relevance goes beyond allocation strategies; it encompasses the need for systems to fetch and utilize data effectively. In real-time systems, maximum availability of pertinent information is essential. Similarly, as human memory tags useful memories to enable quick retrieval, effective memory management techniques must prioritize useful information to be processed in an instant. This analogy reminds one of behavior principles in human cognition, where context and relevance determine memory accessibility (Caprani et al., 2012). Similarly cognitive systems process huge amounts of data without making most-relevant content any more difficult to reach, real-time systems have to make use of memory management techniques maximizing for the most-important information within limited time constraints. Thus, thorough understanding of memory hierarchization can enhance the performance of real-time systems in maximizing the pursuit between artificial intelligence and processing as a human brain. Finally, the constantly evolving nature of technology implies that memory management in real-time systems continually changes to meet emerging challenges. As systems call for larger sizes of data and more complicated demands, static memory management strategies may be bogged down by changing requirements. Advances in algorithmic inventions, such as online environment adaptive classifiers, can transform the way memory is managed (Bonab et al., 2017). Through the incorporation of sophisticated weighting techniques, systems can dynamically allocate memory resources according to existing demand, thereby improving efficiency and responsiveness. As real-time systems evolve, therefore, so too must the methods employed when dealing with memory. An emphasis on continuous improvement in such techniques not only optimizes system performance but ensures that real-time systems can respond suitably to changing conditions without compromising on their critical operational levels. Against this backdrop, memory management is far less a technological imperative than a foundation for operational robustness and adaptability in a metamorphosing technology landscape.

7.1. MEMORY MANAGEMENT TECHNIQUES

Effective memory management is crucial in real-time systems, especially where precise timing and limits on resources are present. Among the various methods adopted, automatic memory management programs have significant advantages towards providing low programming errors. These advantages, however, are typically eliminated in hard real-time systems owing to their intrinsic drawbacks, including being inefficient to provide quick response times and utilization of excessive memory resources. Embedded systems today struggle to leverage such techniques, so others more appropriate to real-time were also explored. One of these others is Real-Time Reference Counting (RTRC), which was modified to address the shortcomings of current garbage collection schemes, and thus automatic memory management for hard real-time systems is now more possible (Bacon et al., 1940). By providing maximized memory use for live objects, RTRC is a profound improvement in memory management methods implemented in real-time systems. Memory management region-based technique is another new method applied in memory management that has been a top candidate for the garbage collection technique implemented in real-time and embedded systems. The method operates by dividing memory into regions or blocks of memory and handling them in batches. Critically, the stack-of-regions discipline ensures that memory deallocation and allocation do not create dangling references, which compromise system reliability. At the core of the approach is a region type inference algorithm that enhances compile-time safety, allowing programmers to automatically analyze and control memory regions without the risk of runtime errors. An official soundness proof has been established for this region type system, justifying its soundness and effectiveness in managing memory in object-oriented styles. Region-based management then further provides safety as well as addressing the specific requirements of real-time systems (Wright et al., 2008). Aside from RTRC and region-based management, hybrids combining methods from automatic garbage collection and memory management by hand are gaining more focus. These hybrids attempt to capture the advantage of both strategies while confining their respective disadvantages. By the intelligent combination of hand control with features of automatic memory management, this hybrid programs seek to provide timely responses required of real-time environments without incurring the overhead usually paid by purely automatic systems. This balance can prove critical in areas where response is an absolute requirement, such as in automotive, aerospace, and medical equipment. As these hybrid frameworks are continued to be researched, they could be the solution to realizing effective and efficient memory management within systems where a millisecond can make all the difference, ultimately providing benefits in performance and reliability for real-time applications (Figure 7.2).

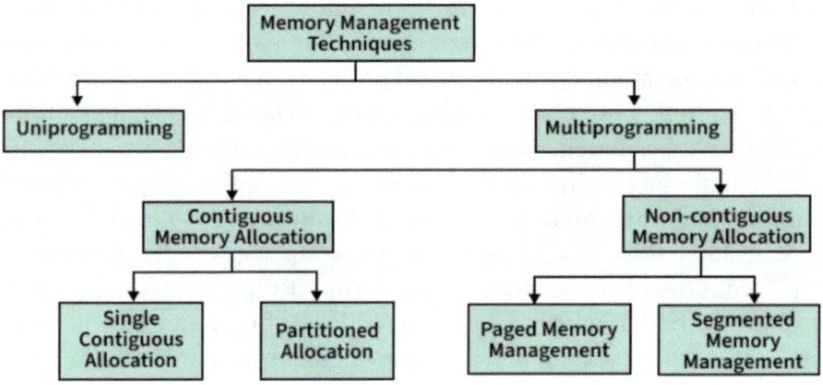

Figure 7.2. Memory management techniques.

Source: https://www.geeksforgeeks.org/operating-systems/memory-management-in-operating-system/.

7.1.1. Static Memory Allocation

Static allocation of memory, which is one of the fundamental principles in real-time memory management, is a method applied to allocate memory at compile time and not at runtime. This method provides a predictable and consistent pattern of use that is essential in real-time systems where predictability of resources and timing is paramount. By choosing the memory needed before execution, static allocation prevents the overhead of dynamic memory management such as fragmentation and potential for allocation failure. Static allocation also simplifies debugging as the addresses of the memory do not shift throughout the life of a program. Such reliability is essential for systems that must meet stringent timing and performance requirements, thereby enhancing the overall resource utilization efficiency of real-time applications. Static memory allocation is also desirable from the point of view of optimizing performance and therefore highly sought after in embedded and response time-intensive systems. By allocating memory statically, program developers can ensure that data structures are access pattern and size optimized, resulting in improved cache behavior and performance. Such optimization is especially vital in real-time systems since any form of delay would cause lethal failures or reduced performance. Moreover, static memory allocation meshes flawlessly with the principles of deterministic programming, allowing one to calculate resource consumption and timing precisely. As new powerful applications and services have appeared in the cloud environment, as evidenced by growing demands for efficient load balancing and resource provisioning in data centers (Ghodke et al., 2018), static memory allocation remains a significant approach to maintaining system behavior under management (Figure 7.3).

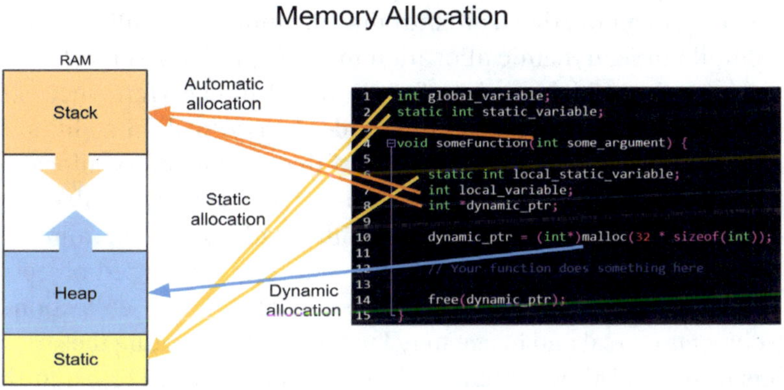

Figure 7.3. *Static memory allocation in real-time systems.*

Source: https://www.digikey.es/en/maker/projects/introduction-to-rtos-solution-to-part-4-memory-management/6d4dfcaa1ff84f57a2098da8e6401d9c?srsltid=AfmBOorm9OxkVacANrP471Co1cSqVr5kahgwPdNQSbgYdZYzn3tzqQy_.

But while static memory allocation has numerous benefits, it even possesses its own drawbacks. The lack of flexibility in re-allocating the resources can prove to be a huge drawback in systems where the requirements of the system may vary over a span of time. This lack of flexibility may lead to sub-optimum usage of memory resources or, conversely, shortages when the need exceeds the pre-allocated value. In real-time systems, the consequences of such deficiencies can be disastrous, threatening system integrity and response reliability. Furthermore, static allocation is unable to accommodate applications with different levels of memory requirements at runtime, hence necessitating careful design considerations at development time. As techniques improve and requirements for multi-threading increase, as have been argued in safety forums on programming languages like Cuckoo (West et al., 1997), the problems of static memory allocation must be addressed with caution so that there is a harmony between reliability and flexibility.

7.1.2. Dynamic Memory Allocation

Dynamic memory allocation is quite crucial in memory management, particularly in real-time systems where efficient and predictable usage of memory is involved. In real-time computational systems, the timely accomplishment of tasks can rely on the utilization and availability of memory resources. Dynamic memory allocation, in which memory is deallocated and allocated as and when needed by the system, can cause unpredictability since fragmentation and memory management overhead are introduced. Unlike static allocation of fixed sizes at compile time, dynamic allocation must be properly controlled to avoid worst-case behavior, which can interfere with real-time performance and cause missed deadlines and system instability under heavy load. In addition, adding the overhead of garbage collection on top of dynamic memory allocation adds yet another layer of complexity to real-time systems. Garbage collection, while useful in unblocking unused memory, generally leads to nondeterministic pause times once the garbage collector identifies and releases unused objects. Mark and Sweep algorithm employed in conventional garbage collection entails memory object traversal and hence may lead to delays violating the strict timing constraints of the real-time system as described in presented research findings. This conflict between the need for efficient memory reclamation and the need for predictability of execution times demonstrates the sensitivity of dynamic memory management in such systems that demand stability and efficiency under varying loads. To offer solutions to the needs of real-time systems, there is a need to explore other memory management techniques that can optimize dynamic allocation with minimized interruptions. More recent research has proposed mechanisms such as reference counting and contamination garbage collection as more deterministic solutions, although these methods also have limitations inherent in them. The research proposes that it would be a good solution to run multiple garbage collectors concurrently because it would allow the system to better manage the availability of memory resources without excessive latency. Moreover, memory allocator choice has a significant effect on performance, scalability, and efficiency as proven in background research where some allocators increased query engine performance significantly. Thus, leveraging advanced memory allocation techniques geared toward real-time applications remains essential for achieving efficiency as well as reliability in such high-demanding applications, leading to enhanced system performance and end-user satisfaction.

7.1.3. Memory Pooling

Memory pooling is a significant memory management technique in real-time systems to address the issue of dynamic memory allocation. For those systems where the time factor is most crucial, both deallocation and memory allocation introduce latency and hence degrade the performance of the system.

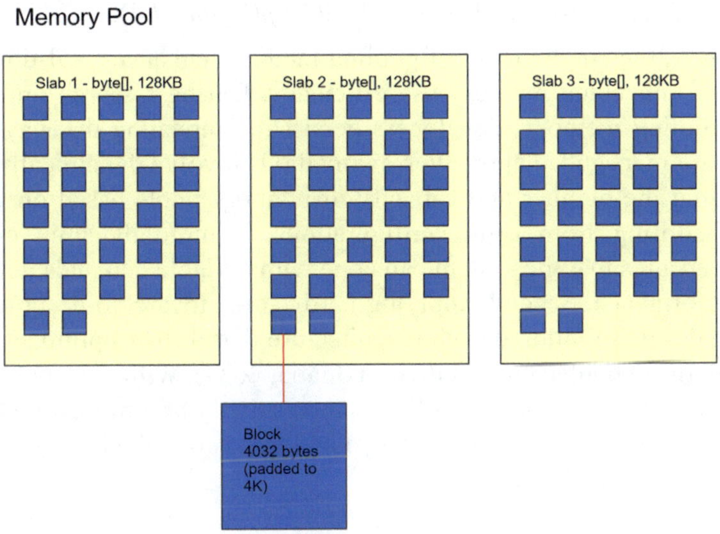

Figure 7.4. *Memory pool.*

Source: https://external-content.duckduckgo.com/iu/?u=https%3A%2F%2Fmgravell.github.io%2Fpipelines.docs%2FMem oryPool%2Fm emorypoo l.png&f=1&nofb=1&ipt=bfc6ed eb301e3b9 30903 f352e7dc af6e2 5c98677 ef08738e55406a30459df7a1.

Memory pooling reverses this issue through the pre-allocation of memory blocks with a fixed size, in such a way that the system can reuse them in an efficient manner. This rigid structure not only enhances performance through minimized allocation delay but also simplifies the memory management procedure. With ongoing demands of real-time support from applications in the fields of autonomous cars and industrial automation, the adoption of memory pooling becomes ever more essential to maintaining strict operation requirements while efficiently managing complex workloads (Bhatia, 2025). Besides, memory pooling offers significant advantages with respect to memory fragmentation, which is usually a problem with traditional dynamic memory management. Memory allocation with frequent calls may cause scattered free memory areas, making it challenging to allocate big memory requests. By utilizing a pooling technique, these systems can effectively reduce fragmentation because memory usage is compiled into defined pools. With fewer random free blocks present, memory allocation becomes deterministic and ultimately improves the responsiveness and reliability of the systems. This is particularly significant in scenarios like monitoring financial transactions, where accurate and timely processing of data is critical (Dave et al., 2025) (Figure 7.4).

Consequently, the employment of pooling methods enhances real-time system integrity by enhancing memory use efficiency. During research on advanced memory pooling methods, developers persist in innovating the way memory resources are managed adaptively. New methods involve dynamically resizing and changing the number and capacity of memory pools based on workload demands, shifting from rigid configurations to more dynamic ones. The flexibility ensures that the system can cope with variable demands without any loss of performance. Second, applying hardware-software co-design concepts allows the design of tailored cache architecture that further optimizes memory access patterns in pooled environments (Bhatia, 2025). With the emerging trend of real-time systems, memory pooling is increasingly becoming a fundamental component of efficient memory management that forms the basis of enhanced performance in critical applications.

7.2. CHALLENGES IN MEMORY MANAGEMENT

The area of real-time memory management is confronted with multifold challenges, particularly in dealing with the extra complexity brought about by multicore processors. The most significant one is the uncontrollability of common resources, which shatters the reliability of worst-case execution time estimation of tasks. Because multicore processors are utilized to facilitate higher computational power, the design aspects of such as the memory cache hierarchy are amenable to unpredictability required in real-time systems. Research has indicated the need for advanced cache management approaches aimed at evading these causes of unpredictability. A thorough analysis and classification of these techniques are of paramount significance to the management of the unique requirements of real-time embedded systems, and yet it remains an open and critical problem among researchers (Alhammad et al., 2015). Another major memory management issue in real-time systems is conflict in the main memory subsystem. The increasing multicore system complexity necessitates the detailed analysis of the behavior of memory controllers, as well as understanding the timing constraints set forth by JEDEC standards. The need for compliance with safety regulations and ongoing system reliability necessitates that developers provide solid proof of task interaction and how one can cause another to be delayed in shared memory environments. Such intricacy is also increased by the understanding that not much is known regarding how different tasks will concurrently utilize shared common memory resources. Without effective contention management, it is very difficult to validate multicore platforms' reliability and performance, most importantly in safety-critical applications (Fernández et al., 2024). Additionally, the design of low-overhead hardware mechanisms is important for enhancing the management of inter-core contention in multicore real-time systems. Such mechanisms can enable real-time feedback on shared resource behavior and hence enhance traceability of task interactions and their implications on timing and performance. Developers can derive valuable information needed to meet associated safety standards by strictly following incidents of contention within the main memory subsystem. The addition of such novel techniques not only improves the nature of timing-related evidence but also facilitates system architects to make informed decisions while optimizing memory management. Hence, these root issues must be resolved to drive real-time systems forward in the aspect of being reliable and predictable within their parameters (Fernández et al., 2024) (Figure 7.5).

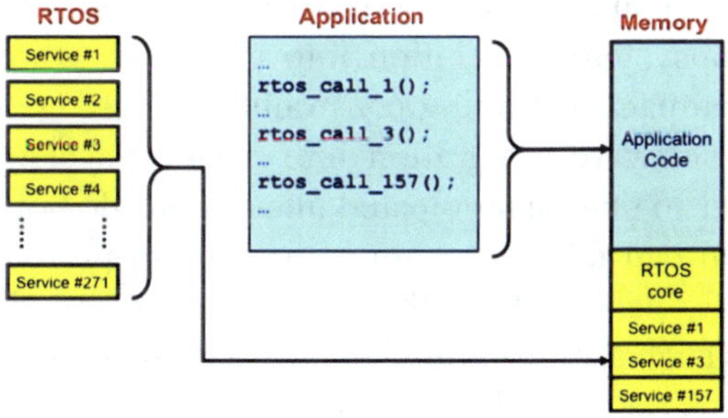

Figure 7.5. RTOS configuration.

Source: https://www.embedded.com/rtos-memory-utilization/.

7.2.1. Timing Constraints

The most significant term in the memory management domain of real-time systems, particularly in terms of predictability and reliability of programs, is the timing constraint. The constraints are significant as they identify the largest period within which some operations must be completed to ensure that the system meets its real-time requirements. The need for precise timing adherence becomes even clearer when considering the complex interrelation between processing capabilities of contemporary systems and memory performance. The disparity in processor and memory speeds, more popularly known as the memory wall problem, highlights how memory access inefficiencies can lead to variable latencies, which conversely affect the overall performance of the system. This unpredictability is especially dangerous for those applications needing hard real-time performance, whose deadline non-adherence causes system catastrophes (Chaparro-Baquero et al., 2018).

In an environment so limited in memory, new scheduling methods are being created in order to harmonize task execution time with memory access patterns. By analyzing differences in execution time as a function of memory allocations, scientists have presented techniques that account for the task relationships through time as well as resultant memory profiles. Such scheduling methods deliver dramatic gains in the practicability of systems, allowing engineers to more predictably meet the tight timing constraints imposed by hard real-time requirements. Advanced scheduling paradigms also include thermal characteristics of multi-core systems, as thermal fluctuations can have a heavy influence on processing cores as well as on memory units and offer another degree of complication in maintaining projects within time-sensitive deliverables (Chaparro-Baquero et al., 2018). Apart from that, considering the growing use of software subsystem integration into electronic control units (ECUs), understanding the impacts of timing constraints in these contexts is extremely significant. New software integration into existing systems also will often necessitate isolation so that unanticipated interactions do not exacerbate timing violations. Isolation can take the form of a memory-protection environment, which is specifically designed for the constraints and working conditions of embedded systems such as those found in the modern automobile. By including efficient mechanisms for enforcing illegal memory accesses, developers can not only preserve the essential timing guarantees but also enhance overall system reliability. Such enhancements, particularly in safety-critical applications like vehicle dynamics control systems, exemplify the necessity of strategic memory management so that performance is not compromised when more subsystems are introduced to established architectures.

7.2.2. Fragmentation Issues

Fragmentation issues are a major issue in the field of memory management in real-time systems. As memory is allocated and deallocated dynamically by systems to cater to various needs, it becomes more probable that memory fragments are formed. These are formed when free memory is split into small, non-contiguous portions that may not be available for large requests, leading to wasteful use of memory. In hard real-time systems where timeliness and predictability take precedence, fragmentation can result in disastrous outcomes, such as increased allocation time and unpredictable latencies. Memory mismanagement not only impacts performance but may also impinge on timely execution of critical tasks, necessitating effective memory management methods geared towards reversing fragmentation. To solve the fragmentation problems inherent in real-time systems, internal and external fragmentation need to be understood. Internal fragmentation results from when memory blocks are larger than necessary, thus causing wastage of space when units of memory are allocated.

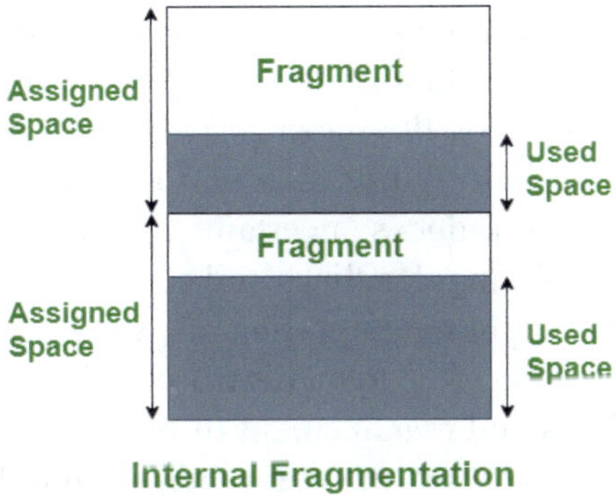

Figure 7.6. Fragmentation issues represent a significant challenge in memory management within real-time systems.

Source: https://media.geeksforgeeks.org/wp-content/uploads/20190924115421/Untitled-Diagram-146.png.

Conversely, external fragmentation results from when a free space is available in numerous distinct locations so that it would be impossible to meet a new demand for contiguous memory. Techniques such as memory pooling, where pre-fixed chunks are handled to cut down the creation of fragments, may enhance memory efficiency. Additionally, employing dynamic memory allocators that can handle memory adaptively at runtime so that allocation and deallocation patterns maintain the status of free memory more contiguous eventually makes support for real-time constraints possible, as described by Durner et al. (2019). Furthermore, management of fragmentation must consider not only the technology deployments but also their impacts on the system architecture as a whole. The performance of real-time systems is heavily reliant on the performance of dynamic memory allocators because poor memory management has a tendency to propagate fragmentation issues. For instance, allocator choice can enhance scalability and influence memory fairness among processes, hence influencing responsiveness within real-time systems. Experiments indicate that selection of an appropriate allocator can greatly improve system performance, emphasizing the need for rigorous analysis while designing memory management devices. Thus, ongoing research on optimizing the performance of allocators and minimizing fragmentation has a crucial role in enhancing real-time systems, making them more reliable and effective in mission-critical systems as expressed by Boardman et al. (2008) (Figure 7.6).

7.2.3. Resource Contention

Resource competition in modern real-time systems has emerged as the core concern, which is often the outcome of workload complexity increasing and competition for limited computational resources. The higher the demand for high-performance functionality, the more systems are operated under various conditions that influence their ability to commit memory and schedule tasks effectively. This variation introduces uncertainty that adversely impacts system performance, leading to missing deadlines and service quality degradation. For instance, in distributed computing environments, workload demands may alter with high velocities, necessitating dynamic adjustment to resource allocation strategies. Hence, analysis and management of resource contentions is critical in ensuring that real-time systems maintain their required performance levels under changing resource availability and operational variability (Bux et al., 2018). The impact of resource contention extends beyond mere performance metrics; they also have a direct impact on real-time service level objectives (SLOs) compliance. SLOs establish specific performance targets that are part of user satisfaction and overall system reliability. However, whenever resource contention complicates task scheduling and memory administration, such targets become harder to achieve. SLOs require systems to execute with strict performance boundaries, but actually, contention for resources in the majority of instances incurs high latency and low throughput. It is observed in studies that the majority of real applications are greatly challenged in meeting aggressive SLOs, particularly when so defined by strict response times and availability targets (Ding et al., 2020). The recognition of such challenges highlights the need for novel techniques that can efficiently predict and overcome the impacts of resource contention in dynamic environments. To overcome resource contention in real-time systems, a number of methodologies have been put forward, from predictive performance modeling (PPM) to tailored resource allocation mechanisms. PPM predicts future resource requirements from past performance history and allows systems to pre-provision memory and computational resources. In the process, they are in a position to effectively reduce contention possibilities and optimize overall system stability. In addition, the classification of the sources of performance variability, as highlighted in recent research studies, provides data that can be employed in optimizing the allocation strategies. Such a precautionary action is not only helpful in enhancing maximal resource utilization but also enables the reduction of delays, hence enhancing the attainment of SLOs in real-time systems (Bux et al., 2018). Lastly, resolving contention for resources is an important aspect for improving memory management activities and enabling real-time systems to meet their operational requirements in a reliable and effective manner.

7.3. IMPACT OF MEMORY MANAGEMENT ON SYSTEM PERFORMANCE

The impact of memory management on system performance is particularly important in real-time systems, where timely task completion is of utmost importance. The methodologies employed in memory management play an important part to play in determining the efficiency with which a system frees up resources and runs tasks. For instance, the task scheduling and monitoring which form part of Adas runtime support represent the dilemma of balancing the requirement for memory allocation with considerations for performance. The problem is a critical one, in that performance may be jeopardized based on the implementation choices utilized by implementers of embedded systems. The intricate relationship between the execution of real-time tasks and memory management practices elucidates that implementers must exercise caution in implementing. Understanding how these parameters interact can significantly contribute to the assurance of systems being responsive and effective in meeting stringent real-time operating specifications (Maule et al., 2025). Additionally, choice of memory management methods, i.e., region-based and garbage collection approaches, heavily impacts system performance in general in embedded applications. Region-based memory management, in particular, has been attracted to its predictability, but it is not without problems. Programmers often have difficulty determining the best number of regions to be allocated before program runs because too many can adversely impact execution time. This is aggravated by the intricacies involved in sustaining performance during memory allocation. Experimental findings have shown that employing more allocated segments can lead to an increase in execution time, which has forced developers to make their code structures optimal in order to meet performance (Hamza et al., 2010). Thus, effective memory management schemes are needed to get optimal real-time performance outcomes. Lastly, memory management implications entail not only execution times but system stability and usage of resources as well. Real-time systems must meet stringent timing and resource requirements since latencies can cause system crashes or non-acceptable performance. Implementers must address both time and space efficiency when defining memory management schemes. The overall impact of these methods is that inefficient handling of memory can result in wastage of resources or uncontrolled behavior and thus reduce the system's reliability. As a matter of fact, identifying the implications of varied memory methods on system performance thus becomes a matter of concern. Therefore, going forward in the area of memory management not only enhances performance measurements but also assists in developing real-time applications to be strong and reliable in nature, emphasizing the importance of ongoing research in this domain (Hamza et al., 2010; Maule et al., 2025).

7.3.1. Latency and Throughput

Throughput and latency are two most important parameters in real-time systems' memory management whose values decide the response and performance of a system. Latency is the time taken before a request is processed to the end, and throughput is the amount of work done in an interval of time. The two interact very strongly, with the improvement in one having an adverse effect on the other. For instance, latency reduction systems prefer quick response time at the cost of overall throughput since fewer system resources are consumed by other tasks. Hence, policies of memory management must carefully strike this balance so that real-time programs meet hard timing constraints and also make efficient use of system resources (Figure 7.7).

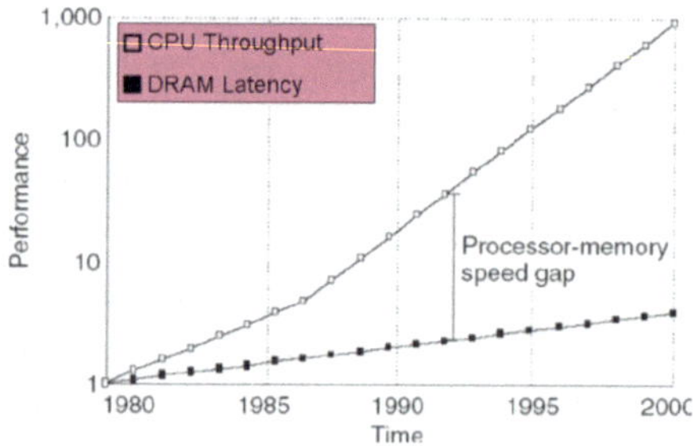

Figure 7.7. Processor–memory latency divide illustrating the memory wall.

Source: https://www.researchgate.net/figure/Processor-memory-latency-divide-introducing-the-memory-wall-5_fig1_224392231.

The latest data handling technologies, particularly in the case of all-flash multi-tiered storage systems, reflect the evolving issues around latency and throughput. While costs are lowered and capacities are enhanced in Flash-based Solid-State Drives (SSDs), traditional Hard Disk Drives (HDDs) are left with the related performance drawbacks. As underlined by Andrews et al. (2017), the development of cutting-edge data placement managers, such as AutoTiering, brings to light how memory allocation can be maximized to achieve increased throughput through the intelligent handling of virtual machine disk files. By reducing unnecessary data migration in such systems, auto-managers can minimize latency during high-priority operations, thereby adding to better overall system performance in real-time systems that require fast and predictable access to data. The significance of optimized throughput and minimum latency is also further explained under in-memory data stream processing platforms such as BriskStream. BriskStream is built with modern shared-memory multicore systems, comprehensively dealing with the complexities of resource management that define real-time scenarios. By means of relative-location factors consideration based on an execution plan optimization paradigm, BriskStream enhances latency as well as throughput, as confirmed through experimental comparisons (He et al., 2019). These technologies underscore the necessity of real-time systems to adopt advanced memory management techniques, keeping both latency and throughput at their highest levels. Ultimately, this balance is one that must be achieved in order to satisfy the performance requirements needed to offer real-time applications and give users seamless experiences within increasingly stressful technology environments (Figure 7.8).

Figure 7.8. Solid-state drive (SSD).

Source: https://res.utmel.com/Images/UEditor/f08d8623-019b-4c8b-ba30-bdfc9a84f715.jpg.

7.3.2. Predictability and Reliability

Predictability and reliability are required in memory management in real-time systems for ensuring that system performance meets rigorous timing constraints. Such environments where timing and order of operations matter, memory management methods must be designed in order to prevent unpredictable delays. Dynamic memory allocation-based systems suffer from memory fragmentation, leading to delay in critical operations and causing deadlines to be missed. The use of deterministic memory management techniques such as static memory allocation or memory pools guarantees the production of a more reliable system for real-time applications. Also, ensuring memory allocation and deallocation operations are time-bound avoids drift from determinism required for the functioning of real-time systems. The predictability issues translate to the hardware aspect of real-time systems, particularly in relation to the utilization of GPUs. These hardware components are increasingly playing a vital role in applications like autonomous vehicles, where they have to be processed immediately. However, as Ferrer et al. (2018) reminds us, common GPU architectures may not be completely compliant with the high safety standards defined in ISO 26262.

As a result, the reliability of such GPUs in automotive use is an issue regarding their loading behavior and their determinism to meet real-time constraints. Consequently, it is also crucial that developers and researchers strive to close these potential loopholes so that not just performance criteria are achieved but safety criteria necessary for dependable utilization in critical applications as well. For achieving added predictability and dependability in real-time memory management systems, research and development into suitable runtime infrastructure also become a significant consideration. The study by Adelantado et al. (2010) highlights the importance of enhancing real-time capabilities in distributed systems, particularly with respect to Quality of Service (QoS) guarantees and scheduling services. With these features, designers can create a more robust memory management system that can accommodate the particular needs of real-time processing. Apart from that, the provision of formal models for verifying real-time simulation processes can provide valuable information regarding potential bottlenecks and latency issues and thus allow better resource allocation. Overall, both software and hardware updates are needed for achieving the necessary predictability and reliability in memory management for real-time systems.

7.3.3. Resource Utilization

Efficient use of resources remains a bedrock principle of real-time system memory management as this directly influences performance as well as dependability. By optimizing memory resources in their utilization, systems can enforce processes to execute under their deadlines without resource conflicts. Dynamic memory deallocation and deallocation are one major way to optimization because they allow the system to adapt rapidly under changing workload conditions. Also, the adoption of advanced memory methods, such as page replacement methods and techniques of minimizing fragmentation, further enhances the use of resources and hence maximum throughput. The requirement to solve all these aspects cannot be overemphasized, particularly in system environments where high efficiency and fast response are primary requirements. Hence, organizations that create real-time programs need to keep their guard up while adopting advanced memory management methods for maximum resource utilization efficiency.

Along with memory management methods, research in architecture to improve energy efficiency is gaining significance in the case of data centers, especially as they strive to meet the relentless demand for data in contemporary computing. Data usage and processing have created enormous power demands in such centers, and innovative methods of power management are required. Techniques such as server consolidation and dynamic voltage and frequency scaling (DVFS) are central to improving energy efficiency while, concurrently, optimizing resource utilization. By classifying these architectural techniques, scientists become better at identifying power reduction strategies without impacting performance. This simultaneous optimization of energy efficiency and resource utilization allows data centers to be sustainable without failing real-time processing needs (Mittal et al., 2014). Field-programmable gate arrays (FPGAs) provide a valuable vehicle for resource exploitation in real-time digital signal processing.

Their parallelism in the internal structure allows for speeding up many algorithms, which in time-critical systems can be determinant. Altering the effective implementation of these algorithms on FPGAs, particularly concerning DSP blocks dedicated to 1-D filter structures, enables designers to achieve high throughput without sacrificing flexibility.

This ability is important in its critical role when applying complicated operations, including high-resolution image large spatial convolutional filters, since keeping functional adaptability makes performance both better in real-time scenarios with dynamics and more feasible for devices to handle (Al-Dujaili et al., 2020). Therefore, incorporating strategies that maximize FPGA utilization results in better memory management, while allowing systems to achieve high throughput and timing requirements simultaneously, all while utilizing resources efficiently (Al-Dujaili et al., 2020).

7.4. CASE STUDIES

Through examining the intricacies of real-time memory management, case studies form a critical tool for model testing and empirical demonstration of theoretical models. Multicore processors, as a case in point, are modern computing demands; however, their use in real-time systems imposes tremendous resource-sharing and predictability challenges. A thorough literature review finds an array of cache management techniques proposed to enhance predictability in such an environment. As noted in an overview of cache management techniques for real-time embedded systems of 1990–2014, a good memory management forms the cornerstone upon which the worst-case execution time estimates are based, thus guaranteeing system efficiency and reliability (Alhammad et al., 2015). This survey not only measures the current practices but also points to the long-standing issues that need more research, so it is a classic case study in real-time computing. Another significant case study to examine is the use of the High-Level Architecture (HLA) standard within real-time systems. A number of research efforts have been focused on the extension of HLA to support the specific limitations of real-time computing by emphasizing the need for QoS assurances and knowledge of worst-case transit times (WCTT).

Such an extension is particularly important while discussing the responsibilities of run-time infrastructures (RTIs) to maintain effective scheduling services in systems. Studies on the achievement of hard real-time properties for HLA federations place high value on a new global bottom-up design strategy for RTIs. Practical applications reveal how scheduling and memory management directly affect system performance in distributed environments and therefore emphasize the necessity of case studies in confirming theoretical abstractions in real-time systems (Adelantado et al., 2010). Also, the results of these case studies not only confirm the necessity of memory management in real-time systems but also highlight the intricacy of research required to address ongoing concerns. Memory management is an ever-evolving topic; therefore, continuous research via case studies allows it to be possible to gain a complete understanding of previous precedents as well as emerging trends.

The classification of research efforts on cache management, in terms of multicore processors, for instance, may be instrumental in informing future research directions. Similarly, a study of the adaptation of HLA to real-time systems provides an example for research into adapting current standards to meet current needs. With such probing questions, the necessity for memory management in order to make real-time systems both efficient and reliable is even more evident, further establishing the necessity of further research in this vital area.

7.4.1. Automotive Control Systems

Incorporating automobile control systems in real-time system memory management has become a focus area of research and development following the progression of vehicles towards increased automation and connectivity. Automative control systems employ sensors, actuators, and sophisticated algorithms heavily to manage vehicle dynamics, safety, and autonomous driving functionality. Since these systems must function properly under tight timing constraints, optimization of memory management is imperative. Meets the constraints of real-time processing to ensure that operations, such as processing data from various sensors, are performed within deadlines. Failure to achieve these deadlines may have catastrophic consequences, particularly in safety-related applications. Hence, one should explore memory architectures that can comfortably meet such strict requirements towards establishing effective automotive control systems.

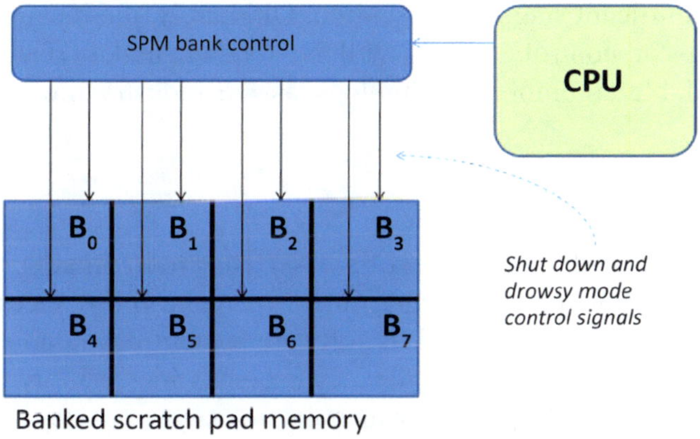

Figure 7.9. *Scratchpad memory configuration.*

Source: https://www.researchgate.net/figure/Scratchpad-memory-configuration_fig2_265865496.

A central problem in the field of automotive control systems is being able to optimize the execution time without compromising on functional safety. The demands of ISO 26262, the functional safety standard for automotive systems, indicate that conventional microarchitectural building blocks like caches and branch predictors tend to complicate worst-case execution time (WCET) analysis. As demonstrated by research, these types of elements are concerned with average-case scenarios and are deficient in providing safe upper bounds on the running of time-critical activities. Automotive engineers are discovering a promising alternative with the advent of software-controlled scratchpad memories (SPMs). SPMs provide explicit control of memory allocation and data transfer, supporting tighter and more accurate performance bounds. This approach not only facilitates adherence to real-time constraints but also facilitates safety-critical features inherent in the automotive industry (Ferrer et al., 2018). In addition, effective memory management methods are imperative to proper implementation of automotive control systems in a cyber-physical system-dominated environment. The requirement to achieve rigorous timing constraints calls for robust means designed to enhance the efficacy of memory usage without sacrificing safety or performance. Through empirical studies, it has been noticed that optimizing the management of stack frames and memory allocation can significantly help enhance automotive programs' performance by reducing WCET (N/A, 2017) (Figure 7.9). For instance, calling on advanced data management techniques, e.g., determining optimal data motion instructions and mapping functions onto SPMs in a strategic fashion, can lower bottlenecks at the most significant stages of execution. Ultimately, the integration of these techniques in car control systems will be fundamental in facilitating safer and more reliable automobile technology as the industry moves toward full automation.

7.4.2. Medical Devices

The use of medical devices in real-time system environments demonstrates the need for optimal memory management to make the devices operational and reliable. As the pace of medical software system development continues to rise, managing data within the devices becomes increasingly complex and warrants strict methodologies. Poor memory management may lead to failure of critical applications with disastrous implications such as misdiagnosis and treatment errors. The safety and effectiveness of such devices highly depend on their ability to manage large volumes of data efficiently. For instance, the integrated methodology in the study demonstrates that rules for sound design are crucial in an effort to mitigate risks associated with software errors resulting from causes other than hardware-software interaction, thereby meeting the need for proper memory handling in real-time systems (Balachandran et al., 2013). Besides, dynamic flexibility in conforming to changing contexts is very crucial for modern medical devices, particularly those that are involved in ongoing monitoring and diagnostic activities. Memory management plays a very significant role in facilitating context-aware programs, which adapt their operations as per real-time data streams. Designing resource-constrained medical devices is particularly insightful, where adaptation in processing the data stream directly influences patient monitoring systems' dependability.

Through the use of context-aware methods, such devices can automatically adjust their operating parameters to sustain performance in the face of changing data rates, highlighting the need for a strong memory management strategy that can support such variances. This flexibility not only maximizes performance but also provides even and proper diagnosis, essential for efficient health provision (Gaber et al., 2009) (Figure 7.10).

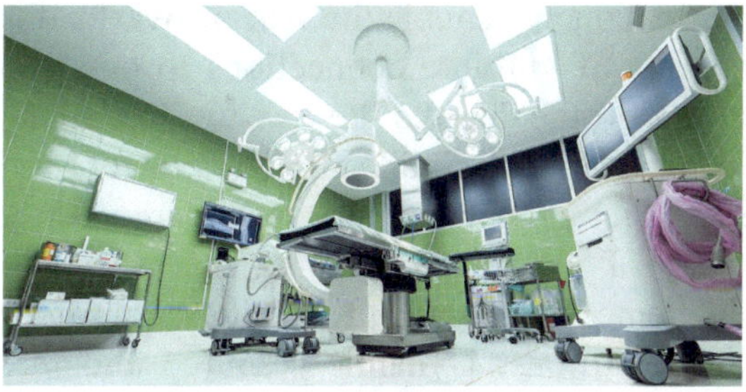

Figure 7.10. Medical devices of real-time systems.

Source: https://www.intervalzero.com/wp-content/uploads/2018/03/ambulance-1822457_960_720.jpg.

In short, the interconnectedness of medical devices and real-time systems dictates the integrated treatment of memory management that is both safe and efficient. The complexity of these systems is still increased by the necessity to conform to industry standards, which stipulate required safety procedures and performance metrics. With medical devices constantly being updated, the ongoing need for new ways of managing memory resources will keep driving innovation in the design and deployment of these technologies. Ensuring error-free software that is safe and reliable is paramount, and as cited in literature, use of methodologies that span across the entire system life cycle will become essential to creating error-free medical device software (Balachandran et al., 2013). Such factors highlight the critical intersection of technological innovation and rigorous management of memory as central to making health care solutions work.

7.4.3. Telecommunications Systems

In telecommunication systems, the combinability of real time processing and efficient memory management is most crucial. Telecommunications networks rely heavily on continuous information flow and hence need systems that have the ability to process and transfer data in short time. With additional growth in demands for high-speed communication, mechanisms for memory management also need to keep up without compromising efficiency. Given the fact that telecommunication networks operate in regions with indefinite data loads, the implementation of sophisticated memory allocation methods is required to ensure no bottlenecks and effective delivery of reliable services. Implementation of sophisticated knowledge management systems has the potential to make it achievable through effective capture and reuse of data that ensures total operational efficacy of telecommunication networks. A serious issue of telecommunication systems is the risk of overloading with resources, particularly in scenarios of multiple connections to one occurrence. As cited in studies on signaling protocols, like the Session Initiation Protocol (SIP), a resource overload can lead to undesirable implications for service continuity and quality, hence the need for proper memory management in real-time systems. Successful processing of incoming signaling messages relies on a delicate balance of available memory space and processing capability, particularly when there are high-load conditions. Dynamic resource and memory assignment algorithms can assist in mitigating overloads by optimizing throughput and enhancing the systems resistance to dynamic user loads. Such interactive scheme not only improves operational efficiency but also user satisfaction by reducing interruptions during usage peaks. Moreover, with changing telecommunication technology, incorporating artificial intelligence and machine learning capabilities within memory management systems is also of vast potential. Intelligent control structures can be utilized to dynamically allocate resources according to real-time needs, improving greatly the responsiveness of telecommunications services. For instance, context-aware framework-integrated systems are able to forecast data flow patterns and redistribute memory resources in time to prevent bottlenecks. The incorporation of such features as automated representation of knowledge and user interfaces can lead to more intelligent management systems that enhance the abilities of operators in real-time decision-making. They not just facilitate easier development of telecommunications systems but also make memory management approaches an essential part in delivering high-quality, dependable communication services in an increasingly interconnected world (Dede et al., 2025; Montazerolghaem et al., 2013).

SUMMARY

With the research of memory management within real-time systems and the intricacies, it is apparent that robust mechanisms are critical to real-time systems' reliability and efficiency. Memory management not only influences the performance measures of real-time applications but also determines their feasibility to meet strict time constraints. As systems get more complex, with efficient memory management skills through innovative buffer techniques, overall efficiency can be enhanced. For instance, adaptive buffering, as illustrated by GreedyDual-Join (GDJ), handles well the natural temporal correlations present in real data streams and helps to demonstrate the necessity for such methods in modern applications. Applications of these methods could significantly transform the treatment of memory allocation in real-time systems, promising the ability to optimize and enhance service quality. Besides, with the ongoing development in technology, the memory management issue in real-time becomes increasingly challenging, necessitating research into other methods. The current literature shows a gap in applying advanced simulation techniques in the study of memory management methodologies, particularly in business and management settings. Using simulation and computational methods, researchers and practitioners can gain insightful knowledge on complex memory behaviors, and thus it is possible to conduct in-depth analysis of possible solutions. The study of such systems within simulated environments has the potential to unlock opportunities for directed improvement in resource utilization and response time, leading to enhanced efficiency in real-world applications. Hence, there lies enormous scope to bridge the existing gaps between theory and practice in this new field. Lastly, the emphasis on the design of context-sensitive and dynamic memory management systems reflects the need for continued innovativeness in this field. Real-time systems are increasingly being used in mission-critical applications, like embedded systems and autonomous automobiles, where failure would result in disastrous consequences. Addressing these needs requires that attention be given not only to improving existing algorithms but also in transcending new paradigms, like the theory of complexity, into functioning models of memory administration. With the help of agent-based simulation methods, the researchers will have the capability of probing the viability of these models in delivering sophisticated solutions for contemporary memory management problems. As the field continues to evolve, embracing such interdisciplinary methods will be essential to enhancing the resilience and extensibility of real-time systems and applications, enabling them to meet the growing demands of an advancing technological landscape.

The intricacy of memory management in real-time systems necessitates an in-depth understanding of basic principles and practices. At the very center of this topic is the necessity for deterministic memory allocation, ensuring that memory resources are committed within bounded time periods. This is a critical requirement for system response, especially where timing failure results in catastrophic failure or in safety hazards. Also, integration of memory management strategies must keep in mind differential hardware configurations and the resultant limitations due to resource availability. Misalignment of memory allocation strategies with real-time requirements can compromise the system's reliability and performance, ultimately eliminating the basic objectives of real-time processing across different applications. In addition, the role of adaptivity of memory management mechanisms cannot be downplayed, particularly in the face of the newly evolving condition of fluctuating workloads and unpredictable usage patterns. Such mechanisms hold the potential to enhance performance by dynamically adapting the allocation, which can help mitigate adverse effects of memory fragmentation and adaptively changing workloads. Above all, the development of efficient algorithms that support such adaptability without violating system integrity remains a key area of research interest. For instance, the development of ensemble methods in order to reduce resource deployment shows some analogy with methods used in machine learning environments, as testified by more recent works offering novel solutions to the challenge. Thorough examination of these methods can provide valuable insights into proper management of memory resources in real-time systems, enhancing their overall efficiency and reliability. Also, security in memory management is an emerging area of concern in real-time systems. While GPUs are powerful computation accelerators, they also bear a number of vulnerabilities posing threats to system security and subjecting them to malware and attacks. Addressing these vulnerabilities demands understanding the intricacy of GPU architecture and building robust security features unique to battling novel threats. These measures can include the employment of aggressive memory scrubbers and advanced monitoring techniques for detection and attack termination targeting memory management vulnerabilities. Considering their significance, researchers need to prioritize improving security frameworks in conjunction with managing performance because memory resource stability also entails protection against unauthorized access and manipulation and system integrity as well as continuous operation (Abhinaya et al., 2018; Bonab et al., 2017).

REFERENCES

1. Abella Ferrer, J., Alcaide Portet, S., Cazorla Almeida, F. J., et al. (2018). Safety-related challenges and opportunities for GPUs in the automotive domain. https://core.ac.uk/download/224976042.pdf (accessed on 29th September 2025).
2. Abhinaya, S. B., Ali, I., Mittal, S., et al. (2018). A survey of techniques for improving security of GPUs. http://arxiv.org/abs/1804.00114 (accessed on 29th September 2025).
3. Adelantado, M., Chaudron, J. B., & Siron, P. (2010). Towards an HLA run-time infrastructure with hard real-time capabilities. https://core.ac.uk/download/12042130.pdf (accessed on 29th September 2025).
4. Aksit, M., & Bergmans, L. M. J. (2000). Composing software from multiple concerns: A model and composition anomalies. https://core.ac.uk/download/pdf/11454348.pdf (accessed on 29th September 2025).
5. Al-Dujaili, A., Fahmy, S. A., & Ioannou, L. (2020). High throughput spatial convolution filters on FPGAs. https://core.ac.uk/download/323057966.pdf (accessed on 29th September 2025).
6. Alhammad, A., Fröhlich, A., Gracioli, G., et al. (2015). A survey on cache management mechanisms for real-time embedded systems. https://core.ac.uk/download/144148885.pdf (accessed on 29th September 2025).
7. Amy, M., De Moura, K., Kelly, J., Kliuchnikov, V., Knight, M., Knill, E., Nielsen, M. A., et al. (2019). Reversible pebbling game for quantum memory management. https://core.ac.uk/download/211998502.pdf (accessed on 29th September 2025).
8. Andrews, A., Bhimani, J., Bolt, R., Evans, A., et al. (2017). Auto Tiering: Automatic data placement manager in multi-tier all-flash datacenter. http://arxiv.org/abs/1805.01988 (accessed on 29th September 2025).
9. Bacon, D. G., Bobrow, D. R., Brownbridge, G. E., Collins, J. M., Barth, J. M., Bull, L. P., et al. (1940). The voluntary adjustment of railroad obligations. https://core.ac.uk/download/62558317.pdf (accessed on 29th September 2025).
10. Balachandran, W., Craw, P., Gkatzidou, V., Hudson, P., et al. (2013). Process of designing robust, dependable, safe and secure software for medical devices: Point of care testing device as a case study. https://core.ac.uk/download/18488619.pdf (accessed on 29th September 2025).
11. Berral, J. Ll., Gavaldà Mestre, R., & Torres Viñals, J. (2013). Modeling cloud resources using machine learning. https://core.ac.uk/download/81579790.pdf (accessed on 29th September 2025).

12. Bhatia, D. (2025). Inference workloads in real-time systems: Optimizing performance. *International Journal of Advanced Research in Science, Communication and Technology*. https://www.semanticscholar.org/paper/a4cd318a3e75a8f02eb40b77290b00e92207f2c3 (accessed on 29th September 2025).
13. Boardman, R., Bruce, H., Csikszentmihalyi, M., Karger, D., Halbert, D. C., Jones, W., Karger, D. R., et al. (2008). Information scraps: How and why information eludes our personal information management tools.
14. Bonab, H. R., & Can, F. (2017). GOOWE: Geometrically optimum and online-weighted ensemble classifier for evolving data streams. http://arxiv.org/abs/1709.02800 (accessed on 29th September 2025).
15. Bux, M., Gusew, W., Leser, U., et al. (2018). Predictive performance modeling for distributed computing using black-box monitoring and machine learning. http://arxiv.org/abs/1805.11877 (accessed on 29th September 2025).
16. Caprani, N., Doherty, A. R., Gurrin, C., et al. (2012). Experiences of aiding autobiographical memory using the Sense Cam. https://core.ac.uk/download/11310692.pdf (accessed on 29th September 2025).
17. Chang, C., Li, F., Bestavros, A., & Kollios. (1997). GreedyDual-Join: Locality-aware buffer management for approximate join processing over data streams. https://open.bu.edu/bitstream/2144/1554/1/2004-028-gdj.pdf (accessed on 29th September 2025).
18. Chaparro-Baquero, G. A. (2018). Memory-aware scheduling for fixed priority hard real-time computing systems. https://core.ac.uk/download/212915545.pdf (accessed on 29th September 2025).
19. Dave, D., Sawhney, G., & Chauhan, V. (2025). *Multi-Agent Stock Prediction Systems: Machine Learning Models, Simulations, And Real-Time Trading Strategies*. https://www.semanticscholar.org/paper/354e91308ce0cbdac81f12e144be1e77a3ba5a07 (accessed on 29th September 2025).
20. Dede, C. J., Scace, J. R., & Sullivan, T. R. (2025). Factors shaping the evolution of electronic documentation systems. https://core.ac.uk/download/pdf/42820992.pdf (accessed on 29th September 2025).
21. Ding, J. (2020). Characterizing service level objectives for cloud services: Motivation of short-term cache allocation performance modeling. https://core.ac.uk/download/305123532.pdf (accessed on 29th September 2025).
22. Durner, D., Leis, V., & Neumann, T. (2019). On the impact of memory allocation on high-performance query processing. http://arxiv.org/abs/1905.01135 (accessed on 29th September 2025).

23. Fernández de Lecea Navarro, A. (2024). Tracking multicore contention in memory controllers and DRAM. https://core.ac.uk/download/613983023.pdf (accessed on 29th September 2025).
24. Ghodke, S. S. (2018). Load balancing and virtual machine allocation in cloud-based data centers. https://core.ac.uk/download/159401018.pdf (accessed on 29th September 2025).
25. Hampton, M. P. (2003). Using contaminated garbage collection and reference counting garbage collection to provide automatic storage reclamation for real-time systems. https://core.ac.uk/download/233233922.pdf (accessed on 29th September 2025).
26. Hamza, H. (2010). The impact of varying memory region number on RTSJ execution time. https://core.ac.uk/download/336567.pdf (accessed on 29th September 2025).
27. He, B., He, J., Zhang, S., Zhou, et al. (2019). Brisk Stream: Scaling data stream processing on shared-memory multicore architectures. http://arxiv.org/abs/1904.03604 (accessed on 29th September 2025).
28. Khan, A., Schäfer, A., & Zetlmeisl, M. (2007). Efficient memory-protected integration of add-on software subsystems in small embedded automotive applications. https://core.ac.uk/download/333479.pdf (accessed on 29th September 2025).
29. Khan, T., Patel, N. V., & Pilla, V. N. (2009). Using agent-based simulation to empirically examine complexity in carbon footprint business process. https://core.ac.uk/download/336097.pdf (accessed on 29th September 2025).
30. Maule, R. A. (2025). Run-time implementation issues for real-time embedded Ada. https://core.ac.uk/download/pdf/42829646.pdf (accessed on 29th September 2025).
31. Mittal, S. (2013). Energy saving techniques for phase change memory (PCM). http://arxiv.org/abs/1309.3785 (accessed on 29th September 2025).
32. Mittal, S. (2014). Power management techniques for data centers: A survey. http://arxiv.org/abs/1404.6681 (accessed on 29th September 2025).
33. Montazerolghaem, A. R., & Yaghmaee, M. H. (2013). SIP overload control testbed: Design, building and evaluation. http://arxiv.org/abs/1307.3411 (accessed on 29th September 2025).
34. N/A. (2017). *WCET-Aware Scratchpad Memory Management for Hard Real-Time Systems*. https://core.ac.uk/download/97830514.pdf (accessed on 29th September 2025).

35. West, R., & Wong, G. (1997). *Cuckoo: A Language for Implementing Memory- And Thread-Safe System Services.* https://open.bu.edu/bitstream/2144/1833/1/2005-006-cuckoo.pdf (accessed on 29th September 2025).

36. Wright, A. K., Pierce, B., Calcagno, C., Bollella, G., Birkedal, L., & Tofte, M. (2008). A formal soundness proof of region-based memory management for object-oriented paradigm. https://core.ac.uk/download/65305.pdf (accessed on 29th September 2025).

CHAPTER 8

INTERRUPT HANDLING AND I/O MANAGEMENT IN RTOS

Contents

INTRODUCTION

In present-day computing, real-time operating systems (RTOS) are an essential part of making responses to external events efficient and pre-defined. RTOS systems are designed to process data as it comes into the system, while simultaneously maintaining important tasks prioritized and performed in a timely manner. Proper handling of interrupts is essential as this allows the RTOS to respond immediately to stimuli such as user input or sensor readings. Interrupt handling, together with efficient input/output (I/O) handling, is the backbone of an RTOS and is therefore utilized in applications ranging from industrial controllers to robotics. In the absence of efficient handling, determinism necessary in real-time applications would be lost, and there might be mission-critical failures, underscoring the need to study and improve interrupt handling processes and methods in RTOS design. Apart from that, I/O management effectiveness in the context of an RTOS reveals how task-to-task communication and data transfers should be smoothly integrated to attain performance levels. Resource sharing and synchronization need to be struck in balance without affecting the high responsiveness level. Absence of appropriate performance metrics discourages the development of complex systems capable of responding promptly to emergent requirements, and implementation of holistic metrics addressing these areas is thus important. As hypothesized in literature, RTOS platform performance and determinism characterization continues to be vital, and this necessitates high-level evaluation metrics that establish response to external stimuli and intertask synchronization techniques (Conde et al., 1996). These measures not only provide insight into the utilization of resources but also channel the developers toward enhancing system reliability for hard real-time applications. Moreover, with the computing paradigm still evolving, the integration of novel programming paradigms into the RTOS design both presents opportunities and brings complexity. For instance, models like Communicating Java Threads (CJT) introduce new methods that can overcome such limitations as non-deterministic execution typical of traditional programming approaches like Java (Bakkers et al., 1998). With such developments, software engineers can enhance the performance of RTOS in a way that makes them catch up with challenges posed by embedded systems today. This intersection of I/O management, interrupt handling, and evolving programming models is the crucial boundary for research and development in real-time systems, stressing the necessity of establishing a solid foundation for future research. Future evolution in I/O methods holds out the promise of not only further efficiency but also reliability in circumstances involving timing.

Importance of Interrupt Handling in RTOS

Effective interrupt handling is among the cornerstones of RTOS since it is an important aspect in maintaining system responsiveness and scheduling tasks. When time and precision are paramount, the ability to respond quickly to stimuli from the outside environment is imperative. RTOS typically schedule tasks based on urgency and deadline, thus the importance of timely interrupt handling in maintaining system determinism. This determinism is crucial for applications like automotive systems, medical devices, and industrial automation, where latency would trigger failures or safety concerns. The challenge lies not just in servicing these interrupts in a timely manner but in addressing the complexity of inter-task communication associated with simultaneous multiple tasks, bringing forth the delicate balance between performance and resource utilization in RTOS environments (Conde et al., 1996).

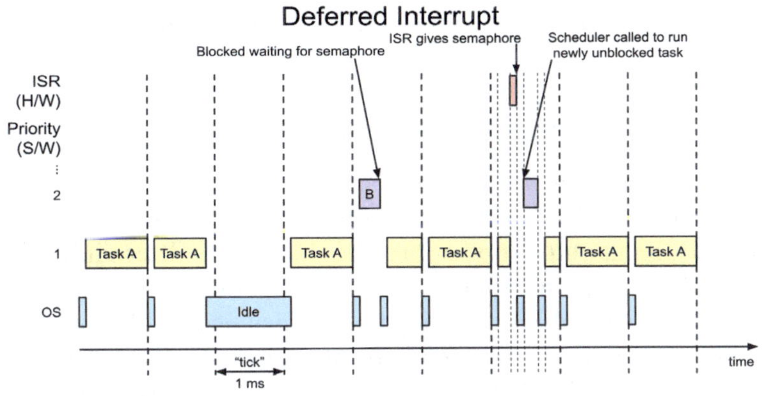

Figure 8.1. Hardware interrupts are an essential part of many embedded systems.

Source: https://www.digikey.com/maker-media/f8a37146-fb16-4815-91a4-f423251c3eda.

Furthermore, having interrupt handling under RTOS enables effective I/O management, and this effectively improves overall system performance. I/O operations have a tendency to determine the efficiency of embedded systems, which continuously manage various peripheral devices requiring asynchronous communication. When an interrupt occurs, an RTOS can suspend the running task temporarily, process the interrupt, and then resume from where it was left, hence minimizing downtime as well as maximizing throughput. This efficient management prioritizes timely tasks and thus latency is reduced. As applications grow in complexity with more I/O devices, sophisticated interrupt handling methods—such as nested interrupts or priority-level interrupt handling—are required to maximize system response time and ensure consistent performance across the system (Pereira et al., 2018). Finally, the influence of interrupt handling transcends performance and efficiency and has implications for system reliability and maintainability of software. Good interrupt handling techniques reduce the likelihood of missed deadlines and system crashes that are cataclysmic for safety-critical systems. By using well-defined procedures to process interrupts, programmers can make software environments more predictable and manageable. Such predictability aids debugging efforts and simplifies maintenance because programmers better understand how interrupts influence system behavior. Further, as embedded systems employ more advanced architectures, including virtualization and multi-core processors, the requirement of systematic interrupt management also arises. Therefore, designing successful interrupt management techniques is at the very heart of any successful RTOS implementation (Conde et al., 1996; Pereira et al., 2018) (Figure 8.1).

Overview of I/O Management in RTOS

Effective management of I/O is a fundamental aspect of RTOS that directly impacts system dependability and performance. Within an RTOS setting, the management of input/output operations should be both deterministic and fast, guaranteeing that tasks run within specified time periods. This necessity comes from the character of real-time applications, which usually deal with high-risk situations like automotive systems or medical equipment, where delays can have serious consequences. For this reason, RTOSs apply specific I/O management methods that place value on response time and reduce jitter, thus allowing predictability in timing behavior in resource consumption. Based on research identified, determinism and performance metrics for I/O operations not only enhance the reliability of an RTOS but also establish that resources in the system are being utilized efficiently to fulfill real-time demands (Conde et al., 1996). Furthermore, RTOS I/O management design entails many interrupt handling protocols and mechanisms as part of the correct operation of input and output devices. Interrupts are necessary for waking up the CPU when an I/O device is ready to provide or accept data and allowing the system to respond immediately to external events without polling resources constantly. The reactive approach minimizes processor cycles and enhances task scheduling. It also presents challenges in priority handling and isolation among tasks with varying levels of criticality. To counteract these issues, the majority of modern RTOSs utilize mixed-criticality systems under which the most important tasks are given higher priorities while making provisions for system throughput in general (Sinha et al., 2018). The success of this balance guarantees that high-priority I/O operations do not have adverse effects on less important tasks, thereby enhancing the overall system performance and reliability. The relationship between interrupt handling and I/O management also has profound implications for inter-task communication and resource sharing within an RTOS environment. Efficient I/O management not only coordinates data transfer among devices and applications but also allows for inter-task synchronization, a key requirement in real-time systems. With the application of mechanisms such as buffers and queues, I/O management enables a reliable delivery of data in correct order, in addition to preventing contention between concurrent tasks competing to use the same resources. As observed in available literature, establishing fine-grained measures for estimating I/O performance can help in measuring the effectiveness of an RTOS to meet its determinism requirements (Conde et al., 1996). Lastly, a properly designed I/O management system enhances the overall execution integrity of an RTOS and offers the underlying support necessary for executing complex timing-critical applications predictably.

8.1. FUNDAMENTALS OF INTERRUPT HANDLING

The underlying interrupt handling principles form the backbone of efficient resource handling in real-time operating systems (RTOS). Interrupts facilitate the processor to react quickly to external occurrences without terminating execution of the main program flow. The RTOS can enable the system to switch into a particular interrupt handler and therefore assign higher-priority tasks by allowing the system to enter a particular interrupt handler. This then helps to distribute processing resources to high-priority activities, like I/O processes, quickly. This flexibility is important in contexts where time is a tight requirement, as it enables the system to execute tasks deterministically. The interaction between interrupts and task scheduling is most important, since how the RTOS handles context switching and prioritization determines the potential to have a big effect on system performance as a whole, ensuring high-priority tasks are completed in a timely manner without detracting from system stability and responsiveness. To grasp the niceties of interrupt handling, one needs to consider what interrupts are signaled, processed, and served. If a device requires service, it requests an interrupt from the processor, which results in the operating system suspending the current task for the moment. The interrupt handler then proceeds and addresses the event, perhaps reading from an I/O device or processing sensor data. This process illustrates the concept of context switching, where the state of the task in execution is saved so that the RTOS can pick it up later. Successful interrupt handling, therefore, requires a high-level design that does not introduce latency and processes high-priority interrupts ahead of low-priority interrupts. Here, ARM-based systems, as observed in research, have shown their efficacy in handling real-time constraints and accommodating heterogeneous requirements of applications, thereby elucidating the significance of efficient interrupt handling in modern embedded systems (Garcia et al., 2014). Moreover, the application of simulation for optimizing interrupt handling techniques is also becoming increasingly popular in studies and implementations. Using methods such as Parallel Discrete Event Simulation (PDES), it is even possible to simulate multiple scenarios of multiprocess logical processes (LPs) and thereby derive knowledge on how interrupts can be effectively managed in a great variety of tasks. Through dynamically load sharing among LPs, systems are able to predict and react to changing workloads or priority demands. This leads to an improved understanding of the behavior of such systems in actual environments (Pellegrini et al., 2012). The use of such simulation techniques not only aids in an improved understanding of interrupt dynamics but also provides a foundation for anticipating problems that may arise in high-performance RTOS systems. Thus, improving interrupt handling through simulation aids in more effective I/O management and improves system efficiency and reliability.

8.1.1. Definition and Purpose of Interrupts

Interrupts are a significant facility in computing systems, particularly in RTOS. They allow processors to process asynchronous events and thereby control tasks and resources in an effective way. An interrupt is a signal that makes a processor suspend its executing task, save its context, and execute a specific piece of code known as an interrupt service routine (ISR). This feature is crucial for managing time-critical operations, like reacting to external device inputs or system requests.

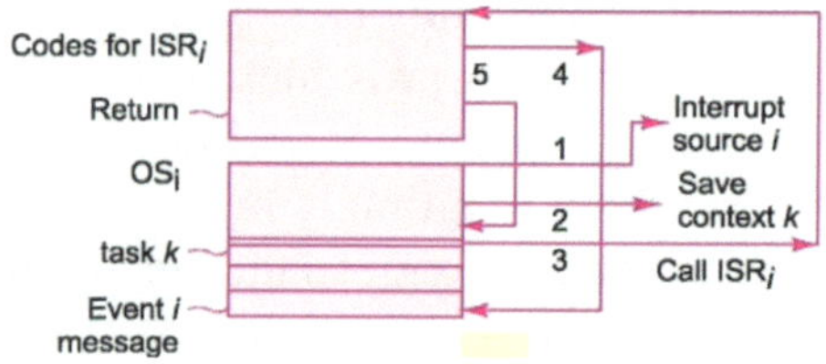

Figure 8.2. RTOS handling the first interrupt.

Source: https://external-content.duckduckgo.com/iu/?u=https%3A%2F%2Fi.ytimg.com%2Fvi%2FrGA83NU-43U%2Fmaxresdefault.jpg&f=1&nofb=1&ipt=0ba85efad3cc6582ea656b78f595f0c7bf442e58eb21d95c97d81e62056039f7.

Through the use of interrupts, RTOS can efficiently prioritize tasks, decrease latency, and enhance overall application responsiveness. As an example of Linux being used as an RTOS by NASA and SpaceX, interrupt management is a prime target for improvement to meet the hard timing constraints typical of flight-critical systems (Madden et al., 2025). Interrupts serve a purpose greater than mere task switching; they play a critical role in enhancing system performance and reliability. In environments where several processes compete for the available resources, interrupts enable dynamic adjustment of processing priorities. For instance, high-priority interrupts may interrupt lower-priority tasks to have pertinent operations addressed immediately. The process is particularly important in real-time systems since failure to respond in time could result in system failure or compromised safety. Moreover, the interrupt configuration and handling support adds an additional degree of flexibility to application developers who seek to optimize application performance. During the development of highly scalable and versatile IoT applications in accordance with Industry 4.0 standards, interrupt handling becomes a critical consideration in achieving the ideal balance of performance, reliability, and resource management (Ahmad et al., 2017) (Figure 8.2). By way of summary, the definition and purpose of interrupts underscore the very important functions of interrupts in contemporary operating systems, particularly in the RTOS environment. They facilitate efficient processing of tasks, better system responsiveness, and make possible dynamic resource allocation required by advanced applications. Because the loads on computer systems keep increasing with the presence of such things as the Internet of Things, the acquisition and application of interrupt handling will still be a valuable skill for programmers and engineers. With the ongoing progress of systems, and with advancements in already existing platforms like Zerynth VM and FreeRTOS, the ability to master interrupts will likely be what will make more sophisticated applications in other fields successful (Ahmad et al., 2017; Madden et al., 2025) (Figure 8.3).

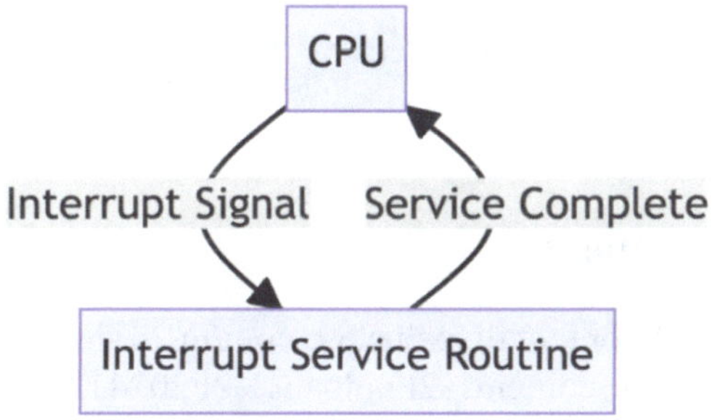

Figure 8.3. *Understanding interrupt service routines (ISR).*

Source: https://external-content.duckduckgo.com/iu/?u=https%3A%2F%2Fthecustomizewindows.cachefly.net%2Fwp-content%2Fuploads%2F2024%2F07%2FUnderstanding-Interrupt-Service-Routines-ISR-768x635.png&f=1&nofb=1&ipt=d312c60c0c6ffeda457e2fecad6f864c6d0cdc5c508188db9b45cf2034507acc.

8.1.2. Types of Interrupts in RTOS

The functioning of a RTOS relies greatly upon its effectiveness in handling interrupts. Interrupts are notifications to the processor that an event must be addressed urgently so that the system is able to respond quickly to high-priority events. In the context of an RTOS, interrupts can be classified into two primary categories: hardware interrupts and software interrupts. Hardware interrupts come from outside devices, like timers or I/O devices, and are intended to notify the CPU that they need processing. Software interrupts, on the other hand, are triggered by programs or the OS itself and are frequently utilized to indicate completion of tasks or notification of certain conditions. It is important to understand these two types in order to create effective interrupt handling mechanisms, which are key to ensuring system responsiveness in real-time systems. One other significant type of interrupt that occurs in RTOS is the exception interrupt, which occurs as a result of unexpected conditions of execution such as division by zero or illegal access of memory. These interrupts are required to maintain system stability and enable error-handling operations (Figure 8.4).

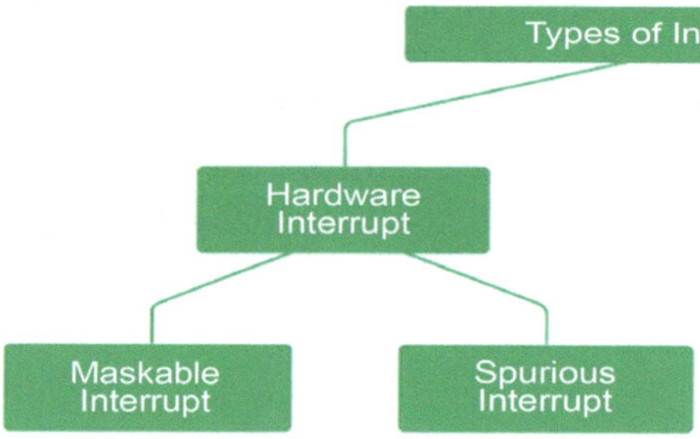

Figure 8.4. Type of interrupts.

Source: https://external-content.duckduckgo.com/iu/?u=https%3A%2F%2Fmedia.geeksforgeeks.org%2Fwp-content%2Fuploads%2F20241210153745065033%2FTypes-of-Interrupt.png&f=1&nofb=1&ipt=c5b71a1364abfee05b906cbd7bd48a7212016dcc11144c29768efdc3209291ac.

The ability to categorize interrupts into these various classes allows developers to employ specialized handling procedures, which are able to interrupt system activities prematurely and ensure that important operations are addressed without undue delay. Notably, the design of such handling procedures normally involves prioritization schemes for granting priority to various classes of interrupts, ensuring that system performance is optimized overall. Such prioritization ensures that the most time-critical operation is dealt with right away, the most important requirement in real-time systems, whose delay could cause system crashes or loss of performance. Accurate interrupt management in an RTOS is also complemented by advances in virtualization technologies. As an example, there have been implementations that enable real-time analysis of systems without modification to their kernel, bridging the analysis-implementation gap. This openness is offered through hardware-assisted virtualization that isolates analysis tools from the running system, thus safeguarding against potential interference. As highlighted in the proposed framework focusing on system-level analyses, tools like HyperDbg allow developers to dynamically debug kernel modules and manage interrupts. Through support of single-step exception and interrupt handler execution, these sophisticated tools underscore the importance of including cutting-edge technology in RTOS design. Such integration not only improves dependability but also guarantees uninterrupted operation in spite of the potentiality of intrusive debugging procedures, further underscores the significance of efficient interrupt handling in real-time systems (Douglas et al., 2009; Fattori et al., 2010).

8.1.3. Interrupt Vector Table and Its Role

The Interrupt Vector Table (IVT) is a significant component in managing interrupts for RTOS.

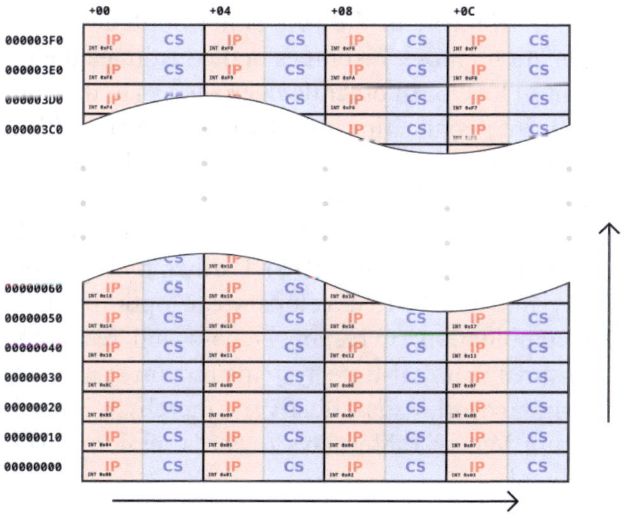

Figure 8.5. *Interrupt vector table.*

Source: https://en.wikipedia.org/wiki/Interrupt_vector_table#/media/File:X86_Interrupt_Vector_Table.svg.

Being well-arranged with an interrupt service routines (ISRs) table, the IVT makes it easy for the processor to find and execute the correct handler in case of an interrupt. Such efficiency is crucial in real-time systems where responsiveness and timing are critical. Not only does the IVT keep interrupts from consuming system performance, but it also enables the prioritization of critical tasks. To this end, the structure and formation of the IVT directly measure overall system latency, governing how rapidly the operating system is able to respond to outside inputs or inside situations requiring immediate response. Furthermore, the IVT's structure must be in concordance with the specific needs of the RTOS it is a part of, involving an individualized approach to interrupt management. For instance, some systems might have a simple lookup table for ISR addresses, while others might have more complex structures such as context- or priority-level-dependent dynamic dispatching mechanisms. It supports different needs that are associated with IoT applications and other systems, which, for maintaining high performance and reliability, rely on efficient interrupt handling. With increasing complexity of systems with the advent of Industry 4.0, there is a need to make the IVT flexible to incorporate other hardware abstraction layers with minimal effort. This adaptability enhances system performance by making it possible for the IVT to accommodate an extensive range of peripherals in addition to dynamic configurations without compromising operational integrity (Figure 8.5). The role of the IVT is not limited to task management; it facilitates coordination among resources and constitutes the core foundation for I/O management in RTOS. In other devices such as in the context of current trends, for instance, interconnection of ARM processors with reconfigurable FPGA devices, the IVT provides an interface between hardware capability and software demands. These architectures enhance performance and flexibility required in high-performance embedded systems for effective dynamic partial reconfiguration (DPR) (Nouvel et al., 2015). Further, by incorporating handling routines seamlessly into the IVT, developers can optimize I/O operations to achieve the best combination of responsiveness and resource conservation. This interaction ensures that real-time systems remain resilient and are able to accommodate changing workloads effectively, thereby reinforcing the pivotal role that the Interrupt Vector Table plays towards modern RTOS designs and administrative protocols.

8.2. INTERRUPT HANDLING MECHANISMS

In the scenario of RTOS, interrupt management is at the core of ensuring timely and predictable responses to external events. Interrupt handling disciplines are the foundation of quality I/O management, allowing the system to interact appropriately with peripherals and real-time tasks. The essence of such a mechanism is to recognize hardware indications of the need for urgent action, thus prioritizing certain tasks over others. With the use of a particular set of performance criteria, i.e., external event response and synchronization between tasks, programmers can evaluate the efficiency with which an RTOS handles these interrupts critically. This analysis technique ensures satisfaction of the deterministic requirements essential for real-time systems, thereby enabling predictable and consistent system behavior (Conde et al., 1996). One of the key aspects of interrupt handling in an RTOS is interrupt prioritization and dispatching. This involves assigning different priorities to interrupt requests (IRQs), enabling the system to handle multiple requests without losing focus of real-time operations. In this context, the interaction between software and hardware resources becomes important. For instance, in those systems incorporating ARM processors and FPGAs, dynamic reorganization of system resources can prove to be a game changer for interrupt handling capabilities. In this context, an optimized microkernel can deliver optimal CPU time and resource allocation, ultimately leading to higher performance and efficiency in interrupt handling and I/O operations (Nouvel et al., 2015). All such advances underscore the importance of a solid architecture in order to provide efficient control over real-time requirements. In addition, interrupt handling mechanisms must not be assessed solely on their efficiency but also on the degree of their flexibility to provide appropriate support in dynamic environments of a real-time system. Diversified hardware support and variable workload requirements call for an inherent understanding of the interrupt handling methodologies. A strict mechanism for evaluation can even identify possible bottlenecks and points that need optimization so that the system will be responsive. Through the analysis of intertask data transfer and resource sharing, developers can fine-tune their systems even more to achieve responsiveness and overall better performance. This is especially important as real-time applications become more sophisticated, necessitating not only durable hardware but also smart software solutions in order to cope with interrupts efficiently (Conde et al., 1996). Under such an environment, the incorporation of sophisticated interrupt handling mechanisms becomes essential in order to attain the desired performance levels in RTOS applications.

8.2.1. Interrupt Service Routines (ISRs)

Interrupt service routines (ISRs) form the backbone of the operation of RTOS since they give instantaneous response to asynchronous events. In a scenario where an RTOS is employed, optimal design of an ISR is critical if system performance and responsiveness are to be guaranteed, particularly in systems where timing becomes of significant importance. When an interrupt is triggered, the ISR takes priority over all other processes, allowing the system to execute the immediate task. This interrupt handling may comprise gathering sensor data, communication with peripheral devices, or other time-critical operations. ISRs must therefore be optimized to execute as fast as possible in order to minimize the overall impact on system latency and delay more critical functions due to too much processing time or having its execution interfered with by other system procedures. Utilization of ISRs requires close consideration of several factors, such as interrupting at different priorities and nested interrupts support. In most RTOS applications, high-priority interrupt preemption of low-priority tasks is enabled, where the most critical responses are handled immediately. ISR design also needs to balance complexity with execution time, employing techniques that do not engage in resource conflicts and maintain predictability of function execution.

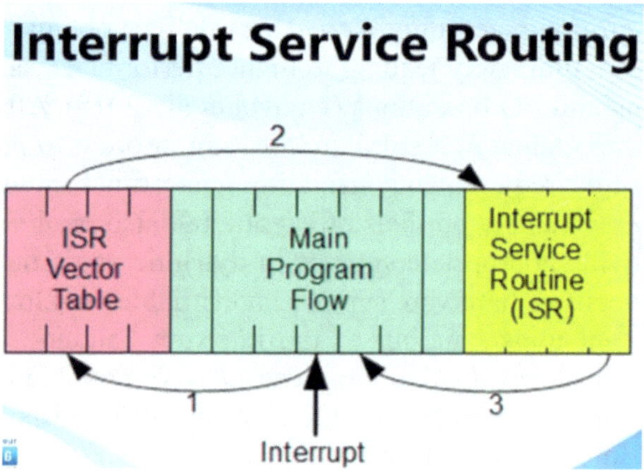

Figure 8.6. Interrupt service routines (ISRs).

Source: https://images.theengineeringprojects.com/image/main/2021/12/IMG-20211202-WA0021.jpg.

For instance, an ISR may need to disable certain interrupts temporarily in order to prevent re-entry, which can lead to unpredictable behavior unless addressed correctly. Thus, the discipline of carrying out ISR is the major contributor in the stability and success of time-critical applications as it provides precise coordination among input/output management in real-time. The interdependence of ISRs and I/O management is most visible in systems that combine diverse operating environments. One can see the synergy expressed in Boomerang, where a traditional non-real-time OS is wedded with a dedicated RTOS for time-critical functions (Golchin et al., 2019). Boomerang uses ISRs effectively to manage time critical I/O while leveraging the underlying libraries and services of the legacy system. This architecture allows for maximizing performance while ensuring high-priority task access to resources. Through demultiplexing the timing-critical tasks from lower-priority operations, Boomerang makes predictable end-to-end processing latency possible, demonstrating how well-drafted ISRs play an essential role in making efficient input and output operations possible in complex system design structures, thus enhancing the capabilities of existing computing systems (De Vos et al., 2003) (Figure 8.6).

8.2.2. Prioritization of Interrupts

Interrupt prioritization is the foundation for the use of RTOS to guarantee that tasks of time-critical nature get executed as efficiently as possible. Interrupts alert the processor to interrupt its ongoing task in order to respond to a more critical event, hence making systems where timing is necessary responsive. Prioritization is the act of assigning various levels of urgency to various interrupts, whereby higher priority interrupts can interrupt lower priority tasks. This mechanism ensures that important processes, possibly related to security or safety, are assigned high priority and are appropriately processed promptly, thus improving system performance. Well-executed interrupt prioritization is highly essential in networks such as wireless sensor networks, where timely response to events can significantly impact the utilization of resources and effectiveness of operation (Duffy et al., 2007). The inherent organization of an RTOS is designed to facilitate this prioritization using various strategies, such as static and dynamic prioritization. Static prioritization obtains fixed priority levels at design time for predictable response but may limit flexibility to respond to changing operational requirements. Contrarily, dynamic prioritization can provide greater flexibility, wherein the system can adjust priorities in line with conditions present, which is particularly useful in cases where task priority will evolve over time. While each method has its drawbacks and benefits, the choice finally depends on the specific requirements of the application environment. For instance, in multi-threaded RTOS such as MANTIS, support for task preemption enables a better balance of energy efficiency and time-critical tasks, demonstrating that optimally ordered threads are critical in the realization of different operational goals (Duffy et al., 2007). Additionally, interrupt prioritization trade-offs extend beyond the performance metrics themselves; they also affect resource management in the system. For instance, interrupt prioritization needs robust memory management and use of power, especially in low-resource settings like sensor networks. Event-driven design tends to consume less memory and processor use, which makes it a suitable design in applications where efficiency is a paramount consideration. In situations with tighter timing requirements, however, a multi-threaded design would be more suited even though resource consumption would be higher. Lastly, the interrupt prioritization choice must not only remember the system responsiveness but also how it will integrate into overall design goals like power saving and application-specific needs (Duffy et al., 2007). Balancing between them is crucial for realizing the complete potential of I/O management in RTOS.

8.2.3. Context Switching in Interrupt Handling

In RTOS, context switching is a major aspect of interrupt handling to facilitate efficient multitasking. When an interrupt occurs, the state of the task running currently must be preserved so that the system is able to service higher-priority tasks that need to be serviced immediately.

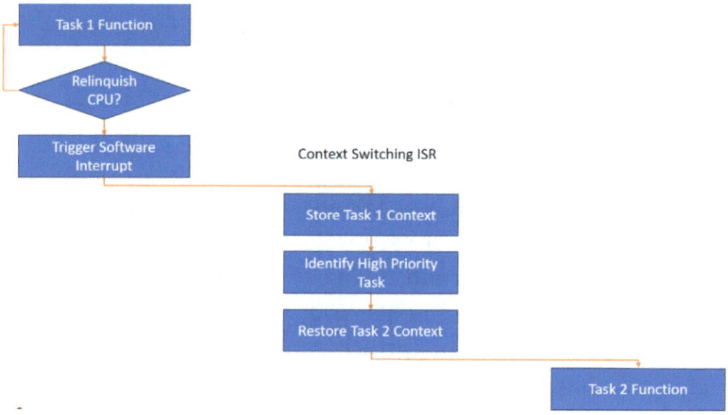

Figure 8.7. Context switching in interrupt handling.

Source: https://www.embien.com/blog/using-interrupts-for-context-switching-in-rtos.

This context saving mechanism preserves the tasks context, i.e., the register values, program counter, and stack pointers, so that task execution can be easily resumed later. Thus, minimizing the overhead of context switching is significant in order to improve the responsiveness of real-time applications. However, as documented in relevant literature, the procedure introduces latency that can be deleterious in real-time systems, highlighting the importance of effective interrupt handling policies at system design (Cheng et al., 2017). Additionally, multicore architecture development has introduced additional parameters to interrupt handling context switching. Current single board computers (SBCs) with multi-core support enable concurrent processing of tasks, so the system can handle interrupts more effectively. Sharing workloads between multiple cores can potentially reduce the context switch overhead in handling interrupts and hence enhance the overall system performance of real-time applications. Such a potential is typically dependent on whether the operating system can schedule tasks and distribute resources among many cores efficiently. QduinoMC, a multicore extension that plug into the Arduino development environment, is an example of how multicore designs can be utilized to process interrupts without breaking timing commitments (Cheng et al., 2017). This aspect indicates the relevance of operating system support in helping to avoid the expense of context switching (Figure 8.7). Finally, an understanding of how context switching impacts performance is important when designing efficient interrupt handling systems. The speed of the CPU, memory latency, and frequency at which context switching takes place can play an important role on an application's performance within an RTOS platform. With more complex applications, the interaction between protocol processing tasks and regular operating system activities must be studied and analyzed in depth. Distributed programs are highly susceptible to performance bottlenecks due to widespread context switching, and this might take away vital resources from primary task execution (Schmidt et al., 1992). By defusing these issues through ingenious design and programming, developers can improve interrupt handling for real-time programs to guarantee their responsiveness and task integrity in progressively demanding computational settings.

8.3. I/O MANAGEMENT IN RTOS

Good management of I/O is one of the fundamentals of RTOS because it influences the system's responsiveness and task scheduling. Where real-time responses are important, such as in industrial automation systems or robots, fast handling of input and output becomes essential. RTOS have a tendency to employ interrupt-driven operations for handling I/O operations to allow the CPU to respond on the fly to external occurrences. The interrupt handling enables low-latency hardware peripheral communication such that data is handled and collected in real-time. Furthermore, with the advent of multi-core single-board computers (SBCs) with mixed interfaces, I/O complexity has increased. Although most SBCs are generally operated on non-RTOS, advancements such as QduinoMC, which enhances the conventional programming platforms, indicate the promise of more mature I/O management under real-time environments (Cheng et al., 2017). Moreover, effective I/O management under RTOS requires a strong structure that can manage multiple device interactions while maintaining the timing guarantees typical in real-time applications. The Modular Operating System (MOSS) is an example, representing software engineering methodology dedicated to real-time systems. The MOSS design emphasizes modularity and adaptability so that developers can assign the highest priority to time-critical operations and control I/O operations synchronously. Each module can be tuned to support specific hardware facilities, which makes the overheads for

I/O operations extremely low. This module-based approach not only enhances utilization of resources but also enhances system scalability and maintainability, two critical factors with increasing complexity in applications. As the experiences through the MOSS project have illustrated, these engineering strategies are instrumental in achieving strong I/O management in upcoming software development efforts (Bounds et al., 2025). In summary, development of I/O management frameworks in RTOS is a reaction to growing demand for high-performance and real-time computing solutions. The use of advanced I/O methods, for example in QduinoMC and MOSS, shows the potential to develop even more complex applications that can undertake several tasks at one time without compromising response times. As real-time apps become more prevalent, particularly in sectors like automation, telecommunications, and medical monitoring, the importance of efficient I/O management should not be ignored. With the use of module, flexible operating systems, developers are capable of overcoming the challenges posed by new hardware and application requirements, paving the way for solutions capable of operating under the most stringent timing constraints. Because of this, further research in this field is crucial in ensuring the functionality and capabilities of RTOS are enhanced to keep pace with future technology development needs (Figure 8.8).

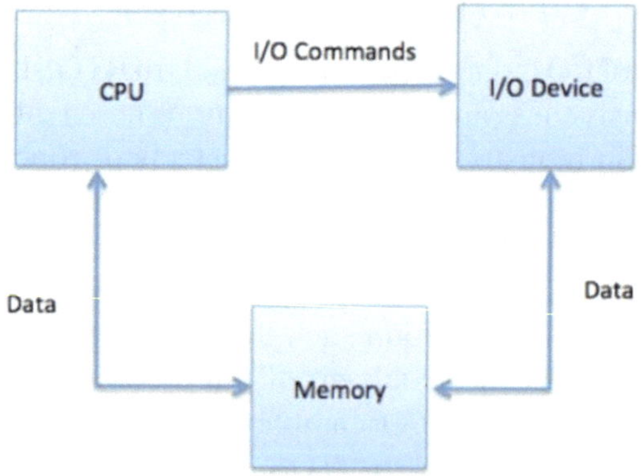

Figure 8.8. Memory-mapped I/O.

Source: https://www.tutorialspoint.com/operating_system/os_io_hardware.htm.

8.3.1. Definition and Importance of I/O Management

Efficient input/output (I/O) operation handling is an integral component of RTOS design. Management of I/O involves the strategies and routines needed to efficiently handle input and output devices in order to allow data to move between the CPU and peripherals smoothly. It is of critical importance in applications where timely execution is given high priority, like in avionics or automotive systems. In such a scenario, quick response times are essential to the system's integrity and functionality. Given that RTOS normally operates under tight timing constraints, efficient I/O management helps decrease delay and boost throughput. This is crucial as any lag or mismanagement can lead to system failure or loss of performance, emphasizing the pivotal role played by I/O management in guaranteeing operating dependability and real-time deadlines being met in high-risk applications. Additionally, the evolution of technologies like the Internet of Things (IoT) has greatly added to the significance of I/O management within RTOS designs. In the context of Industry 4.0, the requirement for interconnected and intelligent devices further emphasizes the necessity for efficient I/O systems capable of handling the swift transfer of data. It is the scalable architecture that high-performance IoT applications require, which can effectively handle workloads with differing needs and provide minimum development time and increased reliability. I/O management in this case not only facilitates seamless communication between devices but also enables effective utilization of resources as well as power consumption. Software like the Zerynth Virtual Machine highlights how current I/O management mechanisms can support diverse programming environments and real-time requirements, further underlining the central role of sound I/O strategies in today's evolving technology landscape, as seen in greater use of systems for smart connectivity and functionality in the IoT environment (Ahmad et al., 2017). Lastly, I/O management is also vital to the point where an RTOS can effectively handle interrupts—the instructions that request the CPU to interrupt what it is currently doing and process other high-priority tasks. Because Linux-based systems are increasingly being used in real-time applications, it is necessary to introduce effective I/O management methods to handle the dual challenge of general-purpose throughput and specific real-time requirements. The inherent design of the Linux kernel is inclined towards data throughput, which contradicts the determinism required in real-time systems (Madden et al., 2025). This calls for customization of the kernel or the application of workaround methodologies to allow for the inclusion of I/O processes requiring strict timing. Therefore, the function of I/O management within an RTOS is not only important for overall functioning but also for matching and optimizing the performance of modern computing solutions where timing and reliability are given top priority.

8.3.2. Types of I/O Devices in RTOS

In RTOS, the classification of input/output (I/O) devices is significant for proper management and process effectiveness. I/O devices can be categorized broadly into two types: synchronous and asynchronous devices. Synchronous devices, such as mice and keyboards, require explicit focus from the processor and are prone to delaying further processing until their input is read. This makes the life of RTOS hard, as it needs to guarantee strict timing constraints. Asynchronous peripherals such as network interfaces and sensors can be executed outside the CPU's main control loop, which allows for more effective interrupt handling, as they notify the operating system only when data is available. Such discrimination not only assists in maximizing interrupt requests but also extends to the overall performance and design of the embedded systems in an RTOS system. The relationship between different types of I/O devices and the RTOS can play a critical role in system responsiveness and resource usage. For instance, while handling multiple device interrupts, the RTOS needs to employ sophisticated scheduling algorithms so that timely servicing can be guaranteed across devices with varying speeds and grades of requirements (Figure 8.9).

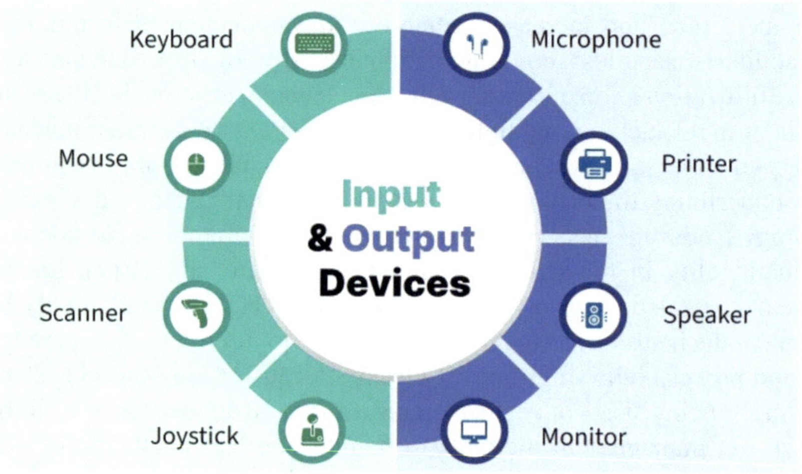

Figure 8.9. Types of I/O devices.

Source: https://media.geeksforgeeks.org/wp-content/uploads/20250315122640215754/Input----Output--Devices.webp.

For instance, chips like digital signal processors (DSPs) are increasingly being utilized in RTOS because they can perform complex data processing functions with real-time needs. They enable quick decision-making while simultaneously accommodating sensor input from various sensors and delivering output to actuators, thereby improving system efficiency and reliability. Therefore, in-depth understanding of the nature and behavior of such I/O devices is important for optimizing interrupt handling approaches and determining whether RTOS can meet real-time demands or not along with superior performance in multi-tasking systems (Angoletta et al., 2008). Moreover, technology has brought about advanced I/O structures in embedded computing that call for superior management approaches in RTOS implementations. With the evolution of technologies, the interaction between I/O devices such as field programmable gate arrays (FPGAs) and application-specific integrated circuits (ASICs) becomes very important. Not only do these devices improve the input/output capabilities of an embedded system but also influence simultaneous processing, thus requiring effective synchronization and communication methods. The design of an RTOS to efficiently handle these diverse types of I/O devices is dependent on the use of state-of-the-art system-level design methods, which support device modeling and integration of diverse device attributes. This modeling is the foundation for reliability support and fulfilling real-time constraints, and therefore the research and understanding of I/O types are more important than ever (Zhang et al., 2006).

8.3.3. I/O Scheduling Algorithms

The role of I/O scheduling algorithms within RTOS is to be at the core of managing the priority and servicing of input and output tasks. The algorithms are designed to optimize the system responsiveness as well as ensure that critical tasks meet their timing demands. Unlike general-purpose operating systems, where throughput might be optimized, RTOS emphasizes determinism and low-latency response. Effective I/O scheduling reduces the bottlenecks that may cause delays in meeting deadlines in time-critical applications, including those that are used in aerospace and automotive systems. How well these algorithms function can make a great difference in the performance of the systems, particularly in situations where events from the outside environment need to be handled within a limited time, thus meeting the challenges of responding to external events as discussed in recent research (Conde et al., 1996). Different I/O scheduling algorithms can be implemented in RTOS systems, including First-Come, First-Served (FCFS), Shortest Job Next (SJN), and Round Robin (RR), with different advantages and disadvantages. FCFS is easy but suffers from latency during heavy loads, while SJN attempts to minimize waiting time by giving priority to shorter jobs but leads to starvation for longer jobs. On the other hand, Round Robin gives a fixed time slice to each task, which is fair but may introduce additional latency in total. Selection and use of an appropriate I/O scheduling algorithm need to be chosen on the basis of the specific requirement of the application, and the extent of real-time requirements. This holds particularly in the case of systems transitioning into RTOS implementations, under which existing algorithms might need to be specifically adapted to guarantee that they meet harsh timing as well as performance requirements (Madden et al., 2025). The determination of the performance of I/O scheduling algorithms in RTOS also includes the establishment of detailed metrics that measure their performance characteristics. Current performance metrics are less specific in capturing the nuances of real-time requirements, leading to potential inefficiencies in system design. By making specific measurements that address response times, inter-task synchronization, and resource sharing, developers can gain a deeper insight into the effectiveness of various algorithms. This is important in ensuring that the underpinning I/O management infrastructure has the guarantee of determinism in actual applications. Lastly, the relationship between I/O scheduling algorithms and performance metrics is significant in achieving reliability and efficiency within RTOS systems, thereby enhancing general system capability in reaction to extremely stringent operational requirements (Conde et al., 1996) (Figure 8.10).

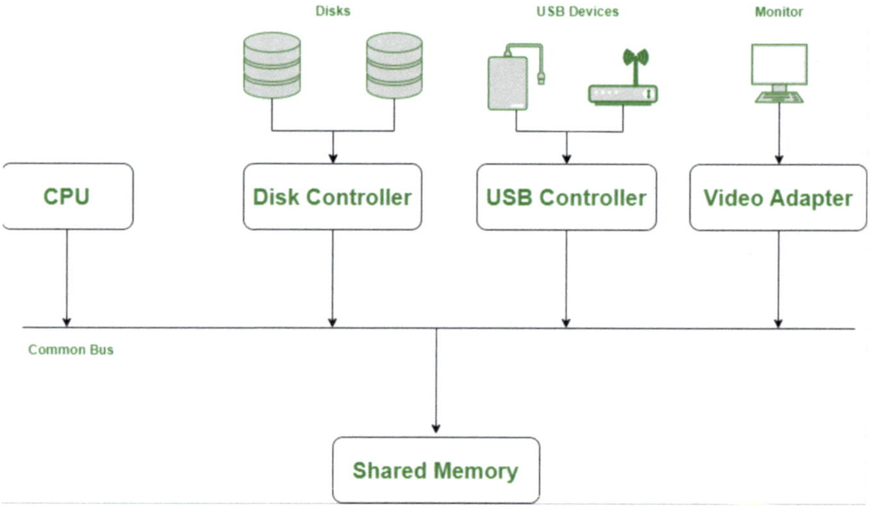

Figure 8.10. I/O scheduling algorithms.

Source: https://www.geeksforgeeks.org/operating-systems/i-o-scheduling-in-operating-systems/.

8.4. INTERACTION BETWEEN INTERRUPTS AND I/O MANAGEMENT

The interaction between I/O management and interrupts in RTOS is a significant concern in the maintenance of the responsiveness and efficiency of a system. Interrupts are notifications to the processor that it needs to give instant attention and are generally triggered by events such as changes in hardware status or completion of data transfer. This procedure allows the RTOS to dynamically schedule tasks so that high-priority processes are assigned resources when they need them without impeding system delays. For instance, when a peripheral device completes an I/O operation, it generates an interrupt, forcing the RTOS to interrupt the ongoing task and service the interrupt. This efficient management is one that the I/O operations are optimized and do not interfere with the overall performance of the system, therefore addressing the determinism requirement of real-time systems as identified in the performance metrics of real-time systems (Conde et al., 1996). Further, the design of interrupt handling mechanisms influences how the I/O management is conducted in an RTOS. Alternative interrupt handling strategies, such as polling versus interrupt driven I/O, have varying strengths and weaknesses in terms of utilizing system resources and response times. In an interrupt-driven approach, the OS can do other work as it awaits data from I/O devices, which equates to higher throughput as well as efficiency in power consumption. Conversely, polling may lead to high CPU activity and the degradation of performance as the processor repeatedly probes devices for status instead of executing other operations. The balance between these techniques comes into play especially in high-performance applications such as those contemplated in the High-Performance Spacecraft Computing initiative, which demands efficiency and flexibility in processing potential (Cudmore et al., 2025). Secondarily, handling simultaneous interrupts from various I/O devices needs sophisticated methods of prioritization. In an RTOS, the operating environment must ensure that more significant interrupts are serviced ahead of lower-priority interrupts, and in a system where I/O accesses are nondeterministic and frequent, this can be very strenuous. Having good interrupt service routines (ISRs) in place is important since badly designed ISRs will introduce latencies and deadline misses in real-time systems. Following the discussion of RTOS performance criteria, an understanding of the nature of interrupts and I/O operations is key to providing determinism and responsiveness at the levels that are required. Thus, careful attention to both the interrupt handling system and I/O management methods is crucial towards maximizing system performance under any RTOS paradigm (Conde et al., 1996).

8.4.1. Role of Interrupts in I/O Operations

In RTOS, interrupts play a very crucial role in performing Input/Output (I/O) operations efficiently. Interrupting the system so that it can act rapidly to external events saves a lot of time and enhances the efficiency of the system. If an I/O device requires the CPUs' attention, it generates an interrupt signal. This message allows the CPU to temporarily suspend its ongoing operations and execute an Interrupt Service Routine (ISR) to service the I/O device's specific needs. Through the use of interrupts, the RTOS can provide a non-blocking system so that the remaining tasks are permitted to proceed with execution until the I/O operation is complete. This efficient I/O resource management is paramount in systems where performance and timing are key, as it maximizes CPU utilization and minimizes response times. How well interrupt handling works also directly influences the reliability and stability of the RTOS overall. All interrupts must be handled with a priority level that will determine how valuable they are, thus preventing lower-priority jobs from interfering with higher-priority events.

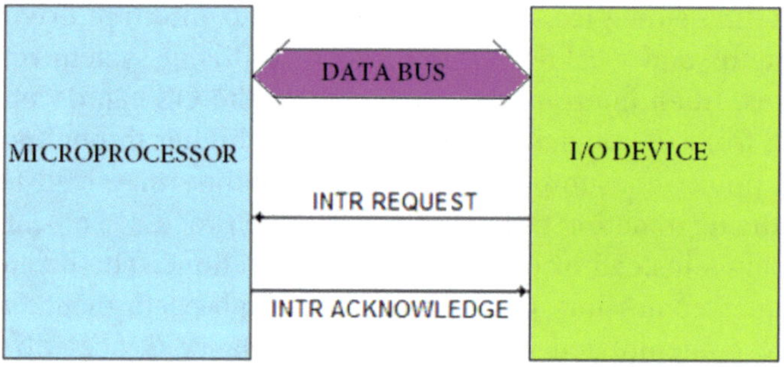

Figure 8.11. The interrupt-driven I/O data transfer method.

Source: https://www.electronicsengineering.nbcafe.in/interrupt-driven-i-o-data-transfer/.

This higher prioritization is important especially in systems that service multiple I/O devices simultaneously. When a number of interrupts are happening at the same time, the RTOS needs to provide schemes such as nested interrupts or prioritization queues so that high-priority interrupts are serviced efficiently. For instance, the fine-grain time-sharing architecture of the Time Warp system proposed in recent studies focuses on event preemption in managing concurrent I/O operations and therefore minimizing the potential for issues through slow handling of high-priority interrupts (Pellegrini et al., 2017). Furthermore, the proposal is keen to point out the need for robust interrupt management models to maintain high levels of system performance even underutilization. Further, interrupt handling mechanism design often involves the utilization of advanced tools that incorporate an additional layer of analysis and debugging facilities in RTOS-based platforms. A case in point is the utilization of virtualization techniques to provide real-time analysis extension without impacting the underlying systems performance. The utilization of tools like HyperDbg illustrates the potential for interactive kernel-mode operation debugging, such as interrupts and exception handlers. This transparency not only underpins more effective interrupt-handling mechanisms but ensures that errors from analysis tools will not compromise system integrity (Fattori et al., 2010). Ultimately, effective processing and optimization of interrupt-driven I/O operations are core to achieving the reliable performance demanded by RTOS applications, specifically in safety-critical sectors such as automotive, aerospace, and telecommunications (Figure 8.11).

8.4.2. Handling I/O Interrupts Efficiently

One of the salient attributes of RTOS is a proper handling of I/O interrupts, and it is important towards a maximum attainment of performance and determinism in real-time systems. Interrupts are essential alerts allowing the CPU to interrupt its current operations and service priority tasks that have to be processed urgently, such as reading a sensor or addressing user input. In the case of RTOS, the difficulty is in finding a balance between responsiveness and system stability. An efficient interrupt handling mechanism reduces the latency experienced during the context switch between normal processing and interrupt servicing. This is especially crucial in systems where delays of even a few milliseconds can cause serious failures, thus the importance of using methods that exercise the performance of these handling processes with precision and comprehensiveness, as highlighted by Conde et al. (1996). Besides simple responsiveness, effective I/O interrupt handling also involves advanced techniques of intertask synchronization and sharing resources. The task interaction between different tasks demands mechanisms that ensure the integrity of data as well as effective process-to-process communication. A fine-grained interrupt handling system should enforce measures that retain the complexity of task interactions, especially in the case of the presence of multiple devices or threads that simultaneously attempt to use common resources. The employment of the measures enables the programmers to design the interrupt handling strategies so that they are suitable for the stringent requirements of real-time applications. Performance metrics that masquerade as response to external occurrences and intertask data transfer are relevant for measuring the efficiency of an RTOS as a whole and hence fostering greater understanding of the extent to which an operating system is capable of handling interrupts (Conde et al., 1996). The introduction of low-power, resource-constrained devices, particularly in the field of the Internet of Things (IoT), has added another level of complexity to handling interrupts. Operating systems of such devices must include real-time features that facilitate proper synchronization among various hardware components. For instance, RIOT OS, with IoT usage in mind, has the feature to make multiple timers on hardware available at the same time, enhancing handling of I/O interrupts by various platforms. This feature facilitates sensors and actuators to operate collaboratively, preserving power while maintaining responsiveness in the system. The development of next-generation MAC protocols, as exemplified by the integration of S-CoSenS onto RIOT OS, demonstrates the salience of effective interrupt handling in enabling huge energy savings and processing boosts, demonstrating the significance of real-time capability in modern I/O management.

8.4.3. Impact of Interrupt Latency on I/O Performance

The impact of interrupt latency on input/output (I/O) performance is a key consideration in RTOS. Interrupt latency is the time period between an interrupt event and the processing of its corresponding handler. This has a critical bearing on the speed at which a system would respond to external events, which is imperative for those applications where processing data timely is vital. For instance, in those applications where robot systems or car controls are controlled in real-time, interrupt processing delays can lead to calculation errors or system failure. Such latencies are generally not well captured by current performance measures, indicating the need for broader metrics that account not only for delay but also for the deterministic response of the RTOS to varying loads, as discussed by Conde et al. (1996). Besides, the architecture of the operating system has a significant influence on the level of interrupt latency one gets to endure. Modern RTOS platforms, even Linux-based ones, have difficulty coping with design decisions favoring throughput over determinism. This type of trade-off can significantly compromise I/O performance, especially in real-time use cases that require very tight timing requirements. As Madden et al. (2025) explains, while Linux has been used for real-time application, its standard-purpose kernel design might inadvertently add latency due to its non-real-time design principles. In environments where high rates of input among devices demand high-speed processing, such interruptions can potentially turn into bottlenecks jeopardizing the responsiveness and overall usability of the systems. Cure of the interrupt latency issue in I/O performance involves analysis of system resources and design choices within the RTOS environment. Efficient interrupt management techniques, including interrupt prioritization in accordance with real-time needs and employment of direct memory access (DMA) for data transfer, can mitigate the effects of latency. Furthermore, adapting the RTOS to cater to the specific needs of an application will ensure interrupt servicing remains timely and effective. Research into precise performance metrics, as advocated by Conde et al. (1996), underscores the need for benchmarks that address not only latency measurement but also the capability of systems to handle numerous concurrent tasks without sacrificing responsiveness. Through these observations, how interrupt latency is interwoven with I/O performance can be handled best, paving the way for more reliable real-time programs.

8.5. CHALLENGES IN INTERRUPT HANDLING

RTOS handling of interrupts is a difficult matter that may have a profound effect on the system overall performance. A significant issue is that most operating systems, including Linux, are designed with throughput as the primary objective at the expense of deterministic behavior. This focus may lead to latencies that compromise an RTOS's ability to meet essential timing requirements. According to Madden et al. (2025), the Linux kernel design is not inherently optimized for the strict timing requirements of real-time systems. Due to this, developers often have to employ workarounds or modify the kernel in ways that enhance its support for real-time at the cost of additional complexity and risks to system reliability. Second, interrupt handling complexity is compounded by the need for synchronization between heterogeneous devices, particularly in networked systems such as the Internet of Things (IoT). According to Roussel et al. (2015), the synchronization needs of high-speed Media Access Control (MAC) protocols require solid real-time features that are not provided by many conventional operating systems. Lacking such real-time features, programs executing in wireless sensor networks risk performance loss and missing deadline. Implementers thus have to do the difficult trade-off of supporting responsive interrupt handling without compromising portability and multi-tasking support essential to current IoT applications. Besides synchronization challenges, interrupt handling must also accommodate priority management so as not to starve low-priority tasks or delay them unnecessarily. This is particularly critical in interrupt-rich and high-rate systems. Prioritization schemes well done can minimize these dangers, but achieving a fine balance between responsiveness and processing overhead is no easy task. Interrupts must be processed inexpensively in order to allow higher-priority work to obtain necessary CPU time without system responsiveness under load being compromised. As real-time systems are made more complex, surpassing these difficulties in interrupt handling is vital to the reliability and performance required of modern applications, and it emphasizes the ongoing necessity for research and development in this area.

8.5.1. Interrupt Overload and Its Consequences

The notion of interrupt overload is of extreme importance in the operation of RTOS, where events need to be processed in a timely manner. Interrupt overload arises when the rate of incoming interrupts exceeds the capabilities of the systems to process them effectively, resulting in a build-up of requests that degrade system responsiveness. In tightly time-constrained systems, e.g., embedded systems or safety-critical systems, things can go horribly wrong with delayed deadlines and non-determinism. An examination of the Quest-V system demonstrates how new architecture can prevent these problems. By the use of multiple sandbox kernels, Quest-V isolates interrupts into different areas of memory, handling I/O and scheduling effectively without overwhelming a global scheduler or clock system and thus ensuring performance integrity under heavy loads (Li et al., 2013). Understanding the consequences of interrupt overload extends far beyond being a matter of theoretical discussion; it has significant design and user interface implications. Ignoring proper interrupt management can lead to system crashes or decreased performance, which in real-time-constrained applications such as aerospace systems, pose a critical risk. The consideration of human-computer interaction should also be noted, as overloaded interrupts have the potential to decrease user confidence in automated systems, particularly in instances where real-time fault management is critical. Here, the guidance in NASAs Technical Memorandum highlights methods of creating intelligent systems that facilitate effective human operator and automated system collaboration (Malin et al., 2025). Such collaborative systems can significantly enhance usability and reliability alongside mitigating the issues brought about by interrupt overload. The consequences of neglecting interrupt overload also result in reworking currently available system architectures. As systems become more and more complex and multifunctional, the architecture must conform to support the sheer volume of interrupts that concurrent operations propagate. Interrupt prioritization through the use of special interrupt handlers or deferring lower-priority tasks are among techniques that can potentially become vital in terms of alleviating the systems I/O management burden. Besides, real-time communication protocols and adaptive scheduling methods can be goldmines in making systems maintain sufficient responsiveness even under heavy interrupt activity. By learning from advanced designs like Quest-V and drawing lessons from intelligent system models, programmers can create more resilient systems that are capable of thriving despite the challenges posed by interrupt overload (Li et al., 2013; Malin et al., 2025).

8.5.2. Real-Time Constraints and Deadlines

In RTOS, constraint and deadline enforcement is essential to ensuring that tasks are completed on time. The systems are designed to respond to external stimuli within a specified time limit, normally determined by the nature of applications being supported. Tasks are typically divided into hard or soft real-time, with hard real-time tasks having to complete on their deadline strictly, while soft real-time tasks can tolerate some degree of failure without having disastrous consequences. The implications of these divisions are manifested in the way tasks are scheduled and prioritized, impacting system design and performance. Missed deadlines in hard real-time systems could result in drastic system failures, thereby validating the importance of efficient real-time constraint handling in automation, medicine, and aviation control systems. The mixed-criticality task model is also generally used for timing-constrained systems to ensure both reliability and parsimony of resources. By prioritizing essential tasks, this model clusters computing resources while maintaining strict performance constraints.

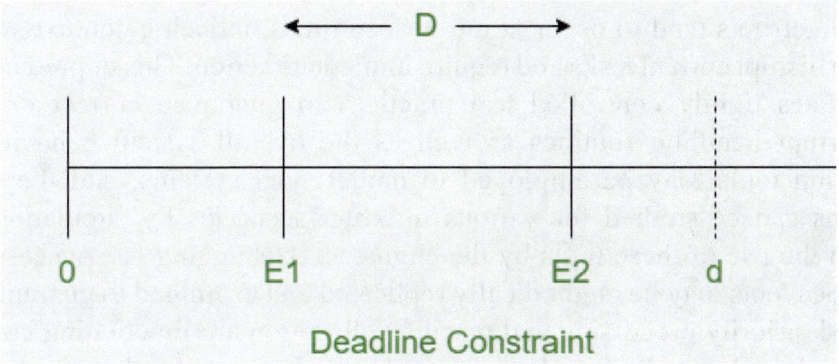

Figure 8.12. Real-time constraints and deadlines.

Source: https://media.geeksforgeeks.org/wp-content/uploads/20200506173637/deadline.png.

As suggested in research, effective resource utilization is critical because systems execute different task-critical levels concurrently. Incorporating robust scheduling algorithms with temporal as well as spatial isolation of tasks to prevent interference from lower-priority tasks upon more vital activities is required. A balance is obtained by employing a well-engineered architecture to manage mixed-criticality environments, which is essential to systems today where the integrity of a system lies in the exact execution of tasks within specified time constraints, according to literature concerning this subject (Sinha et al., 2018). The hardware scheduler function also portrays innovations in managing real-time constraints efficiently. These factors are tuned to achieve the maximum performance of RTOS systems using best-case scheduling algorithm optimizations such as Earliest Deadline First and Least Slack Time. With the addition of FPGA-based systems in this design, flexibility is achieved without the usual limitations pertaining to hardware implementations. As can be inferred from what has been observed, a hardware scheduler can greatly reduce scheduling overhead and scheduling jitter and thus provide a more predictable and efficient response time for critical tasks. The fact that these systems can be customized for specific applications results in improved scaling of resources and ensures that deadlines are fulfilled with increased fidelity, which ultimately results in a more reliable real-time working environment (Bergmann et al., 2015) (Figure 8.12).

8.5.3. Debugging and Testing Interrupt-Driven Systems

Interrupt-driven system debugging and testing is especially difficult due to the inherent non-determinism and complexity inherent in asynchronous processes. RTOS interrupts tend to occur at unforeseen times, inducing context switches that can disrupt current tasks and require immediate action. This unpredictability necessitates tightly controlled test practices to guarantee correct operation of interrupt handling routines as well as the overall system behavior. The simulation tools may be employed to model such systems, and the system reactions can be studied for various interrupt scenarios by simulating them through the use of these tools by the engineers. Debugging is a success if the interrupt events may be methodically replicated and examined to guarantee that both task priority processing and resource allocation are functioning correctly. Interrupt-based systems must be debugged by an integrated technique involving static analysis and dynamic testing. Static analysis examines the source code for potential race conditions, deadlocks, and other concurrency defects prior to runtime, minimizing the chance of faults at runtime. Dynamic testing, however, monitors the system as it executes, tracing events like interrupts and context switches to analyze their impact on performance (Figure 8.13).

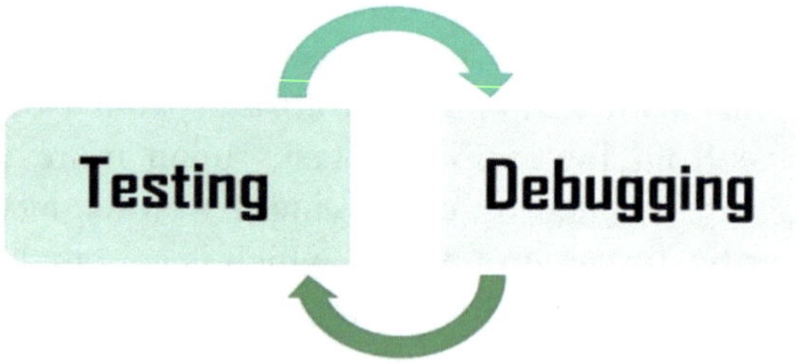

Figure 8.13. The debugging and testing of interrupt-driven systems.

Source: https://techdifferences.com/wp-content/uploads/2019/06/Testing-Vs-Debugging.jpg.

Employing the use of logic analyzers or embedded debuggers facilitates traceability of execution flow and determination of the exact execution path taken during an interrupt. Further, the integration of a Time Management Unit (TMU), as examined in the latest studies, can enhance the capability to observe task execution time and enhance system behavior predictability, eventually minimizing the process of debugging (Gonsholt et al., 2014). Interrupt-driven system testing also must address responsiveness and resource management testing under varying loads. As the complexity of systems increases, determinism and reliability gain increasing importance, especially in areas where timing constraints are tight. Computer-aided testing tools can assist in high test coverage by modeling different interrupt patterns and examining systems response time and accuracy. Incorporating measurement-based methods to measure task processing and error recovery, such as those provided by a TMU, can contribute to the feedback given to programmers regarding the behavior of the system under stress. By dynamic adaptation of system performance based on data collected, as presented in R&D research, engineers can make their interrupt handling policies more sophisticated so that the RTOS meets its intended real-time constraints while contributing to the system's overall robustness (Okyay et al., 2004).

SUMMARY

The subtle relationship between interrupt servicing and I/O management is a feature that distinguishes RTOS. Handling interrupts in the appropriate manner is crucial in providing quick reactions and system stability, particularly in those programs where there are high expectations for reliability and responsiveness. The delicateness of dealing with multiple interrupt sources necessitates sophisticated algorithms and architectures that would handle task prioritization without compromising the overall system performance. As proposed in the studies on integrated concepts for ground systems capable of processing different data from multiple platforms, the availability of efficient interrupt mechanisms is essential towards achieving operational effectiveness and reliability in an environment that is constantly changing (Baldwin et al., 2025). For this reason, effective understanding and utilization of interrupt strategies are pivotal towards fundamental operation of RTOS, determining how data capture and processing is implemented. Further, the switch towards mixed-criticality systems, particularly with the implementation of the Linux kernel adapted for real-time utilization, highlights the evolving dynamics of I/O management within contemporary systems. PREEMPT_RT patch enhances the performance of the kernels by delivering better interrupt response times and system responsiveness critical to both soft and hard real-time systems. This trend represents a point of critical convergence where traditional operating systems meet the requirements of real-time operations, introducing isolation mechanisms to provide the priority of critical tasks while providing overall system stability. According to recent evaluations, these innovations convey that although the Linux kernel includes some limitations, flexibility and development can accommodate several levels of criticality efficiently, which is elementary in modern embedded systems (Onarheim et al., 2024). Finally, the trend of interrupt handling and management of I/O in RTOS will be driven by technological advancements and increased comprehension of the specific demands of real-time applications. Increased complexity in systems will make it essential to address the challenge of assuring timely and reliable responses. That necessity will likely drive further innovation in algorithms and system architecture that enhance performance in the face of load, minimize latency, and support mixed-criticality operations. In the future, constant R&D in hardware and software will be needed to maximize interrupt handling mechanisms and I/O control methods, thus encouraging the creation of stronger and more adaptable real-time systems able to run without any issues in various settings (Baldwin et al., 2025; Onarheim et al., 2024).

Effective interrupt management is a fundamental building block of RTOS since it has significant influences on I/O operations and system performance. The understanding of interrupt handling allows programmers to optimize the execution of tasks, provide system responsiveness, and minimize latency for critical operations. Interrupts facilitate asynchronous communication between the processor and hardware peripherals, providing for the quick servicing of events such as sensor readings or user input. Consequently, a practical and robust interrupt handling system is highly capable of enhancing the effectiveness of an RTOS, particularly in applications involving mixed-criticality task handling. Such techniques are critical to be implemented since system designers must prioritize isolation and usage of resources in their design components to meet specific performance criteria within real-time schedules (Sinha et al., 2018). Furthermore, inclusion of mixed-criticality task models adds an extra layer of complexity to the management of interrupts and I/O in RTOS. The models allow for the servicing of higher-priority tasks all the time without sacrificing system performance even at peak loading. With different levels of criticality designed into systems, scheduling of tasks has to fit in. This is achieved by employing fixed-priority scheduling algorithms that see to it that the highest-priority tasks receive the corresponding CPU resources and handle lower-priority tasks simultaneously efficiently. The temporal and spatial isolation of tasks cannot be overstressed as it contributes to system integrity as well as preventing less-important tasks from interfering with more-important operations in error (Sinha et al., 2018). Additionally, the introduction of Industry 4.0 points towards the importance of interrupt handling and I/O handling in the context of cloud computing and the Internet of Things (IoT) environments. With systems becoming increasingly integrated, the demands for flexible and scalable RTOS solutions become the need of the time. The Zerynth Virtual Machine is a good demonstration of this versatility, offering multithreaded applications the smallest memory footprint while still allowing program developers to program comfortably under Python and C. This architecture is meant to facilitate easy porting on different hardware platforms and RTOS, and the fact that efficient interrupt handling is emphasized as the key to achieving user connectivity and performance speaks volumes. By addressing time-to-market concerns and reliable connectivity, modern RTOS platforms position themselves as core building blocks of the dynamic intelligent technology paradigm.

REFERENCES

1. Ahmad, N. (2017). Porting of FreeRTOS on a Python virtual machine for embedded and IoT devices. https://core.ac.uk/download/79623606.pdf (accessed on 29th September 2025).
2. Andro, M., Farrington, A., Hill, G., Kacpura, T., et al. (2025). Space Telecommunications Radio Systems (STRS) hardware architecture standard: Release 1.0 hardware section. https://core.ac.uk/download/pdf/10543886.pdf (accessed on 29th September 2025).
3. Angoletta, M. E. (2008). Digital signal processor fundamentals and system design. https://core.ac.uk/download/44195315.pdf (accessed on 29th September 2025).
4. Bakkers, A., Broenink, J., & Hilderink, G. (1998). A new Java thread model for concurrent programming of real-time systems. https://core.ac.uk/download/pdf/31151729.pdf (accessed on 29th September 2025).
5. Balas, R., Benini, L., Cuomo, L., Guidieri, A., et al. (2023). Towards a RISC-V open platform for next-generation automotive ECUs. http://arxiv.org/abs/2307.04148 (accessed on 29th September 2025).
6. Baldwin, C. J., Bradford, L. H., Hutson, D. E., Jugle, C., et al. (2025). Functional design for operational Earth resources ground data processing. https://core.ac.uk/download/pdf/42883032.pdf (accessed on 29th September 2025).
7. Bergmann, N. W., & Tang, Y. (2015). A hardware scheduler based on task queues for FPGA-based embedded real-time systems. https://core.ac.uk/download/43368987.pdf (accessed on 29th September 2025).
8. Bounds, J. R., & Pruitt, J. L. (2025). MOSS, an evaluation of software engineering techniques. https://core.ac.uk/download/pdf/42884399.pdf (accessed on 29th September 2025).
9. Buschhoff, M., Falkenberg, R., Friesel, D., Hompel, M., et al. (2017). PhyNetLab: An IoT-based warehouse testbed. http://arxiv.org/abs/1706.09219 (accessed on 29th September 2025).
10. Cheng, Z., West, R., & Ye, Y. (2017). Building real-time embedded applications on QduinoMC: A web-connected 3D printer case study. https://open.bu.edu/bitstream/2144/27914/2/rtas_2017.pdf (accessed on 29th September 2025).
11. Conde, J. F., García-Martínez, A., & Viña, Á. (1996). A comprehensive approach in performance evaluation for modern real-time operating systems. https://core.ac.uk/download/29399340.pdf (accessed on 29th September 2025).

12. Cudmore, A. (2025). High performance spacecraft computing (HPSC) middleware update. https://core.ac.uk/download/pdf/286393153.pdf (accessed on 29th September 2025).
13. Curran, R. T., Fitzpatrick, W. S., Johnson, J. M., Kennedy, K., et al. (2025). System configuration and executive requirements specifications for reusable shuttle and space station/base. https://core.ac.uk/download/pdf/85235074.pdf (accessed on 29th September 2025).
14. De Vos, G. (2003). An implementation of the µC/OS-II kernel and an analysis of its suitability as a real-time operating system for embedded applications. https://core.ac.uk/download/185411354.pdf (accessed on 29th September 2025).
15. Douglas, H., & Gehrmann, C. (2009). Secure virtualization and multicore platforms state-of-the-art report. https://core.ac.uk/download/11434867.pdf (accessed on 29th September 2025).
16. Duffy, C., Herbert, J., Roedig, U., Sreenan, C., et al. (2007). A comprehensive experimental comparison of event-driven and multi-threaded sensor node operating systems. https://core.ac.uk/download/1549498.pdf (accessed on 29th September 2025).
17. Duffy, C., Herbert, J., Roedig, U., Sreenan, C., et al. (2007). Improving the energy efficiency of the MANTIS kernel. https://core.ac.uk/download/390246.pdf (accessed on 29th September 2025).
18. Fahmy, S. A., & Shreejith, S. (2015). Extensible FlexRay communication controller for FPGA-based automotive systems. https://core.ac.uk/download/80790985.pdf (accessed on 29th September 2025).
19. Fattori, A., Martignoni, L., Monga, M., Paleari, R., et al. (2010). Dynamic and transparent analysis of commodity production systems. http://arxiv.org/abs/1006.5845 (accessed on 29th September 2025).
20. Garcia, P. A., Spinelli, E. M., & Toccaceli, G. M. (2014). An embedded system for evoked biopotential acquisition and processing. https://core.ac.uk/download/159301168.pdf (accessed on 29th September 2025).
21. Golchin, A., Sinha, S., & West, R. (2019). Boomerang: Real-time I/O meets legacy systems. https://open.bu.edu/bitstream/2144/43045/2/1908.06807.pdf (accessed on 29th September 2025).
22. Gonsholt, K. E. A., & Ødegaard, L. (2014). Implementing a time management unit for the OR1200 processor. https://core.ac.uk/download/pdf/154667994.pdf (accessed on 29th September 2025).
23. Li, Y., Missimer, E., & West, R. (2013). Predictable migration and communication in the Quest-V multikernal. https://open.bu.edu/

bitstream/2144/11425/1/2013-017-quest-mig-ipc.pdf (accessed on 29th September 2025).

24. Madden, M. M. (2025). Challenges using Linux as a real-time operating system. https://core.ac.uk/download/pdf/323104037.pdf (accessed on 29th September 2025).
25. Malin, J. T., & Schreckenghost, D. L. (2025). Making intelligent systems team players: Overview for designers. https://core.ac.uk/download/pdf/42811927.pdf (accessed on 29th September 2025).
26. Nouvel, F., Prévotet, J. C., & Xia, T. (2015). Mini-NOVA: A lightweight ARM-based virtualization microkernel supporting dynamic partial reconfiguration. https://core.ac.uk/download/52995147.pdf (accessed on 29th September 2025).
27. Okyay, M. O. (2004). A portable real-time operating system for embedded platforms. https://core.ac.uk/download/pdf/324143575.pdf (accessed on 29th September 2025).
28. Onarheim, S. J. (2024). Using the Linux kernel PREEMPT_RT patch in mixed-criticality systems. https://core.ac.uk/download/650685153.pdf (accessed on 29th September 2025).
29. Pellegrini, A., & Quaglia, F. (2017). A fine-grain time-sharing Time Warp system. https://core.ac.uk/download/154948780.pdf (accessed on 29th September 2025).
30. Pellegrini, A., Quaglia, F., & Vitali, R. (2012). A load-sharing architecture for high performance optimistic simulations on multi-core machines. https://core.ac.uk/download/54465509.pdf (accessed on 29th September 2025).
31. Pereira, S. A. G. (2018). A TrustZone-assisted secure silicon on a co-design framework. https://core.ac.uk/download/232201863.pdf (accessed on 29th September 2025).
32. Roussel, K., Song, Y. Q., & Zendra, O. (2015). RIOT OS paves the way for implementation of high-performance MAC protocols. https://core.ac.uk/download/49532959.pdf (accessed on 29th September 2025).
33. Schmidt, D. C., & Suda, T. (1992). Computing infrastructure issues in distributed communications systems: A survey of operating system transport system architectures. https://core.ac.uk/download/287622717.pdf (accessed on 29th September 2025).
34. Sinha, S. (2018). Scheduling policies and system software architectures for mixed-criticality computing. https://core.ac.uk/download/304658766.pdf (accessed on 29th September 2025).

CHAPTER 9

REAL-TIME COMMUNICATION SYSTEMS

Contents

INTRODUCTION

The invention of real-time communication networks has transformed various industries, especially transportation and telecommunications, as far as efficiency and safety are concerned. The networks facilitate real-time exchange of information, which is important for decision-making in situations requiring immediate response. The use of Intelligent Transport Systems (ITS) is good evidence of this revolution, using advanced technologies to enhance traffic control as well as enhance road safety. As highlighted by various research studies, ITS entails autonomous and cooperative systems that both serve their individual functions in improving roadway safety through monitoring and guiding traffic streams (Mol et al., 2008). Such basic understanding of real-time communication systems is a starting point for exploring their broader implications in other fields like healthcare and emergency services. Besides, distributed processing and fault tolerance form the basis of architecture of real-time communication systems, yielding reliability as well as responsivity. For instance, the Tumult system developed at Twente University proves successful with a modular multi-processor design in emphasizing efficient message passing between nodes (Jansen et al., 1988). Such architectures play a vital role in applications that require high accuracy of timing because they provide mechanisms for running processes concurrently without any significant delay. It is thus the importance of conforming to solid standards in communications technology that cannot be overstated as such standards provide the needed protocols for integration and interoperability of systems on varying platforms. The ever-evolving nature of real-time communication systems necessitates ongoing research and development, particularly to mitigate the user adoption challenges as well as technical integration. Today, applications ranging from vehicle-to-vehicle communication and real-time traffic updates are a definitive example of the necessity of joint efforts by stakeholders like government agencies, industry players, and academia. As experienced in the ITS case, complex evaluation processes are necessary in ascertaining the efficacy of new technologies and shaping policy mechanisms on their adoption (Mol et al., 2008). It is thus necessary to do a complete analysis of real-time communication systems to not only declare their advantages but also to tackle the issues that lie ahead in the field of implementation and application.

Definition of Real-Time Communication Systems

Real-time communication systems are largely characterized by the capacity to transmit data with little delay, thereby enabling immediate interaction between users or devices. These types of systems are vital in various applications—from teleconferencing to remote medical consultations—where the sharing of information at timely pace matters. In the working model here, the data throughput and delay are arranged with much care so that data is received as simultaneously as it is transmitted, permitting synchronous interaction. By so doing, design and architecture of real-time systems must emphasize efficiency and reliability in order to have the information relayed effectively and in a timely manner. Their effectiveness in the majority of instances is offered by advanced algorithms and methods maximizing the data transmission efficiency, which just so happens to be closely linked with the exploration of web-enabled technologies such as smart objects and cyber-physical systems explored in current literature (Axelsson et al., 2012). This real-time complexity is further heightened by the convergence of various networks and platforms, as supported by the expansion of the Internet of Things (IoT) and smart technology.

Figure 9.1. Real-time communication.

Source: https://cdn.botpenguin.com/assets/website/Real_Time_Communication_e0da5ad85f.webp.

When the systems combine, the interaction among various communication modalities—e.g., wired, wireless, and cellular networks—results in the environment requiring robust performance metrics. Achieving a subtle balance between efficiency and cost is critical in the creation of economic and high-performing networks. This interdependence is articulated in terms of the creation of new theories, e.g., economic small worlds, which are concerned with efficient information conveyance in addition to cost management (Marchiori et al., 2002). These frameworks facilitate research into the behavior of real-time communication systems, and from that, conclusions are made on how multiple networks can communicate and operate in real-world environments. For real-time communication systems to be scalable and sustainable, researchers and developers must overcome several challenges such as security, interoperability, and user experience. As real-time interaction becomes more necessary, particularly in applications such as healthcare and emergency services, systems must not only operate consistently but also be able to protect sensitive data from security threats. Compatibility between a range of technologies is just as vital;

as technology evolves, ongoing compatibility between devices and platforms is crucial to maintain user engagement and operating effectiveness. Real-time communications encapsulate this subtle balance between performance, security, and human-centered design, and represent an absolutely key area of continuing research and development. This richness of real-time communications culminates in the creation of strong, interconnected infrastructures which facilitate modern society (Marchiori et al., 2002) (Figure 9.1).

Importance in Modern Society

The relevance of real-time communication systems cannot be overstressed in current society since it is of the highest importance in uniting the different cultures and populations. The systems make interaction in real-time possible, providing a platform for information and ideas to be shared between extensive geographical points. With the growth of globalization further affecting social relationships, the real-time communication platforms become an important asset for facilitating more comprehension and cooperation among individuals from disparate environments. These systems are also strong enough to allow people to engage in substantial conversations that are open to learning and cross-cultural communication. In this case, collectivism that is found in different societies, as emphasized in current research, reinforces the value of communication in building a global community. Collectivism studies in the Network Society indicate that encouraging communication can push forward collaborative science and technology efforts, improving overall society progress (Iitaka et al., 2010). Moreover, real-time communication systems pose enormous economic implications for the development of societies, especially in the service sector. The highly dynamic nature of jobs has evoked the demand for seamless integration of communications technology to allow businesses to work and react in response to market demands. While most developed nations shift toward a postindustrial economy, the efficiency of services industries relies more and more on fast communication networks that mechanize procedures, drive customer engagement, and drive innovation. This transition is key to seizing marketplace opportunities and sustaining competitive advantages in today's fast-paced economy. Understanding the services sector as a hyper-sector articulates the pivotal connection between real-time communication and economic growth, laying greater stress on the means through which strategic management can leverage these systems in advancing productivity (Britchenko et al., 2018). The societal effect of real-time communication systems also overflows into enhancing the well-being of its population. Such platforms provide individuals with access to vital services and resources at high speeds, enabling them to participate in civic activities and community events. In a more networked world, access to real-time communication creates opportunities for people to organize, campaign for reform, and collaborate on issues influencing their communities. This participation is vital to democratic processes where informed citizens are able to join together and influence public policy. Further, the suffering that may be inflicted by collectivism's negativities, e.g., stifling personal creativity, as criticisms of Japanese society, may be vanquished through open avenues of communication that promote diverse concepts and forms. Thus, real-time communications systems allow for individual initiative and group effort, requisite for the development of a harmonious and dynamic society (Iitaka et al., 2010).

Overview of Key Technologies

In real-time communication systems, several key technologies are engaged in facilitating instant interaction over distant locations. Among them, the Internet of Things (IoT) is a key technology that enhances connectivity and automation in these systems. IoT devices like sensors, actuators, and smart meters play significant roles in monitoring and controlling communication infrastructure. This is particularly the case in smart grids, which are revolutionizing traditional power grids to support bi-directional information exchange between consumers and service providers. With IoT, smart grids not only enhance energy consumption optimization and reliability but also support real-time data transfer and communication among devices to promote a more efficient and responsive energy management system. These advances in communication technology emphasize the importance of robust infrastructure for enabling widespread connectivity and collaboration in real-time systems (Copeland et al., 2019). Emerging communication protocol technology is another important technology in real-time communication systems. Communication protocols such as WebRTC (web real-time communication) facilitate peer-to-peer communication, and they make high-quality audio, video, and data transfer possible over the internet. Adoption of such protocols has incredibly lowered the barrier for entry of real-time communications so that developers could create more interactive and rich user experiences. With ubiquitous mobile phones and broadband connectivity, the demand for silky-smooth real-time interactions has skyrocketed, nudging developers to build their platforms on an ongoing basis (Figure 9.2). This transition not only raises user satisfaction but also serves as an impetus for innovation in numerous other areas, including education and telemedicine. Through reduction of latency and easier accessibility, complex communication protocols are a decisive factor in shaping the future of real-time communication systems (Leach et al., 2005). In addition to IoT and complex communication protocols, cloud computing has emerged as a foundation technology underpinning real-time communication systems. By offering scalable resources and central data processing, cloud computing offers a nimble base for operating applications and services that require immediate processing of data. With this nimbleness, organizations can deploy solutions without necessarily having to make huge infrastructural investments, further democratizing access to high-end communication tools. Cloud platforms also allow collaboration by the consolidation of various applications, thereby enhancing the overall efficiency of communication. The ability to carry out real-time analytics and feedback mechanisms in cloud systems greatly enhances decision-making across industries. With more demand for flexible, expandable, and efficient systems of communication, cloud computing is a foundational technology that greatly enables the development and upgrade of real-time communication systems (Leach et al., 2005).

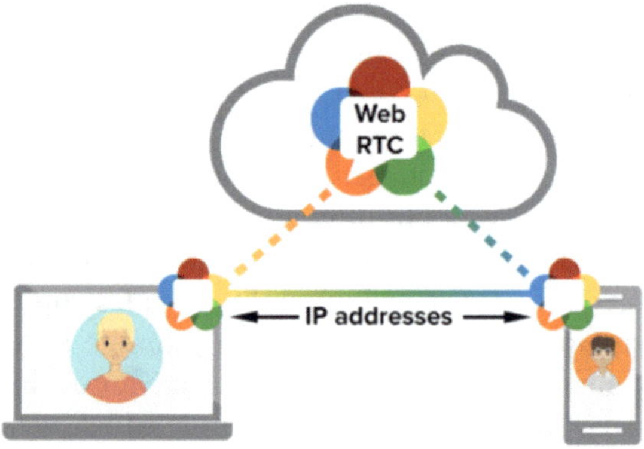

Figure 9.2. *WebRTC (web real-time communication).*

Source: https://www.tonmind.com/js/htmledit/kindeditor/attached/20220106/20220106233617_85696.png.

9.1. HISTORICAL DEVELOPMENT

Historical development of real-time communication systems has been marked by a dramatic change brought about by technological advancements and changing social needs. Communication technology in its early stages was marked by simple telegraph systems enabling real-time text messages over large distances. During the progression of the 20th century, the discovery of telephony and broadcasting unveiled new fields in communication, leading to the evolution of multimedia modes. The advent of the internet in the late 20th century propelled a new era of computer-based communication, with information moving at unprecedented speeds. This revolution paved the way for even more sophisticated systems, with real-time interaction more practical and precise. The advent of wireless communication technologies in the early 21st century continued to revolutionize systems of real-time communication. Developments in mobile technology enabled users to communicate unimaginable ways before, so real-time messaging, video calling, and social media applications emerged. These were becoming indispensable to both business and personal communication, so systems that could process large volumes of data with reduced latency became increasingly necessary. Besides, with the inclusion of Internet of Things (IoT) devices, a network of interdependent systems has been formed, which facilitates increased real-time data exchange. This high-order development raised the critical problems of data processing and communication efficiency that recent systems had to address. To address these challenges, contemporary approaches such as digital twin technology and vehicular fog computing have been devised, demonstrating the continuous evolution of real-time communication systems. Digital twins make predictive modeling possible in sectors such as wind energy, with heterogeneous data streams merged to create successful real-time platforms. Digital twins eliminate inherent inefficiencies and allow better decision-making with hybrid modeling paradigms that merge data-centric and physics-based approaches (Alaliyat et al., 2024). At the same time, vehicle fog computing has been employed within intelligent transport systems to improve real-time collision warning systems and decrease issues like packet loss and communication latency (Feng et al., 2020). These new paradigms show how previous achievements continue to shape the real-time communication landscape, and how innovations in the future are likely to provide even greater connectivity and efficiency.

9.1.1. Early Communication Systems

The evolution of initial communication systems laid the basis for the real-time communication technologies available currently. Early communication at first relied mostly on primitive modes such as smoke signals, drumbeats, and semaphore systems, which had limitations in terms of distance and speed. These systems of communication were essentially meant for short-distance priority messaging and involved a line of sight, hence limiting their application. As societies developed, the invention of the telegraph shattered the long-distance communication barrier by paving the way for messages to travel almost in real-time over vast distances. This revolution laid the foundation for future developments and further asserting the fundamental connection between communication and the advancement of society, ultimately giving birth to the modern real-time systems of communication that we now take for granted in today's interconnected world. The integration of technology into early communication systems was crucial in the creation of communication protocols.

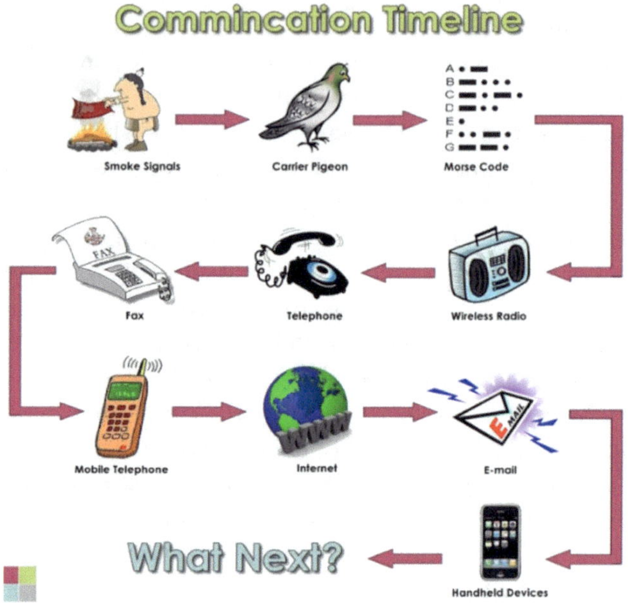

Figure 9.3. *Communication timeline.*

Source: https://i.pinimg.com/736x/a6/4d/e0/a64de03b3218d0ce84ccccf7a8fdcdde.jpg.

The transition of communication from analog to digital communication, made possible by telephone invention, extended the extent of user engagement, enabling instant two-way communication. The telephone's ability to convert sound waves into electricity revolutionized communication, making communication a more intimate experience than the previous nonverbal communication styles. Secondly, early systems focused on user requirements during development. As noted, the communication or elicitation of user requirements is an essential stage of system development, since it demands methodologies that facilitate user participation and tendencies. Therefore, the fundamental features found in primitive systems, such as the emphasis on direct interaction and user-centric approaches, remain essential as we transition into the more sophisticated realm of real-time systems, such as various technologies like the Internet of Things and integrated digital communication systems. Privacy and data integrity are becoming significant concerns in the context of early communication systems, particularly because these systems have expanded to include resource-constrained domains such as the Internet of

Things (IoT). While early systems were groundbreaking, these systems did not have robust mechanisms for protecting user data, which was more vulnerable as digital communication increased. One of the solutions to these issues is the proposal of Privacy-Preserving Data Aggregation (PPDA) techniques designed to preserve data privacy during aggregation in sensor networks. As mentioned, node lifetime is significant in applications from smart healthcare to intelligent transportation systems and directly contributes to such communication system performance. These privacy issues have evolved into necessary matters to handle as organizations implement the initial communication principles into modern environments, so that movement from traditional modes of communication to systems in real-time does not erode user trust and data protection (Ali et al., 2018; Coughlan et al., 2002) (Figure 9.3).

9.1.2. Evolution of Technology

The evolution of technology has deeply impacted the area of communication, particularly in the presence of real-time interactions. The evolution from traditional communication systems to advanced digital systems during the past three decades revolutionized the way people and institutions interact and cooperate. The inefficiency of an outmoded Internet infrastructure has precipitated the efforts to enhance and evolve existing systems. A distinct aspect of this evolution is the programmability of wireless networks, which aims to achieve flexibility and complexity of traditional networks. Such evolution not only makes communication easier but also facilitates new applications necessary to modern connectivity. Through flexibility and programmability being infused into network design, such systems ensure real-time communication can scale up to meet mounting user requirements with reduced lag and greater efficiency in total (Ahad et al., 2014). With the world's urbanization moving rapidly into cities, the integration of cutting-edge communication technologies into the city's infrastructure has become increasingly vital. The Smart City initiative is a model that redefines technology not as an appendix but as an inherent aspect of city function. Using smart communication networks, cities can provide extended services with reduced expenses. Such interfacing creates a supportive loop between data collection and the effectiveness of city services, leading to a greater insight into user needs and habits. For instance, traffic monitoring systems in urban areas can enhance cellular services through anticipating user density and responding with adjusted resources. This innovation is a milestone towards optimizing urban living through enhanced capacity for real-time communication, exemplifying the tremendous impact of technology on social structures (Abrougui et al., 2017). Gazing into the future, the future of real-time systems for communication will likely be shaped more and more by ongoing technological advancements and increased cross-fertilization among various scientific disciplines. New ideas such as SymbioCity encourage a synergistic approach for designing communication infrastructure and urban services where both elements enhance the performance of the other. Besides, with the increase in complexity and diversity of wireless technologies, research into software-defined networks, cognitive radio networks, and virtualized networks will be necessary to create adaptive communication systems. These technologies not only will support current real-time communication demands but will also generate new possibilities for innovative applications to address future requirements. The speeding up of these developments underlines the necessity of ongoing research and development in the area of communications to maintain systems resilient and responsive to the evolving demands of society (Abrougui et al., 2017; Ahad et al., 2014) (Figure 9.4).

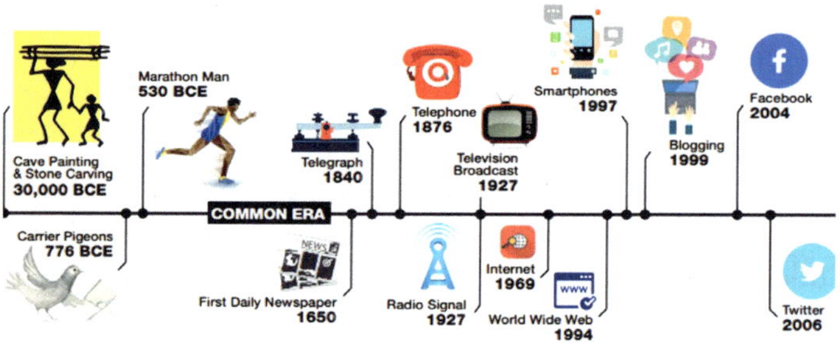

Figure 9.4. Evolution of communication technology from ancient to modern times.

Source: https://external-content.duckduckgo.com/iu/?u=https%3A%2F%2Fwww.myforesight.my%2Fwp-content%2Fuploads%2F2016%2F07%2FTech2.png&f=1&nofb=1&ipt=d46f8a3365297a06fd93b91911ab936fe6029d1e8e5127480078283b61b67bd4.

9.1.3. Milestones in Real-Time Communication

Turning points in real-time communications have evolved a great deal over the decades and have had revolutionary impacts on the way organizations and individuals communicate over distances. Communication was once handicapped by technology-related constraints such as slow data transmission and having to employ asynchronous systems such as email or postal services. The advent of high-speed internet and the invention of instant messaging solutions, however, marked a watershed moment. These innovations delivered immediate, interactive communications that dissolved barriers previously erected by distance and time. As technology developed, so did the mediums available to us for carrying real-time communication, which added to a greater sense of connectedness and collaboration among users. Identifying these milestones—such as the use of VoIP technology and the development of video conferencing—has been instrumental in shaping the language of effective communication in a more digital age. A key aspect of the development of real-time communication is orderly coordination of collaborative projects, typically aided by an assessment framework that ensures appropriate interaction among participants. For instance, in engineering learning, checklists like project definition, tracking, and delivery guide students through complex processes, both project output and communication skill. Such structured framework not only provides the students with clearly defined targets but also emphasizes the importance of teamwork and accountability. The presence of professional skills assessment in such milestones, as illustrated across various learning settings, is designed to feed into a culture that prepares students for real-life challenges while they develop good communication practices. These frameworks build a structured assessment strategy that makes stakeholders confident and clear, especially in areas where there is an emphasis on collective evidence-based work, as described in the study at the Barcelona School of Informatics (Forment et al., 2014). Additionally, the international context of real-time communication brings about the challenges and possibilities for collective work regardless of time zones and different academic calendars. The case study conducted by the authors in Australia, England, and South Africa is a perfect example of new problems in maintaining communication effective in convergent situations because it illustrates how the new communication systems in real-time have knocked down the new walls. Individuals taking part in this scholarly writing process discovered that success relied not solely on technology but also on managing collaboration along with their interpersonal skills. Through project management and individual accountability, these authors were able to bridge their differences and reap maximum from their communication efforts and ultimately yield productive outcomes. This example brings out the significance of transforming technological as well as individual strategies in order to achieve maximum potential of real-time communication systems, a significant lesson for business professionals operating within globally interconnected environments (Heinze et al., 2008).

9.2. TYPES OF REAL-TIME COMMUNICATION SYSTEMS

Real-time communication systems consist of collections of platforms designed to provide real-time communication among users or devices. Real-time communication systems can be broadly categorized into two distinct categories, namely synchronous and asynchronous communication systems. Synchronous communication occurs when the users communicate in real-time, such as using video conferences or VoIP, making it possible to have timely feedback and flow of conversation. That spontaneity is valuable in applications like emergency response coordination or team collaboration, where choices must be made in time. On the other hand, asynchronous systems, as exemplified by email and messaging applications, enable users to trade information without establishing dependencies on receiving instant responses. That flexibility aids in supporting time zone differences or varying schedules, thereby enhancing productivity in various teams. Understanding of such differences facilitates greater practical use based on individual needs in various industries. A second layer of complexity to the realm of real-time communication systems is added by underlying technologies and protocols. Multiparty session types provide a theoretical framework for facilitating intricate communication, particularly within distributed programming environments. Through support for time constraint handling mechanisms as well as exception handling, such systems facilitate fault-tolerant functionality within environments where safety and reliability are required. In particular, the construction of programs like MultiCrustyT demonstrates that modern programming techniques can be employed to develop safe, scheduled protocols, which demonstrate that good design is enough to defeat problems with asynchronous interaction. The focus placed on communication safety and deadlock prevention is important, especially when concurrent interaction is expected to meet high levels of operational excellence in numerous applications. The theoretical foundations and practical applications all converge in highlighting the importance of educated decision-making in system design and implementation. With advances in real-time communication systems, their utilization has become more critical in high-risk environments, such as space exploration missions. NASAs plans for Mars, for instance, encompass significant logistical and medical communication challenges due to the lengthy duration of the mission and vast distance from Earth. Here, real-time communication is not merely a conversation facilitator; it is a mission-success enabler and a crew-independence enabler. The constraint of potential communication delays requires systems that ensure strong operation and quick feedback, or in other words, rapid impact on onboard medical care and emergency response strategies. By comprehending the importance of such systems, mission planners and engineers are able to more effectively develop protocols that ensure crew safety while optimizing the potential for mission success, demonstrating the necessity of careful planning and innovative engineering techniques in the field of real-time communication.

9.2.1. Voice Over Internet Protocol (VoIP)

The addition of Voice over Internet Protocol (VoIP) in real-time communication systems represents the biggest technological advancement that transforms traditional telephony. Unlike traditional telephonic systems based on circuit-switched networks, VoIP employs packet-switched networks, which enable voice communication through the internet. This is achieved by introducing a number of advantages including lower costs for distant calls and the ability to support a wide range of multimedia and communication applications. As a part of a broader technology setting, VoIP has provided access to other innovations such as video conferencing and distant collaboration devices, which are central in both private and business settings. The flexibility of VoIP systems also ensures easier integration with existing internet infrastructure, making it a compelling choice for businesses that want to enhance communication efficiency and reduce operational expenses while facilitating real-time communication (Figure 9.5).

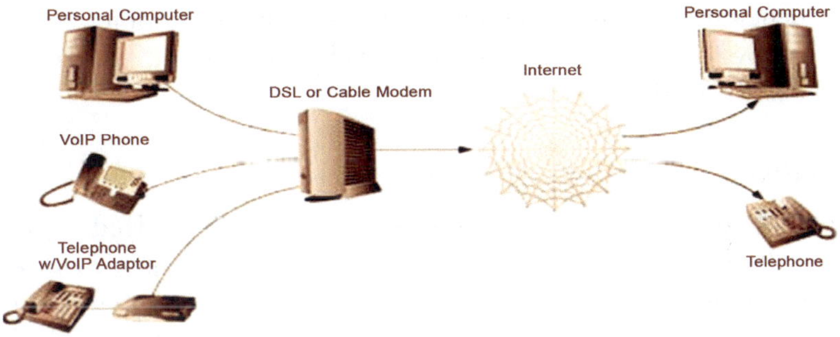

Figure 9.5. *How VoIP works.*

Source: https://external-content.duckduckgo.com/iu/?u=https%3A%2F%2Fassignmentpoint.com%2Fwp-content%2Fuploads%2F2020%2F10%2FHow-voice-over-internet-protocol-VoIP-works.jpg&f=1&nofb=1&ipt=9666199ec5bc3ba06e7c6287129c2006e2e64d3aa706f25b4a3eddd71dccb476.

However, the implementation of VoIP technology is also associated with a series of challenges, particularly in relation to quality of service (QoS). The performance of VoIP systems relies on the tolerance delay, packet loss, and jitter, which directly affect the voice communication quality and reliability. For instance, in bandwidth-constrained environments, introducing security features—such as encryption—may even exacerbate these issues. Lab testing shows that general VoIP performance is generally in the hands of bandwidth present and the particular encryption schemes employed. Even though additional bandwidth can overcome security-degradation issues, limited-capacity environments may experience diminished voice quality due to intermittent communication. Thus, organizations need to maintain a balance between the security needs and the inherent requirements of real-time communication in the interest of ensuring an acceptable user experience (Moreno et al., 2010). Further, the advent of VoIP technology has opened doors for potential usage, one of which is the development of domain-specific systems like the AudioGraph system that incorporates voice activity detection algorithms for sophisticated audio processing capabilities. This dual application of VoIP not only supports real-time communication but also promotes the efficient recording of voice information. The AudioGraph tool is an example of how VoIP can be leveraged to enhance interactive systems by adding functionality such as echo cancellation and sound representation methods. These developments validate the flexibility of VoIP as far beyond voice communication, with its application in supporting synchronous audio applications in various technological contexts. As there is growing demand for high-technology real-time communication systems, VoIP continues to evolve, presenting a chance and challenge for developers and users alike (Liu et al., 2001).

9.2.2. Video Conferencing Tools

The technology of video conferencing has revolutionized systems of communication in real-time by enabling people and companies to alter the means of communication. By facilitating face-to-face communication in a virtual environment, these technologies overcome geographical distance, improving interaction and collaboration.

Figure 9.6. *Video conferencing tools.*

Source: https://external-content.duckduckgo.com/iu/?u=https%3A%2F%2Fcloudinfrastructureservices.co.uk%2Fwp-content%2Fuploads%2F2021%2F10%2Fvideo-conferencing-tools-2.png&f=1&nofb=1&ipt=08d6d2ab7da8e20530d5bd0524b425be43c5b1f03b7f8be1754a8704f035838f.

Offering top-quality video and audio transmission, the participants can become connected as if they were physically present together in one location, which is crucial in schools and companies. As demand for remote communication grows, the capability and sophistication of these devices are improving, offering capabilities like screen sharing, breakout rooms, and real-time collaborative document editing. Not only is this making communications more effective, but it also enables a sense of community, something crucial in an increasingly virtual environment. Furthermore, video conferencing technology has emerged as a key facilitator of effective pedagogy in the education community. They enable tutors to extend their horizons beyond classroom boundaries, building a model of the 'Peripatetic Electronic Teacher' (PET) that supports an active, interactive learning environment. In such a context, teachers are able to adopt several personas—pedagogic, managerial, and commercial—within global networked space, a notion that has been developed through more recent research literature (Squires et al., 1999) (Figure 9.6). The integration of high-quality multimedia capabilities into these platforms supports diversified educational methods and responds to different types of learners. Therefore, the education sector has much to benefit from the application of video conferencing technologies as they not only support diverse teaching methods but also encourage student engagement and interaction in real-time settings. The applications of these real-time communication systems extend beyond the classroom and corporate boardroom. Video conferencing tools play an essential role in facilitating global collaborative work, where teams from across the world can collaborate seamlessly. The psychological and pedagogical foundations of technology-enhanced learning environments suggest that successful communications technologies significantly influence learning (Barker et al., 1995). That flexibility is worth its weight in gold for sectors such as the healthcare industry, in which internet consultation and co-diagnosis can be used to improve patient care. As increasingly more organizations implement these technologies, it becomes important to understand their limitations and potential to best utilize them in various fields. Hence, continuous development and integration of video conferencing technologies will certainly shape the future of real-time communication systems.

9.2.3. Instant Messaging Platforms

The emergence of instant messaging platforms is a revolutionary step in real-time communication systems that radically alters the way users and organizations communicate. Instant messaging platforms provide real-time text-based communication where users can exchange messages in real-time over different devices. Over the course of time, the features of instant messaging have developed to include multimedia sharing, video calls, and integrated services that engage users and make them more connected. Advances in mobile and internet technology have further fueled this revolution, introducing new platforms like WhatsApp, Slack, and Microsoft Teams, each addressing specific communication requirements in personal and professional settings. As the users keep looking for integrated communication experiences, the platforms keep modifying and adding new functionalities in response to stay relevant and keep up with shifting user needs, becoming an integral part of the world of digital communication (N/A, 2006). The architecture of instant messaging platforms typically employs advanced protocols for reliable and efficient message delivery. One of the suitable protocols for implementing IM services is the Extensible Messaging and Presence Protocol (XMPP), which is even capable of being used on low-end devices like set-top boxes. This flexibility extends the use of instant messaging beyond computing environments, thus optimizing the user experience across platforms. XMPP's robust framework not only allows text communication in real-time but also allows for the incorporation of rich interactive features, thereby emerging as a viable choice for developers within digital television systems, for example. Consequently, use of XMPP in such settings enables the creation of feature-oriented applications that optimize user interaction and accessibility, hence proving the protocols applicability in the context of real-time communication systems (Deryckere et al., 2007) (Figure 9.7).

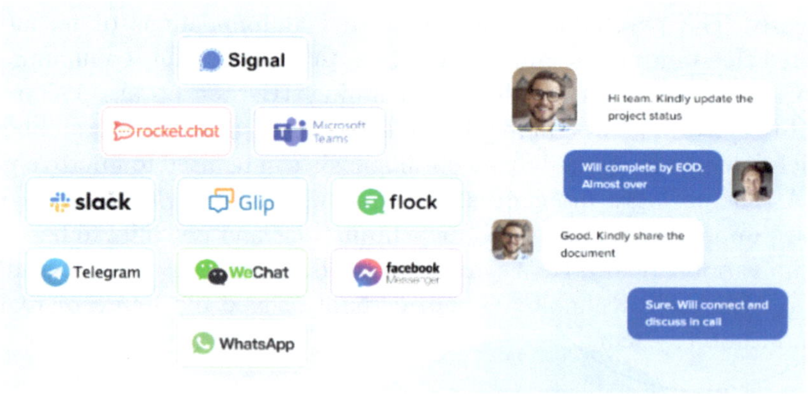

Figure 9.7. *Instant messaging platforms.*

Source: https://external-content.duckduckgo.com/iu/?u=https%3A%2F%2Fwww.mirrorfly.com%2Fblog%2Fwp-content%2Fuploads%2F2024%2F03%2Finstant-messaging-platform.webp&f=1&nofb=1&ipt=dedae81b80c81262353eedd4bbb7cc01b20aeaa6cce95a7a5771b4b108c6a298.

Beyond XMPP, other technological advancements and user demands are shaping the future of instant messaging platforms. With growing concerns for privacy and security, various platforms are making end-to-end encryption a feature, which translates into greater user trust and adoption. Another aspect being brought into the platforms is artificial intelligence to allow personalized user experiences, such as more sophisticated conversation management as well as automated response options. These advances not only simplify the communicative process but also provide information and support in real-time situations. As instant messaging continues to evolve with the shifting landscape of the online world, its usefulness within real-time communicational systems becomes more and more core, meaning that these applications will remain a necessary tool for interpersonal and organizational discussion as society grows more integrated (N/A, 2006).

9.3. KEY TECHNOLOGIES ENABLING REAL-TIME COMMUNICATION

In the background of real-time communication technology of today's era, several pioneering technologies have emerged as the key enabling technologies. One among them is the Internet of Things (IoT) due to its capacity for networking devices to exchange data in an unproblematic manner and get monitored from different platforms. IoT devices, including sensors, actuators, and smart meters, form the core of this communication framework with two-way information flow that enhances functional efficiency. This infrastructure not only supports real-time data control and analysis but also lays the platform for automation procedures required in order to manage changing environments. As defined in current literature, the incorporation of IoT in Smart Grid systems is one such representation of how real-time communication could be combined with advanced monitoring and feedback loops, ultimately leading to enhanced energy management and optimization of resources (Copeland et al., 2019). Furthermore, improvements in wireless technology have been pivotal in enhancing real-time communication systems. The introduction of 5G networks, for example, offers unprecedented data transfer rates and low latency, which are critical for purposes that require instantaneous communication. Such advancements enable other industries, like telemedicine and autonomous transportation, to rely on real-time streams of data for success in their functions. With growing need for real-time connectivity, 5G's ability to support a vast quantity of connected devices simultaneously becomes a matter of urgency. Evolution towards Smart Grids also puts focus on efficient energy distribution and consumption, providing a potential paradigm shift in the engagement of power systems with consumers. This increased connectivity and data sharing capability underscores the necessity of leveraging new wireless technology to deliver convergent communication solutions (Duran et al., 2008). Last but not least, cloud computing is also a technology enabler that enables real-time communication by providing scalable resources and data storage. Cloud facilitation enables companies to host applications that are accessible and updatable in real time, supporting collaboration regardless of geographic location.

This is especially useful for companies with remote employees, enabling immediate information exchange and decision making from multiple platforms. Combined with artificial intelligence and machine learning, cloud computing can process huge sets of data in real-time, providing insights that increase responsiveness and operational tactics. For Smart Grid systems, the adoption of cloud platforms is useful for efficient energy management as well as improved performance monitoring, leading to a more efficient and effective supply of energy. The interaction between cloud technologies and real-time communication services is therefore a critical factor for creating efficient and effective communication systems (Copeland et al., 2019).

9.3.1. Internet Protocol (IP)

Internet protocol (IP) is the underlying communication protocol that supports real-time communications systems, making it possible for devices to exchange data over networks. Essentially, IP gives an addressing system and delivers packets of data among nodes such that information is delivered successfully to its target. IP stability is particularly critical in systems where communication speed and reliability are a matter of paramount importance, e.g., for remote robot control or live streaming. Systems for real-time communication based upon IP must also cope with varying network conditions that can introduce latency; therefore, IP-based communication architecture design should aim for stability and low latency.

Effective measures such as the coupling of IP with real-time transport protocols facilitate fast data transmission necessary in maintaining communication integrity in dynamic systems. With advancing technologies, the robustness of Internet Protocol is more related to technological advancements in wireless sensor networks (WSNs) that support cyber-physical systems. WSNs augment the capability of traditional IP with detailed spatial-temporal sensing and communication without placing too much strain on energy and cost constraints. In real-time communication networks, the use of IP-based transmission in WSNs provides scalable and efficient communication infrastructure. IP solves the expanding system complexity that requires continuous monitoring and regulation, for example, in smart buildings and industrial automation. Reliability is a pressing problem, demanding ongoing efforts in network management and security to ensure that information is being passed on properly and on time (Figure 9.8).

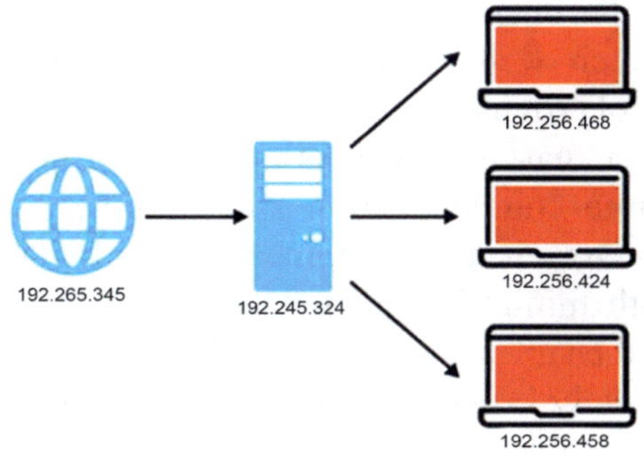

Figure 9.8. Internet protocol (IP).

Source: https://external-content.duckduckgo.com/iu/?u=https%3A%2F%2Fdnycf48t040dh.cloudfront.net%2Ffit-in%2F840x473%2FWhat-is-the-Internet-Protocol.jpeg&f=1&nofb=1&ipt=aad324f86e5aac6facf4eabc6b04dd61691b5ae2dfdb88a7cba047d8b2290d61.

Thus, IPs role towards such complex networks becomes imperative with increasing reliance on real-time data exchange among applications. Establishing a real-time communications medium over IP involves serious exploration of key parameters such as bandwidth and delay, particularly in the scenario where delay-sensitive applications are being supported. For instance, with a passivity-based model reference robust control structure being employed over the internet, understanding the consequences of network topology is crucial to maintaining system stability.

As discussed by Naghshineh et al. (2011), careful site surveys can dictate not only the geographical separation between nodes but even the nuances of communication parameters dictating the virtual terrain over which data flows. These elements ensure control instructions arrive with minimal latency, an aspect fundamental in application domains such as remote control of aircraft or automated machinery. Furthermore, the inclusion of communication as part of secure protocols also further protects authenticity of real-time transactions, ensuring data integrity in the process of exchange. With growing requirements for high-speed and secure communications, the quintessential role of IP in these complicated systems cannot be overstated.

9.3.2. WebRTC (Web Real-Time Communication)

WebRTC is an innovation needed in real-time communication systems. WebRTC eliminates the intermediary servers by enabling direct peer-to-peer communication between web browsers and thus ensures better speed and efficiency. The protocol provides support for any form of data transfer, including audio, video, and data sharing, and thus provides an integrated environment to implement real-time communication applications. As WebRTC operates primarily based on open web standards, it can be easily integrated into existing web applications with minimal adjustments. This factor of easy integration fosters innovation and enables a huge array of use cases, from video calling to online gaming, ultimately bringing sophisticated communication tools within the reach of users across the world.

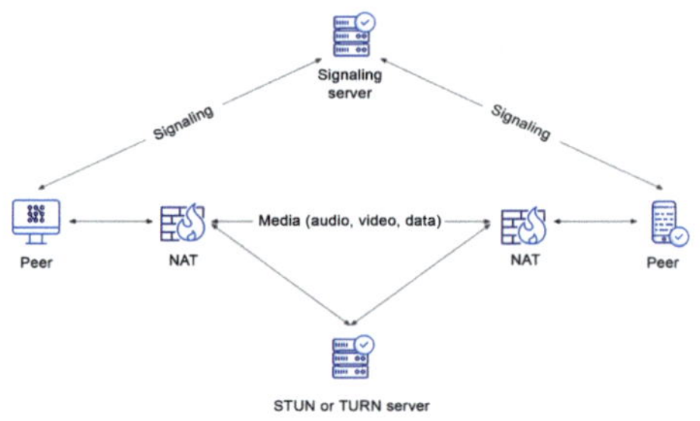

Figure 9.9. How WebRTC works.

Source: https://external-content.duckduckgo.com/iu/?u=https%3A%2F%2Fwww.loadview-testing.com%2Fwp-content%2Fuploads%2FWebRTC-explained.png&f=1&nofb=1&ipt=b96d39fa8bf379cef5e5186a903ceb87b14d75de2033a81ad8636fab3f58b178.

In business environments, especially where instant and efficient response channels are essential, the advantage of WebRTC is evidently far-reaching. For instance, WebRTC use in firefighting and rescue operations has been promising to enhance operational efficiency and safety. With a given application using WebRTC, firemen have been able to communicate in real-time while also recording critical information, such as images and videos, straight from the scene via a Wireless Local Area Network (WLAN) mounted on their fire truck. Such capability is crucial, as it enables the self-documenting of otherwise memory-based communications, immensely improving reporting accuracy. The prospect of effortless multimedia integration into high-stakes situations serves to illustrate the revolutionary promise of WebRTC in real-time communication systems, as evidenced by real-world implementations of first responder applications (Booth et al., 2018) (Figure 9.9). Besides, ongoing advancements in WebRTC functionality demonstrate its lead in propelling interactive multimedia applications. Present research indicates that current P2P applications have encountered constraints in real-time multimedia streaming, but the potential optimization of WebRTCs JavaScript APIs will create opportunities for improving algorithms of streaming. Such an advancement is important, given that demand for quality streaming persists across platforms. By addressing the holes in P2P overlays towards real-time streaming, developers are able to leverage the potential of JavaScript on WebRTC platforms in the support of improved user experience through more intimate, interactive involvement. With the real-time communications universe ongoing evolving, the continued evolution of WebRTC functionality remains an imperative focus for developers and researchers aiming to enhance the effectiveness of communications systems (Cerviño et al., 2012).

9.3.3. Cloud Computing

In real-time communication systems, cloud computing is a background technology that ensures smooth interaction between various platforms and devices. Using clouds distributed architecture, scalability and availability of the services can be immensely enhanced in real-time communication systems. It also helps in offloading the computational and storage operations, which are crucial for those applications that involve rapid processing of data and instantaneous feedback. For instance, in vehicular communication networks, the use of cloud technology enables the execution of advanced signal processing and traffic management algorithms so as to reduce latency and improve overall responsiveness of the system. The capacity of cloud computing to effectively handle large amounts of data is most critical when secure and efficient transmission and real-time processing are essential for safety-critical applications such as collision warnings in vehicular networks (Feng et al., 2020). Given the rising need for high-bandwidth applications, the incorporation of cloud computing in real-time systems of communication becomes increasingly complex yet rewarding. This is so because complicating the handling of large data streams in an effective manner while continuing to provide robust communication complicates the process. The transition from traditional computing paradigms to cloud-computing-based solutions best describes this evolution, as seen through the growing use of distributed systems in computation- and communication-intensive tasks. The evolution of Metaverse applications reinforces this trend because such environments necessitate real-time interaction with data, compelling cloud offerings to become more sophisticated. Consequently, end-to-end process optimization has been made compulsory, integrating data storage, streaming, and processing capabilities in hybrid cloud models that are sensitive to the distinct needs of real-time user interactions (Cai et al., 2022). Also, cloud computing's role in facilitating innovative solutions for real-time communication systems cannot be exaggerated. The fog computing and edge computing paradigms introduce processing in progressively closer proximity to data sources, solving some of the transmission latency challenges. This brings to the fore complex algorithms, such as trajectory calibration for collision warning, which rely on timely data from connected vehicles. These technologies illustrate how cloud computing not only enables real-time applications but also spurs technological development in intelligent transportation systems. Building on the abilities of cloud-based environments, designers can create more reliable and efficient systems that maximize performance and enhance safety in various scenarios of real-time communication (Feng et al., 2020) (Figure 9.10).

Figure 9.10. Cloud computing.

Source: https://external-content.duckduckgo.com/iu/?u=https%3A%2F%2Fstatic.vecteezy.com%2Fsystem%2Fresources%2Fpreviews%2F000%2F435%2F275%2Foriginal%2Fcloud-computing-infographic-vector.jpg&f=1&nofb=1&ipt=bf3cbed5d862c4da58dd72bc81a4ab1208384d5329ca25ade83e995f3e67bb83.

9.4. APPLICATIONS IN VARIOUS SECTORS

Real-time communication systems play a central role in every field of business, with their impact felt across various domains of operation and interaction. In business, real-time communication systems reduce communication lines, enhancing employee teamwork irrespective of locations. Instant messaging, video conferencing, and group project management software foster a flexible workplace. Besides, research has indicated that the penetration of online business platforms significantly affects businesses' net income, with a rise of 37% having been noted as a result of such platforms (Sasvári et al., 2011). Consequently, businesses can utilize real-time communication systems not only to improve internal operations but also to improve their market strategy and customer relations, thereby maximizing financial returns. In medicine, the application of real-time communications is increasingly vital, particularly in emergency response and patient treatment. Telemedicine is an excellent case of this application, whereby medical professionals may interact with patients remotely, hence overcoming geographical constraints and reducing waiting hours. With focused communication channels, medical professionals can share essential information in real-time, hence achieving timely diagnosis and treatments. Applying real-time data enables better resource utilization, which is critical in high-stress situations like emergency rooms. The optimization of these communication systems optimizes patient care and operational efficiency, ultimately translating to better healthcare outcomes and patient satisfaction. Implementing real-time communication in non-traditional domains is specifically making huge impacts in fields like public safety and environmental monitoring. For instance, technologies offering spectrum sharing between cellular networks and fixed radar installations address the issue of efficient allocation of resources in critical communications systems (Abdelhadi et al., 2014). These technologies ensure emergency services' preparedness for communication without interference, upholding information integrity during emergencies. In addition, real-time monitoring systems enable environmental organizations to collect and exchange information on natural processes in real-time, enabling them to respond to events like natural disasters timely. Through these technologies, various industries receive improved coordination, management of resources, and response mechanisms, emphasizing the transformative role played by real-time communication systems.

9.4.1. Business and Corporate Communication

In the contemporary business world, implementation of real-time communication systems as part of business communication planning has come to be a central concern. These systems enable instant messaging, video conferencing, and shared workspaces, bridging organizational effectiveness and decision-making assistance. With an increasing use of smart embedded devices for business operations, these devices interconnect the physical and virtual worlds, creating dynamic platforms on which information is transmitted instantly and accurately. This transition not only enables quick responsiveness but also enables organizations to remain competitive in the fast-paced market. Service-Oriented

Architecture (SOA) is a case in point for how traditional IT frameworks can be modified to incorporate real-time information gathered from embedded devices to ultimately provide enhanced enterprise services. By introducing such innovations, organizations can reduce processes and make inter-department communications not only timely but also contextually relevant and actionable (Kokkonda et al., 2011). In addition, the entry of millennial workers into the labor market demands a re-engineering of business communication processes to meet their particular needs and desires. This age group, who are accustomed to technology, prefers real-time modes of communication that are accessible and simple to use. Notably, even as millennials are capable of exhibiting superior digital competence, they are deprived of the awareness of digital responsibility and its impact on work. As suggested by available research, such a generation is likely to take concerns for environmental sustainability and social responsibility lightly, thus making it imperative that teachers and managers engage students and employees in learning business communications that include such issues. By the intersection of dialogue in digital citizenship, environmental sustainability, and social responsibility, corporate training programs can build a highly proficient and technology-savvy workforce that also possesses broader ethical obligations (Burgess-Wilkerson et al., 2018) (Figure 9.11).

Figure 9.11. Corporate communication strategies.

Source: https://www.digittrix.com/assets/admin_blogimages/Why-Real-Time-Communication-is-Important.webp.

The relationship between corporate messaging and real-time communication systems extends beyond simple efficiency; it also affects organizational culture and values. As more immediate and interactive forms of communication are adopted by companies, they reinforce a transparent and open communications culture. This model fosters trust between employees and management, motivating participation and collaboration. Further, by garnering feedback through real-time channels, companies can better adapt and respond to employee needs, enhancing job satisfaction and productivity overall. Such forward-thinking communication practices are particularly relevant in today's dynamic business environment, where having the ability to change direction rapidly based on feedback or market conditions is key. Therefore, embedding real-time communication systems within organizational frameworks not only streamlines processes but also formulates an interactive, adaptive organization culture that can survive despite continuous change (Kokkonda et al., 2011).

9.4.2. Education and E-Learning

The introduction of real-time communication technologies has greatly changed the context of education and e-learning. By enabling immediate interaction between the teacher and student, these technologies create an interactive and lively learning environment that transcends the bounds of the classroom. The practice of video conferencing, instant messaging, and collaborative platforms adds to the sense of immediacy in terms of feedback, making it easier for learners to access the support they need in order to cope with complicated topics. Real-time communication systems not only facilitate participation but also enable the teacher to adjust the teaching style to meet different learner needs. It is thus significant that these systems be included in pedagogical designs to enhance the accessibility and quality of learning opportunities.

In teacher education, addressing the twin challenges of quantity and quality is essential. The need for effective and scalable teacher training methods is critical in regions such as Sub-Saharan Africa, where institutions are struggling to meet educational demands. New methods based on real-time communication systems can play an important role in meeting this need. With decision to utilize distance education and ICT, as explained by Leach et al. (2005), the institutions are not only able to increase the number of trained teachers but also improve their teaching methods. Moreover, effective implementation of these technologies is able to bridge spatial divides, allowing experienced instructors to mentor new teachers remotely, thereby improving educational attainment across the board. The continuous development of e-learning necessitates a robust infrastructure for distributed learning system design. Instructional design needs required technological elements that support the learning process while meeting intended competencies. A conceptual structure blending these elements, as proposed by Bell et al. (2006), offers an integrated education design with significant emphasis on the importance of real-time communication. In an effort to circumvent the intricacies surrounding the provision of education, instructional designers and educators need to put significant emphasis on research and development on an ongoing basis. Collaborative efforts towards enhancing such systems can yield creative solutions that not only solve the immediate requirements of today's education but also follow principles of accessibility and inclusion in inclusive learning environments (Figure 9.12).

Figure 9.12. E-learning.

Source: https://sertifier.com/blog/wp-content/uploads/2022/07/e-learning-definition-and-concept.jpg.

9.4.3. Healthcare and Telemedicine

The rapid evolution of telecommunication technology has had a great influence on the health environment, particularly through the advent of telemedicine. Telemedicine, a novel mode of access to care, allows patients access to healthcare professionals remotely without necessarily having to see them in person. It increases the availability of quality care while reducing in-person consultations. The integration of real-time communication technology has played a key role in introducing on time consultations and monitoring the patients' conditions easily. For instance, the application of Service Assurance (SA) and Real-time Monitoring Systems ensures excellent reliability in communications among patients and providers, ultimately contributing to improved health outcomes. The technologies, besides streamlining operations within healthcare facilities, contribute significantly to patient satisfaction, making access to medical advice convenient and efficient. With the health industry slowly switching over to such new-age technologies, the move towards telemedicine is the integral move towards a more networked and sensitive healthcare system (Nadella, 2025). The use of telemedicine in the healthcare industry is also supported with artificial intelligence (AI) and advanced imaging technologies that facilitate robust diagnostics as well as patient care. AI technologies are being developed to optimize medical imaging so that quicker and more accurate data transmission is possible for significant medical evaluations. This includes a new image compression system capable of allowing transmission of radiology scans, and convolutional neural networks are employed for enhanced transmission efficiency with reduced latency. The implications for telemedicine are significant, as such technologies allow more precise real-time diagnostics, thus allowing healthcare providers to make informed decisions remotely (Dodda et al., 2024).

In addition, such AI tools not only streamline clinical functions but also enhance the interplay between telemedicine and integrated patient care, reducing total healthcare costs and alleviating pressure on medical facilities. As telemedicine continues to evolve, it should be valued and managed for the built-in challenges of the new paradigm. Digital equity, cybersecurity, and issues of interoperability must be well managed to preserve the effectiveness of telehealth systems.

Disparities in access to technology have the potential to restrict the promising benefits of telemedicine to vulnerable populations. Moreover, patient data privacy and integrity of real-time communications concerns can undermine public faith in such digital health applications. Evaluation of these concerns is at the heart of integrating telemedicine into existing healthcare frameworks in a sustainable manner. By addressing such issues, stakeholders can maximize the potential of real-time communication systems to enhance patient outcomes and make telemedicine an actual alternative to traditional models of healthcare (Nadella, 2025) (Figure 9.13).

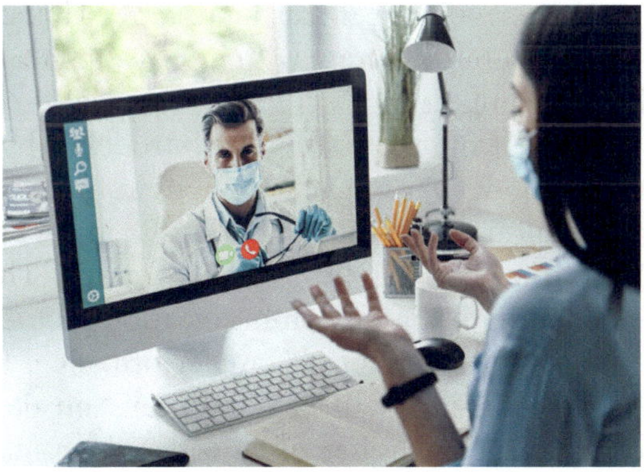

Figure 9.13. Telemedicine.

Source: https://www.atnetindia.net/wp-content/uploads/2023/04/video-conferencing-in-telemedicine-scaled.jpg.

9.5. CHALLENGES AND LIMITATIONS

The installation of real-time communication systems, particularly within the application of smart grid technology, is dominated by enormous challenges and limitations that must be addressed to ensure maximum operation and reliability. An important challenge lies in the widespread connectivity requirement, which is essential to facilitate the interconnection of Internet of Things (IoT) devices such as sensors and smart meters into the system. The dense deployment of these devices requires high-level automation and robust tracking capabilities to facilitate seamless operations in any power generation, transmission, and distribution networks. According to Copeland et al. (2019), while bi-directional energy flow is more efficient, it also renders communication protocols more complex with greater likelihood of latency and data loss in real-time applications. Thus, the development of robust network solutions for enabling trustworthy data exchange in varying conditions remains a persistent challenge. Furthermore, the cyber-physical nature of real-time communication systems, particularly in smart grids, poses vulnerabilities susceptible to attacks, which can bypass system integrity. As shown in previous incidents like the recent shutdown of the Ukrainian power grid, cyber-attacks exploit multiple points of entry at communication and networks. Recognition of these vulnerabilities is of utmost significance in creating effective security measures. The complexity of these cyber-physical attacks is further compounded by the networked aspect of devices, which enables the impact of a single vulnerability to be amplified. In agreement with Biswas et al. (2016), such security threats are mitigated not only by the thorough analysis of potential attacks but also by innovative defensive practices suited to an ever-evolving threat landscape. This calls for a holistic strategy for cybersecurity commensurate with improvements in communication technology. Finally, the limitations associated with real-time communication networks are likely to arise from the challenges introduced by maintaining data consistency and integrity under varying network environments. The requirement for real-time communication can introduce trade-offs in data processing power, particularly in high-traffic or machine failure scenarios. This is additionally complicated by the adoption of digital communication protocols, where packet delay and loss can significantly disrupt system performance. To overcome these issues, researchers and engineers will have to focus on developing resilient architectures that can manage changing situations and yet maintain sound data communication. As noted by Copeland et al. (2019) and Biswas et al. (2016), this underscores the need for continued research and innovation to address the shortcomings of real-time communication systems, particularly in the rapidly evolving field of smart grid technology.

9.5.1. Network Latency Issues

In the case of real-time communication systems, network latency issues pose serious challenges that can compromise the efficacy and efficiency of such systems. Latency, or time delay in data delivery, could be attributed to several factors like network congestion, node-to-node distance, and processing delay per network component. For instance, in the context of factory settings for mobile robots, reliance on conventional wireless communication can amplify these delays. As the research has noted, autonomous guided vehicles benefiting from available enterprise networks can suffer both economic as well as performance penalties, calling for new solutions in the way of more responsive communication architectures. Latency's impact forcefully comes to the fore when such applications are subject to immediate feedback, since delays can compromise operating efficiency and lead to dangerous situations in automated systems (Schneier et al., 2016) (Figure 9.14).

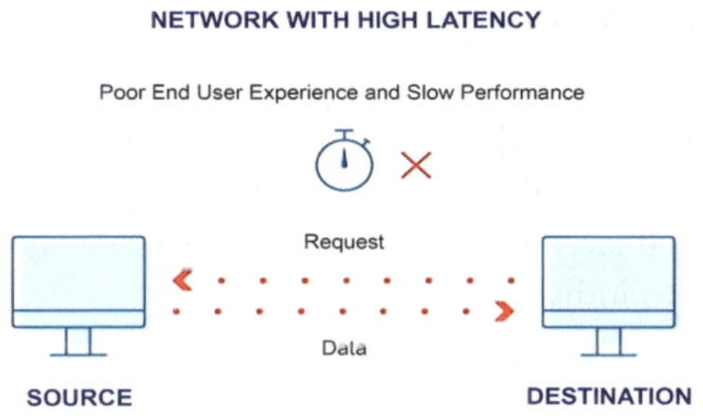

Figure 9.14. *Network latency.*

Source: https://www.dnsstuff.com/wp-content/uploads/2019/08/what-is-network-latency.jpg.

Moreover, the emergence of new networking technologies like Software Defined Networking (SDN) and Network Function Virtualization (NFV) provides opportunities as well as challenges with regards to latency. While the two technologies provide better network management and resource utilization for 5G networks, their integration creates complexities that add to latency rather than relieving it. Challenges surrounding the softwarization of the RAN underscore the importance of effective latency management; otherwise, organizations risk adopting suboptimal solutions that fail to harness the full potential of SDN. As stated, interworking among existing technologies with new SDN infrastructure complicates the effort towards minimizing latency, particularly in fronthaul operations where the transmission of data must be performed in real-time fashion to support real-time communication (Aghvami et al., 2018). To counter latency effectively in real-time communication networks, a multiple-angled approach is needed. This includes not just the adoption of new technologies but also the transformation of network infrastructures and protocols to optimize responsiveness. For example, deploying mesh networking capabilities can lead to reduced latency through improved data routing, which decreases the path that information travels. Besides, real-time monitoring and adaptive traffic management concepts can actually mitigate congestion, ensuring critical communications remain uninterrupted. Based on studies, simulation of several situations and experimenting with various settings might be worth knowing in terms of optimizing the network. By actively mitigating latency, organizations can enhance the efficiency and dependability of their real-time communications systems, leading to improved operational performance across various industries (Schneier et al., 2016).

9.5.2. Security and Privacy Concerns

Security and privacy are of utmost importance in the scenario of real-time communication systems. As these systems provide real-time communication between various platforms, there is a high likelihood of being hacked online. Online criminals find it easy to exploit loopholes of such systems and hence risk unauthorized access to individuals' information.

Figure 9.15. *Internet of medical things (IoMT).*

Source: https://healthtech.decos.com/sites/default/files/styles/webp/public/2023-10/IoMT.png.webp?itok=FMA1kLgb.

For instance, in medicine, communication systems used to connect medical equipment can be invaded, compromising patient safety and privacy. For example, the Internet of Medical Things (IoMT) is revolutionizing patient care, but its implementation has serious issues in ensuring the safety and security of data that is being transferred. Safe frameworks like OpenICE-lite must be created for enhancing interoperability while providing security assurances, eventually enabling both patient safety and data integrity in real-time communication systems (Ivanov et al., 2018) (Figure 9.15). Moreover, privacy concerns of real-time communication systems extend beyond technological vulnerabilities; they touch upon the ethical considerations of data collection and purposes. The widespread use of wearable technologies and smart technologies has enabled more extensive surveillance of health metrics and daily activities, with potential benefits and challenges. As much as these technologies have the capacity to give users valuable insights into their health, they raise essential questions about user consent as well as control over data. The users may not be cognizant of the manner in which their information is collected, stored, and disseminated, leading to vulnerability and a feeling of mistrust. Measures like user-managed data collection and transparent privacy policies are crucial in instilling a feeling of security among the users as well as promoting reasonable use of real-time communication mechanisms (Abad et al., 2023). Hence, addressing both security and privacy concerns in real-time communication systems must involve a multi-faceted approach that incorporates technological innovations along with robust policy structures. Even as organizational measures to enhance cybersecurity are being planned, they must also prioritize user awareness and education of privacy habits. Incorporation of encryption technologies along with regularly upgraded security measures can keep threats to data egress and cyber-attacks in check. Furthermore, industry players and service providers should cooperate in the establishment of knowledge standards that support the privacy rights of users without undermining the authenticity of real-time communication. By coming up with an ideal ecosystem that is centered on security and privacy, stakeholders will achieve trust in such systems, thus enhancing large-scale adoption and secure use by industries (Abad et al., 2023).

9.5.3. Accessibility and Digital Divide

Accessibility is a core concept when real-time communication systems are involved, especially when it involves bridging the extensive digital divide that engulfs the globe. While technology has driven the development of new and cutting-edge communication platforms, unequal access to such communications systems continues to be widespread. People lack the necessary digital gear, operational internet connections, or computer literacy to take full advantage of modern communication tools. This inequality not only disables personal connectivity but also directly affects education, health, and economic opportunity. As educational materials become increasingly online, as highlighted by the open educational resource's movement, the gap between those who are able to leverage these resources and those who are unable grows larger, highlighting the need for addressing accessibility comprehensively (Lane et al., 2009). Apart from this, initiatives to enhance accessibility, whereby governments and institutions step in, are crucial to bridging the digital divide. The launch of e-Office concepts under its e-Government modernization initiative by the Madinah government is one such instance of initiatives to simplify access to government services. By opening electronic offices in various departments, the government not only encourages civic participation but also forces citizens into e-Services. Although these efforts are aimed at making information and services more democratic to access, disparities in adoption rates and technological acumen persist, creating new barriers to access. Thus, with an eagerness to improve accessibility, attainment of such goals happens more slowly than anticipated, revealing the already present divides (Al-Sobhi et al., 2009). Addressing the digital divide requires a complex campaign to enhance not just physical access to technology, but the skills and confidence necessary to make effective use of it. The open education debate indicates that while opportunities for access may be expanding, many remain excluded on the basis of individual circumstances or structural factors in society. The competencies and confidence necessary to engage with computer-based systems can also vary widely along demographic fault lines, often further complicated by socio-economic status. These interventions must therefore be multi-faceted in nature incorporating training programs, community outreach, and support networks which empower individuals with both the capability and confidence to cross such fault lines. It is only through the enactment of such extensive strategies that we might aspire to create a setting where real-time communication systems are made available to all (Lane et al., 2009).

9.6. FUTURE TRENDS IN REAL-TIME COMMUNICATION

With the rise of technology, the landscape of real-time communication systems is poised for dramatic change. Among the prime movers of such transformation is the deployment of fifth generation (5G) networks, promising never-before-seen levels of speed and reliability. With ultra-low latency capabilities, 5G is redefining communication paradigms, opening doors to a wealth of applications in multiple industries, from self-driving cars to telemedicine and augmented reality. As highlighted in recent surveys, such growth implies huge investments on the side of network operators and stokes concerns about the economic sustainability of new business models under mandatory infrastructure costs and possible market advantages. Therefore, exploring how changes can be economically viable for operators but improve user experience remains a matter of challenge when it comes to real-time communication systems (Cuevas et al., 2017). Outside the technology advancements that 5G will bring, the meshing of artificial intelligence (AI) within real-time communication networks holds the promise to re-engineer how users communicate and how effectively data processing will be done. AI can enhance user experiences by personalizing communications and optimizing network action through predictive analysis. This convergence of AI and real-time communication not only streamlines message delivery but also empowers users to tap and process huge volumes of data in real-time. For instance, AI-fueled algorithms can screen shopper behavior and preference, which can lead to more effective audience targeting in ad campaigns. These innovations are prime examples of the significant effect of AI on improving the functionality and attractiveness of real-time communication systems, which has caught the imagination of businesses aiming to stay in the business with a rapidly changing digital scenario. Further, the onset of ecologically oriented communication plans is a reflection of the impending trend towards sustainability in real-time communication systems. As per research detailed, there is an appreciable trend in utilizing the huge amount of environmental information generated by populations for enriching real-time communications. Through integration of environmental observation from diverse sources like sensors and people, communication systems can become inclusive platforms to support well-informed decision-making for environmental problems. This transition from traditional sensor networks to an Observation Web is a significant paradigm change that can potentially facilitate increased collaboration among communities. Such innovation, in addition to facilitating user participation and involvement, also aligns with the broader sustainability agenda—a consideration that is especially important as society continues to center responsible and environmentally conscious practice at the forefront of technology development and use (Berre et al., 2011).

9.6.1. Integration of Artificial Intelligence (AI)

Artificial intelligence (AI) application in real-time communication systems is the major advancement in the aspect of enhancing interoperability and efficiency. AI technologies allow data processing and analysis of vast amounts of data generated throughout communication as well as real-time insights instantly. Such integration facilitates enhanced decision-making processes, wherein AI algorithms analyze patterns of communication, predict potential issues, and present solutions in real-time. Such responsiveness is, in turn, particularly critical in sectors such as healthcare and emergency services, where timely information can have a significant impact on outcomes. Institutions are also increasingly recognizing that they have to embed AI in their models of learning in order to prepare future professionals for this new reality, as demonstrated by active learning programs situated in the industry 4.0 technology framework (Prieto et al., 2019). With real-time communication frameworks evolving alongside AI technology, the IDSS is a standout spotlight area. With the integration of AI and IDSS, decision-makers can process complex sets of information more effectively and create usable insights at rapid velocities. This advancement is of monumental significance in scenarios of immediate response, e.g., financial trading or automated customer service deployment. Recent research indicates that such integrated systems have more performance by synergies between communication technologies and AI, which allow the organization to streamline operations and achieve maximum efficiency (Kaklauskas et al., 2010). New findings on such integration not only improve the ability of existing communication systems but also create new paths to expansion in various industries. Secondly, the companies and individuals that adopt AI-enabled communication practices will gain revolutionary benefits, highlighting the importance of a strategic integration strategy. Keeping training and development in AI technology at priority, stakeholders can equip themselves and their employees with the required skills to gain maximum benefit from these technologies. Since real-time communication systems continue to be a defining aspect of interactions in sectors, AI adoption promotes a continuous discourse on technology ethics and data privacy. These factors, combined with the assurance of improved working efficiency, indicate the varied impacts of AI adoption in communication systems and underscore the necessity of bridging the gap between technology and ethical practice in the expanding digital sphere.

9.6.2. Advancements in 5G Technology

5G technology is an evolutionary leap in the arena of real-time communication systems. Far exceeding its predecessors, 5G guarantees improved bandwidth, reduced latency, and improved connectivity—key features for use cases that demand instant response time. Real-time communication is highly reliant on such developments because they provide seamless interactions across segments such as healthcare to transportation and entertainment. For instance, the ability to stream high-definition video and data in a virtually real-time fashion in telehealth allows for effective remote consultation and monitoring. Further, with improvements in 5G technology, it becomes possible to introduce others such as Artificial Intelligence (AI) and Internet of Things (IoT) and integrate them, creating a robust ecosystem for real-time applications to thrive in an ever more connected world. One of the essential applications of 5G technology is through its capability to provide Vehicle-to-Everything (V2X) communication. This allows traffic management and road safety enhancement through sharing of real-time information between pedestrians, infrastructure, and vehicles. 5Gs low latency and high data rate enable the implementation of V2X, which allows for delayed alerts of traffic congestion, crashes, and optimal routes, hence significantly reducing congestion and enhancing the driving experience. As discussed in existing research, including Bintoro (2025), the integration of 5G and V2X technologies promises to enhance safety and drive innovation in autonomous vehicles, making them more reliable in real-time situations. 5G is thus a cornerstone pillar for the Intelligent Transportation Systems of today, positioning itself at the middle of innovations in road transport in the future. One other key field of 5G technology lies in its comprehensive influence on Unmanned Aerial Vehicle (UAV) functionality. Originally meant for military applications, UAVs have emerged in civilian sectors for activities ranging from disaster relief to crop monitoring. The incorporation of 5G has revolutionized the application of UAVs, particularly in image streaming, where advancements in data compression algorithms and wireless transmission make it possible to stream high-definition images in real-time. This is crucial for real-time data analysis and decision-making purposes. According to recent research, as denoted by Shi (2024), the combination of 5G with upcoming technology like AI enhances the capability and independence of UAVs, thereby opening up more areas of application. The rapid evolution of these technologies will further integrate UAVs into smart cities and transportation networks, highlighting the complex role played by 5G in real-time communication systems.

9.6.3. Potential for Virtual and Augmented Reality

The advent of Virtual Reality (VR) and Augmented Reality (AR) technologies has vast potential to enhance real-time communication networks. Such simulated environments have the potential to change the manner in which users communicate with one another and the environment, offering more engaging and interactive experiences compared to conventional interfaces. With the use of advanced graphics and spatial audio, VR and AR provide users with a better intuitive understanding of information and improved collaboration. For instance, in the workplace, its members spread across the globe could engage in meetings that mimic a face-to-face environment, generating more interaction and innovation. This convergence of technology not only supports effortless communication but also engages participants actively, thereby increasing general productivity and innovation across industries like education, business, and healthcare. Apart from that, the potential for haptic feedback in virtual and augmented reality extends the limits of communication modalities. With the addition of wearable technology relying on haptic feedback to offer tactile information, immersive experiences are highly enhanced. Haptic interface-instrumented users can be offered real-time physical feedback that is connected to virtual activities, thereby offering an elaborate means of interaction. A technical development such as the flat cone dielectric elastomer actuator (FCDEA) array is one great case in point. Such technology enables users to be provided with tactile information with ease when interfacing with virtual space, developing force and texture-like sensations, for improved emotional engagement in virtual sensations. This capability means that AR and VR communication can override the conventional limits of audio and visual channels to afford richer multi-sensory contact and interaction. In AR, real-time communication is particularly important because it enhances the capacity of users to manage and understand complex data. The ability to project vital information onto the actual world means that users can engage with digital data in a natural and spatial manner. For instance, in architectural design, AR can project 3D models that augment spatial knowledge such that users can experience a direct interaction with their surroundings. As the algorithmic processes become better and technologies improve, AR applications enable easy access to accurate projections such that it is more interactive. By tapping into the spatial knowledge and mental awareness of the user, AR amplifies the communication process, an indispensable use across various fields. Ultimately, as AR continues to evolve, it holds the potential to revolutionize how individuals connect and collaborate in real-time, a significant improvement in communication processes and practices (Baglioni et al., 2019; Hwang et al., 2025).

SUMMARY

As an introduction to the key features of real-time communication systems is provided, it is obvious that technology evolution enormously enhances not only connectivity but also efficiency and dependability in the systems. As can be observed throughout the essay, real-time communication enables a lot of applications ranging from vehicle networks to telemedicine, highlighting the pivotal role that real-time communication plays in modern society. The addition of predictive analytics, particularly through the application of machine learning techniques, as noted in previous studies, indicates that additional differentiation of trajectory prediction understanding will impact significant safety and comfort use cases in cars. Specifically, greater situational awareness has a direct correlation with greater performance in situations like Forward Collision Warning (FCW) and Cooperative Adaptive Cruise Control (CACC), affirming the need for ongoing research on robust frameworks that handle inaccuracies in data correctly and facilitate user safety using these technologies (Fallah et al., 2018). Furthermore, research into real-time communication systems transpires over into the field of human-computer interaction (HCI) to a wider cultural and applied context. Research from all over the globe, including the characterization of HCI activity in China, reports that there are basic gaps to bridge in addressing bigger, macro-level models of interaction. These factors position real-time systems not just as technology but also as cultural artifacts that must consider the user's experience and access. The fourth HCI paradigm thus challenges researchers to merge methodologies, with emergent user requirements and many levels of access to technology. As discussed, a balanced approach can enhance the overall effectiveness and inclusivity of real-time communication applications (Ayobi et al., 2019). In conclusion, the promise of real-time communication systems lies in the manner in which they can change and develop according to user requirements and technology advancements. As seen through various examples, the dynamic nature of such systems necessitates continuous innovation to deal with emerging challenges like managing data, security, and consolidating dissimilar communication paradigms. The interaction of predictive modeling in vehicle networks and sociocultural frameworks in HCI research can enable paradigm-revolutionary advances in systems that balance safety and user experience. Ultimately, specifying the future of real-time communication relies on collaboration across disciplines, which will enable the creation of systems that are not merely efficient but also equitable in serving a global user base.

As part of real-time communication system research, it is important to investigate the multi-dimensionality of security vulnerabilities that are intrinsic to these systems. Such systems that facilitate data transmission in real-time are exposed to a myriad of attacks at different layers of the communication protocol stack. The physical, link, network, transport, and application layers specifically present unique security concerns. Analysis of these vulnerabilities is essential as it forms the foundation knowledge necessary to build resilient defense mechanisms needed to secure user privacy and system integrity. Additionally, existing key management, user authentication, and access control protocols are examined to identify areas of improvement necessary to neutralize potential attacks. These detailed analysis of security mechanisms, as presented in several studies, call for prompt addressing of these weaknesses at the design and implementation stages of real-time communication systems (Gupta et al., 2013). Further, the unification of Software Defined Networking (SDN) and Network Function Virtualization (NFV) represents a major shift in paradigms in real-time communication systems, particularly in the context of the urgent development of 5G technology. SDN and NFV offer new answers to all management issues, with the potential of more flexibility and efficiency in network management. However, the softwarization of the RAN also raises questions about the completeness of such implementations, as the industry may experience fragmented rather than unified integration of SDN solutions. Problems such as backward compatibility, latency concerns in comparison to general-purpose processors, and emerging security threats due to softwarization warrant serious consideration. In-depth knowledge about these issues is essential to ensure the advantages of SDN and NFV are utilized without jeopardizing the security and reliability of an infrastructure for real-time communication systems (Aghvami et al., 2018). Lastly, the evolving nature of real-time communication systems calls for continuous research and innovative solutions, especially in terms of new technologies. The convergence of communications and security calls for constant debate among researchers, practitioners, and policymakers in solving the problems of real-time data transmission effectively. As greater dependence is being heaped on such systems, so is the necessity for enhancing security defenses with a perspective toward upholding privacy of users in spite of technological progress. Research into trust management schemes, such as reputation-based schemes, becomes increasingly important as such structures have the potential to enhance security in wireless networks. Continuous discussion on these unresolved issues provides an exhaustive overview of the matters at hand and provides scope for future research in secure real-time communication systems (Gupta et al., 2013).

REFERENCES

1. Abad, H. (2023). Privacy concerns and proposed solutions with IoT in wearable technology. https://core.ac.uk/download/595866282.pdf (accessed on 29th September 2025).
2. Abdelhadi, A., Clancy, C., & Ghorbanzadeh, M. (2014). A utility proportional fairness resource allocation in spectrally radar-coexistent cellular networks. http://arxiv.org/abs/1406.2631 (accessed on 29th September 2025).
3. Abrougui, A., Aloi, G., Araniti, G., Batty, M., Biral, A., Centenaro, M., Checko, A., et al. (2017). SymbioCity: Smart cities for smarter networks. https://core.ac.uk/download/77066421.pdf (accessed on 29th September 2025).
4. Aghvami, H., Dohler, M., Fletcher, S., Friderikos, V., et al. (2018). Will SDN be part of 5G? https://core.ac.uk/download/157863188.pdf (accessed on 29th September 2025).
5. Ahad, N., Ahmed, N., & Qadir, J. (2014). Building programmable wireless networks: An architectural survey. http://arxiv.org/abs/1310.0251 (accessed on 29th September 2025).
6. Alaliyat, S. A. A., Hasan, A. I., Kandemir, E., Kvamsdal, T., et al. (2024). Predictive digital twin for wind energy systems: A literature review. https://core.ac.uk/download/646167159.pdf (accessed on 29th September 2025).
7. Ali, I., Khan, E., & Sabir, S. (2018). Privacy-preserving data aggregation in resource-constrained sensor nodes in Internet of Things: A review. http://arxiv.org/abs/1812.04216 (accessed on 29th September 2025).
8. Alier Forment, M., Cabré Garcia, J. M., Climent Vilaró, J., Corbalán González, S., et al. (2014). Evaluation and assessment of professional skills in the final year project. https://core.ac.uk/download/41776612.pdf (accessed on 29th September 2025).
9. Al-Sobhi, F., Kamal, M., & Weerakkody, V. (2009). Current state of e-services in Saudi Arabia: The case of intermediaries in facilitating government services in Madinah city. https://core.ac.uk/download/336505.pdf (accessed on 29th September 2025).
10. Anonymous. (2006). TechNews digests: Jan–Nov 2006. https://core.ac.uk/download/4151586.pdf (accessed on 29th September 2025).
11. Arnedo Moreno, J., Domingo Prieto, M., Radmand, P., Singh, J., et al. (2010). VoIP: Making secure calls and maintaining high call quality. https://core.ac.uk/download/9628442.pdf (accessed on 29th September 2025).

12. Axelsson, J., & Kobetski, A. (2012). Federated embedded systems–A review of the literature in related fields. https://core.ac.uk/download/11434985.pdf (accessed on 29th September 2025).
13. Ayobi, A., Bi, T., Wang, C., Zhang, Y., et al. (2019). Characterizing HCI research in China: Streams, methodologies and future directions. https://core.ac.uk/download/519715846.pdf (accessed on 29th September 2025).
14. Baglioni, L., Menconero, S., & Russo, M. (2019). Parametric surfaces for augmented architecture representation. https://core.ac.uk/download/188831772.pdf (accessed on 29th September 2025).
15. Barker, P., Benest, I., Elliott, G., Moss, L., et al. (1995). Reviews. https://core.ac.uk/download/6937.pdf (accessed on 29th September 2025).
16. Bell, B. S., & Kozlowski, S. W. J. (2006). Distributed learning system design: A new approach and an agenda for future research. https://core.ac.uk/download/5124433.pdf (accessed on 29th September 2025).
17. Berre, A. J., Havlik, D., Lorenzo Mon, J., Mazzetti, P., et al. (2011). From sensor to observation web with environmental enablers in the future internet. https://core.ac.uk/download/8653076.pdf (accessed on 29th September 2025).
18. Bintoro, K. B. Y. (2025). Overview of Vehicle-to-Everything communication: Technological advancements, applications, and future prospects in intelligent transportation systems. *JISA (Jurnal Informatika dan Sains)*. https://www.semanticscholar.org/paper/804a83695a0952958afc67f4b33b2197c8c978f4 (accessed on 29th September 2025).
19. Biswas, S., Guvenc, I., Saad, W., Sanjab, A., et al. (2016). Smart grid security: Threats, challenges, and solutions. https://core.ac.uk/download/322809289.pdf (accessed on 29th September 2025).
20. Booth, S., Goodpaster, N., Hurley, J. P., Moede, C., et al. (2018). Communication system for firefighters. https://core.ac.uk/download/215442530.pdf (accessed on 29th September 2025).
21. Britchenko, I., Cherniavska, T., & Machashchik, P. (2018). New trends in development of services in the modern economy. https://core.ac.uk/download/323058294.pdf (accessed on 29th September 2025).
22. Burgess-Wilkerson, B., Garrison, C., Hamilton, C., Robbins, C., et al. (2018). Preparing millennials as digital citizens and socially and environmentally responsible business professionals in a socially irresponsible climate. https://core.ac.uk/download/214444219.pdf (accessed on 29th September 2025).

23. Cai, Y., Llorca, J., Molisch, A. F., Tulino, A., et al. (2022). Compute- and data-intensive networks: The key to the Metaverse. http://arxiv.org/abs/2204.02001 (accessed on 29th September 2025).
24. Cerviño Arriba, J., Rodríguez Pérez, P., Salvachúa Rodríguez, J., Trajkovska, I., et al. (2012). Opportunities and challenges of implementing P2P streaming applications in the web. https://core.ac.uk/download/148664786.pdf (accessed on 29th September 2025).
25. Copeland, R., Crespi, N., Rehmani, M. H., Saleem, Y., et al. (2019). Internet of Things-aided smart grid: Technologies, architectures, applications, prototypes, and future research directions. http://arxiv.org/abs/1704.08977 (accessed on 29th September 2025).
26. Coughlan, J. A., & Macredie, R. D. (2002). Effective communication in requirements elicitation: A comparison of methodologies. https://core.ac.uk/download/333154.pdf (accessed on 29th September 2025).
27. Cuevas, M., Dohler, M., Laya, A., Lema, M., et al. (2017). Business case and technology analysis for 5G low latency applications. https://core.ac.uk/download/96762095.pdf (accessed on 29th September 2025).
28. De Mol, J., Van Leeuwen, T., Vandenberghe, W., Vlassenroot, S., et al. (2008). Intelligent transport systemin ITS in verkeersveiligheid. https://core.ac.uk/download/55814175.pdf (accessed on 29th September 2025).
29. Delgado Prieto, M., Fernández Sobrino, Á., Fibla Biosca, P., Romeral Martínez, M., et al. (2019). Active learning-based laboratory towards engineering education 4.0. https://core.ac.uk/download/294830056.pdf (accessed on 29th September 2025).
30. Deryckere, T., Hoekman, K., Ide, M., Martens, L., et al. (2007). XMPP and iDTV or how to make television a social medium. https://core.ac.uk/download/55732064.pdf (accessed on 29th September 2025).
31. Dodda, S., Narne, S., Chintala, S., Kanungo, S., Adedoja, T., & Sharma, S. (2024). Exploring AI-driven innovations in image communication systems for enhanced medical imaging applications. *Journal of Electrical Systems*. https://www.semanticscholar.org/paper/a9e7b6063631e34c93883fe3e5b26d6ec37efbdf (accessed on 29th September 2025).
32. Duquennoy, S., Höglund, J., Misra, P., Mottola, L., et al. (2013). Supporting cyber-physical systems with wireless sensor networks: An outlook of software and services. https://core.ac.uk/download/17037990.pdf (accessed on 29th September 2025).
33. Duran, L., Ebrahim, T., Faulhaber, K., Serface, P., et al. (2008). CleanTX analysis on the smart grid. https://core.ac.uk/download/211336585.pdf (accessed on 29th September 2025).

34. Fallah, Y. P., Kazemi, H., Mahjoub, H. N., Tahmasbi-Sarvestani, A., et al. (2018). A learning-based framework for two-dimensional vehicle maneuver prediction over V2V networks. http://arxiv.org/abs/1808.00516 (accessed on 29th September 2025).
35. Feng, L., Guo, S., Liu, K., Wu, H., et al. (2020). Vehicular fog computing enabled real-time collision warning via trajectory calibration. http://arxiv.org/abs/2005.11508 (accessed on 29th September 2025).
36. Fleming, N., Lehnhardt, K., McGuire, K., Urbina, D., et al. (2025). Medical system concept of operations for Mars Exploration Mission-11: Exploration Medical Capability (ExMC) Element - Human Research Program. https://core.ac.uk/download/pdf/288485181.pdf (accessed on 29th September 2025).
37. Gupta, A., Mishra, A., Naveed, A., Perrig, A., Shamir, A., Franklin, A. A., Wood, A. D., et al. (2013). Security and privacy issues in wireless mesh networks: A survey. http://arxiv.org/abs/1302.0939 (accessed on 29th September 2025).
38. Heinze, A., Lynch, K., & Scott, E. (2008). Scholarly collaboration across time zones. https://core.ac.uk/download/1666503.pdf (accessed on 29th September 2025).
39. Hou, P., Lagaillardie, N., & Yoshida, N. (2024). Fearless asynchronous communications with timed multiparty session protocols. https://core.ac.uk/download/613711686.pdf (accessed on 29th September 2025).
40. Hwang, I., Jang, S. Y., Kyung, K. U., Pei, Y., et al. (2025). Skin-attached haptic patch for versatile and augmented tactile interaction. https://core.ac.uk/download/649473549.pdf (accessed on 29th September 2025).
41. Iitaka, T. (2010). Open source, collectivism, and Japanese society. https://core.ac.uk/download/pdf/16436388.pdf (accessed on 29th September 2025).
42. Ivanov, R., Lee, I., Nguyen, H., Sokolsky, O., et al. (2018). OpenICE-lite: Towards a connectivity platform for the Internet of Medical Things. https://core.ac.uk/download/219378697.pdf (accessed on 29th September 2025).
43. Jansen, P. G., & Smit, G. J. M. (1988). The communication processor of TUMULT-64. https://core.ac.uk/download/pdf/11473576.pdf (accessed on 29th September 2025).
44. Kaklauskas, A., Kusiak, A., Marquez, A. C., Duffy, A. H. B., Chae, B., Lopez, B., et al. (2010). Integration of decision support systems to improve decision support performance. https://core.ac.uk/download/9023194.pdf (accessed on 29th September 2025).

45. Kokkonda, B., Kumar, P. P., & Rajesh, G. (2011). On demand web services with quality of service. https://core.ac.uk/download/234676759.pdf (accessed on 29th September 2025).
46. Lane, A. (2009). The impact of openness on bridging educational digital divides. https://core.ac.uk/download/4701.pdf (accessed on 29th September 2025).
47. Leach, J., Moon, B., & Stevens, M. P. (2005). Designing open and distance learning for teacher education in Sub-Saharan Africa: A toolkit for educators and planners. https://core.ac.uk/download/81717.pdf (accessed on 29th September 2025).
48. Liu, F. (2001). The voice activity detection (VAD) recorder and VAD network recorder: A thesis presented in partial fulfilment of the requirements for the degree of Master of Science in Computer Science at Massey University. https://core.ac.uk/download/162617230.pdf (accessed on 29th September 2025).
49. Marchiori, M., & Latora, V. (2002). Economic small-world behavior in weighted networks. *Physical Journal B*. https://core.ac.uk/download/20671571.pdf (accessed on 29th September 2025).
50. Nadella, V. M. (2025). The backbone of modern society: How telecom technologies drive societal transformation. *World Journal of Advanced Research and Reviews*. https://www.semanticscholar.org/paper/9cf697905f2c792d1f68b8ee7dd851175412c72f (accessed on 29th September 2025).
51. Naghshineh, S. (2011). Teleoperation of passivity-based model reference robust control over the internet. https://core.ac.uk/download/4832695.pdf (accessed on 29th September 2025).
52. Sasvári, P. L. (2011). The economic impacts of information and communication technology in the Hungarian economy. https://core.ac.uk/download/11857620.pdf (accessed on 29th September 2025).
53. Schneier, M., Drath, R., Arumugam, S., Wang, Z., & Yan, Z. (2016). To mesh or not to mesh: Flexible wireless indoor communication among mobile robots in industrial environments. https://core.ac.uk/download/55822886.pdf (accessed on 29th September 2025).
54. Shi, H. (2024). In-depth analysis of UAV image transmission and communication systems: Principles, models. *Science and Technology of Engineering, Chemistry and Environmental Protection*. https://www.semanticscholar.org/paper/ec7a18a729f29beb621b232baa64ec521f8f3ac3 (accessed on 29th September 2025).

CHAPTER 10

RTOS SECURITY AND RELIABILITY

Contents

INTRODUCTION

The real-time operating systems (RTOS) are very much applicable to the fields of reliability and security, particularly because the systems are finding their way into numerous applications, ranging from industrial automation to automobile systems. The primary activity of an RTOS is to schedule task execution in a timely and predictable manner, and the task is very critical for those applications were delay results in disaster. With other industries increasingly relying on such systems, there is more cause for alarm at the vulnerabilities in their complexity. This complexity can serve to pose security threats, hence the need for there to be a close examination of how such systems can be made resilient to internal and external attacks. The understanding of the intricate relationship between security and reliability is critical to ascertaining that RTOS can carry out their essential functions with no interference or compromise. Moreover, the use of Commercial Off the Shelf (COTS) components in developing safety-critical systems adds another challenge that has to be accommodated. The use of COTS products is usually welcomed to offset development time and cost, against the fast pace of technology advancement. However, as noted through recent arguments, the incorporation of such components brings about challenges of system reliability and safety, especially in deep supply chains. There needs to be a detailed evaluation to establish the effect of the incorporation of these factors on the operating reliability of RTOS. Additionally, regulation of safety is evolving to include an integrated safety life cycle in concert with the system development life cycle. This mirrors the importance of considering safety concerns all the way from the initial stages of design in order to ensure the strength of RTOS during real deployments (Caseley et al., 2017). Lastly, as businesses embrace the use of RTOS in various sectors, legislation and regulation and best practice have to keep up with emerging threats. The drive towards greater security controls, along with maintaining operational reliability, is not merely a matter of technical necessity but also a fundamental socio-economic concern. In the expanding universe of networked devices and automated systems, the consequences of security breaches have the potential to inflict significant financial damage as well as compromise user safety. By exploring the relationship between RTOS security and reliability, researchers and engineers strive to develop frameworks that provide assurance against cyber-attacks while ensuring that systems are reliable during operation. This simultaneous consideration is important, as sustainable technological progress needs to value both security measures and stable performance in order to instill confidence in users and stakeholders (Gundlach et al., 2017).

Importance of Security and Reliability in RTOS

The paramount need for security and reliability in RTOS cannot be overemphasized in light of the rising convergence of connected systems between industries. With Industry 4.0-driven forces of convergence compelling industries to become more connected through cyber-physical systems and IoT, the requirement for robust security measures has increased. With RTOS running in everything from automobiles to health-care devices, they handle sensitive information and mission-critical operations. Security vulnerabilities not only affect data integrity but also threaten the safety of users, so efficient vulnerability fixing becomes imperative for developers. The multi-layered software framework exhibited by offerings like Zerynth Virtual Machine also puts the issue of compatibility with heterogeneous RTOS in perspective along with ensuring integration of security protocols without any interruption, thereby enhancing the overall reliability and trustworthiness of such systems (Ahmad et al., 2017). Reliability of RTOS is also highly dependent on the ability to ensure predictable performance over varying loading conditions, especially under real-time conditions where timing is critical. For instance, in electric utility grids, the deployment of DER relies on strong RTOS to handle demand flexibility and maximize grid services. The economic impacts of such reliability are considerable; they form a platform for improved strategies that balance stakeholder interests in energy-efficient buildings and systems. By developing a strong base with the focus on the importance of reliability, stakeholders are in a position to develop programs that not only optimize performance but also allow for investments in technology that promote resilience in grid services. The integration of flexible demand solutions into utility infrastructure aids to amplify this idea, hence making it feasible for RTOS to serve as legitimate agents in facilitating innovative energy management (Eckman et al., 2021). Besides, the ever-changing nature of cybersecurity threats necessitates on-going efforts towards enhancing security protocols within RTOS systems. As more and more devices are networked, the exposure surface to cyber-attacks enlarges, and consequently, manufacturers need to adopt proactive security controls. These include enforcing encryption, access controls, and regular updates to safeguard against exploitation. Moreover, RTOS developers must prioritize making systems secure and trustworthy when they are attacked, so they keep functioning despite being compromised. Methods that include security best practice at the design stage can help significantly minimize risks, giving people and stakeholders confidence. With increasing dependence of industries on sophisticated RTOS, reliability and security should be of highest concern for sustainable growth and faith in digital infrastructures, which are the backbone of modern-day technological settings (Ahmad et al., 2017).

10.1. SECURITY CHALLENGES IN RTOS

The security of real-time operating systems (RTOS) is gaining prominence in an age where networked devices and the Internet of Things (IoT) prevail. Among the challenges in securing RTOS is in their design and operational limitations that exist in such systems. Relative to general-purpose operating systems, RTOS must prioritize performance and timing and thus forfeits security mechanisms in most instances. For instance, limited memory and processing power can restrict the use of intensive security measures, leaving systems vulnerable to attacks. Further, employing Commercial Off the Shelf (COTS) components also adds complexity to security, given that such components are not automatically designed with RTOS security in mind, placing them at greater risk of exposure to various forms of security threats, particularly in safety-critical systems) (Caseley et al., 2017). As RTOS solutions are becoming ubiquitous, the possible scope of security breaches underscores the immediate need for more robust security frameworks. Another key issue arises from the threat profile inherent in RTOS systems. Attackers often exploit vulnerabilities in the software framework and communication protocols that RTOS employs to gain access to systems. As an example, issues of buffer overflows, race conditions, and illegal access to vulnerable resources can compromise the system's reliability and integrity. The use of old or unpatched components in legacy systems can also further hasten these security vulnerabilities. The unprecedented growth of cyberattacks during the last few years emphasizes the growing imperative for the RTOS community to develop and implement effective countermeasures. Security loopholes in RTOS can lead not only to data loss but also to catastrophic failures in safety-critical systems such as those employed in healthcare or transport, where failure is unacceptable. Thus, it becomes essential to solve these loopholes for the purpose of ensuring operational trustworthiness and safety compliance. Moreover, the need for a common policy towards security and safety in RTOS design cannot be overstated. Current industry debate suggests application of an overall safety life cycle within security design considerations (Caseley et al., 2017). This integration allows for repeated analysis of the systems security posture to ensure that potential threats are approached early in the development process. Adding security to the safety lifecycle also encourages collaboration among stakeholders, improving mutual knowledge of safety and security requirements. With environments in RTOS becoming increasingly complex and dependent on communications with the outside world, security concerns neglected as a whole could undermine system dependability. Therefore, the embracement of standards that guarantee both security and safety throughout the complete development process is crucial in an effort to develop resilient RTOS programs that are immune to the evolving threats.

10.1.1. Vulnerabilities in Embedded Systems

Embedded systems form the backbone for thousands of applications ranging from automotive control systems to medical devices. Their inclusion within critical operations, however, exposes them to a plethora of vulnerabilities that undermine both reliability and security. With these systems relying increasingly on more sophisticated components—anything from sensors to actuators—their attack surfaces have broadened to expose them to malicious interferences. Security decisions, in most cases, are being made in the early stages of systems life cycle, typically neglecting adequate threat modeling and vulnerabilities analysis. An adequate response requires a properly composed model that is comprised of a taxonomy of system attributes and therefore allows discovery of potential attack vectors and assisting strategic architectural mitigations before deployment (Bakirtzis et al., 2018). This pre-emotive measure is key to deciding that embedded systems must have the capability to operate safely in this high-risk environment. Problems with mixed-criticality systems are most evident in embedded systems where duties of varying importance and urgency exist on the same platform. This commingling, while resource-efficient, can compromise system integrity unless proper provisions are made. Without appropriate partitioning techniques, lower-criticality subsystem failure or exploitation would result in failures to higher-criticality operations. The MultiPARTES project shows an effort towards resolution of this problem through providing mechanisms enforcing hard temporal and spatial separations among partitions (Mu et al., 2013). Through the employment of virtualization techniques specific to heterogeneous multicore processors, the project demonstrates the potential for greater reliability and security in mixed-criticality systems. Hence, addressing partitioning and integration problems is essential for the effective system design and effective certification processes in embedded systems (Figure 10.1).

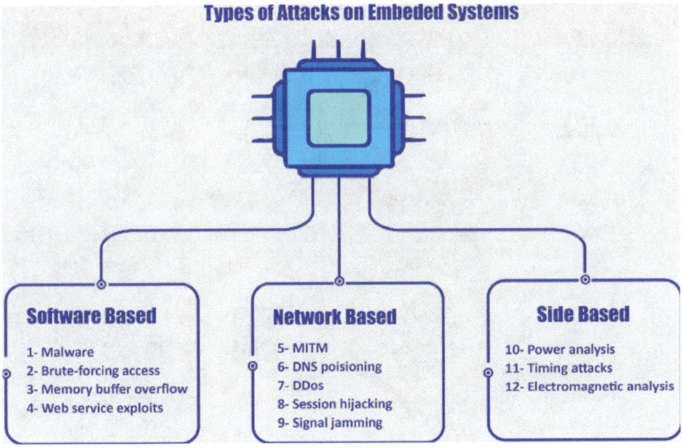

Figure 10.1. *Types of attacks on embedded system.*

Source: https://rsk-cyber-security.com/wp-content/uploads/2022/08/embeded-system-graph.png.

Besides, the importance of continuous monitoring and adaptation of embedded system architectures cannot be overstated since cyberattacks evolve at a dynamic rate. Ongoing updation of security policies and utilization of advanced verification techniques are the prerequisites for maintaining the integrity of the systems. The developers should remain vigilant against known exploits while, at the same time, considering novel attack vectors that can emerge with technological advancements. Due to the inherent interconnectedness in modern embedded applications, it is important to have a layered security approach. Apart from adhering to vulnerability analysis practices, it ensures that life-critical applications such as those within the aerospace or healthcare sectors remain secure against probable intrusions (Bakirtzis et al., 2018). By fostering an atmosphere that prioritizes security as well as reliability, risk can be alleviated and embedded system trustworthiness as a whole increased.

10.1.2. Threats from Cyberattacks

The propagation of cyberattacks poses enormous threats to the security and dependability of RTOS in critical applications such as healthcare, transportation, and defense. Cyber-attacks frequently exploit weaknesses in RTOS environments where timing constraints and resources further complicate security measures. These environments usually gather and process sensitive data, making them prime targets for hostile operators eager to exploit system integrity or confidentiality breaches.

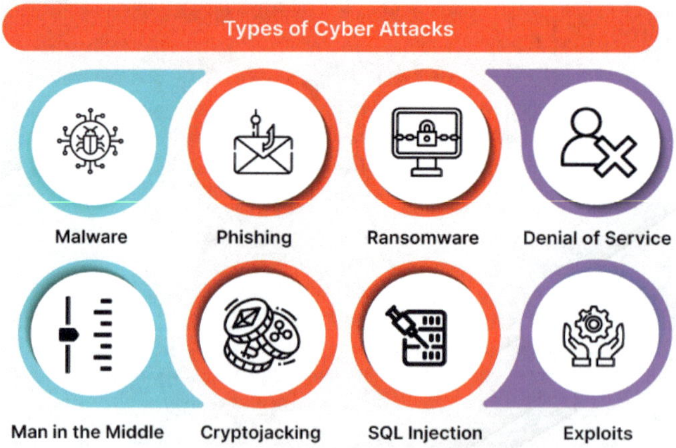

Figure 10.2. Types of cyberattacks.

Source: https://external-content.duckduckgo.com/iu/?u=https%3A%2F%2Fwww.fortinet.com%2Fcontent%2Fdam%2Ffortinet%2Fimages%2Fcyberglossary%2Ftypes-of-cyberattacks.png&f=1&nofb=1&ipt=2768982f0f37a47aa172e3ae778c8f83f737b8e6910cd02690b135fa1b31ae53.

With increasing integration of cyber-physical systems, threats can enter through external interfaces and lead to potential invasions when the system is in use. Such integration requires end-to-end security solutions that consider both intrinsic and emergent threats, with a focus on the early stages of system development life cycle to ensure effective mitigation strategies are in place (Bakirtzis et al., 2018). Furthermore, denial-of-service (DoS) attacks represent an exemplar of a significant threat to RTOS reliability, especially for those installed in wireless communication contexts. Through challenging the systems resources with unnecessary requests, these attacks undermine normal operation and lead to failures of crucial functionalities. The ease of their performance is a reflection of the importance of robust protection schemes tailored to the wireless architectures that dominate most RTOS applications. Wireless network dependence also introduces complexity in security solutions, as these networks are normally less secure and more prone to unauthorized use. Hence, effective security measures must be incorporated into hardware and software so as to block possible exploitation (Бурячок et al., 2018) (Figure 10.2). This demands ongoing research and development to advance prevailing models in a bid to better address the unique requirements RTOS presents. Furthermore, safety and reliability for RTOS mean adopting a lifecycle approach to system development and security testing. Preliminary estimates of system vulnerabilities can lead to the development of prophylactic solutions that can comprehensively enhance resistance to cyber-attacks. Using formal methods, such as the Systems Modeling Language (SysML), designers are able to create a comprehensive model that characterizes system properties and potential attack patterns. Such models allow designers to visualize vulnerability and risk of individual components, thus facilitating architectural mitigations design before deployment. This proactive security stance not only reduces the chances of successful cyber-attacks but also maximizes overall reliability of RTOS in mission-critical operations where failure is not acceptable (Bakirtzis et al., 2018). As threats change, such strategies will become increasingly important to maintaining operational integrity.

10.1.3. Lack of Standardized Security Protocols

Inadequate and inconsistent security measures in RTOS critically affect their reliability and integrity of operations. With industries creating increasingly more sophisticated applications on RTOS, such as autonomous vehicles and industrial automation, the problems with inconsistent security fall increasingly into focus. Greater deployment of networked devices makes this issue worse because security implementation inconsistencies can offer platforms for cyber-attacks. Lacking standard procedures, developers are not able to ensure their systems will be capable of protecting against dynamic threats and maintaining data integrity. Not only does this non-uniformity impact system performance, but it also leads to mistrust among users and stakeholders who view security as their number one priority in the operational environment. Moreover, the lack of uniformity in security protocols makes it more difficult to identify and prioritize vulnerabilities effectively. Current methods are lacking comprehensive frameworks under which RTOS security is evaluated, leading to random utilization across different platforms. As a prime example, advancements in artificial intelligence show that there is a need for a single unified security framework that includes data privacy and algorithmic openness. Such a framework would go towards reducing the risk of the extensive deployment of AI in RTOS-dependent industries, as discussed in the proposed solution to the expanding threat horizon and trust deficit in AI deployment (Gudlur, 2025). To this end, one solution to security would go towards increased levels of trust among users, leading to an increase in the usage of such technologies while addressing critical security gaps. The problems regarding the lack of standardized procedures point towards the imperative of developing dedicated frameworks for RTOS security enhancement. Current methodologies do not even touch upon important aspects such as firmware vulnerabilities and their effects in embedded systems, which are prevalent in vehicular networks as well as other critical infrastructures (Fang et al., 2025). Standardized processes would enable effective communication and interaction between different RTOS and their modules to provide improved vulnerability recognition and response. As the demand for secure and reliable RTOS grows, carrying out comprehensive and standardized security measures will be important for maintaining operational integrity and enabling innovation in an increasingly changing technology landscape. These futuristic strategies will not just make the overall security position of RTOS robust but will also contribute to building a secure community for users and organizations.

10.2. RELIABILITY ISSUES IN RTOS

The reliability of RTOS is critical due to the specific performance needs of time-constrained applications. An RTOS must guarantee the execution of tasks of higher priority within precise time constraints and eliminate latencies that would lead to system failures. The classic reliability issue originates from the complexity in dealing with multitasking environments, where multiple processes could contend for limited resources such as CPU time or memory. The uncertainty of resource assignment, especially under burdens, is a source of concern with respect to system responsiveness and task completion. Moreover, the absence of standardized metrics for RTOS performance makes it difficult to assess reliability, such that developers are often at a loss for choosing an operating system that satisfies the rigorous demands of their applications. RTOS system failures have typically been attributed to inadequate error handling and exception handling and have direct effects on critical system stability. RTOS is applied in cases where timing is critical—automotive or medical equipment—and any failure would have disastrous consequences. The robustness of the error handling mechanisms included in the RTOS design plays a pivotal role in ensuring uninterrupted operation and rapid recovery from failure. Additionally, the reliance on various hardware platforms and communication interfaces can hold certain vulnerabilities that undermine reliability. Hence, rigorous testing protocols simulating actual operating conditions must be embraced to determine the reliability of RTOS in depth. These protocols must concern not only the task execution but the system behavior when the system fails, so the design paradigm is strong. Moreover, the integration of security functions into RTOS will have an unforeseen effect on reliability. For instance, employing advanced encryption algorithms or access management mechanisms may add additional processing overheads, thus causing delays critical to real-time operation. This is a paradox that emphasizes the need to balance security and reliability because overly strict security measures could undermine an RTOSs ability to meet its timing guarantees. This challenge calls for an interdisciplinary collaboration involving real-time systems experts and computer security specialists, who must collaborate to develop solutions that enhance security and reliability without compromising performance. This is a critical effort as demand for secure and reliable real-time systems continues to rise, particularly within industries reliant upon tight operation controls such as healthcare, aerospace, and automotive systems (Gundlach et al., 2017; Joskow et al., 2025).

10.2.1. Fault Tolerance Mechanisms

Fault tolerance techniques are a critical component of maintaining reliability and integrity in the RTOS environment. Fault tolerance techniques are brought in to enable RTOS to withstand failures of various types and recover from them without interrupting the vital processes. By means of voting mechanisms, for instance, multiple instances of a computation can be checked against each other so that the consensus figure based on the majority is implemented. These mechanisms are critical in systems whose failures could have catastrophic consequences, and which emphasize the necessity for robust fault detection and recovery techniques (Butler et al., 2025). This fault tolerance background forms the background for a further exploration of more sophisticated and nested protective schemes within the framework of RTOS designs. Enhanced communication protocols and hardware further enhanced fault tolerance in embedded systems. Specifically, time-triggered protocols, such as FlexRay, have taken a great step forward in the dependability of in-car networks with determinist behaviors that are essential to safety functions. The protocols enable synchronous data exchanges, minimizing the occurrence of data loss or corruption that can arise from traditional event-triggered systems (Fahmy et al., 2015). As application complexity goes up, the incorporation of advanced mechanisms—like configurable communication controllers on FPGA structure—has enhanced the capability not only to successfully tolerate faults but to include features like security and timeliness. This enhancement in the fault tolerance landscape is reflective of the rise in demands on modern-day RTOS. Moreover, fault tolerance mechanisms' adaptability and flexibility are of most importance to the dynamic needs within the domain of embedded systems. With more interconnectivity and reliance on distributed compute nodes, fault response and adaptability are important. High-capability fault tolerance mechanisms facilitate not just recovery from failures but also persistent service delivery, ensuring operational integrity even under stress. The future deployments of fault-tolerant systems will also need to consider their interfacing with security systems, so that vulnerabilities exploited by criminals to their own benefit do not compromise fault tolerance itself. To this end, understanding of the interplay between fault tolerance with overall system resilience will be important to further advance RTOS technologies (Butler et al., 2025; Fahmy et al., 2015) (Figure 10.3).

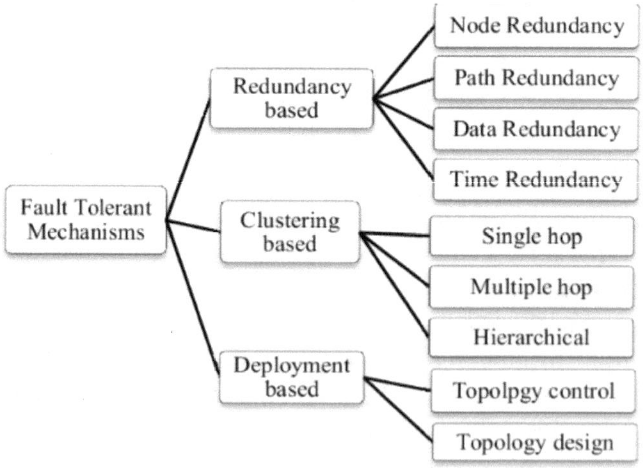

Figure 10.3. Fault tolerance mechanisms.

Source: https://www.researchgate.net/profile/Gholamreza-Kakamanshadi/publication/291831673/figure/fig1/AS:669351619342359@1536597270921/Fault-tolerance-mechanisms-taxo.png.

10.2.2. Impact of Hardware Failures

Hardware failure effect on RTOS is of paramount concern, particularly for safety-critical systems. As the trend goes toward more dependence on complex, off-the-shelf hardware components, the likelihood of encountering hardware failures that would compromise system integrity increases as well. These failures can take many different forms, from errant memory, thermally overloaded processors, to device failures in peripherals. These issues disrupt communication and processing functionality of an RTOS and can lead to system crashes or even more disastrous system failure in those applications where responses are vital. Commercial off-the-shelf (COTS) components, though enticing in reducing cost and facilitating rapid deployment, further escalate the effort to make it reliable, emphasizing the importance of good safety lifecycle management throughout the entire system development lifecycle (Caseley et al., 2017).

Reducing the impact of faults in the hardware in an RTOS setting is a key factor in the quest for safety and dependability. A good method is through the implementation of fault tolerance mechanisms, where faults are perceived and recovered from by the system without severe performance degradation. Techniques may include redundancy, whereby additional hardware components are used to take over in the event of the primary unit failing, or watchdog timers, which reset systems upon recognition of unresponsive responses. The proposed design technique from ongoing research focuses on a central cluster of proven software used for fault administration with the timing demands for safety-critical tasks remaining satisfied (Abdi et al., 2017).

This proactive fault management strategy not just enhances RTOS-based systems' operational resilience but also fosters trust in their utilization in high-reward environments. Finally, the consequences of hardware failure are much broader than mere technical interruption; they raise fundamental questions regarding compliance with regulations and public safety. The intricacy of modern embedded systems elevates the regulatory inspection profile to a level where any malfunction can be disastrous.

To address these needs, engineers and developers have to adopt a single safety engineering approach where rigorous safety standards control design choices from initial design stages. A phased safety lifecycle running concurrently with development can generate evidence-based safety cases minimizing risks from hardware malfunctions (Caseley et al., 2017). By such integrated engineering practices, stakeholders are in a position to enhance the reliability of RTOS applications to ensure that they satisfy not just performance expectations but also safety criteria in operating environments.

10.2.3. Software Bugs and Their Consequences

In the age of software systems being an essential part of everyday operations in diverse industries, the incidence of software bugs has assumed top priority, particularly in RTOS. The ramifications of these bugs can spread far beyond mere inconvenience, impacting system reliability, security, and user experience. Organizations often need to implement speed-optimized software to be able to meet market demands at the expense of compromising the completeness of testing cycles. Consequently, the significance of ongoing testing cannot be ignored in spite of pressure for fast delivery. In opting to perform patch deployments following release for security vulnerability or bug patches, organizations show how there is a trade-off between short-term market demands and long-term software integrity (Singh et al., 2025). The consequences of such bugs are tremendous, not just affecting individual systems but also user trust and industry standards in general. The growing reliance on software, particularly in safety-critical systems like automobile and aviation, emphasizes the serious consequences of software bugs. In both industries, engineers are tasked not just with maximizing performance but with keeping systems reliable and safe as well. Security vulnerabilities may lead to catastrophic failures and hence emphasize the importance of rigorous testing processes from design to deployment. One such instance is the creation of tools which can verify software as safe and secure, and this has been invaluable in identifying cybersecurity vulnerabilities in safety-critical systems. First implemented in Department of Defense systems, these tools have now been extended to automotive and embedded software, underlining their utility in contemporary uses (Awadhutkar et al., 2025) (Figure 10.4).

Figure 10.4. *Software bugs.*

Source: https://blog.noticeninja.com/hs-fs/hubfs/Finding%20And%20Fixing%20Bugs%20%281%29-1.jpg?width=1000&name=Finding%20And%20Fixing%20Bugs%20%281%29-1.jpg.

Systematic software testing is not only beneficial but a necessity in the advancement of reliability within bug-prone RTOS systems to safeguard user interests. Fixing software bugs in RTOS therefore has a double-edge challenge: a call for enhanced software reliability and the call to stay agile in deployment. Developing sophisticated overall models that integrate testing activity with patch deployment processes represents a software engineering milestone. These models allow ongoing fault detection and remediation even post-release, making it possible for a proactive bug management approach. Additionally, by applying statistical approaches and real data sets, developers can create insights that drive decision-making on software releases. Comparative analyses between model performances show that a systematic approach towards software quality management can play an important role in reliability and satisfaction enhancement. With increasing reliance on RTOS in critical infrastructures, the issue of minimizing software bugs is even more significant in ensuring operational safety and system dependability as a whole (Singh et al., 2025).

10.3. SECURITY MEASURES FOR RTOS

Security features for RTOS play a crucial role in safeguarding the integrity and functionality of systems running under stringent timing constraints. As RTOS are typically used for safety-critical applications such as automotive control systems, industrial automation, and medical devices, it is necessary to make them more resilient against cyber threats. One of the most significant precautions is the implementation of strict access controls that limit user privilege in accordance with the principle of least privilege. By constraining access rights, the likelihood of security exploits can be reduced, and unauthorized elements cannot utilize intrinsic weaknesses in firmware and software levels of RTOS. Furthermore, interoperability gaps between system components have the ability to introduce attack surfaces, necessitating rigorous vetting and validation exercises at system development integration, hence guaranteeing operational reliability and security (Nuthula, 2025). Additional security is introduced through the use of strong encryption standards for data transmission as well as storage. In the RTOS case, data integrity and confidentiality must be stringently guaranteed because sensitive information is openly exchanged between elements in a networked system. Secure communications technologies such as Transport Layer Security (TLS) can be integrated to prevent eavesdropping and data tampering during inter-process communications. Dynamic code update features are important for patching vulnerabilities at the point of discovery, enabling live security updates without impacting system performance. The ability to quickly deploy security patches is crucial, subjecting potential risks to timely correction and to upholding trust in safety-critical applications where even a minor delay may have disastrous effects (Oklander et al., 2025). Additionally, evolution of RTOS security strategy must account for emerging threats created by increased system complexity and connectivity. With technologies such as edge computing and Internet of Things (IoT) going far and wide, the attack surface of RTOS applications increases proportionally. Implementing threat modeling and risk assessment strategies while designing the system can foresee potential weaknesses and direct the architecture to include security measures with context-dependent implementations. Ongoing training for developers and operation personnel is also crucial because human mistakes often result in system security loopholes. Conducting regular audits and penetration testing on the RTOS ensures the effectiveness of the implemented security measures and adaptive response to new security paradigms, thereby making RTOS both dependable and secure in their respective environments (Nuthula, 2025) (Figure 10.5).

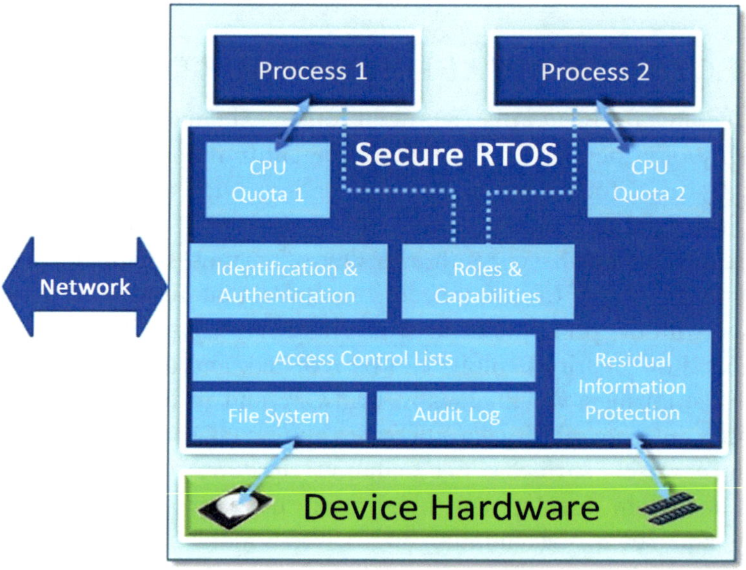

Figure 10.5. *A diagrammatic representation of a secure RTOS offering a number of built-in security features.*

Source: https://militaryembedded.com/cyber/cybersecurity/securing-connected-embedded-devices-using-built-in-rtos-security.

10.3.1. Access Control Mechanisms

Access control mechanisms are a fundamental support framework in the context of RTOS security, in which system resources are utilized solely by valid entities. Access control mechanisms are heterogeneous in character and encompass techniques such as authentication, authorization, and auditing. Effective authentication mechanisms validate the identities of users or processes requesting access to resources within the system, while authorization techniques determine the rights allocated to recognized entities. A robust access control system not only simplifies threats of unauthorized access but also facilitates adherence to security policies that are governed within a given implementation. With the use of RTOS applications growing more common across industries like healthcare and autonomous vehicles, the use of robust access control systems is key to the maintenance of reliability as well as protection against confidential data (Figure 10.6).

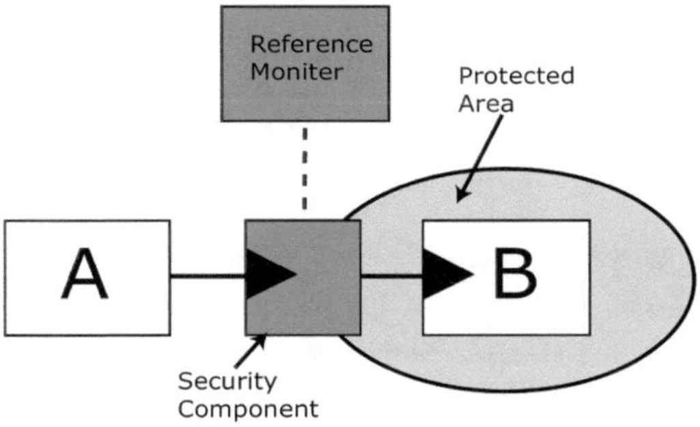

Figure 10.6. *Access control mechanism.*

Source: https://www.researchgate.net/publication/4355551_Generic_Memory_Protection_Mechanism_for_Embedded_System_and_Its_Application_to_Embedded_Component_Systems.

The diversity of access control models allows system designers to tailor mechanisms for specific application requirements. For example, discretionary access control (DAC) grants resource owners' authority to control access policy, whereas mandatory access control (MAC) uses system-level policies restricting user ability to modify permission. Role-based access control (RBAC), on the other hand, associates' rights, and permissions with specific user roles, facilitating easier management of access in larger systems. Each model has a different set of benefits and problems, which need a clear investigation and understanding of how these mechanisms support security objectives. These are particularly relevant, particularly in RTOS systems, where the absolute nature of real-time constraints would be able to influence the enforcement of advanced access control policies. Furthermore, access control mechanisms in the RTOS environments present a delicate balance between security and reliability, particularly taking into account the prevalent trend toward interconnection of systems. Access control failure offers a chance for a weakness that can lead to system intrusions, data theft, as well as disruption of service delivery. An effective access control mechanism has the potential to guarantee not only the enforcement of permissions but also, they ought to react to emerging security threats. Therefore, persistent monitoring and adaptive access control calibration are essential for the operation security of RTOS. This constant evolution aligns with broader regulation and compliance models, such as the development of energy regulation and market design, where the intermixture of security and operation procedures in important infrastructure (Gundlach et al., 2017; Weinmann, 2025) (Figure 10.7).

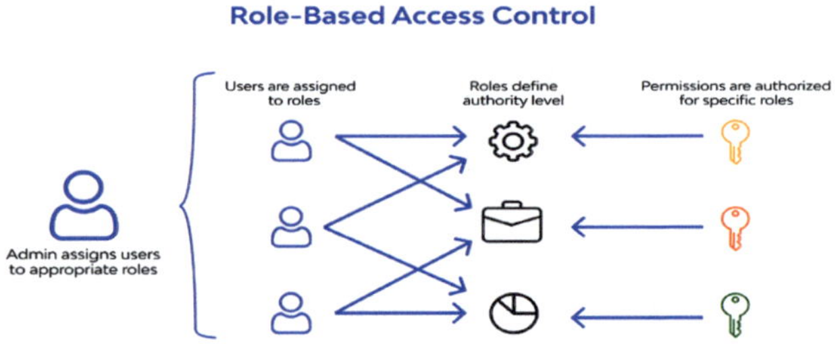

Figure 10.7. Role-based access control (RBAC).

Source: https://cdn.prod.website-files.com/5ff66329429d880392f6cba2/67ab6226372b182be4e12169_60a23b06b2d3123baf7c305d_RBAC.png.

10.3.2. Encryption Techniques

The importance of encryption techniques in securing and making RTOS reliable cannot be overstated. With increasing use of embedded systems in the mission-critical areas of healthcare, defense, and automobile technology, safeguarding sensitive data from misuse has gained well beyond momentum. Among numerous encryption algorithms, RSA (Rivest-Shamir-Adleman) is specifically known for its robust security due to the intractability of factoring large primes. Hardware-based RSA with Field Programmable Gate Arrays (FPGAs) is a fine way to provide a balance between speed and security requirements. Development of low-cost RSA-based crypto embedded systems as in recent work illustrates how to utilize such hardware to employ it in efficiently executing encryption processes without compromising responsiveness needed for real-time systems (Ahmad et al., 2006). Apart from RSA, there are some other encryption approaches gaining popularity in RTOS environments. Symmetric key algorithms such as the Advanced Encryption Standard (AES) offer fast processing, which is very important in applications that demand fast data encryption and decryption. The use of AES with RTOS can significantly enhance security without compromising system performance. Moreover, integrating cryptographic protection into the software layers of the operating system can neutralize the threats from outside attacks. As FPGAs allow various encryption schemes to be incorporated into other computational operations, their programmability in hardware renders them an appropriate option for designing secure embedded systems to execute multiple applications simultaneously (Srikanth et al., 2007) (Figure 10.8).

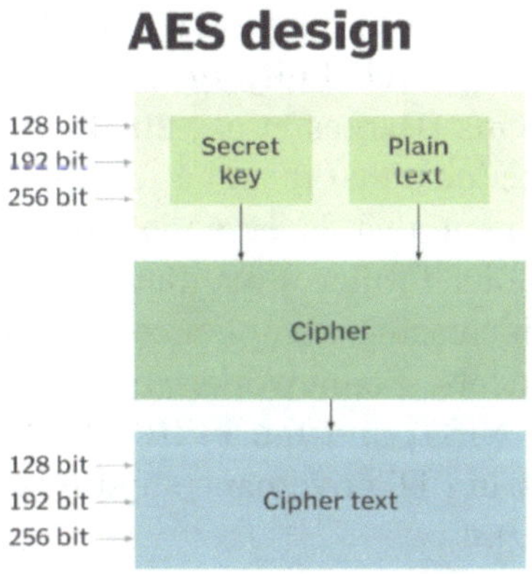

Figure 10.8. *Advanced encryption standard (AES) design.*

Source: https://external-content.duckduckgo.com/iu/?u=https%3A%2F%2Fcdn.ttgtmedia.com%2Frms%2FonlineImages%2Fsecurity-aes_design.jpg&f=1&nofb=1&ipt=fe57762bb37d2b30bf3e356ee770e99b89d62bf4e0c2b46eb9e8ec06110878df.

Encryption testing should also be based on current security vulnerability patterns and mitigation strategies in RTOS systems. Preemptive encryption is a priority as malware and cyber-attacks advance. Hardware Security Module (HSM) functions and secure key management practices can be the basis of encryption implementation dependability. By ensuring that encryption keys are appropriately safeguarded and available only to legitimate processes, the overall system integrity is ensured. Furthermore, studies on adaptive encryption algorithms, whose parameters can adapt to detected threats, hold potential for enhanced RTOS security. Such a strategy that is multi-pronged towards encryption, with both algorithmic efficacy and real-time reaction to threats in mind, is essential in ushering secure and reliable RTOS implementations.

10.3.3. Regular Security Audits

The implementation of regular security audits is essential in guaranteeing the reliability and integrity of RTOS, particularly in the wake of increased cyber threat complexity. Security audits allow for a systematic approach towards identifying vulnerabilities in the RTOS system, allowing organizations to assess their security position in advance. Such audits take into account both system configurations and the inherent procedures that govern security norms, with an eye to compliance with current regulations and stated policies. The data gained through regular audits enable firms to close loopholes before they are exploited, thereby minimizing the potential for breaches that could severely impact system operation and reliability of utmost concern in healthcare and automotive control systems (Barnes et al., 2004). In addition, the results can inform the security procedures that must be refreshed, which creates a culture of continuous improvement that is essential in today's dynamic world of technology. Periodic audits further strengthen the security model of RTOS in addition to further increasing compliance with many industry standards and regulatory requirements. Frameworks which are at the core of security audits such as COBIT, NIST, and the FFIEC IT Handbook offer extensive methodologies for assessing IT governance and risk management (Bharathan et al., 2025) (Figure 10.9).

Figure 10.9. *Regular security audits.*

Source: https://external-content.duckduckgo.com/iu/?u=https%3A%2F%2Fwww.compuquip.com%2Fhubfs%2Fwhen-to-conduct-a-security-audit.jpeg&f=1&nofb=1&ipt=2b6bd5a9786c317fab148734cd2b77164f287dfc53e1bdf60840b263530ed8d9.

By conforming to these accepted standards, organizations are able to coordinate their security procedures to best practices and operational metrics. Synchronization is crucial not merely for compliance with regulations and the avoidance of possible fines but also for rendering security provisions not merely reactive but integrated in the RTOS lifecycle. This organized audit process stretches organizations to adapt to evolving technology and regulatory settings while systematically addressing vulnerabilities that compromise system reliability. Furthermore, the findings of regular security audits extend beyond the identification of vulnerabilities; they also foster stakeholder confidence in RTOS deployments' security and reliability. Transparent disclosure of audit findings and consequent corrective action demonstrates an organization's commitment to proper security practice. Stakeholders like investors, customers, and regulatory bodies increasingly expect that organizations be proactive in their security practices, especially as digital transformation accelerates at a faster rate. By reporting public audit results and improvement measures, organizations can be relied upon and establish a robust reputation as secure and dependable organizations. This strategy not only anticipates future interferences with system operation but also delivers a strong operating environment capable of adapting to defeat emerging threats and challenges (Bharathan et al., 2025).

10.4. RELIABILITY ENHANCEMENTS IN RTOS

Reliability of RTOS is critical in applications where the accurate timing and predictable behavior are required. Improvement in reliability can significantly impact the systems capability to withstand failures and abnormal operation, which is critically vital for industries such as aerospace, automotive, and industrial automation. Applicability of robust fault tolerance mechanisms ensures that even in failures, the system is operative and can recover gracefully with no discontinuation in operation. Techniques such as watchdog timers, duplicate execution of tasks, and error detection codes enhance reliability by monitoring system states and responding rapidly to anomalies. They not only minimize downtime to the barest minimum but also build confidence among users by maintaining the integrity of critical operations under poor conditions, thereby building the overall security framework of the RTOS system. Besides that, strict test procedures incorporated into RTOS design provide system functionality consistency through verification of system ability in any possible situation. Formal verification and model-based testing enable developers to anticipate system behavior across various scenarios and identify possible areas of lack of reliability before deployment. Through simulation of various working conditions, developers can test resource usage and scheduling of tasks by the RTOS without bottlenecks and resource conflicts. This forward-looking approach aligns with industry best practices and regulatory standards, making the RTOS not only reliable but also safety-critical standards compliant. Therefore, the implementation of enhanced testing processes is the need of the hour to ensure the RTOS maintains high performance and reliability levels, ultimately catering to the interests of developers and end-users alike. Furthermore, collaboration between industry players goes a long way in enhancing RTOS reliability on a continuous basis. Knowledge sharing and collaborative effort in the standardization facilitates the development of benchmarks that enhance reliability across implementations. As reviewed by Eckman et al. (2021), the focus on economic value creation through demand flexibility in electric utility systems underscores the significance of the same in the context of RTOS. Through building a network that shares knowledge on failure modes, redundancy practices, and adaptive strategies, stakeholders can build more dependable RTOS solutions. Additionally, integrating experience from real-world applications enables iterative improvements, building an environment in which reliability can advance in conjunction with technology advancement. Through this, an active community for collaboration guarantees not just security but also improves the overall dependability of RTOS in an increasingly sophisticated operating environment.

10.4.1. Redundancy Strategies

Redundancy methods are crucial in enhancing the dependability and security of RTOS. As embedded systems expand to accommodate demands for enhancing performance and capabilities in safety-critical systems, there is greater danger of faults that could compromise system integrity. In response, redundancy mechanisms, such as dual modular redundancy and triple modular redundancy, ensure that if one component fails, other components can take over seamlessly. These strategies not only maintain operational continuity but also facilitate fault detection and recovery processes. By implementing such redundancy strategies, designers can systematically address vulnerabilities inherent in RTOS architectures, thereby reinforcing overall system safety. In addition, the strategies contribute to the overall goal of creating safe-by-design embedded systems, whereby proactive methods are utilized in the design process to undo any existing failures (Abdi et al., 2017). Task scheduling within an RTOS framework also becomes essential to guaranteeing that redundancy strategies are engaged. Utilizing proper schedulability analysis assists systems in managing multiple redundant parts in a timely manner in severe timing constraints. This technique is employed so that safety-critical activities are in operation, even during fault recovery operations that can include platform-wide restart and software reloading. From the analysis of different restart-tolerant models of tasks, developers are able to decide which disciplines of scheduling are most appropriate for their specific situation, using the resources to the greatest possible extent and achieving reliability during operational outages. Such careful handling of scheduling mechanisms, as well as redundancy techniques, also enhances the system's resilience to unexpected events, providing an environment capable of ensuring safe operation across varying conditions (Abdi et al., 2017). Aside from standard redundancy techniques, middleware solutions such as the Data Distribution Service (DDS) offer new methods of supporting reliability for embedded systems. DDS operates on a publish-subscribe model with loose communication between decoupled components. The modular architecture facilitates fault tolerance by enabling components to publish their states so that observers have grounds to respond based on up-to-date data despite parts of the system being able to fail. A comparison of the performance of different DDS implementations illustrates how such systems can enhance responsiveness and security in a system, particularly in safety-critical environments. By critically analyzing the various implementations' performance and security features, system architects can choose the best middleware technologies for their applications, thereby providing general RTOS dependability through enhanced data dissemination mechanisms.

10.4.2. Real-Time Monitoring Systems

Real-time monitoring systems (RTMS) are crucial in improving the reliability and security of RTOS. RTMS are designed to provide instant feedback and analysis of data, allowing for timely intervention and correction. As software complexity grows in safety-critical systems, such as those used in automotive and aerospace applications, utilization of effective monitoring is even more critical. By integrating RTMS within the RTOS framework, developers can have the ability to guarantee any potential vulnerabilities are identified and fixed in real-time. This pre-emptive strategy not only lowers risk but also addresses the evolving safety standards that necessitate strict evaluation of system performance throughout its lifespan (Caseley et al., 2017). As such, RTMS is a significant contributor to ensuring the establishment of a safe operating environment, being a landmark innovation in safety engineering practice. Installation of real-time monitoring systems is not so much a question of risk management as enhancing general system operational efficiency. By means of advanced analytics and machine learning technologies, RTMS can predict future failures before they happen. This forecasting functionality enables optimizing system resources and reducing downtime. Moreover, real-time data feeds facilitate decision-making activities by reacting dynamically to shifting environments and system needs. For instance, in cases like power grids, combining monitoring systems that work in real-time to accommodate variability can significantly improve reliability (Gundlach et al., 2017) (Figure 10.10).

Figure 10.10. *Real-time monitoring systems (RTMS).*

Source: https://external-content.duckduckgo.com/iu/?u=https%3A%2F%2Fwww.hiotron.com%2Fwp-content%2Fuploads%2F2021%2F10%2FReal-time-monitoring-800x360.png&f=1&nofb=1&ipt=077c5ede77902e2f03522079ece88c490d9a98cb14b37e57decb918b137da0b1.

It should be noted that the deployment of such systems needs to incorporate a sophisticated knowledge of technical capabilities and limitations in order not to introduce new vulnerabilities to the RTOS architecture. Also, the effectiveness of real-time monitoring systems is dependent on their integration with other available safety mechanisms as well as operational paradigms. The relationship between monitoring technology and safety-critical designs requires a comprehensive safety life cycle that incorporates continuous review and enhancement. According to case studies, the use of commercially off-the-shelf (COTS) components creates complications in system integrity maintenance while increasing functionalities (Caseley et al., 2017). Accordingly, the utilization of RTMS becomes critical to not only ensure compliance with safety standards but also yield actionable intelligence that can inform system engineering operations. With the increasing demand for reliable and secure RTOS across sectors, the creation of real-time monitoring capability will be an important decider of future security and operational planning.

10.4.3. Update and Patch Management

Effective update and patch management is absolutely essential to the security and reliability of RTOS. Implemented in mission-critical applications like automobile control, medical equipment, and industrial automation, these systems are open to cyber-attacks if no updates are performed regularly. An effective patch management practice must encompass not just the deployment of updates but also the verification of their integrity and authenticity. A systematic implementation of processes allows firms to address found vulnerabilities in good time, thus removing latent dangers. As RTOS environments may carry stringent performance requirements, the updating procedure via updates must be designed to introduce minimal disruption to installations. A current patch management process supports greater system resilience to the ever-evolving environment of security attacks, which is the foundation for operational dependability as well as device functionality. The patch and update management issues in RTOS are multi-faceted when considering the constraints of operation unique to embedded systems. Traditional downtime is not supported in most RTOS environments; therefore, the application of updates needs to be carried out in such a way that continuous availability of the system is possible. Solutions such as hot updates or the Cetratus architecture provide dynamic update infrastructures in which changes can be applied while the system remains operational, with real-time monitoring of the new software versions in quarantine until they are verified as reliable (Inchausti et al., 2019) (Figure 10.11).

Figure 10.11. *Patch management process.*

Source: https://external-content.duckduckgo.com/iu/?u=https%3A%2F%2Ftechpio.com%2Fblog%2Fwp-content%2Fuploads%2F2023%2F12%2FPatch-Management-Process.jpg&f=1&nofb=1&ipt=c40556da7e18f7e1878a282148177cddbea4093c0fff92b170da2990456c4804.

This pre-emptive measure ensures that whatever can be the problem from a patch, it does not propagate and compromise the integrity of the entire system. Hence, it is important to have a clear understanding of such methodologies to ensure the safeguarding of core operations, thereby enhancing the reliability of the RTOS. In addition, the level of regulatory compliance and cyber-attacks further increases the importance of proper patch management in RTOS. As new vulnerabilities develop, particularly in sectors like energy and critical infrastructure, delay in applying timely updates has disastrous consequences to system integrity as well as public safety. For instance, abolishing net neutrality regulations has been termed as a zero-day vulnerability that exposes critical services to additional vulnerabilities that deteriorate their cybersecurity posture (Sandoval et al., 2019). Thus, regulatory bodies and industry stakeholders must make patch management a central part of their cybersecurity policy. Keeping systems secure against emerging threats, organizations secure their operational integrity and conformity with industry standards. Not only do they fill existing vulnerabilities but also set a template for long-term resistance and reliability in RTOS installations.

10.5. CASE STUDIES OF RTOS SECURITY AND RELIABILITY

For RTOS, security and reliability should be of the highest importance, particularly in safety-critical environments such as aerospace, automotive, and medical equipment. RTOS deployment case studies usually highlight the intricate interdependence of timely execution of tasks and strong security features. For instance, introducing security protocol involves overhead that may compromise the real-time character of the system, causing unacceptable latencies for mission-critical activities. Examining these case studies reveals how RTOS structures apply alternative security models to mitigate vulnerability while maintaining task scheduling efficiency, hence both system reliability and safety. These studies stress the need for continuous evaluation and adaptive security responses relative to evolving threats, particularly since these systems increasingly rely on networked technologies. Moreover, commercial off-the-shelf (COTS) component utilization in RTOS applications presents grave threats to reliability and security. Case studies highlight the manner in which safety-critical systems are increasingly turning to the utilization of COTS components in an attempt to control development time and cost effectively. This application complicates matters in regard to the safety and security guaranteeing across the supply chain. The study identifies the need for an integrated safety lifecycle that can align with the RTOS design and development processes. Through the use of full-cycle safety standards, developers can guarantee that considerations of safety are integrated into every stage of system development. Such a comprehensive approach has proven to be effective in delivering the necessary evidence for building safety cases that ultimately lead to the reliability of RTOS implementations in safety-critical systems (Caseley et al., 2017). Realistic case studies also reflect the efficacy of adaptive security measures under

RTOS environments. With the rising demand for networked devices comes the risk of security attacks that can render functionality and user safety in a state of impairment. For example, a study demonstrated how an RTOS that was used in the automotive system used real-time anomaly detection techniques that were capable of detecting and responding to abnormal behavior without compromising the performance of the systems. By examining the effective use of such a practice, the case study identifies the importance of proactive and dynamic defensive mechanisms in maintaining operational integrity. In addition, exposure to case studies presenting both success and failures in RTOS implementations provides valuable lessons, funneling future development activity towards effective adoption of reliability and safe operation (Gundlach et al., 2017).

10.5.1. Analysis of RTOS in Automotive Systems

Over the last few years, the use of RTOS in automotive systems has gained momentum due to the increasing demands for performance, reliability, and better safety features. As cars have evolved into complex devices filled with state-of-the-art technology, their management has become more complicated. RTOS is essential to the guarantee that several subsystems operate within their established time budgets, hence enhancing the overall efficiency of car systems. An uncompromisable approach to managing these time-constrained operations is of the essence, especially in relation to safety-relevant systems such as autonomous vehicles and ADAS. By providing assured timing behavior, RTOS enables software developers to provide strict performance guarantees, critical in order to achieve a seamless user experience as well as to prevent the risks that come with cutting-edge automotive technology. The use of RTOS in automotive systems also raises grave security and reliability issues. The increased connectivity between vehicle systems offers new entry points for vulnerabilities, exposing them to potential cyberattacks. With safety guarantee as the top priority, it is essential that the RTOS used not only meets standards but also provides secure strength. As a case in point, Abdi et al. (2017) underscores the necessity of verified safety guarantees in addition to requirements for performance. This places the spotlight on the implementation of design methods that surround basic verified software to effectively regulate faults and recovery processes. Having RTOS capable of responding to failures without compromising the integrity of the system is an essential contribution towards making automotive applications more reliable. Furthermore, the need for effective fault management in RTOS is further enhanced by the stringent need for maintaining operational safety in automotive systems. Utilization of sophisticated fault detection and recovery mechanisms are central to these objectives. Schedulability analysis, as introduced by Abdi et al. (2017), becomes a necessary mechanism for ensuring timing constraints are still respected even with the occurrence of faults. Creative strategies such as full platform restarts and software reloading can recover successfully without affecting strict safety standards. Overall, by analyzing and enhancing the reliability characteristics of RTOS, automotive systems can make significant strides toward meeting their safety goals, allowing more sophisticated cars to be functional as well as safe in a dynamic driving environment.

10.5.2. RTOS in Medical Devices

The application of RTOS in medical devices has been extensively used due to the need for high reliability and performance in healthcare operations. The sophistication of medical devices with the integration of advanced functionalities such as data analysis and patient monitoring is founded on RTOS to ensure timely completion of critical tasks. The safety guarantee requirement is the highest; thus, an integrated safety engineering methodology is essential in developing such systems. The methodology demands that it have a life cycle of safety that is fully integrated in the overall design and development processes. Through the process, the developers make sure that factors of safety are given a critical role in determining design decisions for the entire length of the project, thus preventing risks of installing Commercial Off the Shelf (COTS) components into advanced medical supply chains (Caseley et al., 2017). RTOS-powered medical devices is not only a matter of technical need but also regulatory. The regulatory bodies impose rigorous requirements, and thus it is necessary to have stringent verification procedures in place so that the systems operate as expected under all projected circumstances. However, the verification process can be excessively time-consuming and expensive, especially for the embedded systems used in safety-critical situations. An approach using safety-by-design techniques is thus necessary. Safety-by-design methodologies prefer the use of a small number of guaranteed software with adequate fault detection and recovery provisions. This allows developers to leverage the benefits of RTOS and ensure the timing constraints of the safety-critical tasks are adequately met even under operation perturbations, thereby enhancing overall system reliability (Abdi et al., 2017). Besides, application of RTOS in medical devices extends beyond task scheduling; it encompasses the entire aspect of patient protection and device efficacy. Effective deployment of an RTOS involves diligent schedulability analysis in order to guarantee that a system's essential operations will still operate even with faults. This involves careful consideration in establishing how much a system can meet its timing requirements without affecting the integrity of its output. With the aid of restart-tolerant task models and comparison of performance through the employment of simulation tools, developers will be able to enhance task scheduling for medical devices. This initial focus on operation reliability not only ensures patient health but also ensures compliance with the industry, ultimately fostering a culture of responsibility and faith in healthcare technology development (Abdi et al., 2017).

10.5.3. RTOS in Industrial Automation

Inclusion of RTOS in industrial automation systems has increasingly been crucial both in providing security as well as ensuring operation reliability. An RTOS ensures timely scheduling and execution of the tasks, which is crucially significant for applications where machine and process control is needed exactly. The ability of an RTOS to guarantee response times, usually given in microseconds or milliseconds, makes it particularly well-suited for complex automation tasks, such as those in Supervisory, Control, and Data Acquisition (SCADA) systems. In a recent project, for instance, a meshed High Voltage Direct Current (HVDC) grid had real-time visualization of electrical variables presented by an RTOS, allowing operators to monitor data streams without loss. Effective handling of multiple tasks at the same time and the provision of low latency demonstrate the way in which an RTOS enhances security and reliability in rugged industrial environments, resulting in better security and more secure, efficient operations (Comas et al., 2016). Secondly, the widespread application of Industrial Wireless Sensor Networks (IWSNs) demonstrates the importance of RTOS to counteract security threats caused by more advanced automation systems. IWSNs, applied across various industries such as oil and gas and process control, bring significant advantages like flexibility, scalability, and cost-effectiveness. However, these networks are vulnerable to threats and attacks because of their dynamic and largely unpredictable nature. In this context, RTOS is instrumental in offering security solutions that ensure data integrity and system reliability. By utilizing strong scheduling algorithms and effective resource management, an RTOS can mitigate the threats of insecure communication paths as well as unexpected behaviors generally posed by IWSNs, thus fostering uninterruptible and safe operational performance (Aslam et al., 2018). Finally, RTOS-Industrial automation interaction includes creating stronger manufacturing processes. The deployment of an RTOS facilitates compliance with safety standards as it allows fail-safe programs to execute in real-time. With the pace of technological innovation, business is placed under added pressures of modernization while maintaining stringent safety controls. An RTOS supports both of these objectives by offering continuous monitoring and immediate response to aberrations in the system. Efficiency to maintain operational integrity and adapt to new conditions improves overall process reliability in industrial processes. By incorporating security features into RTOS's operational framework, industrial automation can achieve higher efficiency at the cost of safety but without it, eventually becoming a more resilient paradigm susceptible to modernization (Aslam et al., 2018; Comas et al., 2016).

SUMMARY

In encapsulating the research on RTOS security and reliability, it is evident that there is a need to fight the intricate problems in these areas for the sake of offering robust performance in mission-critical software. The increasing reliance on RTOS across different industries necessitates the need to include rigorous security structures. With the rising complexity and interconnected nature of systems, so are vulnerabilities amplified, and the redrawing of existing security measures becomes necessary. Indeed, the implications of failing to satisfy these security conditions can be disastrous, particularly in safety-critical areas such as automotive or healthcare technology. A vision-oriented strategy in combining both reliability and security from the earliest design stages allows a more solid foundation that is essential for long-term success in embedded systems. Secondly, the use of safety lifecycle methods, as discussed in safety-critical systems, imposes the necessity of integrating security with reliability processes. By merging the two primary areas, organizations are capable of creating a synergistic environment that enhances system dependability. The need for safety standards, as defined in recent studies, indicates the growing consensus on the necessity of a robust safety life cycle that is parallel to development processes and eventually influences design decisions throughout the process of engineering. The integration is particularly important with systems becoming more dependent on Commercial Off the Shelf (COTS) components, which, although economically attractive, can have unexpected vulnerabilities if not properly evaluated and followed through in their life cycle. Such measures not only increase security provisions but also result in a more secure and reliable operating setting for real-time systems. Finally, if we view the argument regarding RTOS reliability and security, there seems to be a continuous evaluation and adaptation necessity in a continuously evolving technological landscape. The ability to institute testing that adequately aligns with both state policy and market behavior, as illustrated in the conversation around carbon pricing strategies, becomes a model for how we are able to proceed with RTOS security. By establishing prudent policy and adjusting procedures in relation to real-world implications, organizations are able to enhance their security position without compromising on reliability within operations. This two-way approach—integrating regulatory requirements with engineering methods—

will not only make the robustness of RTOS that much stronger but also pave the way for innovative solutions to thrive, ultimately setting the bar higher for innovations to come.

RTOS security and reliability heavily depend on several fundamental concepts that underscore the critical roles they assume in contemporary embedded systems. Of utmost importance, the absence of a generalized approach to design among RTOS models tends to cause disparities in security techniques and reliability methods, with widespread implications for system performance. The dynamic between regulatory competition, as seen in electricity markets, is an apt analogy; divergent frameworks affect market reliability, and divergent RTOS implementations affect introducing vulnerabilities or making defenses more secure from cyber-attacks. By examining such dynamics, one discovers that upholding robust security measures and end-to-end reliability calls for a common strategy embracing best practices amidst varied RTOS implementations within various industries, thereby making the entire framework more reliable. Moreover, the quantification of economic value concerned with RTOS security follows closely with increased demand for RTOS flexibility and responsiveness. As much as valuation of distributed energy resource investment enables enhanced grid services, so can measurement of RTOS security measures enable policy and protocol optimization to leverage system reliability to the highest degree. By prioritizing economic values of a fundamental character of RTOS security, stakeholders can harmonize interests so that security enhancements do not come at the expense of real-time applications' operational effectiveness. This ensures it also facilitates broader discussion between developers, policymakers, and users to establish a safety and reliability culture for RTOS installations with a view to ensuring secure operation of critical infrastructures. Finally, it is essential that stakeholders take extra care in assessing RTOS security provisions by conducting constant analysis and fine-tuning optimal practice. With technology continuously evolving, the demand for adaptive models within real-time systems becomes increasingly important. Efforts aimed at improving current methodologies for RTOS security analysis should strive to reconcile economic considerations with overall societal impacts. Such coordination is possible through joint efforts of regulative organizations, industry players, and academies, as in the case of regulatory networks for the power industry. These synergies would not only strengthen RTOS reliability and security pillars but also form the foundation for future needs meeting innovative solutions, resonating with conclusions drawn from current trends and report analysis of reliable demand flexibility and how it adds to utility systems (Eckman et al., 2021; Weinmann, 2025).

REFERENCES

1. Abdi, F., Caccamo, M., Mancuso, R., Tabish, R., et al. (2017). Restart-based fault-tolerance: System design and schedulable analysis. http://arxiv.org/abs/1705.02412 (accessed on 29th September 2025).
2. Ahmad, I., Hani, M. K., & Thamrin, N. (2006). Crypto embedded system for electronic document. https://core.ac.uk/download/11778281.pdf (accessed on 29th September 2025).
3. Ahmad, N. (2017). Porting of FreeRTOS on a Python virtual machine for embedded and IoT devices. https://core.ac.uk/download/79623606.pdf (accessed on 29th September 2025).
4. Alonso Muñoz, A. A., Crespo Lorente, A., & Trujillo González, S. (2013). MultiPARTES: Multicore virtualization for mixed-criticality systems. http://oa.upm.es/25770/1/INVE_MEM_2013_160490.pdf (accessed on 29th September 2025).
5. Anonymous. (2025). And the state-of-the-art. https://core.ac.uk/download/pdf/24067697.pdf (accessed on 29th September 2025).
6. Aslam, N., Cao, Y., Hussain, S., Khan, M., et al. (2018). A critical analysis of research potential, challenges and future directives in industrial wireless sensor networks. https://core.ac.uk/download/96885354.pdf (accessed on 29th September 2025).
7. Awadhutkar, P., Tamrawi, A., & Sauceda, J. (2025). Detecting cyber-security vulnerabilities in legacy safety-critical software with tight performance constraints. *SAE Technical Paper Series*. https://www.semanticscholar.org/paper/f92ad16e256a199364502923ad0b0db984869f52 (accessed on 29th September 2025).
8. Bakirtzis, G., Carter, B. T., Elks, C. R., Fleming, C., et al. (2018). A model-based approach to security analysis for cyber-physical systems. http://arxiv.org/abs/1710.11442 (accessed on 29th September 2025).
9. Barnes, K., Johnson, B., & Nickelson, R. (2004). Introduction to SCADA protection and vulnerabilities. https://core.ac.uk/download/71312422.pdf (accessed on 29th September 2025).
10. Bharathan, R. (2025). Mastering technology audit quality assurance: A framework for auditors. https://core.ac.uk/download/658903290.pdf (accessed on 29th September 2025).
11. Blazek, P., Fujdiak, R., Misurec, J., Mlynek, D., et al. (2020). Security and performance trade-offs for Data Distribution Service in flying ad-hoc networks. https://core.ac.uk/download/233029868.pdf (accessed on 29th September 2025).

12. Butler, R. W. (2025). A primer on architectural level fault tolerance. https://core.ac.uk/download/pdf/10541936.pdf (accessed on 29th September 2025).

13. Caseley, F., Hall, J. G., Jackson, P., et al. (2017). Safety engineering with COTS components. https://core.ac.uk/download/82983623.pdf (accessed on 29th September 2025).

14. Eckman, T., Leventis, G., & Schwartz, L. C. (2021). Determining utility system value of demand flexibility from grid-interactive efficient buildings. https://core.ac.uk/download/322493960.pdf (accessed on 29th September 2025).

15. Fahmy, S. A., & Shreejith, S. (2015). Extensible FlexRay communication controller for FPGA-based automotive systems. https://core.ac.uk/download/80790985.pdf (accessed on 29th September 2025).

16. Fang, X., He, K., Wu, Y., Chen, R., & Zhao, J. (2025). Balancing accuracy and efficiency in vehicular network firmware vulnerability detection: A fuzzy matching framework with standardized data serialization. *Informatics*. https://www.semanticscholar.org/paper/9b2e5fb4cadc68ea5f01ed1703208e18ce157fbe (accessed on 29th September 2025).

17. Gudlur, V. V. R. (2025). Proposing a secure framework for industrial AI security in 21st century. *2025 IEEE International Conference on Robotics and Technologies for Industrial Automation (ROBOTHIA)*. https://www.semanticscholar.org/paper/c763564dad082224d387a739e08b2048731c6419 (accessed on 29th September 2025).

18. Gundlach, J., & Webb, R. (2017). Carbon pricing in New York ISO markets: Federal and state issues. https://core.ac.uk/download/212892574.pdf (accessed on 29th September 2025).

19. Joskow, P. L. (2025). Comments in response to FERC rulemaking on regional transmission organizations. https://core.ac.uk/download/pdf/6665083.pdf (accessed on 29th September 2025).

20. Mora Comas, G. (2016). Development and implementation of a LabVIEW based SCADA system for a meshed multi-terminal VSC-HVDC grid scaled platform. https://core.ac.uk/download/81577752.pdf (accessed on 29th September 2025).

21. Mugarza Inchausti, I. (2019). Quarantine-mode based live patching for zero downtime safety critical systems. https://core.ac.uk/download/547404147.pdf (accessed on 29th September 2025).

22. Nuthula, S. (2025). Decoding real-time operating systems in automotive software: A systematic analysis. *World Journal of Advanced Engineering Technology and Sciences*. https://www.semanticscholar.org/paper/

c41fd58481133aa2661914b4f14f4b1da960c1b4 (accessed on 29th September 2025).

23. Oklander, M., & Harnyk, M. (2025). Optimization of response team deployment: Logistical solutions for security companies. *Business Navigator*. https://www.semanticscholar.org/paper/5597aaff07a0fbb8fc228f5cda276219cf51f75c (accessed on 29th September 2025).
24. Sandoval, C. J. K. (2019). Cybersecurity paradigm shift: The risks of net neutrality repeal to energy reliability, public safety, and climate change solutions. https://core.ac.uk/download/227285459.pdf (accessed on 29th September 2025).
25. Singh, V., Kumar, V., Singh, V. B., & Agrawal, A. P. (2025). Unveiling the evolution: Multi-patch multi-release software reliability growth model with testing effort. *Journal of Reliability and Statistical Studies*. https://www.semanticscholar.org/paper/fdc213546275f02d52409183d74af1895103258e (accessed on 29th September 2025).
26. Srikanth, P. K. A. S., & Srinivas, K. (2007). Implementation of FPGA in the design of embedded systems. https://core.ac.uk/download/53186862.pdf (accessed on 29th September 2025).
27. Weinmann, J. (2025). Agglomerative magnets and informal regulatory networks: Electricity market design convergence in the USA and Continental Europe. https://core.ac.uk/download/pdf/7139849.pdf (accessed on 29th September 2025).

INDEX

D

E

F

G

H

S

T